From lonely TO SINGLE

Laura Bauman

Balboa Press books may be ordered through booksellers or by contacting:

Balboa Press
A Division of Hay House
1663 Liberty Drive
Bloomington, IN 47403
www.balboapress.com
1 (877) 407-4847

Print information available on the last page.

ISBN: 978-1-5043-7208-4 (sc)
ISBN: 978-1-5043-7209-1 (hc)
ISBN: 978-1-5043-7221-3 (e)

Library of Congress Control Number: 2016921021

Balboa Press rev. date: 12/30/2016

Dedicated to my beloved daughter

CHAPTER 1

It was on a Saturday evening. Eva was watching *The Saint* with Roger Moore on TV together with her mother and her husband, Camil. It was in the sixties. Not many families had a TV set back then. And those who had one, could watch only one channel, the national TV, official channel of the communist state led by a dictator. Usually, the TV programs just praised him. When a foreign movie was on, it was a real treat. And on Saturdays, Eva could watch one of her favorite actors, in a TV series that she wouldn't have missed for the world. Literally she wouldn't have missed it for the world, because on this particular evening, she was already in labor, but she was standing behind a chair, grabbing its backrest with both hands, because she was hardly able to bear the pain.

Eva was on the brink of giving birth to her second child. She already had an eight years old son, Eduard. She had quite a troubled marriage with her husband Camil. But on this evening, all she wanted was to see the series up to its end, then she was going to go to the maternity, which was quite close to her block and then she could give birth to her child. Her mother and Camil were aware that she could hardly bear the pain already and were telling her every other minute:

"Come on, Eva, let's go already! You'll give birth here, in the apartment. Come on, let's go!"

"I am not going anyway until the film is not over...." She was giving birth to her second child, she knew better not to go so early to the maternity. She knew that the labor could go on and on for hours and hours. Why stay in that cold, unfriendly hospital when she could stay a little longer at home and watch her favorite TV series?

Eva had very few pleasures in life. She has been born in thirties, in an Eastern European country. She grew up in a very poor family, in Mineville.

Mineville was the main city in the region in the county. This area has always been inhabited by a very strong, hard-working, proud, untamed people. The region is mountainous, people are working hard to earn their living. They work a lot, they eat a lot and they drink a lot. And, besides the work at home, they for a few months every year, all over the country to work some more, to gain some more money. With the money they bring home, they build huge, beautiful houses.

This region has always been sustained by the mining industry. Miners were not afraid of death, they were not afraid of anything. They went every day down into the guts of the earth, being fully aware that is very possible they will never come back on the face of the earth. The communist dictator did not like miners. He visited the region less often than other regions of the country, people could only thank God for that. What the dictator hated most about the miners was that they did not pretend to be so enthusiastic about his speeches as others did and the oppressors had to play ovations and applauses on huge loudspeakers at each break in his speech. And gossip was that most of all, he was afraid of miners.

The location of the city is beautiful. It is situated in a depression, surrounded by mountains. The mountains hold and surround Mineville, as if they are holding it in their arms. Actually, if you look at the city from a distance, you think it is placed in the palms of God's hands. And God did always protect this city. No serious earthquakes, no serious floods. A lot of gold and copper underground. In the old days, there was so much gold in Mineville that women could find it in the river that crosses the city. And a lot of citizens that love this city more than any other place on earth.

Eva's father worked in a gold mine near Mineville. Her mother stayed home to raise the children. Eva had a brother and a sister. They were all living of the miserable salary of her father, who also drank more than half of it every month after he received it. At least they had a house of their own, even if it was small. You entered in a small kitchen, after that in a first room and then in a second room. All the house was around 30 square meters and they were all living there. Until her father worked, the situation was hard. But her father was also a Union member. As he had the bad habit of speaking out his mind, he got locked away for a few months by the capitalist regime. Then, after the second World War, again he could not keep his big mouth shut, so he got locked away also by the communists.

The family lived a very hard life. Eva woke up early in the morning and went to the woods to bring home some branches and other fallen wood for the fire. She had a brother and a sister, but they were not sent for wood as they were weak and always ill. Eva was strong and healthy. She ate anything and worked hard like a grown up. She got the worst shoes if any and the worst cloths and she worked the most of all children. Eva was her father's favorite, but her mom took care more of her siblings because she always felt Eva was strong enough to take care of herself.

Eva always wanted to become a school teacher but only attended eight years of elementary school. Her parents could not afford more. They tried to buy her at least some better cloths and shoes so that she can go to school. More fortunate children were going to school with an apple or a bagel. The poorer ones relied on the occasional food they received in school – a little milk or some biscuits. The state gave this food to the children, but they were told Daddy Stalin sent them the food.

Eva was sent to earn money when she was about sixteen. She got a nice job as a clerk and she started to contribute to her family's income. Eva was very proud that she had a good job and she could help support the family. Her job was in a clean, warm office, she did not have to work in a factory or out on the field. And, one day, a nice young man came to the company where she worked. He looked well taken care of and also he seemed like he knew what he wanted. His attention was captured by Eva, this very young girl, with long wavy black hair and beautiful blue eyes. A few more meetings in her office, and then, one day, he asked her out on a date. He told her he would go home to ask permission from her family to let her and he did. He came to her house and stopped at the gate. Everybody was curious to see Eva's date. He even came on his motorbike. Back then, in Eva's neighborhood not anybody had a motorbike. Eva was blown away. They went on their date. And a few dates later, Camil asked her hand from her father. Soon after this, Eva's father died, at the age of fifty. All those years of hard work in the mine, the months spent in jail, the drinking and poor eating finally got to him. The family remained without his support, only with the pension received by Eva's mother and Eva's salary. Camil went to the army. All the healthy men were obliged to go to the army for three years. After he returned, they got married. For a while, they stayed together with Eva's family, in that small house of them. After two years, their first son was born. They named him Eduard. When Eduard turned two years old, they received an apartment with two rooms in a block of flats. Everybody received a place to live during the communist regime. All you had to do was to make an application, after a year or two, the state assigned you a place to live, depending on the number of members of your family. You did not have to buy it, and you could live in it for ever. Electricity, gas and water were very affordable. This was one of the things that appealed to the masses. In this little apartment, you entered in a hall and from there to one of the rooms, then to the other room. The quieter, more isolated rooms was Camil's, the passing room was for Eva and the children.

The Saint finally ended. Eva took her coat and with her mother and husband started to walk towards the maternity. At the entrance, there was an old doorman. It was Saturday night and he was a *little* intoxicated. He offered his arm to Eva to help her up to the second floor.

"*Come on m'am, let me help you up the stairs*" said the old doorman.

"*Oh, thank you, it's not really necessary, I can manage*" said Eva, as it looked more like he needed some help.

"*Oh, m'am, please let me help you, it's my duty. There are two floors to climb*" he insisted.

So they started to climb the stairs. It was just like Eva thought, actually she helped him up to the second floor and not the other way around.

The labor did not take very long, Eva came to the maternity pretty late. At eleven o'clock, she gave birth to a baby girl. She named her Valerie. Valerie was a big, strong and healthy, little baby. She was crying loudly, Eva was sure that her little girl came to the world very hungry. Camil was waiting outside, as soon as her little girl was born, one of the nurses went and gave him the good news. Mother and child were healthy.

Camil went home happy, even though a little disappointed. Actually, he would have liked to have another son. But he had an unfailing method to deal with an emotion, disturbance, change in his life. He was drinking. The birth of his daughter was a big event in his life, so the few days Eva was in the maternity with the baby, he drank a lot. His first son, Eduard, was very used to see him like this. At least now he was preoccupied with the event and he was not aggressive and abusive.

The three days in maternity went by pretty fast. Eva was sent home with Valerie. They went home with Camil, who was carrying little Valerie in his arms. When Eva arrived home, she found the house in a terrible state. On all the furniture, one bottle, one glass, one bottle, one glass. So, she put Valerie on a bed and she started to clean up the house. Then, she remembered it was her turn to clean up the stairwell of the block where they were living. So, she did that too. Then, she put all the dirty laundry to soak in hot water and detergent. Until they were soaking, she cooked also dinner for family. Finally, she washed all the cloths with her hands. Of course, she did all this and she fed her little girl and her older girl in the mean time, then also bathed her little one. When her husband arrived home, everything was in order.

After six weeks, Valerie was baptized as a Roman Catholic child. Eva was Roman Catholic, while Camil was Greek Catholic. Camil never declared weather he believed in God or not, religion did not interest him whatsoever. Eva, on the other hand, believed in God and wanted to baptize her girls after her faith.

Camil appreciated Eva's efforts, better yet, he demanded it loud and clearly, but he did not want to show it. He was convinced that if he shows the slightest sign of emotion, gratitude or love towards his wife or children, they will walk all over him and he will lose their respect. And he managed to get a lot of respect this way. His wife, Eva, that gorgeous, blue-eyed, long black haired, untamed, bold girl respected him. She was really afraid of him and she managed to transmit this fear also to her children. Also, a great part of the fear they felt of their father was due to all the beatings she applied to her wife and also to his son whenever he dared to intervene to defend his mother. The official reason of Camil was always jealousy. He was jealous of everything and everybody. This always started the family crisis, which ended invariably with the beating of his wife and son. And this always happened when he was drinking. It was a strange thing also about the drinking, he could go on and on for months without as much as a drop of alcohol, but as soon as he tasted the stuff, he was not able to stop. And he drank and tortured them until he fell ill. Until the smell of alcohol was oozing out of his flesh. Then, Eva was taking care of him and called his boss to excuse his absence from work, until he got back on his feet. And everything went on.

After little Valerie was born, there was kind of an untold agreement between them, they all wanted to keep her away of all these scenes. Valerie's first encounter with her father, with a man actually was while she was still in her mother's womb. Eva and Camil had to go to a wedding one evening. Camil dressed up faster than Eva. Eva wanted to wipe the floor before she left, so there she was, on her four, pregnant, wiping the floor. Camil got angry she was not ready so he kicked her in the womb with his foot.

"Come on, come on, move it. I don't want to be late. Is this the most important thing for you to do now? Why do you like to keep me waiting?"

Even so, Valerie was a healthy little girl. She was always hungry and her mother was happy for this. Mothers always worry when their little ones don't eat. Eva had to go back to work as soon as little Valerie was three months. Back then, maternity leave was three months. Eva searched very much for a good nanny. She found an old lady, but she had to take her daughter every morning to that old lady, as she was not willing to come to them. The other thing was that back then, in Mineville there were not so many bridges over the river that crosses the city as there are now. Eva had to wake up every morning at 4 o'clock. After the morning preparations, with her baby in her arms, she walked to the nanny, she left her baby there, then she walked to her job. She worked the nine –ten hours. Then, the way back to the nanny and back home. But not this was the hardest part of her life. After she arrived home, she began to cook, to clean the house, to wash the cloths. She fed her children. She checked her son's homework. Not even this did seem hard to her. What was hard for her was that in the evening, when she was beat, she could not go to sleep, she had to stay and wait for her husband. Camil finished his job around six o'clock in the afternoon, but from work he went straight to the pub, where he drank with his friends. And his friends knew very well that his weakest point was jealousy, so they filled his head with all kind of lies about his wife. How she was cheating on him. How he is the man in the house and he had to teach her some respect. In this state, given by his aggressive nature, combined with the booze and all these lies, he went home. He never had a fix hour when he arrived. Eva had to expect him with the warm food. If the food was too hot or too cold, it meant Eva did not love him and did not respect him, so the violent scene began. Therefore, Eva kept the food on the stove and waited on the window. When the food got a little cold, she warmed it up again. And so she continued on and on, until late in the night. Then he arrived, he ate, and in the best case, he went to sleep. In the worst case, he started the scene, triggered by jealousy.

He even alleged that he did not father Eduard and Valerie. Eva was very offended by this. She reasoned on and on that the two children were his, she never cheated on him. And the more she pleaded, the more he hit her. He beat her and asked her:

"Admit it, you whore, you cheated on me. The children are not mine. Don't you respect me at all? Why don't you admit it, you dirty whore?"

And after hours of beating and barking at her, she broke down and admitted crying:

"Alright, the children are not yours. You're right, you're always right. Just please stop this, you're killing me."

At this point, it seemed that he calmed down and he started complaining, especially to the children if they were around:

"Now you see, you see how much I suffer? I love your mother very much, but she doesn't love me. What can I do in this situation? I love her, but she loves someone else."

Then followed his crocodile tears. These scenes were the most damaging for Valerie. Seeing her father torturing her mother like this and then pretending that he is the victim, that he is the one hurt. To see such an aggressor actually shedding tears after terrorizing his own family. Did he actually think his children were so stupid and believed that he is a good, feeling person? Or just he was so stupid and thought they will buy anything from him…

Sometimes, Eduard intervened to try to protect her mother, so he got beaten too.

By dawn, he finally fell asleep. In one or two hours, Eva had to wake him, so that he could go to work. If she was not able to wake him up, she had to speak with his boss and tell that he was feeling sick and could not go to work. Of course, everybody knew what was going on. They knew his temper. They saw Eva going to work all beaten up and with the broken nose and with a black eye. But everything went on unchanged, his friends still did not feel any compassion for Eva and the children and they went on filling his head with trash.

There were also calmer periods in the family. Camil had always been a difficult person, but when he was sober living with him was bearable.

He left them alone, just retired in his room and occupied himself with his hobby. He liked to work on electric and electronic appliances and he has learned everything about mending TV sets and radios on his own. Eva cooked for them and they all ate together and there was no fighting between them.

Valerie especially liked the Sunday mornings spent with her parents when her father was sober. Eva cooked a large pot of soup with a big cow bone and with meat and a lot of vegetables in it. She gave a smaller pot to Valerie and she could also cook a soup, copying exactly what her mother did. Eva finished the soup around 9 or 10 o'clock in the morning and then all sat down at the table and Camil ate some of Valerie's soup and some of Eva's soup and used to say that Valerie's soup was better than the one cooked by her mother. This made Valerie very happy and proud of herself and encouraged her to cook with great pleasure. Other times, Valerie woke up later, just when the meal was ready. So, she came directly to the kitchen and ate together with her father the tendons and bone marrow and the vegetables from the soup. After the meal, Valerie went to play, Eva went to take a nap as she was up since 4 o'clock to cook and Camil went quietly to his room. This happy life took place only in his periods of soberness.

However, in the other periods, the drunk ones, Valerie started to understand, or better yet to feel, how things were going. She learned that her father's anger could be triggered by anything. In her little mind of a child, she was searching for rules like: «*If I do bad things, my daddy will get angry and he will beat up mammy. So, I have to be a good little girl, not to upset him.*» But this rule did not apply. She learned that if for example she fell and hurt her knees and she started to cry, her father would get angry and beat her mother because it was her fault her children were so stupid and so weak. She learned to study her father as soon as he stepped into the house. She was using all her senses for this. If he was in a good mood (that is, not intoxicated with alcohol) she could breathe freely and speak a little if necessary. If not, she just hid in the further corner of their little apartment and played quietly with a toy, taking care not to ask anything from her mom, neither food, nor water. Just staying there still and breathing very quietly. Valerie didn't have many toys either. There was no money for toys. And the balls were taboo in the house. Whenever Camil found a ball, he kicked it as hard as he could into Eva. Every single time he found a ball in the house.

Another little thing Camil enjoyed to do with Valerie was to lift her up about 50 centimeters from the ground. Valerie instinctively would reach out to a table or a door or something to hold on to it, as she knew his next move was to pretend he will drop her. Then, he used to say:

"*What's the matter, you don't trust me? You don't trust your own father? Do you think I would drop you so that you hurt yourself?*"

So, Valerie, let go of the object she was holding on to, to please him. And then, of course, he pretended to drop her. And then he laughed looking at her how she struggled to get her balance back, in order not to fall from his arms. The moments when Camil was the happiest were the ones when Eva and the girls were afraid or in difficulty. So, Valerie thought she should change the tactic. Whenever her father pulled this of, she just crossed her arms and totally relaxed and looked at him.

"*OK, dad. I trust you. I'm not afraid you drop me. Just do whatever you want with me.*"

Eventually, this is how she made her father stop doing this.

After she became four – five years old, it wasn't so easy anymore to hide from her father. He called her to speak with her. Now these talks were real interrogatories. He asked apparently harmless questions, but some of the answers could escalate into dangerous situations. Valerie learned pretty soon that she had to analyze every word, before she let it out her mouth. Some words could lead to conclusions such as:

"*You know, your mother is a whore. But what can I do? I love her, even if she does not love me.*" Valerie would remain petrified, as she knew what was to come. Other words could lead:

"*How can you be so stupid? Mom, how could you teach them to be so stupid? Am I the only intelligent person in this house? What would you do without me?* "At least after this conclusion, there was no beating, just contempt.

Eva never confronted him upfront, he was a terrible man. On the contrary, she showed him submission by any means. There were occasions when she washed his feet when he came from work and she asked the children to do the same. Or, after am outburst of aggression, Eva asked the children to go to him and kiss him on the cheek and tell him that they loved him. These scenes were more devastating for the psychic of the children than the beatings. The beatings were delimitating clearly good from evil and they understood clearly how to relate to them: sympathy and compassion towards mom – who was good; antipathy and opposition towards dad – who was bad. But these scenes were perverting. In these scenes, the good was making a pact with evil to take them down.

For some years in her early childhood, Eva could not find anyone to stay with Valerie. She was too small for school, her nanny refused at some point to stay with her. Eva's mother refused to help her. She had also other grandchildren and she had to take care of those grandchildren, she did not have time for Valerie too. Valerie always found her grandmother as a very cold woman. She never felt love or any kind of sympathy from her grandmother's side. Furthermore, her grandmother always told her how much she is like her father. How she walks like her father, how she looks like her father, how she eats much like her father. For Valerie, her father was pure evil, the fact that her grandmother saw her father in her was probably the worst thing she could tell her. Nobody else from the family had the time to help with little Valerie. So, Eva and Camil decided to leave her home alone, every day, for a few hours, until Eduard was at school. Of course they trained her very well, that she should not answer to anybody knocking on the door, that she should not play with matches and so on. They closed her in the apartment. Nobody could go in or out without a key. Valerie stayed for hours crying in the window, looking out for her sister or her mother coming home. Then, she went to the front door and cried there too. She was crying so loud, that some neighbors that passed by the door, every time they received postcards by post, slipped them under the door. Valerie stopped crying every time. And she looked for hours and hours to the colored postcards.

When Valerie was six and a half years old, she started school.

In school, Valerie was a clever and diligent pupil, even though a rebel, a real tomboy. A few days after she started school, Eva asked her:

"Do you have homework to do?"

"No, no homework."

"OK, maybe a few days later. You know, all children have to do homework. Your schoolmistress will tell you."

"Alright."

A few days later, Eva asked Valerie again:

"So, do you have homework?"

"No, no homework."

"Hmmm, that's strange. Your schoolmistress did not give you homework to do?"

"No, she did not tell me anything about homework."

Another week passed by, Valerie still did not have any homework to do. Eva got concerned about this, so she went to talk with the schoolmistress to ask what was going on.

"Hello, I am Valerie's mother."

"Hello, nice to meet you. I am glad you came to talk to me."

"Yes, well, I am little concerned. Valerie never has homework. I asked her several times, but she said she has none. Don't you give the children homework?"

"Of course I give them homework. I give them homework every day. I was wondering actually why Valerie does not do her homework. She is a smart girl."

"She tells me she does not have homework to do."

"Really? Well, let's go speak with her."

The schoolmistress and Eva went and confronted Valerie.

"So, how come you tell me you have no homework? Your schoolmistress tells me she gives you homework every day."

"She did not tell me to do homework. She said it to the children. She never told me personally «Valerie, do this and that.»"

"When I tell children to do homework, I refer to you too. It means you have to do it too. I cannot speak only with you personally. I have to teach all the children from your class. Do you understand?" clarified the schoolmistress, smiling.

"Yes, OK." said Valerie.

Eva was giving tasks to Valerie, usually what she did not like to do. Once, she made herself a pair of pants at a friend of hers, who was a tailor. She went for the first time, her friend took her measures. Then, when the pants were ready, she sent Valerie to bring them home. She tried on the pants. She said one leg of the trousers was longer than the other. So, she went Valerie back. Valerie went back, the tailor lady measured the legs, they were equal. So Valerie went back home with the trousers. Told her mother what the tailor said. Her mother got angry. She told her she was stupid, why didn't she tell the tailor one leg was longer than the other? What, she was not able to solve such a minor issue by herself? Valerie made 3 trips between her mother and the tailor and the thank she got for this was that she was stupid and incapable of anything.

Camil had as a hobby electronics. Every month he demanded to have the electronics magazine. One month Eva forgot to buy it so she sent Valerie to search it everywhere.

"*You go and search the magazine. You will not find it easily, as it probably was sold out. But you don't come home without the magazine. Do you understand me?*"

"I have to go and find the magazine. Otherwise I am not allowed to come back home."

"Right. Here you have the money. Go and buy it."

Valerie left. She stopped at every newsstand. She walked and she walked. She could not find the magazine in her town, so she actually went by foot 10 kilometers to a smaller town, right next to Mineville. Valerie was terrified. At her age, in her young mind, she took her mother's words very seriously. Seeing she could not find the magazine anywhere, she actually started to think where was she going to spend the night? Will they even come to search her? Finally, in the little town near Mineville she found the magazine, bought it and returned home.

Eva used to lend money to friends or relatives of her. Once she lent money to her sister in law and asked the money back several times, but she did not get it back. So she said Valerie:

"*You go to her and ask for my money. Tell her I need it back and tell her you are not allowed to come back home without the money.*"

Valerie was absolutely horrified.

"*But mom, what will I tell her? How can I go there, to the store where she works and tell her something like this?*" tried Valerie to reason with her.

"*You have to do it. You go and do what I tell you to do. Otherwise, you will be punished. You have to do what I ask you to.*"

Valerie had the best time when she was learning. She was a good pupil, the second in her class. Of course, she wasn't the first because she was wild, and undisciplined, more like a boy than a girl. Teachers were divided in two groups: one group liked her a lot. The other group just hated her. Valerie never cared too much what people thought of her. She was very badly dressed. Camil did not allow Eva to buy her nice cloths, she was not allowed to spend money for anything besides his booze. Even though Eva also worked and had a pretty good salary, almost half of the family income was spent for alcohol and cigarettes. Valerie's hair was always cut very short. Camil's opinion was that it was more hygienic like this. Valerie was always walking with bad shoes. Always when it was wet outside, her feet were wet inside her shoes. Valerie did not look much like a young girl, she looked more like a boy. At home, Valerie was always told:

"*Who do you think you are? You are nothing. You are just a worthless piece of dirt. We can do whatever we want with you. You think you're smart? You don't know anything! You think you look nice? Your sister is much prettier than you are. Don't you dare not listen to us, we have all the power over you!*"

So, Valerie thought to herself: "*Well, if on top all this, there are some persons who don't like me, that's their problem.*"

She did her homework, she was very conscious. She always did what she was asked to do. She never wanted to give reasons to the grownups to punish her. What she liked the most about learning, was that when she was learning, Camil left her alone. Even if he was coming behind her and was looking over her shoulder to see if she was really learning or just pretending to do so, while wobbling in his drunk state, he did not say anything to her. So, Valerie, tried to breathe as silently as possible and to write as beautiful as possible until her father was leaving from there.

Valerie had a real natural talent for English. Although back then, in the seventies, it was not a good quality to have talent for English. She wrote some love poems in English and learned very easily. Her English lady-teacher just adored her. Once, at a reunion of the teachers with the parents, she asked Eva:

"*Please allow me do some private lessons with Valerie. She has an inborn talent for English, I don't want any money from you, I just want to teach her more.*"

"*I have to discuss with her father. We'll let you know.*" Eva replied.

So she asked Camil about this. Camil said:

"*So, Valerie are good in English? Let's see. You think that I cannot check this? Bring me an English dictionary.*"

Valerie ran and brought her father the English dictionary. Camil took the dictionary and he started to read several random words from different pages and he asked Valerie:

"Do you know what this means? And do you know what this means?"

Valerie did not know even half of the words he asked. She was just a second grade pupil and this was how her father checked what she knew. He refused the teacher's offer to teach her more English:

"Why does she need more English? It is not important to know English. And what does that woman want with our child anyway? Tell her we don't want her private lessons."

So, Valerie continued to read in English whatever she could put her hands on and continued to solve grammar exercises, as this is what she liked to do most of all. It was her favorite subject in school and she dreamt of becoming an English teacher.

Valerie knew since she was young that she could cope better during hard times if she found something to raise her moral, something to lift her spirit. That something during her young years was the Swedish band ABBA. She absolutely adored them. When she listened to their music and looked at their pictures, she just rose beyond everything and felt happy. The problem was that on the communist radio it was broadcasted rarely. Pictures with ABBA were smuggled into the country and Valerie got them however she could. They meant the world for her.

With Valerie growing up, things were changing in her family. Her father became less violent physically. Even so, he still drank almost all of the time. He had those periods of him when he drank like crazy, not going to work, just staying at home tormenting them with his never ending speeches and aggressiveness. Once Valerie was studying on the floor and her father stumbled in the room and looked at her for a minute to check if she was learning. Valerie accidentally lost the smile of her face (she had to smile at him always, no matter what) and looked at him expressing exactly what she felt. As drunk as he was, he immediately said:

"Why are looking at me like that? You know that I can kick your face with my foot right now? Are you aware that this can happen in only one second? Don't give me that look. Don't think you're any better than me."

Eva started to drink along with him: "*So that less booze remains for him.*" Eduard also drank with them, on the same principle. Pretty soon, young Eduard started to have a drinking problem too, just like his father.

Many times, Valerie found herself feeling lonely and isolated with her intoxicated family. Again, all she could do to keep her mind away from this was to learn. Even if they made comments like: "*What good will learning do for you? You will never be smarter than we are. You think you need to learn to become a simple worker in a factory?*", at least they left her alone.

Camil and Eva did not have friends, nobody came to visit them. Camil was jealous of everybody. If something broke down in the house, Camil was not in the mood to fix it. He complained:

"*What would you do without me? You are so stupid, all three of you.*"

After this, if Eva called somebody else to fix the problem, of course when Camil and everybody was home, he accused her that all that she wanted in fact was to sleep with the guy.

Valerie never had many friends either. She wasn't allowed to go anywhere and she wasn't allowed to invite anybody home.

"*It's too dangerous. Who knows what can happen? Don't you see what's going on in the world? Well, after all, you do what you want, I don't want to get involved. But I will not be responsible if anything happens with you. Mom, do you let her do this?*" said Camil every time she asked if she could go out. Eventually, Valerie just stopped asking. She preferred not to ask, than to ask, get this lecture over and over again, and finally not getting permission.

Once at school Valerie went out in the schoolyard like all other pupils. In a corner, a boy was beating a girl. All the children were standing in circle around them and laughing. The sight of a male beating a female was always causing Valerie to slip into a state in which she did not act rationally. She felt the fear in her guts and her mind reacted like in a typical survival situation. Her instincts were taking over. So, Valerie jumped on the boy, who was few years older than her and much bigger, pinned him down and started to kick him with her fists as hard as she could. She beat up the boy pretty good. She could hardly be taken off the boy by two teachers. And as a result, she was the aggressive problem pupil. Eva was called to school and the teachers complained about her. Eva told her:

"*Thank God they did not call your father. Don't you dare tell him about this. If he finds out, it will be all my fault, he will say I taught you to be so bad.*"

The boys from the school hated her more after this incident. They waited for the right moment, and six boys found her walking once alone a long dark hallway. They surrounded her and started to threaten and offend her. Fortunately, her classmate saw the whole scene and ran for a teacher, who came and chased the boys away.

When Camil was not around, Eva complained to her children:

"*I don't have any money left. Your father drinks more money than he brings home. Now, I have to go ask for a loan again. I can't stand him anymore. Every month is the same story, we always remain without money and in debt. It's unbearable what he does with me.*"

"*Why don't you just leave him? You can divorce him, you know...*" Eduard replied.

"*What do you know? You're just a snotty kid, you'll understand when you grow up. I can't just divorce like that. What will everybody say? Besides, I'm catholic, I can't divorce.*" Eva argued back.

Valerie just thought for herself: "*Than shut the hell up and stop complaining!*" Of course, she could not say it out loud, she did not want to hurt her mother. She knew how much she suffered because of her father. She just could not understand why all this torment: if she could not stand him anymore, she should leave him. If she could not leave him, than she had to bear it.

Eduard had no problem in hurting his parents. On the contrary, he liked to do this. He studied them and tried to do what he knew would hurt them most. He lied to them, he was stealing money from them. If Valerie wanted something, for example something nice to wear or a decent pair of shoes, she didn't even ask her parents. She knew they wouldn't buy her that thing, and on top of everything she will hear over and over the same speeches. On the other hand, if Eduard wanted something, he asked his parents. Insisted with them. If this did not work, he blackmailed his mother to buy him what he wanted, otherwise he would tell Camil some things he did not know. And if this did not work either, he waited for the right moment, when his parents gave him money to pay for a bill or something, and with that money he went and bought what he wanted.

It was the 70's in Eastern Europe. These were the best years of the communist regime. People could still find food in the stores. They had electricity and heating all the time. One could live very well from an average salary. Moreover, the state was giving everyone a place to live and a job.

Camil and Eva were both working and they had decent salaries, but were never able to save anything. No money was invested in the house, they did not own a car. Eva was not allowed to buy anything for the children, in Camil's opinion this meant only throwing money out the window. Camil was convinced that he will die young, just like his mother. Camil's mother had died very young. He was only six when she died. She was walking outside bear foot like all the peasants back then and she stepped into something and cut her foot. She never went to a doctor and she died of the infection. Camil remained with his younger brother and his father. His grandmother took care of the two boys until his father re-married. Camil was a very agitated little boy, his grandmother had a hard time watching over him. At nights, she used to give him some spoonfuls of wine to make him sleep already. In time, this mistake turned into a real drinking problem. As a grown up, he was always saying:

"*Why should I save money? Then, I will die young just like my mother and you will bring your lover boy to live of the money I leave you. No way! I'm not stupid to do such thing*"

Everything was spent on booze, food and cigarettes. Eva was cooking every day for her family, always Camil's favorite meals. The more he drank, the hungrier he was.

The most difficult periods were the holidays, such as Christmas, New Year or Easter. Camil was drinking during the entire fest, Eva and Eduard were accompanying him. Valerie innocently hoped every year that Santa Claus will leave presents for everyone under the Christmas tree.

"*Mammy, I was a good girl this year, wasn't I? Do you think I deserve to receive something this year?*" asked Valerie her mother.

"*I don't know, I don't know if Santa has any money.*" answered Eva.

"*How can you be so naive, how can you still believe in such stories? There is no Santa Claus. There is no God. These are just stories made up by Christians*" continued Eduard.

"*Don't tell her there is no God. These are the things they are teaching you in school?*" replied Eva.

"*Yes, in school they teach us real scientific facts. It is proven, there is no God. Religion is just opium for the masses.*" replied Eduard.

"*Don't listen to her, Valerie. Her mind is poisoned by the communists. Of course there is God and there are angels of God.*" said Eva.

Valerie did not know what to believe. But she would have liked Santa to come and leave some presents. So, first thing in the Christmas morning, when everybody was still sleeping, she rushed out of bed and went straight to the Christmas tree. There she found her shoe. It looked empty. So, she stuck her hand into it and searched. And she found a rotten potato. Camil used to put her a rotten potato in a shoe, under the tree. If she wanted so badly to get a present under the tree, well, her wish was granted...

Despite all this, Valerie was convinced she has to send out love and kindness from her heart. Whatever they told her at home or in school, she knew deep in her heart that what goes around, comes around. Rarely she received some money from her mother, without Camil knowing it, She always saved these small amounts of money and on Christmas she bought little presents for Camil, for Eva and for Eduard. The result was that everybody had a present under the tree, except for Valerie. But Valerie was happy anyway, happy that she could surprise them in a pleasant way, happy that she could bring a little joy in the house, happy that she could bring a little smile on their faces, even if for a short moment.

Valerie started secondary school in the eighties. The family got from the state a bigger apartment. This one had three rooms, two bathrooms, a big kitchen and a big hall. One room was Camil's, another room was Eduard's and the third room was for Eva and Valerie. Camil got a job away from the city, he was coming home only on Saturday afternoon and went again to work on Monday morning.

During the communist regime, schools were always against religion, but during the eighties they became quite aggressive in this sense. The dictator's portrait was on the wall of every classroom. And not only they were declaring out loud that the communist principles were the only ones to follow, not only they forced these principles on the young minds, they started to play subtle mind games with the children. Now, it became a shame if you believed in God. One Sunday, Valerie dressed up nicely and went in the morning to the church. On the way there, she met with one of her teachers.

"*Where are you going dressed up so nicely this morning, Valerie*?" asked her teacher.

"*I'm going to church, Madam*." answered Valerie.

Next day in school, in front of the entire class the teacher started:

"*Well, children, let me tell you what I did yesterday. As it was Sunday, I* *went out for a walk. Guess who I met? I met Valerie. She was all dressed up. You think she doesn't have nice clothes? Oh, you are so wrong. She does have nice clothes, but she only wears them at church. So I asked her << Where are you going, Valerie? >>*"

And in this point, the teacher started to walk affected through the classroom, like she was imitating Valerie's walk: "*<<I am going to church>> she said.*"

All the children started laughing. Valerie was processing the event in her head. What did she do wrong? Why was her teacher mocking her? She could not understand, but she thought: «*Well, she's always bragging how her pupils come to visit her after they finish school. I'm sure I'll never come to visit her after I finish school.*»

At home, Eva eventually reached her limit of endurance. One night, Camil arrived home drunk and mad with jealousy and beat her up badly. After he fell asleep, on their tiptoes, Eva, Eduard and Valerie escaped from home. Little Valerie was in her pajamas, Eduard rolled her into a blanket, took her in his arms and off they were. Outside it was dark and raining. They went to live with Eva's brother and she filed for divorce. It was very hard to divorce during the communism. Just like the dictator did not like to admit that there are mental patients, therefore the psychiatrists were not necessary under the communist regime, he gave strict orders that people should not divorce, this was not in accordance with the communist principles regarding the family. A divorce could take years and years, and several times the lawyers tried to convince the parties not to divorce. Eva went through the divorce for months and months, but at the final hearing, she changed her mind. She accepted to remain Camil's wife.

The children felt disappointed and betrayed after this. Eduard was managing the formation of Valerie's mind. Valerie was persuaded that she is worthless, and there is no God. The games of words and phrases by Camil and Eduard, to which any answer would Valerie give was stupid, and hence meant she was just a little idiot. And if Valerie spoke out her opinions and beliefs, they were even more fierce in their mind attacks. In school, the teachers were making huge efforts to demonstrate there is no God and if any of the children declared they still believed in Him, the reaction of the system was furious. Looked a lot like the inquisition. All this convinced Valerie that she should believe in God. She understood completely how wrong the ideas at home and in school were, so if these two institutions were against something, that particular thing had to be good. Also, Valerie believed that even if she was not allowed to say whatever she wanted, she was not allowed to do whatever she wanted, she was not allowed to dress as she wanted or eat what she liked, nobody could stop her to think whatever she wanted. Her mind was free and it was up to her what she created in her mind: love and peace and logic, or hatred, aggression and chaos. For Valerie, communism did not have logic. First of all, it started out from the idea that all men are equal. This made no sense: how can you reward a person that works 14 hours a day, with consciousness and intelligence the same as you reward a person that pretends to work 8 hours a day? How can you take all properties from everyone and make it one common property, and then expect everyone to take care of that common property as if it was their own? How can you impose the selling price of a specific commodity and expect the several factories producing it to compete to make it better and at a lower price? Why should they compete for that? The state imposes the price anyway and if the factory has losses, the state will pay for the losses. So, why struggle? Despite all the bombing from around her, Valerie had very clear and strong beliefs in her head and nobody could take that away from her. And she believed strongly that things have a way of getting into their normal and logical state, no matter how hard some people were fighting to alter them for their own interest. She was convinced that communism will eventually end, as it was against logic and common sense.

In the eighties, life was getting harder and harder in Eastern Europe. The country had too many debts, so the dictator decided the people should make sacrifices until the debts were paid off. Electricity was interrupted several hours a day, didn't matter if it was night or day. When it was dark outside, the towns looked spooky. All those huge blocks of flats, totally in the dark. The streets all dark. The blocks were rarely heated. Every afternoon, it was dark and cold in the house. Valerie was learning at candle light, with gloves on her hands, with a knitted hat on her head, with two pairs of woolen socks, with several knitted blouses on. In the stores, one could not find anything to eat. On all the shelves, there was only cheap champagne and canned beans. Literally, there wasn't anything else. You could not find in the store basic hygiene articles, such as toilet paper, soap, tooth paste or cotton. The bread, the flour, the sugar, the oil and the meat were sold to the population only in limited quantities. The dictator had appointed a doctor who informed the population that eating too much was not healthy, so every person was allowed to eat 300 grams of bread every day, 1 kilogram of flour a month, almost 1 liter of oil every month, 500 grams of meat every month and so on. Every person received coupons with for basic food and hopefully, after staying for hours in queues in front of the groceries, they managed to buy these quantities. One could not find real coffee in the store, there was only surrogate coffee, made of chickpeas and oat. One could find real coffee only in the so-called "shops" and only with foreign currencies. But it could be bought only by the strangers, as the people was not allowed to possess foreign currency. What the people could eat was vegetables, second class vegetables of course. The first class vegetables were exported to Russia, the regime needed the money for the well fair of its corrupted leaders and for the building of the dictator's megalomaniac ideas. If you were lucky and you stayed in a long queue, you could buy some eggs. Milk and dairy was sold only half an hour in the morning. If you wanted to get some, you went in the front of the store in the middle of the night and you stayed in queue until seven o'clock in the morning when the store opened. In this way, you could buy two liters of milk and maybe a little glass of cream or of yoghurt.

The TV program was reduced to 2 hours a day, so that the people could save electricity. It consisted of half an hour news – what else did the brilliant mind of the dictator come up with – a new totally inefficient factory to build, some new agricultural ideas, like for example planting fir trees on the coast of the sea. He was an expert in all the fields. Then half an hour of actors reciting poems dedicated to him. And finally, a film that demonstrated once again how good communism was to the people. If you wanted to see a foreign movie or listen to some foreign music, you had to install an antenna on the block you were living and sometimes you could catch some foreign channels, Mineville was pretty close to the western border of the country. Of course, this was forbidden, but everybody was doing it.

The content of the newspaper was pretty much like the TV programs with the picture in front and then just articles about the bright years of communism and the brilliant genius of the dictator. Even the books had on their first page a picture of the dictator, did not matter the subject they were treating. The personality cult was pushed to the extreme. The most evident displays were when he visited different regions of the country. On the way he went, they planted near the road high corn, so that he can see how flourishing is agriculture in the country. They were mending the roads and painting the signs. The towns were cleaned where he passed, the factories all freshly painted. People had to dress in uniforms and stand one after the other on the side of the road he passed and they had to wave with the little flags and to chant his name happily. Everywhere, the informers were watching. Anybody could be an informer. Your brother, you mother, your best friend, your neighbor. They just had to tip the secret service and afterwards a number of bad things could happen. You could wake up in the middle of the night with the secret service pounding on your door. They took you away for questioning, you disappeared and nobody heard from you again. You could go next day to work and find out you have been fired. Your children could be expelled from school with no reason whatsoever.

The hardest winter of the 80's was the winter of 1984-1985. There was a joke going around: <<those who survived this winter will be arrested by the secret service. It is obvious they are from the resistance. >> Temperatures went to almost -30^{0}C for several weeks and the communist apartments were not heated. The gases were stopped, the electricity was interrupted several hours per day to save the energy. If you left a glass of water on the table during the night, the water froze. Valerie's family had some neighbors with who they managed somehow to get along well. One evening, after several hours without electricity and gases, the little four years old girls of the neighbors came to them, knocked on the door, on the dark staircase and Eva opened the door. The little girl started to tell Eva very happily: "*Eva, Eva, we have gases. They turned on the gas, we can heat with the cooker stove*". This was Valerie's one the saddest moments of her life. How sad that a little child was happy to receive something so basic as gases for heating...

After four years of primary school and four years of secondary school, most of the children were starting high school. The first eight years of school ended with a ball. Almost every girl had a new, beautiful dress tailored for this occasion. They went to a hairdresser and got even a makeup with this occasion. Valerie did not get a new dress, she had never been to a hairdresser and she was not allowed to wear make-up. She got an old dress, remained from her mom. Her hair was always cut short, it was more hygienic this way. And she was not allowed to wear make-up.

Some children finished school after eight classes and became workers. Those who continued, had to sustain an admission examination to the high school they wanted to attend. Valerie was aware of the cross examination she will be submitted by Camil with this occasion, so she thought to change the strategy a bit. She prepared very well her speech and approached Camil when he was not expecting this. Valerie would have liked to attend a high school with philology profile as she was passionate about English, but Camil would have never agreed. Generally, during communism the only talent one could have had in school was mathematics. No other subject had any importance. And if you liked English, you definitely were in trouble:

"*Why do you like English? You want to get away from the country and escape in some decadent capitalist country?*"

Valerie thought it over and over and she decided what she wanted. She waited for the right moment, a quiet Sunday afternoon, when her father was sober. So, she went into his room and started boldly:

"*Look, dad, they told us in school that we should decide as soon as possible what high school we want to attend. And I thought it over and you know, I like Chemistry a lot. And Chemistry has a good future in our country with all the factories and all. And maybe I will have a chance to find a job in our city with the chemical plant. So, I would like to attend the high school with chemical profile. What do you think, you agree?*"

Camil was impressed. He did not expect this maturity from his younger daughter and generally speaking, he never expected any intelligence coming from his family. So he replied:

"*Well, I see you're determined and you know what you want. Go for it.*"

Valerie was admitted into the high school with chemical profile. She was becoming a very strong opinioned, naughty, rebel young lady. She had the bad habit of speaking out loud her opinions and again some loved her for this and others hated her. Her favorite subjects were English and Chemistry and she spent hours every day studying these two subjects. She was a good pupil, doing well on all subjects. She understood she never could be in the group of nice girls, she wasn't sweet, she wasn't feminine, she did not come from a "good" family, she wasn't preoccupied with the issues of the nice girls. So, she joined the group of naughty girls. At least, these were less hypocrite. She tried some cigarettes, some sleeping pills. When she was 15, she reached the conclusion that there was nothing out there to live for, so she tried to kill herself. Once by cutting one vein on her right arm, and the second time by taking a full box of sleeping pills. She failed, both times. Nobody in her family or at school noticed any of this. She became more convinced that nobody cared what happened with her.

Camil was getting older, he became less aggressive physically, moreover he was home only in the weekend and on holidays. When he was away, Eva, Eduard and Valerie were relieved. Valerie felt free and started to understand how important freedom was in her life. Eva became more cranky every day. She left every day a long list of chorus that Valerie had to do after she got back from school. Even if Valerie did everything, Eva criticized her and was always dissatisfied. The cleaning of the apartment was Valerie's duty. Eduard was cleaning only his room. Eva was not cleaning, she was working and commuting to the job. At night when she arrived home, she was beat. So, Valerie was left with the cleaning of the windows, cleaning of the ceramic tiles that were covering the walls of the bathrooms and the kitchen, beating the carpets, taking out the trash, buying the daily bread and vegetables, also going to collection point with the empty bottles and jars, after she washed them of course. The state had collection points for the glasses and jars and paid some cents for every bottle and jar. Valerie did not receive not even the small amounts of money resulted from this. She gave it all to her mom.

Furthermore, the painting of the apartment every few years was the job of the two children. They had to gather all the stuff in the middle of the room, than cover them with a plastic foil, and then they had to paint the rooms. After that, they had to clean and put everything back. All this with no help whatsoever from their parents. This was a job for two strong men, not for two teenagers. Camil was drinking through the entire event. He was nervous. And convinced that the they will ruin the entire house. So, he got drunk and stood wobbling in the door of the room and watching every move they made. Eva had to cook for him, over and over. And listen to his pointless babbling, for hours about his childhood with his stepmother, and the three years spent in the army and the first years as a worker. And the top was that after the painting and cleaning, the doors and heating elements and the glass doors had to be painted. This was exclusively Valerie's job. Eva had managed to get (this is a typical expression – it is used when get something, but you don't buy it and you don't receive it from others; it can be interpreted in any way) some cream-colored paint and Valerie had to paint everything with it. The problem was that the paint was way over the expiration date and it was hard to apply on the surface. All the three experts, Camil, Eva and Eduard criticized all her work, but none of them helped her. She could do at least this for the family, now couldn't she?

Eduard was working at the same factory as his mother. He was spending a lot and drinking and smoking. His salary was never enough for him from one month to the other, even if he still lived in his parents' house. He was asking money from Eva regularly and never returned it. The three of them were not united, Eva did nothing in this regard. Valerie would have liked to have a united family. With her father ok, she understood that it was not possible to make a team, but why couldn't they, the three of them be a team? Valerie thought:

"*Why does mom allow Eduard to do all those nasty things? To compensate his terrible childhood? She could compensate it, but in the meantime she also could discipline him. She is our mom, our alpha female, why doesn't she unite us in a family?*"

Whenever Camil went away, they just retired in their corners and their thoughts. They never discussed anything meaningful. When Eduard was in the mood, he made a long speech, almost like he wanted to totally demoralize Valerie. Future looked always lugubrious and there was no hope for anyone. Valerie listened to these speeches, after all Eduard was her older brother. But her ideas and beliefs were not altered at all by them. She saw how many things she already has been through and she ended up just fine in the end. She could not be convinced that the world is going backwards, towards chaos and evil. On the contrary, the world could only evolve towards love and spirituality and good sense.

When Valerie turned sixteen, her older brother Eduard got a small apartment from the state. Immediately he moved out, happy that he could get away from home. The small apartment was not much, it was on the fourth floor in a block with four floors. When it was raining heavily, the walls got wet. The windows and the door did not close well. It was in a pretty bad shape, with no furniture and in a dangerous neighborhood, but it was still better than staying under the same roof with Camil. Valerie remembered how many times her brother promised her when she was little that as soon as he gets away from home, he will take her too and they both will be free from Camil. Now, it was all forgotten. After he left, Eduard never mentioned this again. After he left from home, he could focus totally on his lover, a married older woman. All promises made to her little sister, in the nights when Camil was abusing them were forgotten.

Valerie had to study a real lot in high school. The marks are between 1 and 10. Well, Valerie never had only marks of 10, but her average degree was over 9,00. She didn't have the right image either to be the best of her class – her parents were not teachers or doctors or anything. They were just regular workers. But she always came out with the second or third average mark at the end of the year. Moreover, she studied for admission to university. Most of the children studying for admission were taking private lessons, in school the preparation was pretty general. But these private lessons were quite a big expense for the parents. Camil has asked once Valerie:

„I see you want to take the exam for admission in university. Do you want to have some private lessons?"

In just a fraction of second, Valerie weighed all consequences: what if I succeed at the admission exam? That will be the happy case. What if I fail the exam? I will never hear the end of it. All his life, he spent the minimum possible with me, imagine if he makes this investment and I fail... So she replied to her father:

„Thanks, dad, but it's not necessary. I will study on my own. Thank you though."

Valerie decided to try the admission to University in Steville, the Chemical Faculty. There was a lot to study for this examination. The examination consisted of three tests: mathematics, physics, chemistry. A total of ten manuals to learn. The admission examinations were difficult back then and the stake was very high: if you were admitted, you came out a college graduate and you automatically entered the middle class of the communism. You most probably got from the state a nice, warm job, in an office. You did not become a worker in a factory or in the field.

In last year of high school. Valerie made a bet with herself to come out first at the end of high school – she liked the way the kid with the highest average mark was called „chief of promotion" at the end of high school. So she went for it. She focused a little more, studied in a more disciplined way, paid more attention also to the subjects that did not interest her so much. She woke every morning at 4 o'clock because she could focus best in the morning. She studied very hard a couple of hours in the morning and then another 4-6 hours in the afternoon. By this time, she became addicted to coffee. She drank quite a lot of it, but she could not imagine her life without coffee.

Finally, the last day of school arrived. All the pupils were gathered in the schoolyard. All the teachers were there and all the parents. Camil and Eva also were there, Eduard didn't show up. After the usual speeches, the moment Valerie was waiting for has arrived. The headmaster started with the ninth grade, he called out the pupils with the best average marks. Then the tenth grade and the eleventh grade followed. Finally, the twelfth grade. The head master announced her name. She did it, she came out first. She was declared "chief of promotion" in front if the entire school. In front of her parents. This time she felt self-confident. This time she felt her parents were proud of her. Valerie obtained this little success only by her own work. Not because for being beautiful, not for wearing fancy dresses, not because her parents were friends with the teachers. She achieved this because she learned seriously for twelve years, without trying to cheat herself, her parents or her teachers. It seemed unreal to her that she obtained this success. Knowing what the children were doing in school. Most of them were cheating at the exams. The most intelligent of them all was considered the one that cheated best without being caught. The boys were mainly interested in girls. The girls were mainly interested in dresses and makeup tips. It wasn't very cool to study hard. There were however, few pupils who wanted to study because they wanted to be admitted in a good university. These ones got all the support from their families, they had calm and loving homes and they have taken private lessons. Valerie did not have any of these, all she got was her mind and her will.

Her happiness lasted for one day. She had to start immediately to arrange everything for the admission to university. She had to make copies of her birth certificate, identity card and high school graduation diploma and go to the notary public to legalize them. Then, she had to buy a train ticket to go to Steville. The train ticket was a very tough thing to get.

There were thousands of people travelling to Steville in those days, many of them by train. The queues for buying the tickets were huge, you had to wait in line for hours.

For most of the pupils, their parents did all these. But Valerie did them by herself. It took her a few days of walking from one place to the other in the warm and dusty summer and staying in long queues for hours, but she managed to obtain all the papers needed for the admission exam. They were all in her purse, hanging on her shoulder. She took a bus to get home with them, next day early in the morning she was going to leave to Steville to compete with all the rich, well adjusted and well trained kids. After about twenty minutes, she got off the bus, in the station near the block where she lived. She made two steps and looked into her purse. It was open. And everything was stolen! Her wallet with the money for the trip to Steville, the train ticket and her identity card. The legalized documents necessary for registration, her keys to the house, all gone! Her mind was trying to process the event. She could not go next day to Steville, she had no ticket. But even if she went to Steville, she had no documents, it was impossible to get everything again and still go to the exam. This meant she had to stay one year at home and go to the exam only next year. Her parents will not let her stay at home and not get a job. And if she did get a job, she will not be able to study again for the exam.

CHAPTER 2

One day before her trip to Steville, where she was about to take the examination of admission to university, all her documents, the train ticket and her money were stolen. Valerie went home, nobody was there. She remembered that her mom said she would go to Eduard that day. So Valerie went also to Eduard and found her mother and her brother there. She told them the whole story. They were talking.

"*There's nothing we can do. Even if we did something, it's too late.*" said Eva.

"*It takes days to get copies again to everything. And to get a new identity card from the police, it will take days. And those declarations why it was stolen and so on…*" said Eduard.

"*OK, so that's it. I am not going to Steville, it wasn't meant to be.*"

"*We have to change the lock to the door. The thief has got the keys, the address. We have to explain everything to your father. Oh, we'll never hear the end of it.*" said Eva.

"*I can already hear him: <<why couldn't you be more attentive. I told you to take care. Especially in such crowded places like a bus. You should have hold your purse in your hand. You knew you had important documents there>>*" continued Valerie.

Suddenly, they heard a knock on the door. Eduard went to open the door. It was a policeman. He presented himself, then:

"*Can I speak with Valerie?*" he asked.

Valerie answered: "*Yes, of course, it is me.*"

"*Did you lose anything today?*" he asked.

"*Yes, as a matter of fact my purse was stolen on the bus and I had in it very important documents, my identity card, my keys, money and my train ticket to Steville.*" explained Valerie.

"*Well, you are one lucky girl. I was walking down town, near some shrubs and for no reason I looked down. Between two shrubs I saw a wallet thrown down together with an envelope with documents, open. I picked it up. The money and the keys were gone, but there were the documents, the identity card and the train ticket. Seeing the train ticket, I thought you are going to Steville tomorrow, for the admission. I looked up the address in your identity card and went to your house. I knocked on the door, but nobody answered. I was preparing to leave, when a neighbor of yours passed by me. I asked him if he knew where everybody is gone. He said he didn't know, but there is a chance to find you at your brother's place and he indicated me the block and the apartment. So, I came here and I found you. Here are your things.*"

Valerie could not believe her eyes and her ears. «*What were the odds? Is this true?*» she thought. And the policeman finished with a smile:

"*Good luck with the exam. And take care of your stuff, somebody may steel it.*"

Valerie thanked the man and he left.

Eva and Valerie went home, together with Eduard. Eduard was supposed to go to Steville with Valerie the next day. In the evening, Camil also arrived from work. They never told him what happened. Camil was nervous anyway because his little girl was going to university. And now this other story, with the lost and found documents. It would have been too much, he could cope with it the only way he knew. He drank the whole night. Eva and Eduard had to keep him company. At least, they let Valerie sleep.

Next day, early in the morning everybody was preparing the big trip. Except for Camil. He was sleeping drunk, he has had a very hard night. The three of them prepared everything and were ready to leave. Eva and Eduard haven't been sleeping the whole night. Before leaving, Eduard drank some more wine. He took the bottle and drank directly from it. Right before going out the door. Valerie looked at him stunned. She was thinking: "*Why is he doing this? We are just about to leave. How are we going to go in that train full of people for three and half an hour? He will smell of alcohol. And then, when we arrive to Steville, we shall have to go by foot a lot, with all the bags and with him in this state....*" Valerie was looking at her brother and understood that their father has defeated him. He became just like him.

Eduard thought that he got back at Camil by acting like him. But the truth was that Camil defeated him by making him become just like him.

They got to the train. As expected, it was crowded. There were those little compartment with eight seats each. Every seat was taken, there were people even on the corridor. Eduard smelt of alcohol, everybody in the compartment was looking at them. Valerie was so ashamed to go with him in that state. But, after the three and a half hour trip, they arrived at Steville and Eduard seemed to sober up little by little. From the train station, they went by foot to the apartment where they rented a room for the few days they were going to stay in Steville. Valerie and Eduard were walking, carrying the big bags they came with. Valerie did not see one friendly face. They were all looking at them like: "*Now look at these two. They came to Steville like it's their backyard. We'll show them. Dirty peasants…*"

They walked and they walked. It was summer. Warm and dusty. The bags seemed heavier than they really were. They knew the direction, but it seemed they will never get there. Finally, they saw from a distance the corner of Street Seaville. They had to get to street Seaville, number 2. They stopped for a moment and put down the bags to rest. Valerie said:

"*Look, Eduard, that must be the street! That's the corner of street Seaville! And number 2 should be right on the corner. We're almost there!*"

And Eduard replied:

"*Yeah, and on this corner is number 200. We just have to get to number 2.*"

They laughed so hard, that they could hardly walk on. And they got to the corner. And luckily, it was the house with number 2, and not 200 …

The rented room was in an apartment that belonged to an old lady who lived alone. Everything in the apartment was old and smelly. Lots and lots of old, smelly stuff. At every step you made, everything was squeaking and cracking. The price was very high too, but they could not find anything better, especially in that period.

The next three days Valerie sustained the exams. There were around 1.000 competitors competing for the 150 places of chemical engineers. The examination consisted of three tests: on the first day she had the math test, the second day the physics test, and the third day she had the chemistry test.

With the Math, she was aware she did not know anything. In high school, her teacher was a very ill, old woman who did not have any energy for teaching. She remained with virtually nothing.

With the Physics, it was almost OK. In the first two years of high school, she did not learn much Physics, as her teacher gave birth to two children in two years, and nobody replaced her in maternity leave. They played during the physics classes in those two years. In the last two years however, they got a very good and exigent teacher and this had a good effect. Valerie recovered everything in these two last years and she felt she was well prepared for the examination.

With the Chemistry, Valerie was very confident. Chemistry, together with English, were her passions and she was very well prepared for the Chemistry exam. She was aware however that also the other children were well prepared, most of them got private lessons, that prepared them exactly for these exams, while she had learned only alone at home, what she thought was important.

After she sustained all the tests, in the very same night, the two of them returned home to Mineville, this time with the night train. At night, they did not have a direct train, they had to take two connection. It was a terribly tiresome night, they did not find any place to sit down, they had to stand all night long in a dark, dirty, stinking train.

Camil welcomed them home by drinking some more. Eva's only concern continued to be cooking for her husband and listening to his never ending stories. Valerie fell ill. She broke down from the stress and the tiredness. Her left foot swelled up and it hurt so much, she could not stand on her feet. Valerie had to lie in her bed for several days. As her leg was swollen and hurt, she put a rolled blanket under it, so that it was elevated. This annoyed Camil extremely. He did not say anything directly to Valerie, but she heard him telling her mother:

"Look at her, she just sustained the exam, she hasn't been even admitted yet, and she already thinks she's better than us."

"Why, what did she do?" asked Eva.

"Look how she lies there, with her leg elevated. Who does she think she is? I think we should teach her a lesson, I think we should beat her up, we should give her the lash. We have to put her in her place." said Camil.

Eva did not reply anything. She just looked at him in horror. Even after all these years of terror, Camil was still able to surprise her with his evilness. Eva just went into the room and whispered to Valerie:

"Hey, my little one, I know your foot hurts. But your father doesn't like how you are lying here. Take that blanket away from under your foot and sit up. Pretend you are reading or something."

Valerie did this immediately. Fortunately, she was a very strong girl, so the problem with her foot disappeared after a few days, she could walk normally again.

One day, she had to go to town, her mom left her some chorus to do. Camil asked for a few days off, at work he said that for the admission exam of her daughter. In fact, all he did those days, was to drink and torment some more his family. When Valerie returned from the town and opened the front door, Camil was on the phone with somebody. After a few seconds, Valerie understood her father was on the phone with the Faculty of Chemistry. Somebody has told him that the faculties are already posting the results from the exams and he was curious to see how Valerie did. On the other, he did not trust the information he got from his wife and children. He thought it was possible that Valerie will lie to him that she succeeded, just to go to Steville and live of his money, without being actually admitted. So, he called the faculty himself and asked what result Valerie obtained.

After a few minutes of waiting, the person on the line told him that his daughter was admitted. He thanked politely and hung up. He told Valerie:

"You are admitted."

"I am? Hmmm ..." answered Valerie. She did not feel any joy whatsoever. On one hand, she was sincerely surprised, she knew how many competitors there were on those 150 places, on the other hand she was waiting with fear her father's reaction. How will he take it? What if he gets mad that he was a worker all his life and now his daughter will become and engineer?

Summer holiday went by fast. Soon, it was autumn and Valerie began her first year in university. The school year started on the 15th of September, but the students had to go to register for lodging a few days earlier. The wealthy ones rented apartments in Steville. But most of them, just like Valerie, received lodging in the student halls. At the university, a list was posted indicating where every student was to be lodged. After consulting the list, the students went to the hall assigned for them. They went early in the morning and stayed in queue until late in the afternoon. There were hundreds of students lodged in one hall and only one person was registering them. A lot of documents had to be filled in and it all went very slowly. Of course, those who managed to pay off the intendent, got the better rooms. Those like Valerie, got the worst rooms, those with badly closing windows and doors, on the ground or last floor and those situated at the end of the hallway, as those were the coldest. Valerie got a room at the last floor, with three roommates she didn't know.

There were around 30 rooms on a floor. In each room, there were 4 girls. They had common toilets and shower, around 10 at each floor, where 80 girls lived. There was also a common kitchen on each floor. It wouldn't have been so bad, but there wasn't always hot water – nowhere in the country wasn't hot water all the time- so in the evening there were long queues at the showers. The common showers did not have any shower curtains. Every autumn the administrators put shower curtains, but they were stolen after a few days, so during the entire year the showers remained without curtains. So, everybody in the queue was looking patiently to the girl that was showering exactly in that moment. Also, the drains were usually clogged, so everybody was standing in a big pool of miserable stinking water. From time to time some nut of the street came inside the shower room and looked at the naked girls. They knew there were no curtains and they knew between which hours there was hot water, so they could come exactly in the perfect time.

The rooms were not heated. Even if it was forbidden, everybody brought homemade electric hot plates. These were homemade by putting an electric wire on a ceramic support. The thicker and longer the wire was, the more heat it produced, and of course the more electricity it consumed. The electric consumption was so high during cold season that the fuses from the electric board were burnt out every day. The girls went and replaced them and everything continued unchanged. From time to time, the hall administrator came to check in anybody was heating the rooms. All the electric hot plates were hidden under the bed. Then the administrator commented:

"How come it's so warm in here? Do you have one of those electric hot plates?"

"*No, we wouldn't bring one of those here. They are forbidden!*" answered the students.

"*Yeah right...*" mumbled back the administrator.

Valerie did not feel good in university. She missed her mom terribly, she had no friends. Her roommates hardly spoke with her. In Steville, people were very different from those in her home town. She always had the feeling that her presence annoyed them. She never saw a friendly face in that town. She never went out, just to school and back in the hall. Her parents gave her a monthly allowance of 1.000 crowns for her expenses. This amount was enough for eating one month at the buttery and the lodging expenses. After paying these two, she remained with nothing. Valerie decided not to eat anymore at the buttery, so she remained with the greater part of her allowance. Eating was tricky, as you could not buy a bread without the ration book. The only things you could buy freely were the local vegetables and fruit, so this is what she ate. She managed to save 500 crowns every month. She put aside the money carefully, not spending anything for herself. She never bought any cloths or shoes, never went to a hairdresser, never went out. The only things she bought of this money were presents for her family for their birthdays and Christmas.

Eduard was working and had a pretty good salary. Unfortunately, he managed his money just like Camil. He always spent a more than he earned. He never had money, even if Eva gave him many times money without Camil knowing it. Once, when Valerie came home, Eduard approached her.

"*Well, tell me some more, how is it in university*?" started Eduard.

"*You would say if it's university, you learn something interesting. But the courses are so boring I can hardly stay awake. And I absolutely hate Steville. I don't know anybody there.*" answered Valerie.

"*Yes, but you go out, right? With your friends? I know there are a lot of nice places where you can go out.*" continued Eduard.

"*I don't have friends. And I don't like to go out and spend money foolishly. I better stay home and read or knit.*"

"*Well, I would go out if I were in Steville. But I'm not. I'm here, in Mineville. And I have to come to work every day, except Sunday. And on Sunday, I have to clean, to cook, to wash and iron, all the housework. And if I work so hard, you would say I should have enough money to get by from one salary to the other. But my salary is not enough to live for one month. Plus, I have the debts."*

"How much do you owe?"

"It's not that much. 3.000 crowns. But I can never pay it back. I pay it back one month, than I remain with no money and I have to borrow again. It's like a vicious circle. If I could get a little help, just until I get back on my feet."

"Well, all you have to do is cut back on the expenses a few months and pay off the debts little by little, every month. What is your salary? And what are your expenses?"

"Well, my salary is 3.500 crowns. I pay for food 2.000 crowns a month. Than for the utilities 1.000 crowns. I hardly spend for anything else. I haven't bought a book for months now. Or cloths, or anything. I still did not buy anything for the apartment, the important things I needed. I need a new blanket, the one I have is rag. I should buy a new bed, you know I brought from home my old bed, it has a lot of broken springs and it smells. If I could just pay back my debts and get rid of them…"

"Well, hmm… I could loan you some money. I can give you 3.000 crowns. You can pay back the debts and get back on your feet. And I can give you 500 crowns a month for a few months, so that you can buy what you still need in the house. And then, when you can, you can pay me back. What do you say?"

"I think it could work out fine. It would help me."

"But please, I insist you pay your debts first. Don't throw the money on useless stuff. OK?"

"Of course, don't worry."

Valerie lent him the money and continued giving him the 500 crowns monthly. She ended up lending his working brother the amount of 5.000 crowns.

Eduard told the whole story to his married lover.

"Can you imagine? I convinced her to give me all her savings. How stupid can she be? I have always said this: stupidity must be scoffed" Eduard said to him.

"I don't know if she is stupid. She tried to help you, right?"

"Yeah, this is what I told her, that I want to pay back my debts. I will not pay back anything! But, this is not the point. The point is that she is so stupid she does what anybody asks her to."

"Not anybody, just her brother."

"Yes, but still. She doesn't buy herself anything. She only buys us presents. What does she think? She can turn back time in this way and make up for all the pain father caused us at every Christmas and birthday? No way! I will never forgive him for that! Never! And I will pay them back everything they did to me, to her and to my mother. I'll show them. And now I taught one more lesson to my little sister. Everything that she knows, she knows from me. But hopefully, now she also learned she does not have to do what anybody asks her. I'll never pay her back this money!"

Valerie did not get the highest marks in the first year of university. It was very much to learn and she was not convinced that all that stuff will help her later on in her career as chemist engineer. Of course, she learned the best she could, but she could not compete neither with the privileged children, whose parents were teachers or some local celebs and they got the highest marks literally not knowing anything, nor with the geniuses that knew absolutely everything, those who learned every minute of every day and knew all courses by heart.

The schedule was hard. She had courses from Monday to Saturday, from eight o'clock in the morning until eight o'clock in the evening, with a lunch break of 2 hours. Not all the faculties had so many courses, but at the chemical engineering faculty they had a lot of laboratory hours and practical training hours and the students had to attend all of them. On the top of all this, all the girls had one day a week when they had to dress with army cloths and they were trained theoretically and practically like men in the army. The dictator considered that the women had to be prepared and kept in reserve and in case of war, they had to contribute to the defense of the country just like the men. True gender equality. He was a real humanist, right? And all those people who accused him of not being humanist… But Valerie, together with all those girls back then did not appreciate his humanity the way the state expected them to do. They could hardly get dressed in those uncomfortable cloths, which kept warm in summer and cold in winter. They did not like all those hours spent to learn about army, when they knew they will never be in it. They did not like the obligatory medical checks for army they were subjected to and how they were treated like animals.

In the holiday after the first year, Valerie went home, to Mineville. The most interesting thing in that vacation was that Camil started to notice similarities between Valerie and one of his younger brothers. Suddenly, Valerie started to take after him and his family. Now this was quite strange, considering that he always claimed he did not father the two children. Valerie discussed with Eva and Eduard:

"*How come that I have become his daughter only after I was admitted in faculty? Now isn't that interesting?*"

She started the second year, a little better adjusted, there were some colleagues with whom she exchanged some words every now and then. She got a nicer room this time, with nicer roommates, two of which were her colleagues also in faculty.

One of her roommates had her birthday in December, so they thought they should throw a party. They invited around twenty students, cleaned up the room nicely and prepared some food. Valerie was staying in a corner and watching the guys entering their room. One particular guy caught her eye. He was just as poor and badly dressed like she was, just that he tried to show something else to the world. He tried to show that he was self-confident and that he did not care very much how people judged him.

Of course, as soon he noticed that she is watching, she looked away and danced and laughed with other guys. But, as the hours went by, she felt more and more sorry for him. He was just sitting in a corner, drinking alone, not dancing, not participating to any of the fun. Looked like nobody understood him. So, she sat near him and they ended up talking. She started to feel a strange connection with him. He looked like a twenty years old scared, neglected and abused child, with those bad teeth and those old cloths. Valerie's instinct to protect any abused child was instantly triggered. She actually turned down the others who came to call her back to party, just to stay near Alan and at least try to keep him company.

They met once accidentally after the party and they talked a little. Then, the Christmas holiday and every student went home. After they returned from the holiday, Alan came quite often to the hall Valerie was in. Many times he came to her, but sometimes he went to his colleagues who lived in the same hall. Valerie was watching out the window and she saw him coming every time. And she was praying in her mind:

"*Oh God, please, let him come to me. Please*!"

She was falling more and more for him. She thought this is a guy who doesn't have anything. He won't mind that I don't have anything ether.

He will not judge me because of my family, probably his family is pretty much the same. How could she go out with a well dressed guy from a decent family? She could never meet his standards. And how could she take a normal guy back to her parents? What would he say seeing Camil drunk almost all the time? This Alan however seems is he deeper than that.

Alan, on the other hand, was playing with her. He felt she was interested in him and it was the first time in his life when a girl was so interested in him, so he decided he will enjoy the play.

In the end of January the session of examinations started. Valerie felt she could not take any longer this game, so she decided to confront him directly. Once, when he came to visit her and they were all alone, she told him directly:

"*Look, Alan, maybe you noticed. I love you. I would like us to be closer friends than we are now. What do you say?*"

Alan was quite surprised, but his poker face did not give anything away. This is what he wanted, but he never expected to get it so easily and quickly. So he answered:

"*Well, I'm surprised at this. I thought we were only good friends. I am not looking for love. I just like to talk to you every now and then.*"

"*Really? You're not looking for love? So, what are you looking for?*"

"*Frankly, the thing I want most is that my mother comes to me and strokes my back. You know, when I was a boy back home and I was doing my homework in the afternoon, my mom used to come behind me and she just put her hand on my back and watched me writing. This is the closest physical contact I need right now. I don't want more, especially not from you.*"

"*Alright then, it's a good thing I asked. At least now I know where I stand. Well, I should go back to study now. We have a lot of exams this session and I should start learning. Good luck then and see you around.*" ended Valerie the discussion, trying to hide her emotions and to calm down her heart that was ready to jump out her chest.

Valerie remained heart-broken after this. In the session that followed, she could not focus much on the studying. So, she failed two exams. It wasn't a big tragedy, she could sustain the two exams again in the summer session.

After the session ended, the students had a one week vacation and they all went home to their families. Valerie used this time to heal her wounds.

She was a passionate person and because of this she tended to suffer a lot, but on the other hand, the good thing about her was that she had an exceptional power to leave everything behind her and move one. Whenever she was in crisis situations, she repeated in her mind: «*If you cannot walk, than crawl. But never ever stop moving forward. Never ever give up. No matter how many times you fall down, always rise and keep on going ahead.*»

The one week holiday passed quickly and she returned to school. She and her roommates had a deal to wait for each other when they came from home, as they had to carry a lot of bags, there were not many taxis in those days in Steville and the public transportation vehicles only took them from the railway station to the center of Steville, but not up the hill where their hall was situated. So, when the train arrived in Steville station, she saw one of her roommate waiting for her. Surprisingly, Alan was waiting for her too. She got off the train with all the baggage and after the greetings she asked Alan:

"*How come you are waiting for me?*"

"*Well, after we left on our holiday I missed you.*" Alan answered.

"*I don't understand. I told you I loved you, you said you don't want love, how come you missed me? Aaah, you mean you missed me as a friend, right?*"

"*Let's go, shall we. You want to remain here in the station and keep talking? Shouldn't we go home?*" ended Alan the discussion.

"*Alright, alright, let's go. But I'm not through with this.*" mumbled Valerie.

Alan spent the whole day with Valerie.

"*Do you know I was heartbroken after you rejected me? Do you know I could not study the whole session?*"

"*I am sorry for that. I didn't mean to hurt you. It's just that I felt we're moving too fast.*"

"*Alright, but you should have said this and we could have slowed down, but you just rejected me. And I don't think I deserved that.*"

"*OK, so can we get over this?*"

"*Aah, it's easy for you to say. You don't understand how much I suffered. I wish you have a session just like I had the last one because of you, so that you understand the hell I went through.*"

Alan wasn't very impressed with that, now he was just focusing on seducing her. The days that followed, he visited her every day. They ate together, they discussed a lot about everything. It didn't take much to seduce Valerie either, she was head over heels for him.

When she was in his company, Valerie felt like her soul has finally arrived home. She felt totally confident in him. Alan had absolutely no aggressiveness in him. If a man was taller or bigger than she was, Valerie felt subconsciously threatened by him. She always felt threatened by her father, so any male that physically was bigger than she was, represented a danger for her. Alan was slightly shorter than she was and also thinner. He was more a child than a man, a suffering child too. Valerie felt that underneath his naughty comments there was a lot of hidden pain, originating from his childhood. Valerie felt she found her soul-mate.

They became inseparable. They did not have much money. Valerie received her monthly allowance from home, Alan did not receive anything from home, as he had a scholarship. He did not receive any amount of money as scholarship, but in compensation with this, he did not have to pay for food and lodging. So, they got by as they could. They were taking care of each other, Valerie was cooking, Alan washed the laundry. They were learning together, spending together all the time when they were not in school.

Neither Alan, nor Valerie have ever felt noticed in their lives. They knew they did not have nice cloths, they were never allowed to go out ever because:

"*We have no money!*"

They never had money and never were part of the group of favored kids. They were used to be kind of on sufferance. By having this love affair however they got noticed. All their friends and colleagues were envious of them. They were twenty years old and they formed an indissociable couple. When you were around them, you could physically feel the love bond that connected them. And nobody could find any occult reason why they were together, which was even more annoying. They were both poor, so nobody could say one of them had any kind of interest.

The only time they could not be together was during the holidays. Valerie had to go to Mineville, 150 km north of Steville and Alan had to go to Streamtown, 120 km south to Steville. These were the hardest times, they missed each other terribly. Alan couldn't come to Valerie, Camil wouldn't have allowed it. On the other hand, Valerie couldn't go to Alan, again Camil wouldn't have let her. All that they had during the holidays were the daily talks on the phone. And the hope that school will begin soon and they will be together again.

In June 1989, Valerie was starting the final session of exams of her second year of university. Her close relation with Alan was hard to swallow by her roommates. He was always there with her and the girls did not like this. So Valerie decided it's better to go home for the session. As usual, she took the train home. Most of the students travelled with no ticket, they just gave some money to the conductor and that was it. Valerie bought a ticket. When she got up on the train she discovered, like many other times, that her seat was already occupied. Many times, the Railway Company used to sell out one seat two times, they were stealing from the customers by any means they could. Normally, Valerie would have fought for her seat. But this time, an old lady was sitting there, who travelled from 450 km away and she was going to get off the train at the next station. So, Valerie stood on the aisle. All the windows were open, it was hot outside. The train windows did not stay open by themselves, they had to be held open. Valerie put her elbows on the window near which she was standing and she was looking out. In a certain point, the railway doubled, and from the opposite direction another train came, a goods train. It was loaded with planks. Valerie was looking out the window, to the train passing by them, in the opposite direction. Suddenly, she felt very afraid. She thought:

«*What if something bad happened?*» Then, a couple of seconds later « *Neah, what could happen?*»

She hardly finished her thought and something hit her so hard, she was thrown back into the wall of compartment. She could hardly understand what happened. She looked at her right arm. It was hanging in a strange way. And blood was pouring from her elbow. Then, she looked on the floor and saw a piece of wood, full with blood. After a few seconds, she understood what happened. A plank flew off the goods train and hit her in the right elbow, crushing it.

Coincidence was that in the same compartment with her, two doctors were travelling, brother and sister. They were going to Mineville. The man doctor insisted that Valerie gets down in the first station and goes to the emergency room. Valerie refused. Alan remained in Steville, her parents were in Mineville. She did not want to get off in a station in between. She told the doctor:

"I refuse to get down. If I lose my consciousness because of loss of blood, you can throw me down on the field, anywhere, I don't care. But until then, I continue to travel to Mineville."

Indeed, she was losing a lot blood. She was able to sit down in her compartment and the doctors were discussing.

"I think we should put a tourniquet to her arm. She is losing too much blood. She will not make it to Mineville." said the woman doctor.

"I think we should not put a tourniquet to her arm. In two more hours, her right arm will receive no more blood and she will lose her arm. She is losing blood, but I think the damage would be bigger if we put her tourniquet."

Finally, they did not put her tourniquet. Fortunately, in the same compartment, there was also a retired nurse who happened to have with her 20 meters of sterile bandage. So they bandaged her and that was it. Nobody had any pain killer and soon after the initial shock, her arm started to hurt.

After one and a half an hour the conductor appeared, asking her if she needed anything. She said:

"Yeah, I need some pain killer. My arm hurts a lot. And bring your first aid kit, you see my bandage is already full of blood."

"We don't have any pain killers and no first aid kit. Anything else? Do you need some water?" replied the conductor.

"No, I don't need water, thanks a lot."

This was the only reaction of the railway company to an accident that happened because of their gross negligence. Actually, Valerie thought for herself:

"I am lucky I did not get a fine. As I know the state, they could have fined me for staying with the arms on the open window. This is how the laws are made in our country: they punish the victims."

After three more hours of travelling, Valerie arrived to Mineville. Eduard was waiting for her in the railway station. They found in the station some acquaintances and they went straight to the hospital, the emergency room. When they arrived in front of the emergency room, a male assistant was getting out of it, with a cigarette in his hand. He wanted to take a break. That Saturday was a rough day in emergency. When he saw Valerie coming, with that big bandage full of blood around her arm, he put his cigarette back in his pocket and returned with her in the emergency room.

Eduard went in the room with her. There was also the doctor on call who immediately took care of her. After he finished the first aid, he looked gratefully at them. They did not make any sound. Usually, people make a big drama in the emergency room. And the accompanying persons make a bigger drama than the victims. But these two acted very courageously and he could do his job.

After this, Valerie was transferred to the Intensive Care Unit. The things that preoccupied her most were:

«What will father say about this? He will get angry with me that I wasn't careful. He will say I shouldn't stay in the open window, now look what problems I caused. And Alan, oohh, he will be devastated. Poor little thing. He will be so worried…»

After some time, also Camil and Eva came to the hospital. Valerie couldn't look to her father, she was afraid of his reaction. But this time, he did not say anything. Eva acted like nothing happened and this helped Valerie more than anything. She felt she would not have the power to encourage her mother if she were devastated.

Most of all, Valerie tried to process what happened. Whenever something bad happened in her life, in order for her to be able to move on, she had to understand. She had to find a reason. And this time she found God. Better yet, she found God again. She understood how close she was to death. Just 20 centimeters upper, and the plank would have hit her temple and she would have died. Or, what were the chances that in a crowded train, she will be in a compartment with two doctors? What if they put her the tourniquet? She would have lost her right arm.

On Monday, Valerie went to surgery. The operation took more than two hours. The surgeon found her elbow crushed. The bone was crushed, the muscle and the tendon were crushed, only the nerve was continuous and untouched. He took out several wooden chips from her arm and he did not close her up, because he was not sure the cleaning was total. He wanted to operate her again on Wednesday. So he did and seeing the evolution was good and there was no infection, he put her a metallic rod to keep her elbow in a right angle, then he closed her up. Then, her arm was put in plaster, the inner side of her arm, the part that was not cut.

For Valerie, it was a shear miracle that she did not die and that she did not lose her arm. She bore everything courageously and without a sound of complaint. The only time when she broke down in tears was when she returned from the second surgery in her ward and found there Alan. She cried and complained like a little child, all her defenses broke down and she revealed her fears and the pain she was going through. Alan had the power to touch her soul. He stayed in the hospital with her and took care of her. As her right hand was plastered, Alan was feeding her. He was writing for her. He was combing her hair and brushing her teeth. All this happened during the summer session and Alan spent more of the time with Valerie in hospital. Alan did not sustain some of his exams and he failed some of them. At the end of it all, they both realized that the wish of Valerie came true: "*I wish you have a session just like I had the last one because of you, so that you understand the hell I went through.*" She never meant to harm him when she said it. The words just came out of her mouth and it looked that they were very powerful.

While Valerie was in the hospital, he spent all the days with her. But he could not sleep also in the hospital, so he went to sleep at her house. Camil did not make a big deal out of it because of Valerie's condition. Valerie thought in normal conditions, Camil would have never accepted a stranger to sleep in their house. And how come Valerie has got a boyfriend already? When she is only 20 years old. After she came home from the hospital, Camil even allowed her to go to Alan's parents, to Streamtown. Alan and Valerie enjoyed all the time spent together.

In autumn, after they got back to school, they practically lived together. Alan was sleeping in a bed with Valerie, in the hall she was living, even if it was forbidden, as it was a hall exclusively for girls. They did not have any plans for future. They did not want to get married, they just did not think what will happen after they finish university and they will have to return home.

In December 1989, something happened and they got their holiday earlier than expected. Nothing was declared officially, but everybody was discussing that the Revolution that began in the country. The army and the police was shooting people on the streets for manifesting against the communist regime. It seemed unbelievable. People had lost all hope, they dared not dream they will get rid of the dictator. He led the country since the sixties and now there were persons who had the courage and go out on the street and say out loud their opinion.

As most of the students, Valerie and Alan went home, glad they got the holiday earlier. In Mineville, there was no shooting on the streets. The miners just gathered in the center on the city, they went to the local authorities and changed the mayor and chiefs of the party and burnt some pictures of the dictator. This was pretty much it.

One day, they came out of school and went for a coffee in a coffee shop in the park in front of the faculty. It wasn't very cold and the owner placed a TV set out on the terrace, on a shelf. It was a color TV set and the channel was MTV. A music video clip was on and it was color! Valerie thought she died and went to heaven. Also, slowly, food started to appear in the shops. Every now and then, when they had a little money, Valerie bought a chicken and she cooked it for Alan. She would have liked to cook it in one piece, in the oven. But they did not have an oven so she cooked it on the stove, in a stew pan, covered and with a little water under it. It was just as good as the cooking in oven. Or they bought a bottle of Coca Cola and a little bag of peanuts. This was pretty much the greatest luxury they could afford.

Alan and Valerie were living together and there were many persons around them annoyed by this. Especially Alan's mother, who approached them several times regarding this subject.

"*People are talking, they are asking all kinds of questions. What is with you? You are living together and you are not married.*"

"*They should mind their own business.*" used to answer Alan.

"*Yes, but I want to know too. What are you going to do? Do you love each other? If yes, you should get married. If not, it's better if you end it right now. You cannot continue like this.*"

One afternoon, when Alan and Valerie were in Steville, she called Valerie on the phone and told her:

"*Look, tomorrow morning we are going to your parents to discuss about your wedding. You will come with us. So be prepared, tomorrow we come to pick you up and we go together to Mineville.*"

Valerie informed Alan about this and that was it.

Next day they all went to Mineville. The meeting between Valerie's parents and Alan's parents was quite interesting. Camil was pretending he did not know why those people went to his house, as no formal proposal has taken place. Eva did not understand why Alan's mother is insisting for this marriage.

"*She acts as if she was the mother of the bride and the bride was pregnant and the marriage has to take place urgently. But she is not the mother of the bride, and you are not pregnant. What is the big rush?*" said Eva to Valerie.

Alan's father knew that he had to pose the question, but he was avoiding this by any means. He started like:"

"*Look, these kids love each other and they won't separate.*"

"*So, what are you saying?*" answered Camil.

"*He says they have to get married this summer. And we have to make it before the 1st of August, because between the 1st of August and 15th of August no marriages can be performed as it is the fast of the Virgin Mary.*" intervened Alan's mother, who was used to organize things, as everything always had to take place as she wanted.

After this Alan's mother decided and informed everybody also that the bride's dress has to bought by the bride's parents and that the wedding expenses should be divided between the two families. Camil did not object, he just said that if this is in the best interest of his daughter, he agrees.

After these aspects were decided, they continued with irrelevant conversations. The next day, Alan's parents went home and everybody remained trying to process the events. Alan and Valerie did never thought of marriage. Alan just wanted to please his mother and Valerie wanted to please Alan. So they went along with his mother's decision. Valerie's parents did not agree with this, but they declared they will not get involved. It's her life, it's her mistake, she will pay for it.

The next months went by pretty quickly.

As the wedding was closing in, the first unpleasant surprise was the fact that the orthodox priest refused to marry them because Valerie was not orthodox. Alan was orthodox and his priest said the only way he could marry him was for Valerie to be baptized orthodox too. Eva and Valerie were quite affected by this, but could not back out now.

Valerie asked her mother-in-law for just one thing. She did not like the custom to cry out at the wedding, in front of everybody, what amount of money has everyone given as a gift to the newly wed. She felt it was much more decent that everyone leaves an envelope with what they can and if they could and that is it. Alan's mother promised they would do so.

The wedding was scheduled for the end of July.

At the civil ceremony, among other things, the registrar read the following:

"*-the state protects the family;*

-the marriage is based on the freely given agreement of the husband and wife;

-in the relations between the husband and the wife, as well as when they exercise their rights in relation with their children, the husband and the wife have equal rights;

-the parental rights are exercised exclusively in the best interest of the children;

-the family relations are based on friendship and mutual understanding, and the members must support each other both morally and materially;

-the husband and the wife decide together in all the matters of the marriage"

Alan's parents insisted for an orthodox religious wedding, even though Valerie was catholic. The priest said he cannot wed a catholic with an orthodox, therefore Valerie had to be baptized as an orthodox. This was disturbing, especially for Eva:

"*Why should the priest baptize you? You're not a pagan. You're Christian. You have been baptized.*"

Valerie agreed to this, as she had no choice. So Valerie confessed before the wedding and the priest baptized her. At the confession, the priest explained:

"*You don't have to feel bad about this. This is the custom. The orthodox religion is very similar to the catholic religion. There are only slight differences. On is that the boss of all catholics is the Pope of Rome and the boss of the orthodox is our Archbishop. The catholics make the cross sign up, left, right, down, while the orthodox make the cross sign up, right, left, down. The catholics say the Holy Spirit, and the orthodox say the Holy Ghost. But they really are very much the same. And important thing is that you have faith in God and go to church when you have the time. Orthodox or catholic, whichever you want.*"

The priest won her over with this. He was the only person friendly with Valerie and this made her feel good. She made the mistake of telling Alan's family what the priest said at the confession.

"He should not have said that. It was not proper. What kind of confession was that? He should have asked you about your sins, not say these things."

Their disapproval made Valerie like the priest even more. At the religious wedding, he spoke about love and togetherness.

Alan's parents invited around 200 persons, from Valerie's side only their parents came and a couple of friends. Regarding the wish of Valerie, they did according to the custom, not according to what they promised her.

Valerie hardly knew anybody at her wedding. From the 200 persons present, maybe she knew 20. She felt stranger and lonely, with all the eyes watching her. She could hardly keep herself from crying. It was a terribly stressful event for her. The next day, she got her foot again swollen up like after the admission to faculty and again she had to lie in bed for several days, as she could not step on her foot.

The money raised at the wedding was mostly used to pay off all the expenses. Not much remained and all that remained at Alan's mother, she was going to manage it, as her opinion was that Alan and Valerie will not be able to manage it themselves.

Alan and Valerie did not enjoy at all the holiday after the wedding and they were looking forward to the beginning of school, in September when they could return to school. They spent the holiday at Alan's parents, trying to cope with the hard work that was required in their household. Alan's parents had regular jobs, besides that they had a lot of land to work and four cows. Then, there was Alan's younger sister who was still in school.

Valerie did not have anything against hard work, but this was a little too much. She has been raised in a big city, she never had to do such hard physical hard work, most she had to do at home was to clean, to cook, to wash the laundry, to buy groceries, maybe paint the house. But is still was much, much easier than the work in Alan's parents house.

Finally the school started again. Alan and Valerie got along very well when they were by themselves. They spent quality time together and almost one guessed what the other one thought. If Valerie was in the mood to drink a coffee, she did not have to say anything, Alan just got up and made a coffee and they drank it together. Valerie was always cooking what Alan liked and what they could afford, on the other hand Alan helped her by washing the dishes. They were a quiet couple, they did not cause any trouble.

At faculty, there was a lot of material to study. The chemical faculty was a pretty hard one, with lots and lots of courses, laboratories and practical hours. They also studied computers, but there were no modern computers yet in the country. They learned to work with BASIC, which allowed them to make short simple, computer programs, but they did not learn any user programs yet. Alan was quite passionate for computers and Valerie liked to please him in any way that she could. She insisted to control very well their expenses and managed somehow to save the money necessary to buy their own little computer for home. It cost 10.000 crowns and it was produced in the country. The computer consisted only of the central unit and the keyboard. You had to have a cable and TV screen to connect it to the computer. You also had to have a tape recorder and tapes with programs you uploaded on the central unit, connected to it with a cable. They could learn a lot more computers than at school and Alan could play in his spare time.

After the marriage, Valerie's parents reduced her monthly allowance. They considered: "she is married now, so her husband should support her." Alan's parents have never gave him a monthly allowance, he had to survive only of the scholarship from the state. Life got very tough for them. They had very little money and could hardly survive from one month to the other, even if they did not spend foolishly for anything. Eventually, they took a night job together at the milk distribution company. This consisted basically of taking the bottles of milk from the point the car left them to apartments situated in several blocks in Steville and taking back the empty bottles from the customer to the car that took them back to the factory. At nights they had to work and during the day they were in school. And on top of this, they were literally starving, they never bought any new cloths, they never went out and for holidays they just went home to work some more. Nobody protected the marriage, neither the state and society, nor the parents and the family.

Valerie suffered a lot with her teeth. She had some cavities since her early childhood, but nobody ever took her to the dentist. Now, as a student, things got much worse and she had several rankled grinders that hurt terribly. She had no money to go to the dentist, so she just took the cheapest pain killers and suffered. From time to time, her teeth swallowed up and all her face was distorted. But this is not what bothered her, it was the pain that was unbearable.

Then her tummy was aching quite frequently. She never went to a gynecologist, but she was sure it was gynecologic problem. The tummy pains were so strong, that she could not even walk while she was having them. Still, she never went to a doctor.

Until they were students, they could live together in the student hall. It was a modest life, but at least they were together. Finally, they finished university. Again, all the colleagues were dressed with new dresses and suits. Valerie and Alan were wearing again their old cloths, they could not afford to buy anything new. They had to leave eventually the hall and an aunt of Alan who was living in Steville agreed to let them live in her apartment until they could find something by themselves.

Valerie and Alan were both chemical engineers. Alan found a job immediately in a factory from Steville. Valerie applied for several jobs in Steville. The answers were:

"*Well, you know the position is already filled. We had to place the announcement in the newspaper, because you know, it's required by the law. But, we actually already have a person in that position.*"

"*We are looking for a man engineer, not for a woman engineer.*"

"*We are looking for somebody with experience. What experience do you have? Aah, you have just graduated? Well, we are sorry, but we really need somebody with experience.*"

"*We are looking for a high school graduate. You are totally over trained for our need.*"

Valerie's self confidence was seriously shaken. She has studied hard all her life, it was hard for her to accept that there was absolutely no company that needed her. Alan did not help her either to find a job. He was ashamed that her wife was unemployed. He was ashamed to go with her to the unemployment office. Indeed, it was a very depressing sight. There were queues that lasted for hours, a lot of documents to register there and then, after you finally got the unemployment aid, you had to go again every month to stay again at that never ending queue and apply for a new prolongation. Even so, one could receive the unemployment aid for maximum 9 months, after which you were out there on your own. With absolutely no income and no hope.

With every rejection, Valerie broke down in tears. She came home and cried for hours. After each queue at the unemployment office, she got terrible stomach aches. She prayed every day for a job. She would have accepted anything, just to have a little income of her own.

She felt totally useless and there was nobody there to lift her spirit. She worked a lot at Alan's aunt house. She thought maybe like this he will accept that she is unemployed. Alan's aunt was working, she had a husband and three children. So, Valerie and the children were the only ones staying at home. Valerie tried to help the best she could. She cooked, she washed the dishes, she cleaned the house, she washed the laundry as often as she could for all of them with her hands, as there was no washing machine. When the children came home from school, she helped them with the homework. And this wasn't easy either. The children could not focus very easily and Valerie felt it was her duty to make them somehow interested by school and learning. This however, is an impossible mission when the children have parents that don't think learning is very important.

Valerie and Alan were living from his salary. He was an engineer on probation. The money were hardly enough for the food they were eating. They could not rent anything with that money.

Even so, Alan insisted they should have a child.

"*We don't have a place of our own. You know I don't have a job. We cannot afford a rented apartment. How shall we raise a baby?*" asked Valerie.

"*We'll manage somehow. I think you should have a baby, you just stay home and do nothing. At least, have a baby.*" replied Alan.

Valerie did not get pregnant easily. She did not know what the problem was, she couldn't afford to go to a doctor. She also had terrible belly-aches and she knew they were somehow related to her gynecological problem. If she got the aches at home, she could just hide and lie down until they passed. But if she got the aches on the street, she felt she will faint so she sat down wherever she was, on the border of the footway. This condition went on for months. She also had terrible toothaches. Periodically she had dental abscesses and she did not go to the dentist either, again for not having money. She felt even more useless because she could not get pregnant. What good was she for Alan? With no job, no income, no help from her parents and not this. Not even capable to have a baby.

All she could afford to do was to pray. God never let her down and she needed no money to go in a church and kneel down and pray. She felt sometimes she has a little life, a little soul inside of her with whom she could communicate in her mind, and after a few weeks it disappeared and then after another few weeks, she could speak with it again. She couldn't share with anybody this experience.

"*You are going mad, you know? How about finding finally a decent job instead of talking with the spirits?*" would have said Alan or her parents and brother.

Finally, totally desperate, Valerie asked God in one of her prayers:

"*Please God, if You consider it is good for me to have a baby, please give me this baby now and let him or her be healthy. If You don't think it is good for me, than just stop all this now, all this trying of having a baby and the pain and everything.*"

This was right before the Christmas of 1993. Valerie and Alan went to Mineville, to Valerie's parents for the holiday. Alan stayed just a few days and had to return to Steville. They decided Valerie should remain some more in Mineville, this would reduce their expenses in Steville.

So she remained. She remained until the beginning of March when she returned to Steville. With the train, as usual and Alan waited for her in the railway station. They went to the tram station and in the few minutes they waited there, Valerie told Alan:

"*I'm not quite sure yet, but I think I am pregnant. We are going to have a baby.*"

"*Now you got pregnant? Now, when I have just decided to divorce you?*" answered Alan.

Chapter 3

Alan and Valerie have tried for several months to have a baby, but with no success. When she finally got pregnant and she gave the good news to Alan, he replied her that he has just decided to get a divorce.

Valerie was shocked by his reaction. Because it was him who insisted they should have a baby as soon as possible. Because usually a couple gets married when a child appears, it does not get a divorce with this occasion. Because he has never ever spoken of divorce until now. Because he has always told her that he loves her.

"*But why? Why do you want to get a divorce?*" Valerie asked him.

"*Because you don't have a job, and we can hardly get by with my salary, because we don't have a place of our own and we cannot afford to rent anything. Because your parents don't help us at all. Al least my parents give us food if we go home, your parents never gave us at least one sack of potatoes.*" answered Alan.

"*But at least can we wait until after the baby is born and then we divorce?* "asked Valerie.

"*No, we have to divorce immediately.*" answered Alan.

"*But why?*"

"*Because I say so. No matter how much you cry, you don't impress me. I won't change my mind. I want a divorce right now.*"

She cried and cried. Not to make him change his mind, but of shock and pain and despair. She felt like it was the end of the world. What will happen with her and the little baby? Where will they stay? How will she raise the little child with no income?

The discussion between them was repeated several times the days after that. Valerie was crying almost all the time. She knew this was not good for the little child, but she couldn't help herself. What shocked her the most was that Alan was totally cold and inconsiderate seeing her like this. As if he was a totally different man from the one she married once. The weeks went by one by one and there was one last discussion about this issue that ended like this:

"I understand that you want to get a divorce and you want to get it before the baby is born. It is OK. I understand. But then, why did you insist to have this baby if you knew you wanted a divorce? You insisted for months << Let's have a baby. Let's have a baby>> and when we got the baby, you want a divorce. It's just that I don't understand."

"It's nothing to understand. This is the situation. And if you don't like it, go and have an abortion" replied Alan.

In this particular moment, when Alan said this, Valerie had a revelation. She understood Alan had lost his mind. This was not a normal person and she had to get out of that relationship as soon as possible. So she replied:

"Alright then. We shall get a divorce. Regarding the child, I will not have an abortion. I have tried for months to get pregnant, you know how difficult it was. If I get an abortion now, maybe I will never have the chance again to get pregnant. So I will keep the baby. Don't worry, you will not be affected, we shall divorce anyway."

She decided not to cry anymore, to lift her own moral and manage the situation the best she could. She used to sing "It's alright" by East 17 in her head. When Alan will drive her away she will go home and find a job and she will manage somehow.

Valerie went to the doctor too to see if everything was OK. The doctor confirmed her that she was pregnant. He also said:

"Didn't you have problems? Any pain? Did you get pregnant easily?" asked the doctor.

"As a matter of fact, I have had pains in my tummy all my life, but I did not know the reason. And we have tried for months now to have this baby, but only now I got pregnant. Is there anything wrong with me?"

"Your uterus is not fully developed. You have the uterus of a little girl and it does not have the right shape either. It cannot hold a baby. You probably got pregnant, but you miscarried at the first cycle. Also, you have a huge cyst. This is what caused the pain. Did you know about it?"

"No, I didn't."

"It happened that this time, the cyst positioned itself so that it blocked fetus

inside and you could not lose it. The fetus had a few weeks to develop and this is how it survived. It is quite a miracle you remained pregnant without any outside intervention. You know that?"

"*I know.*" answered Valerie.

When she got out from the doctor, Valerie rushed to Alan to tell him the whole story. She thought she could raise his interest for their baby. His answer to all this was:

"*Yeah, that's interesting.*"

At the next medical check, Valerie wanted Alan to see the little fetus on the screen of the ultrasound device. Maybe if he saw the little life inside her, his heart will melt. Maybe he will open his heart and they could work out somehow the situation. She thought how she could convince him to go in the gynecologist's cabinet and look to the baby. She got an idea, but she did not say anything to him. She just asked Alan to go with her to the check. Alan agreed. He remained outside the clinic and smoked until she went in. Valerie waited her turn and she went in to the doctor's cabinet.

"*Hello doctor. Do you mind if I call in my husband to see the baby?"*

"*Hello. You want to show him what he has done?"* asked the doctor smiling. "*No, I don't mind. Go ahead and call him.*"

Valerie put on the most serious face she was capable of and went out to Alan and told him:

"*Alan, the doctor said you have to come in. He wants to discuss something with you.*"

"*With me?*" asked Alan, putting out his cigarette. "*What is the problem?*"

"*I don't know. He said he wants to speak with you.*" continued Valerie very seriously.

So Alan went in with her. Valerie raised her blouse and let down her pants and jumped on the doctor's bed and the doctor started to show them on the ultrasound device their little baby. Valerie thought if this does not melt his heart, nothing will. But it did not melt his heart, he continued to be frozen.

Not long after this, Alan's aunt started to insist they should move out as soon as possible. She considered she had helped them more than enough and she could not help them anymore. Before the baby was born, they had to move out. She could not accept them anymore in the apartment with the little child. This meant Valerie had to start looking for a rented apartment.

Alan did not have time for this, he had to go to work. Alan's aunt offered to help and she brought phone numbers every day where Valerie had to call and ask about the location and the price. Also in order to help her, Alan was asking her every evening what locations did she see and what was the price. They could not afford 90% of the rents and the ones they could afford were not acceptable for Alan. Valerie had to check them all out anyway. By summer, she was six months pregnant and she had to go every day to the telephone boot with the list of telephone numbers. She had to call every number and write down the address and the price. Then, she had to visit the one or two locations that fit in their price range. By foot, as they could not afford to travel with taxi or bus. Valerie walked in Steville around 10 km every day in search of a rented apartment. And it happened that as they saw her, the owners told her upfront:

"*We don't accept pregnant women.*"

So she had to turn around and leave. It seemed to her that she became totally unacceptable to everybody as soon as she got pregnant.

Then she had to buy alone grocery, vegetables, fruit and bread. She had to go to the biggest market downtown as there were the lowest prices, but they lived at about 5 km away from downtown. It was warm outside and because of the heavy physical effort, her blood sugar dropped dramatically and she could not even sit down on the street. So she just leant against a wall and sometimes bought a glass of juice. Back then, they were selling on the streets some very artificially flavored and colored juices from machines called TEC. A glass was very cheap and totally unhealthy, but at least it was cold and contained some sugar, so it helped her continue her walk back home. When she afforded to buy half of kilo newly appeared fruit, such as strawberries in May or cherries in June, she carefully kept it for husband. She thought he is the one who's working, he should eat what's best. She remembered her grandmother telling her and the other grandchildren stories:

"*We were so poor, we could not afford to buy oil. When I was able to buy half a liter of oil, I hid it away from the children and I put it on bread and packed it for lunch for your grandfather, otherwise the children would have eaten it.*"

Eva did the same, all that was best was kept for Camil. And Valerie felt it was natural for her to do the same for her husband. Even so, Alan was not pleased. He looked at her disappointed and with contempt. Hardly speaking with her. Very serious all the time, as if carrying all the responsibility of the world on his shoulders.

She was making efforts to cope with all of this, but it looked that Alan was bothered by her efforts too. Now, he passed from the discussion about divorce to a new issue: he will divorce her and take away her baby.

"*You cannot take my baby, no judge will give you the baby.*" said Valerie.

"*Yes, the judge will give me baby if I prove you are not fit as a mother. I will tell the judge you have no place to live and no income, you cannot raise a child. You'll see. Just give birth to the child and I will take it away from you.*" answered Alan.

It looked as if Alan was disturbed by the fact he could not break her by saying he will leave her. Valerie encountered this situation also as a child, many times Camil was even more angry with them when he saw they were strong and wouldn't give up to his tortures. And now the same with Alan. Most likely he felt he was a weak man, who was not able to defeat a pregnant, totally helpless and unprotected woman. And this made him more angry with her.

Even though she did not let anything show, Valerie was terrified that he would take her child away from her. She even had thoughts like: "*I'd better die giving birth to the child. In this way, he will remain with the child and everybody will be happy. I won't disturb anybody anymore.*" She decided however just to wait and see how will he attack at the divorce and prepared herself for the battle of her life, as she was not going to give up her child to this man, who first wanted a child, then he told her to get an abortion and now wanted to take away the child from the her.

In the beginning of August, in the eighth month of pregnancy, Valerie finally found a cheap place which they could afford. It was a very small, one room apartment, with no kitchen, no gas, only electricity and a small bathroom. She visited the apartment with Alan's aunt, Alan was too busy with his job. She agreed on the price with the owner and set the date when they could move in.

After she gave the initial deposit and the rent for the three months in advance, she went home and started to pack their things on her own. After three days, the owners called Alan at work and they informed him that the rent is more than they initially agreed, because the initial price agreed was for one person, but they say that in fact two persons were going to move in and the third person is on the way, so they have to increase the rent. Alan and Valerie agreed, they had no other choice. They searched for months and could not find anything with their income and the aunt was pushing them every day to move out, so they had no choice.

Valerie packed all their stuff by herself, carried everything in the car hired for the move and again from the car to the newly rented apartment. She cleaned the place and put everything in order. They noticed they did not have warm water on the tap, even though the owners told them there was warm water on the tap. When confronted, they said:

"*Well, it was warm water on the tap, we didn't know it isn't anymore. Nobody lived here for a long time, we couldn't know.*"

If they wanted to wash, they had to heat water on an electric heating plate. Fortunately, it was summer, because the apartment did not have heating either.

After all was in place, and when Valerie started her ninth month of pregnancy, Alan decided Valerie should go home, to Mineville. He told her:

"*Valerie, you should go home, to your parents.*"

"*I don't want to go home, I want to stay with you. You're my husband. We should be together when our child comes to this world.*" replied Valerie.

"*No, no. I will be at work. I cannot take care of you. You have to go home. I have already spoken with my cousin, he will take you to Mineville with his car. You cannot remain here in Steville.*"

And so she did. She went home to her parents. She wasn't sad anymore. She decided to focus totally on the child that was about to come. Camil has become older and wasn't physically violent anymore. If she was a little careful, she could get by with her parents.

In her last month of pregnancy Valerie continued to have a very active life. She helped her mother in the house with all the works. Every week, they went for a long walk on a mountain nearby Mineville. They gathered mushrooms, berries and herbs. She helped her mother by going with her to the market and the shops, she continued to clean the house and also helped her mother with the laundry. Valerie also sewed with her hands and her mother's sewing machine all the swaddling clothes, blouses, pants and hats for her baby. She had no money, so she did all these from old clothes and bed clothes her mother did not need anymore.

Camil has never been ill in his whole life, but now, as he was close to sixty years, he was starting to have some medical problems. Once he had to go to a medical check in the same time when Valerie had to go for her check. Valerie said:

"*OK, dad, we'll go together.*"

"*Hmmm, I don't think it's good. You go ahead, I'll come after ten minutes.*" answered Camil.

"*But why? We go in the same place. The doctor is there only for a few hours. At least we can walk there together. It's been a long time we did not walk together. With mom, I walk every day, but with you dad, I think I haven't been anywhere since I was little.*" insisted Valerie.

"*Not now, maybe some other time. You go ahead, I will come a little later.*" said Camil.

Valerie went by herself of course. But she thought a lot about it. Whatever happened in her life, Valerie had to understand the reason. And she could accept any kind of reason: logical would have been the best, but she accepted also spiritual or occult or karmic reasons. The important thing was that she had to find a reason for everything so that she could digest the events. And she found it this time too, even if she did not like it. Her father was ashamed to go by her side on the street because she was pregnant. In her father's eyes, just like in Alan's eyes, a pregnant woman was a weak, stupid, defeated woman with whom they should not be associated. But Valerie did not feel that way at all when she was pregnant. She felt strong and beautiful and proud of herself that she could not be defeated neither by her father, nor by her husband.

On a Wednesday evening, Valerie was watching TV with her mother, when suddenly her water broke. She did not say anything to her parents and she did not go to the hospital. She was afraid of the birth and very determined to go to the hospital in the very last minute possible. The next morning she did not go to the market with her mom as she did fell very well. After her mom returned, they ate a little fish. Valerie finished to sew the last pillow case for her baby and at noon she laid down with her mom for a nap. She could not sleep, as she already felt the contractions. She got up only when she felt the contractions at every four minutes. She took her little bag, said good-bye to her father and went to the hospital together with her mom.

The hospital was ten minutes away from her parents block. They walked and at around 1 p.m they arrived there. In the hospital, Valerie was admitted immediately. The nurse asked her when did her water break and why she came only now to the hospital. She answered:

"*Yesterday evening.*"

The nurse looked at her and said:

"*Why are you afraid? This is not an illness, you just give birth to a child. Women give birth to children every day, there is no need for you to be afraid, you will be fine.*"

As she wasn't dilated enough, they took her to the labor room. There were three women already there, who have been in labor for hours and hours already. Valerie tried to behave as good as possible. She got the bed under the window. As outside it was sunny, she felt it was too warm for her. The nurse drew the curtains. Then, Valerie got cold. She was all trembling, and the nurse had to draw the curtains again. Valerie tried to walk through the room, she thought maybe the pain will be bearable. In a certain moment, she heard her mom shouting her name:

"*Valerie, Valerie!*"

She thought she was hallucinating, she thought she was hearing voices. She looked out the window and down, on the alley next to the hospital she saw her mom and her sister.

"*Hey, how is it? How do you feel? Does it hurt?*" her mom asked joking.

Valerie started to laugh, but she couldn't, because of the pain. So, she just held her tummy and laughed and answered:

"*Ohh, I'm fine, it's not bad. It doesn't hurt so much. I'm going in now, see you after it's over.*"

Valerie closed the window and lied down again. Then, she felt very sick and ran to the bathroom and threw up. She felt extremely bad and could not control herself anymore. The nurses were sympathetic and understood right away that all this was caused by her fear of giving birth, therefore they were trying to calm her down. She decided to say the prayer "*Our Father*" in her mind through the whole thing. So she repeated it, again and again, focusing only on the prayer. And this worked for her, she finally was able to control her body and the pain she was feeling.

At seven p.m. the lady doctor on call decided Valerie should be taken into delivery room. The delivery room was quite a scene. Even though the medical staff kept it clean, the municipal hospital of Mineville was built in the 70's and had not been renovated until Valerie was admitted. The medical devices and instruments were old. The hospital did not have money to buy the minimum supply of medical materials and drugs, so the patients had to bring in what they needed while in the hospital. The room was white and unfriendly, all metals and white tiles. Valerie continued to pray in her mind and not long after, she heard for the first time the cry of her newborn baby. The nurse told her:

"*You have a healthy and beautiful little girl, just like you.*"

Valerie waited until the nurse cleaned her little daughter. Meanwhile, the lady doctor on call took care of her. Another nurse asked her:

"*What will be name of the little girl?*"

Valerie answered;

"*Victoria.*"

"*What about the father?*"

Valerie hesitated for a moment. "*Does this child have a father? Will he recognize her?*"

"*Well?*" insisted the nurse. "*We have to fill in the form, you know, and then send it to the Registrar's Office, so that you receive the birth certificate.*"

"*Aaahh, OK. Alan is his name.*"

Another nurse came with Victoria in her arms and showed the little girl to her mother. From that angle, Valerie could see only her baby's eyes, and her eyes looked exactly like Alan's eyes.

The nurse asked:

"*Who does she take after?*'

"*Her father.*" Valerie could not believe how disappointed her voice must have soundrd. She felt sorry for that, but she couldn't take her words back.

The nurse answered:

"*Well, don't be disappointed. In one year, you will be back here and you will have a son that will look just like you.*"

This really amused Valerie. She thought: «*Just sit tight and wait until I'm back here with another child of Alan.*»

After one more hour of observation, they finally sent Valerie to her ward and little Victoria to the special room of the little babies, where they were kept under observation during the night.

Valerie felt exhausted, but at least most of the pain was gone. She could not sleep all night. She got out of the ward and walked on the long corridor of the hospital. It was dark and quiet, everybody was sleeping. She felt she had to be awake and walk, if she fell asleep, maybe something bad would happen to her. Then a nurse saw her and sent her back to her ward. It was dangerous for her to walk alone on the corridor after the birth, what if she fell? So Valerie went back to her ward and continued to walk in it.

She could hardly wait to be four a.m. and call her mom on the phone, she knew Eva was getting up at this hour. When the time was right, she went to the pay phone from the end of the corridor and called her mother up.

"Hey, mom? How are you doing? I hope I did not wake you up. I was so anxious to call you, I was waiting all night to be four o'clock already, so that I can call you"

"I am fine, but how are you? Are you OK? How do you feel? How is the little one?"

"I'm fine, fine. I feel a little tired. I could not sleep all night. Victoria is OK, but she did not spend the night with me. They took her in the room with infrared light after she was born and they said they will her to me this morning. I named her Victoria. What do you say?"

"Ohh, it's a beautiful name. And what does she look like?"

"She is so beautiful, just breathtaking. She's like a little doll. She has a wonderful pinkish skin."

"Do you want me to call Alan or his parents to let them know?"

"No, don't call them. They don't care about her or me anyway."

"OK then. Take care. Go get some rest. I will come to visit you later on. Do you need anything besides food and milk? Should I bring you some coffee?"

"Yes, please bring me some. I know I'm not allowed to drink coffee, but I would kill for a cup. And if I remember anything else, I'll call you back. Love you, mom."

"I love you too, my little one. See you later."

At around eight o'clock they brought Victoria to her. The moment when Valerie took her baby in her arms the first time was the happiest and warmest moment in her life. She was so tiny and helpless and so beautiful. Little Victoria was not crying, just laid in her mom's arms and enjoyed the moment. Valerie looked at her and could not get enough. Her eyes indeed were like Alan's, but the rest of her face, the nose, the mouth, the conformation were exactly like hers. Valerie kissed her over and over again and hugged her and spoke with her.

"I love you so much my little one. I have waited for you so much, so I will not be lonely anymore. You know, I felt you inside of me and then I felt I lost you and then I felt you again. And they were all laughing at me, they said I was crazy. But I knew you were there. And the doctor confirmed what I said. He told me I got pregnant several times and I had miscarried. I know every time I got pregnant, your little soul was inside of me. Nobody can convince me that this isn't true. You're the love of my life, my little angel. And please forgive me that now I am so poor and I cannot buy you anything. I promise you I will work hard, all day and night if necessary, and buy you everything you need. I don't care if your father leaves us. I will never leave you and I will never let you down. We'll win together my little one, my little Victoria. I promise you this."

Valerie felt completely transformed after the first encounter with her little girl. She felt her being passed on the second place and her daughter passed on the first. It was quite strange, it was like her being transformed in two separate beings, her daughter and herself, and her very self came only second. Her way of thinking transformed, the first most important became the best interest of her child. She felt stronger and strangely, holding her little girl in her arms, or sleeping next to her and hearing her breathing, she felt safe and protected. Valerie thought her little girl will feel protected in her presence, but actually, it was the other way around. Valerie was the one who felt protected, and it was great to feel protected, because as a girl, as a young woman, as a wife and as a pregnant woman she did not feel protected at all.

Victoria was a very quiet little girl. She almost never cried. She was the most happy when she was in her mother's arms. Valerie liked to hold her in her arms, but she kept in mind that she shouldn't hold her in her arms all the time. She did not want to spoil her little girl, she wanted to raise a strong, resilient and tough fighter.

Valerie felt better every day. Then a problem appeared with the electrical system in her ward and she had to move in another ward. She already was sick and tired of moving and now again it happened with her. Otherwise, everything was OK in the hospital. The medical staff was very professional and nice. She has heard all kind of rumors before she was admitted that you have to give gifts and money to the staff, otherwise they don't take care of you. Well, Valerie did not give anything to the medical staff simply because she had absolutely no money. And they still took good care of her. Moreover, one of the nurses did something that really impressed Valerie. It was the end of September and the room was a little cool, as the central heating was not turned on yet. One of the nurses brought her personal radiator in Valerie's ward, so that she and little Victoria were warm. Valerie did not see so much kindness at her own husband since she got pregnant, and now this from a total stranger. The hospital of Mineville was very clean, compared with other healthcare facilities from the country. There were a lot of things she liked a lot about this hospital. One was that nobody could enter by chance in the newborn section. It was on a floor where you could get only with the elevator and the elevator was accompanied always by hospital staff. The other thing was that unlike other hospitals from the country, in Mineville, the next day the little baby was born, they brought in the mother's ward. Most hospitals did not do it and the children were kept in a separate ward, apart from the mother, so that the mother can rest and they brought the child to the mother only for the feeding. Valerie was happy this was not the rule there, she couldn't have rested without her child close to her.

Victoria was losing weight. All the babies lose weight right after they are born, but Victoria lost more and more weight. She has been born with 3,3 kilograms and now she was under 3 kilograms. The doctor was very concerned. She asked Valerie:

"Does she eat?"

"I think so. I keep her at my breast for hours."

"Well, we must check if she eats. We'll weigh her before she eats and after she eats. Today she should eat 40 grams of milk at a meal. We'll see how it goes."

So they weighed Victoria and they saw she did not eat anything. Valerie did not have any milk. The doctor decided that the little girl has to receive milk from a feeding bottle. Valerie felt very guilty. She knew she had to nurse her little girl with mother milk. She tried everything. But with no success. Whatever she did, she still had no milk.

After she was fed with milk from the feeding bottle, Victoria started to gain weight. And after ten days, Valerie could finally go home. Camil and Eva came to help her. Camil took home all the things from the hospital and Eva took little Victoria home in her arms. They all walked as the hospital was very close to their apartment. After the first walk of her life in the arms of her grandmother, Victoria slept like an angel for several hours.

After a few days, Eva's family wanted to come and visit little Victoria. Victoria had to work for hours in the kitchen with her mother to prepare food for ten persons. They had no help neither from Camil, nor from Eduard. Valerie felt she could hardly stand after all those hours, but somehow it all passed and she got over this too.

She tried not to bother her parents with her little daughter, especially her father. He seemed to be disturbed by everything. Valerie could not afford to buy disposable diapers. She used the diapers she sewed of old bed clothes. Because of this, she had to change little Victoria almost every half an hour. She had to rush to the bathroom with the wet diapers and rinse them quickly in cold water, so that her father will not smell anything. Then she rushed back to the room, to dress up the little girl, who most probably already started to cry. Once a day, Valerie had to wash with her hands all the diapers and put them to dry. Some of the days, her mother helped her do this, but most of them she did all this work alone.

The Orthodox baptize their children when they are six weeks old. Alan's parents insisted to baptize little Victoria at their church, in Streamtown. They decided that Alan and his father will come to Mineville to take Valerie and Victoria to Streamtown.

Camil never had a car, even though he had driving license since he was in the army. He always insisted that Eva or Eduard get a driving license too, so that he will not be the only one in the family who drives. Eva and Eduard did not want to get a driving license because they knew how things would have gone: Camil would get drunk and criticize every move they made while driving. They just did not want this complication.

Alan's father had a car, produced in 1980 in the country. These were simple, good cars, quite appropriate for the people. They used them for everything. To go to work, to go on holiday. To go on the field and carry home the crop. On the bumpy roads of the country, these were the ideal cars. Of course, from time to time they had some technical problems, but every person that owned a local car knew the basic "first aid" for his car.

Alan arrived with his father to Mineville at around noon. Valerie cooked lunch for them as best as she good. She prepared little Victoria for the long trip of 280 km from Mineville to Streamtown, where Alan's parents were living.

Victoria did not like very much her first trip by car. She got sick, she cried a lot, even though Valerie held her in her arms the whole way. Then, when climbing on a hill, the car broke down. It was quite usual for this to happen. There was really a local story that stated that on that hill there is an area where all cars break cars due to a paranormal phenomenon. This locality was right before Steville. To pass through it, you have to climb the hill first, and then descend. So, as the car could not start anymore, Alan's father remained at the wheel, Valerie remained in the back with Victoria, and Alan had to push the car until they reached the highest point of the hill. Afterwards, at the descent, luckily, the care started up again and they could continue their trip. It took them almost six hours to arrive to Streamtown.

Alan's parents invited almost 30 persons to the baptism. First, the ceremony at the church was made. The same priest who married Valerie and Alan baptized the little one. Valerie trusted and respected him, because of the way he spoke with her at their first encounter. The ceremony lasted around 30 minutes and the most important role was the one of god mother. She had to undress the child before the baptism, then to dress her up again and then she had to hold her in her arms until the ceremony ended. For the act of baptism itself, the priest held the child with his two hands and submerged him or her quickly three times in the holy water. The holy water was in a 20 liters capacity brass pot and it was a little heated when prepared for the baptism. After the child was baptized, he or she were dressed up quickly by the godmother in the new cloths she bought especially for this ceremony.

Valerie did not have much money. She dressed up Victoria as best as she could to bring her to the church and she was happy the little one received some brand new cloths. Also, Alan's mother received a lot of cloths from her colleagues, little cloths remained from other children. Many times, the children grew out their cloths before they were worn out, so people used to lend it to other little children. This came in very handy to Valerie who suddenly got a lot of cloths for Victoria, as she did not afford to buy any new cloths for her, Victoria was wearing only the cloths sewn by her mother.

After the church ceremony, they went home for the dinner given to all the guests. Victoria was more and more agitated. She was not used to so many people and all she wanted was to sleep quietly with her mother. All the guests wanted to see her and she could not retire yet. Only late in the night it all ended and finally they could go to sleep. Valerie was quite happy. Besides the cloths, she also received some money as gift from the guests and with that money she intended to buy a buggy for Victoria.

Right the next day after the baptism, Alan had to return to Stevilleto work. Valerie and Victoria remained in Streamtown. Valerie was shocked to see that Alan's parents helped her more with the little one than her own parents. Unlike with her own parents, she could go out from the house for half an hour, they did not shout after her:

"Hey, you forgot to take the child. What if she wakes up?"

Or, if she went to the bathroom, they would not shout to her:

"Hey, the child is up, what should I do with her? Come and look after your child, she's crying."

Alan's parents were different. They took her out to fresh air every now and then, and even more than that, every morning they washed and hung out all the diapers gathered in bathroom since last day.

Alan's sister were also helping with the little one, they were all very glad they had a little niece.

Still, Valerie was not home. She missed terribly her parents and her home. Alan and his parents were making plans for them. One plan was that Valerie and Victoria will go to Stevilleto live with Alan. The other plan was that little Victoria remained in Streamtown, to be risen by his parents, and Valerie will go to Steville to live with Alan. The third plan was that Valerie will return with Victoria to Mineville. Valerie considered that for the best interest of her family, the best was to go with little Victoria to Steville. Alan found a two rooms apartment at an affordable price, so they would have a place to live. They would get by somehow only with his salary, until Valerie would find some work too.

Alan came again with a car to Streamtown and took his wife and his daughter to Steville. The apartment he rented was on the third floor in a block of flats in the cheapest district of Steville. Victoria started to make her little habits already. At four o'clock in the morning she was up. Rested, in a very good mood. Valerie changed her diapers with dry ones. Then,

Victoria ate. After this, Valerie prepared her husband so that he could go to work. She made him the coffee and prepared his sandwich. She would have wanted to pack him more than a sandwich, but he always opposed this idea:

"Everybody comes with a sandwich. I will not bring with me more than a sandwich. What do you want from me? To unpack there in front of everyone packs of food so that they can laugh at me? No way! Just pack me a little sandwich."

So Valerie packed him only a sandwich. She tried to put as much as possible in that sandwich, but Alan criticized her for this too. He pointed out that the sandwich should have the maximum thickness less than maximum opening of his mouth. He was an engineer, right? So Valerie did not make him very thick sandwiches.

After Alan left to work, Valerie started to wash the cloths and diapers. She also knitted all the time. Now she was knitting a blouse for Alan's sisters sisters. Valerie stayed up until around 10 o'clock in the morning, after which she fell asleep. While she was sleeping, Valerie could clean up the house. At noon, the little one woke up and Valerie took her out for the daily walk. No matter how cold it was outside, Valerie took Victoria out for the walk. She wanted her little one to be healthy and used to any kind of weather. During this noon walk, Valerie also bought everything was necessary in the house. This was a bit tricky, as she could go by foot only in the little shops from the neighborhood. Valerie was afraid to let Victoria out in front of the shop in her buggy, as most mothers did. All the threats of Alan during her pregnancy that he would divorce her and take away her child had a dramatic and lasting effect on Valerie's psychic. In that period, MTV was broadcasting frequently the video clip of Soul Asylum with *Runaway train*, and Valerie thought that final scene when the little baby was kidnapped was horrifying. As a result, Valerie never let little Victoria unsupervised. She went only in shops where there was place for the buggy or to the market, where she could buy everything outside. The other hard thing was to carry home all the bags and the buggy with the child and then to take them up by foot to the third floor, with no help whatsoever. She used to put all the bags with grocery to Victoria's feet, then lifted the buggy and took them up to their apartment. After they got home, Valerie started to cook, the special cream soup with all kinds of vegetables for Victoria, so that she could eat everyday something else, besides milk. Then she cooked dinner for her husband. Alan used to come home every day around 3 or 4 o'clock from work. He ate and then he went back to another job, he said to a second job. Every single day he went to his second job, also on Saturday and on Sunday. Valerie was wondering:

"What kind of a company is that where you go every day in the afternoon to work, even on Saturday and on Sunday?"

"We work something on computers. I have to go to a second job, you know you don't work and how hard it is to get by of a single salary."

"I know, I know, but every single day? What company is it?"

"Come with me and you'll see if you don't trust me."

Valerie did not go with Alan, but she did not believe it at all. Alan came home from this second job late at night and he went right to sleep. Valerie could not fall asleep until he was not home. Then after she fell asleep, many times Victoria woke up and then next day at 4 o'clock it started all other again. The biggest problem of Valerie was that she slept very little. Everybody was telling her to sleep when the baby was sleeping, but during the day, when the baby was sleeping she cleaned and washed and cooked. And at night, after the little one woke her two or three times, she could fall back asleep. She could not sleep when the baby was sleeping, she had to do everything by herself.

It was a hard life for Valerie and she was terribly unhappy. But the top of all this was the Christmas of '94. Alan said he had to go to work even on Christmas Eve. Valerie could not believe this was happening. She remained home with her little one and after Victoria fell asleep, she stayed in the dark and looked out the window. She could not control her tears anymore, she stayed in the window crying, in the dark house, waiting for her husband to come home. This was the worst Christmas of her life and she suffered terribly, but she wiped off her tears and decided not to give up. She prayed that night to God to give her strength to go on without Alan if he chose not be with her. She knew she had to be strong for her daughter and this was the decision she took that night: no matter what, she will fight and work as much as she could and provide for her daughter.

Late at night Alan came home. On the first day of Christmas he left home again all afternoon, and on the second day of Christmas the same way, even though these were national holidays and nobody was working.

Valerie made huge efforts to control herself and did not fight with him because of this. It made no sense. She could not change him anyway and she could not keep him near her forcefully. If he preferred to spend his time with someone else, Valerie could not chain him to her and her daughter.

Valerie continued to go to the regular medical checks of the little one to a pediatric doctor from Steville. This time, it was a lady doctor and Victoria did not like her at all. They had to make the periodical vaccinations. Valerie insisted that Alan went with them and stayed in those long interminable queues. Alan did not like to go with them, he had much more important things to do. He supported the family, now he had to go to the doctor too with the little one? Even if he went with them, he waited outside.

Valerie told him:

"*Come in with us, Victoria has to get her vaccination.*"

"*I don't want to come to see her getting an injection. No way.*"

"*Why not? She is your daughter too you know.*"

"*I cannot see her crying like that. I feel sorry for her.*"

"*Really? Wow, that's strange. When I was pregnant with her and I was crying because you wanted a divorce, you did not feel sorry for her. You know my crying affected her directly? How come back then you did not feel sorry for her or for me by the way?*"

Alan did not reply anymore after she got really angry, he just concluded Valerie was treating him very bad.

In January, one evening the lady owner of the apartment paid them a visit. She started with the usual "politeness".

"*How are you? You're fine. Ohh, I'm glad. I'm really glad. And how is the little one? Is she quiet, does she sleep well at night? She's grown since I saw her last time.*"

Valerie could not answer one question, she went right on to the next. They were that kind of questions, when people ask them and they don't even wait for the answer. And you try to answer, you just say the first words and they go on and on and you feel like an idiot you even tried to answer. So, she stopped answering and let the lady get to the real issue why she came.

"*You know, I've been a widower for a long time. And two years ago I found this man. We get along very well, we've been together ever since. He lives with me, at my old aunt. I am taking care of her. Of course, I have this apartment. This was mine and my late husband's, may God rest his soul."*

Valerie and Alan were just looking at her, not saying anything.

"She's OK. My aunt I mean, she's OK to live with. But she has some moments. You don't wanna know. Sometimes we have fights like you would not believe it."

By now, they were wondering how long is this going to last?

"*Well, yesterday, me and my aunt, we had a big fight. It was stupid, actually, with no real reason whatsoever. Anyway, she said she does not want us there anymore. She wants us to move out. I know she'll blow over. This happened many times in the past. After a time, she changes her mind and calls me back, to take care of her. But now, she wants us to move out. We have to come here on Sunday the latest, me and boyfriend. We have no other place to go.*"

"*You mean here? In this apartment?*" asked Valerie.

"*Yes, here. We have no other place to go.*" repeated the owner.

"*How are we going to live here all of us? We are three, and you two come? In two small rooms?*" asked again Valerie.

"*It'll be fine. We'll take one room and you and your husband will take the other. We'll get by somehow.*"

"*And I suppose this will be at the same price, right? Or at a higher price?*" asked Valerie.

"*You don't have to ironic. Of course it will be at the same price. Did I say it will be at a higher price? And it will be only for a time, until my aunt changes her mind.*"

CHAPTER 4

In January 1995, Alan and Valerie have been living together, in Steville, with their daughter Victoria for two months in a rented apartment. One evening the lady owner of the apartment came to visit them and she told them that on the same Sunday she has to move in with them, together with her boyfriend, as she did not have a place to live.

Valerie knew she could not remain in the same apartment with those two people. Finding another apartment at their budget could take months and months. She remembered her experience of searching for rent while she was pregnant. She was not accepted anywhere in Steville because she was pregnant. How will they accept them with a little child? Valerie decided the best thing for Victoria was to go back to her parents, to Mineville. Alan was never home with them, he was better off by himself, with his first job and second job. Valerie decided to go with Victoria to her parents. As usual, Alan had no reaction whatsoever.

Alan called again the car and took Valerie and Victoria back to Mineville.

Valerie was actually happy she left from Steville and the holidays were over, she felt extremely tired and wanted to settle down finally. She took care of her little daughter and in the meantime started to look for a job. She needed to have money. Alan was giving her an amount every month and Valerie gave half of it to Eva to contribute to the incomes of the house. Eva was very unhappy:

"This money you give me it's not enough, Valerie. The coffee you drink is more than what you give me."

Valerie was calculating in her mind. She received from Alan the money to buy 400 grams of instant coffee every month – coffee has always been kind of a currency for Valerie throughout her life. It was the one luxury she could never give up, no matter how poor she was. OK, if she gave half of this money to her money, it meant she gave her mom the money for 200 grams of coffee. She did not drink that amount of coffee every month! She thought for herself: «*What is she talking about?*» But she just lowered her head and replied:

"*I know, mom, and I'm sorry, but I cannot give you more money. I give you half of what Alan gives me. I need the rest to buy milk and some fruit for Victoria. Please understand me. I will get a job as soon as possible and then I will be able to give you more.*" tried Valerie to defend herself.

Victoria was a healthy and smart little child. She didn't want to eat anything else but milk in the first months of life, but Valerie knew it was important for her daughter to eat fresh fruit every day. As she could not afford much, she made a puree every day of half a banana, one kiwi and the juice of one orange. Victoria ate this puree every day for her daily portion of vitamins. Valerie never gave her sweets. As long she was little, at home with her, Victoria could not know about sweets and Valerie took advantage of this. The little one never ate sweets in her childhood. Valerie was concerned because her daughter was eating only milk, and it was not even mother milk, as she had no lactation. She was trying hard to introduce as much aliments as possible in little Victoria's diet. First she managed to make her eat eggs, then some vegetables, as potatoes baked in the oven, or spinach, or carrots boiled in soup.

Victoria was growing up and she was a healthy and intelligent child. When she was three months old, she said her first word:

"*Ma-ma-ma-ma-ma*"

It happened at a medical check. Victoria got her vaccine from the nurse and Valerie was two steps away from her, discussing with the doctor. One of the nurses said:

"*Listen mam, she's calling you.*"

Another word Victoria said at only a few months was the answer to one her mom's questions. Valerie asked:

"*You're the most beautiful girl in the world?*"

And Victoria answered:

"*Yeah!*"

Valerie took Victoria to long walks out of the house and as much as possible in not polluted areas, parks or quiet streets. She spoke with

Victoria a lot and even if the little one could not speak yet, she knew her daughter understood her better than anyone.

Alan came once a month to visit them. He was 150 km away, in Steville, but he could not come more often. He did not have the time, he did not have money, he did not have a car and so on and so forth.

Valerie was looking for a job but could not find anything related to her profession. In Mineville there was a huge chemical plant, but she could not get even an interview. There were some persons who promised her they would help her get in, but these remained only promises. They were always hinting that she should bribe somebody to get in and she would have accepted this, she just begged them to get her in contact with somebody, but still nothing happened. She applied wherever she saw job openings. As sales assistant, as secretary, as chemist operator at an alcohol production plant, she went to several interviews, but still she got no job. The only ones who were interested to hire her were an alcohol distribution company, who needed a sales person to go all over the country with samples of their products. She was so desperate, that she would have accepted this job, but Camil did not agree. He said situation is not so desperate and she still has time to look for something better.

But for Valerie, the situation was quite desperate. She was very short with money. She could not afford to buy herself anything. She received a small amount of money from Alan and she gave half of it to her mother. She also received the monthly allowance from the state, of which she could buy around 10 liters of milk. This was pretty much it. Valerie could buy the milk, the fruit Victoria ate and the special soap and shampoo for children and this was pretty much all. She could not afford to buy disposable diapers. She rarely bought one pack and used it only in special occasions, for visits to doctor for example. The doctor and the nurse came often to visit Victoria at home and she was always with diapers made by Valerie of old cloths. Valerie felt very ashamed for this. The nurse noticed this and told her:

"It is very good you don't use disposable diapers. The child will learn faster to use the potty, as she will faster understand the difference between being dry and being wet and what causes it. And it is good that you made the diapers of old cloths as these are softer than new textiles."

The doctor asked her if she was breastfeeding Victoria. Valerie answered very ashamed

"*I'm so sorry, I don't have milk. I tried everything, in the hospital already.*" answered Valerie, lowering her head.

The doctor was consulting little Victoria, and suddenly looked straight into Valerie's eyes and he asked:

"*Do you have some problems with your husband?*"

Valerie thought «*How does he know this?*» and she replied again lowering her head:

"*Yes, we have some difficulties.*"

"*That's why you don't have milk. Don't feel guilty about this, it's not your fault. If a woman feels loved and protected and understood during her pregnancy and lactation, everything goes normally. She lactates and she can breastfeed her child. Otherwise, her body cannot function normally. Don't worry about this, try to think positive. You cannot get sick now, Victoria needs you.*"

Valerie was so grateful for these words and all this showed on her eyes and her face. She almost started to cry. Once again in her life she got more support and understanding from a total stranger than from her husband. The doctor looked back at her reassuring with his smiling eyes and he was rewarded in full by her gratitude. He said:

"*Don't worry, things will work out. Everything will be OK.*"

"*Thank you doctor…*"

Valerie felt a lot better hearing this. She could not afford to buy a baby walking chair. Everybody had one, but she didn't. She spent hours and hours bent and holding little Victoria's hands to teach her how to walk. She could not buy any new cloths for the little one, she had to use whatever she had received from her mother in law and Victoria was growing. Fortunately, she did not have to spend for food and lodging for herself, as she lived with her parents. But this did not make her feel better, she felt totally useless and stupid. She tried to help her parents with the works in the house as much as she could, she sewed, she knitted, she repaired and cleaned the shoes of her mother and father, she cleaned the house, she helped her mother in her little garden that she owned at around 6 kilometers from their home. Valerie went with her mother almost every day to the garden, by foot as the bus was too expensive by her. Valerie pushed the buggy with Victoria and carried the bags with her milk, cloths and diapers to change her, food and water for herself and her mother. Then, when they returned home from the garden, she carried back everything and also what they gathered there: some tomatoes, onions, carrots, apples or grapes, depending on the season. Or they went on the mountain and gathered herbs, berries and mushrooms. For these walks, Valerie carried little Victoria with her baby carrier, as the buggy was unusable on the mountain tracks. Even though she was not a big or heavy child, to carry like this a six- seven months child was back breaking. But the communion, togetherness between them made it all worthwhile.

When Victoria was around eight months old, Valerie managed to find finally a job. It was an undeclared work at a family that was bootlegging alcohol. They needed a chemist engineer (sic!) to check the concentration of alcohol. The alcohol concentration was measured with a densitometer. This was a glass apparatus that was sunk in the mixture and the level until it sunk showed the concentration of alcohol. Actually, this was all she had to do. The other people there were doing the hard part: they had to wash manually the bottles, rinse them, put them to dry, then place them manually on the machine that filled them with the alcohol (they were counterfeiting rum), then take the bottles of the machine, put them in boxes and then carry them in the storage room, where they stayed until the little pick up van came to take them. The loading in the pick-up van was again done manually by the people working there. Women and children mostly. Valerie could not look at them and do nothing. So she helped in all processes. Washing bottles, loading boxes, whatever. This actually impressed the owners and they promised her she will be "promoted" and will get to work in the office of the big house, to take care of all the documents involved. In the meantime, Valerie was searching hard to find another job, she wanted a declared, legal job at a serious company. She found an IT company that was hiring so she applied for a job there. While she was waiting for the answer from them, she was so nervous that she broke a densitometer. The owners told her she will have to pay for it, as it was very expensive. Valerie paid for it with the money she earned in two weeks of work. But finally, the IT company called her to the interview and she went there decided to get a job no matter what.

The interview at the IT company went OK, but there was a catch:

in order to work there, you had to make a series of courses, because knowing to work with Windows was a prerequisite condition. Valerie had not worked with computers since faculty. Their old computer, bought when they were students, had remained at Alan and it was anyway totally obsolete. She was very frustrated because she wanted to learn, but she had no money to make the course. She discussed this with Alan. On the phone of course, their marriage was unfolding on the phone. He only came once a month to Valerie and Victoria.

"*Look, Alan, I have been to an interview. They are an IT company. It looks OK, I think they have a future.*"

"*Well, that's good, go for it.*" answered Alan.

"*Yes, but I cannot work there unless I know how to use Windows with Word and Excel and so on.*"

"*So? What's the problem?* "asked Alan.

"*I don't have the money to make the course they are offering. So, I can't do it. I have to find some job to make the necessary money and then come back to them.*" answered Valerie.

"*Don't worry about it, I'll give you the money. Just go for it. You have to learn computers, there's no other way nowadays.*" told her Alan,

"*Really? You'll give me the money? Thank you! Thank you so much! Ohh, I'm so glad I'll go and register to the course right now! Thank you!*"

This way Valerie learnt to work on computer. After she finished the course, that company told her they are considering to hire her, but she would have to work for a trial period. The work was unregistered labor and it was basically editing of various texts in Word. They paid her by the page. Valerie wanted to have a registered job, but for now she accepted also this unregistered labor, as she did not have anything better. She took advantage of those weeks and absorbed as much information as she could. This happened in July 1995. In August 1995 the company closed for the summer holidays. Valerie asked them if they will call her back after the holidays, they replied they are going to think about it. So Valerie went home and continued fiercely to search for a job.

She did not buy the newspapers, but one day, Eduard told her that the Mining Research Institute announced in the local newspaper that they were organizing a competition for several job openings. Valerie immediately went to the Mining Institute to ask for more details. They gave her the bibliography for the competition and told her the date of the exam. Valerie went straight to the Public Library, got the books she needed and started immediately to study.

Victoria was a sweet little child, the more she grew, the cuter she was. Totally attached to her mother as they were together literally all the time. When her father came to them however, Victoria behaved almost like with a total stranger. She did not know very well who this man was and why was he getting so close to her mom. If he tried to get close to her too suddenly, she started to cry. He had to approach her very slowly and carefully. And then, after 24 hours, he went back to Steville and she did not see him again for another month. Eva adored her granddaughter and Victoria had a special relationship with her too. Valerie remembered her own childhood and how her grandmother was always cold and critical with her and she was happy Victoria was so close to Eva. With Camil however, things were different. He was always disturbed when she cried, he was disturbed by the smell in the house. He never came in close physical contact with the little one, so Victoria treated him back with the same coldness. Raised in this spirit, Victoria felt comfortable only in the presence of women. She cried if she was left alone with men, she cried if she was taken in the arms of a man. Funny thing, when Valerie took her to the periodical medical check, Victoria never cried when the nurses undressed her, gave her injections or whatever and then they dressed her up, but as soon as the male doctor approached her, she started to cry. The doctor was amused by this and said there was nothing wrong with her, he adored her and he thought she just possessed "*too much character*". The doctor was an amazing one, very professional and he always got the diagnosis right. Valerie respected him very much and totally trusted him. He also was a good thought reader and always reassured Valerie when she was concerned about something.

The exam day came. Valerie studied hard all the bibliography. She was very determined to get a job at the Institute. It was a state company, surely it will be a registered job. She went to the exam and wrote as well as she could. And when they posted the results, she was happy to see that she got a job. She was living with her parents, so she could leave Victoria with them when she went to work. Alan could stay in Steville where he wanted to be. Valerie could have now her own money, not being dependant on him anymore.

After another two weeks, Valerie started her new job at the Research Institute. She was very enthusiastic about it. It all started with the labor protection routine. It took several days of trainings until she actually went to the department she was going to work in. This was a small research team, made up of three women, of which one senior researcher, her assistant and a lab assistant. Valerie was going to be prepared to take over the position of senior researcher, as the old lady had to retire soon.

The Institute was a typical state company, not very different to how it was during the communist regime, even if the Revolution took place 6 years before. It stretched out on a huge land, it had more than 20 building and a big front building with the highest management. The research group in which Valerie was distributed consisted of 3 persons and a boss. Several research groups had another boss, which again had her bosses. If you counted the persons well, there were more bosses, than people actually working. Nobody was working very hard. There was also a saying: "*We are pretending we are working, they are pretending they are paying us.*" There were persons that were actually dozing off with their heads on their desks, others were chatting for hours. Then the interminable lunch breaks. Truly, it was a wonder the Institute was still functioning. Nobody went out to bring more contracts, nobody fought to increase the turnover. The buildings were pretty much in decay, both outside and inside. They never had money to invest, to renovate the working places, to buy new instruments and machines, to train the people.

Valerie saw the state of affairs and it did not strike her as a very profitable, long lasting company, but at least it was registered job and she could have some experience in her CV. She was determined to learn as much as she could, was happy to help with anything they needed. She edited on the computer the research papers. She translated into English or from English. She made any laboratory analyses were required. She cleaned the office or the lab. After a short time, however, the old lady, the senior researcher started to show her adversity towards Valerie. Nothing Valerie did was good enough.

"*You're stupid you let your husband alone in Steville. You should be in Steville with him. What are you looking for here? Go to Steville and stay with your husband. He'll find another woman who stays with him and he'll leave you, you'll see.*"

The boss did not know any English whatsoever. Valerie helped a lot as she translated everything was necessary. But she got no recognition or thanks from her boss, on the contrary:

"How well you know English anyway? I never heard you really speak English well. What? That you translate from English? I can do that with a dictionary and I don't claim that I know English. Let me see how much English you know. Bring me a dictionary."

This last sentence actually brought a smile on Valerie's face. She remembered her father checking her English knowledge when she was a child. He also checked her knowledge with a dictionary. "*Well, we know what the result of this check is going to be.*" thought Valerie smiling.

Anything Valerie did, could not please her boss. No matter what she said, no matter how hard she worked, it was not good enough. Valerie analyzed herself, trying to figure out what she was doing wrong. She wanted to be a good employee, she wanted to be helpful and reliable for her team, but could not find any way to get the acceptance of her boss. She figured out eventually that her boss felt threatened by her – she was hired to replace her at retirement, right? Understanding this, Valerie calmed down and tried to survive in the team, avoiding her boss as much as she could. They had at their disposal an office, where the boss, the assistant and Valerie had the desks, and a laboratory where the laboratory assistant had her desk. So Valerie took some notebooks and pens and moved to the laboratory, without saying anything. In the laboratory was much colder and not so comfortable as in the office, but at least there was nobody there to criticize her.

Even if she did not enjoy going to work with that particular team, Valerie was happy to have her own salary, as small as it was. First of all, she could buy little Victoria the minimum she needed. Then, she could give her mother more money to try to help with the expenses of the household. Also, Valerie started to save money. A very little amount, but she still saved money every month. She liked to prepare herself for rainy days, having a little amount of money in the bank gave her a feeling of safety.

Valerie did not say anybody that she saved money, she knew they will try to take the money away from her. Alan would take it away from her, Eduard would want to take it away from her. She learned her lesson in the past, she understood it's better if people don't know anything about her money.

Eduard on the other hand never saved any money his entire life. Not when he was working, not now, after he was fired from her job at the state company, where he worked during the communist regime. Moreover, he even pulled Valerie's leg:

"*Why are you saving money? To lend it to somebody else and then not get it back?*"

"*I'm not saving money. What's your problem?*" answered her Valerie.

"*And what good did it do to you to get married? Does your husband give you any money?*" continued Eduard.

"*He gave me money until I did not work, now I take care of myself.*"

"*Hah, how stupid you are! You realize that my lover gives me more money than your husband gives to you?*" laughed Eduard at her.

"*I realize that. You're very smart. Much smarter than I am. But let me ask you this: from the little money my husband gives me I am raising a child. You receive more money than I do: what do you do with it? Where is it? You always complain you cannot afford to buy anything. Where's all that money?*" asked her Valerie.

"*We drink it and eat it.*" answered Eduard with the laugh disappearing of his face.

A month after Valerie got her first registered job, Victoria became one year old. Valerie tried to celebrate this as well as she could. She had no friends, no guests for the celebration, but she prepared a special dinner with her parents and the little one and took a lot of nice pictures, to keep them as a memory. Not long after that, Victoria learned how to walk. In the beginning, the little one learned how to move around the apartment on all fours. She was a smart, curious little girl and wanted to see and try everything. She discovered the whole apartment like this – and it was a big apartment too, around 120 square meters. The only room where she was not allowed to go was Camil's room. Whenever she got to the door of Camil's room, he told her:

"*Go away from here!*"

So, Victoria went away. Valerie did have a baby walking chair, so she taught Victoria to walk by holding her two hands and walking behind her.

It was breaking her back and she could hardly wait her little daughter to learn to walk by herself.

Both Valerie and Eva involved little Victoria in all kind of works around the house. Whatever they did, they brought Victoria nearby to help them. Once Eva was washing the laundry with the old washing machine. These old washing machines were only doing the washing, not the rinsing, neither the spinning, unlike the modern ones. You put in warm water and detergent and the laundry. You closed the top and let the machine wash the laundry for how many minute you wanted. Then you stopped the machine, took the top off, took out the laundry and put it in the tub to rinse it. After the machine was stopped, Eva brought little Victoria help her take out the washed laundry and put it into the tub. She put a little chair under Victoria's feet, as she was still too small to bend over and take out laundry from the machine. The larger pieces were taken out by Eva, Victoria had to take out the little socks to help her grandmother. At a certain point, Victoria took a larger piece of laundry and tried to pull it out from between the others. As she couldn't do it, she fell into the machine with her feet up. Eva has turned to the tub for a couple of seconds to put in some laundry, when she turned back to the washing machine, she just saw the legs of little Victoria sticking out of the water. She took out the little one immediately. Fortunately, it all happened in a few seconds, but she got really scared. After the initial shock passed, they all laughed about it.

Valerie took Victoria out in the fresh air every single day. No matter it was raining or sun shine, no matter it was warm or cold. When she had more time, they went up on the surrounding mountains. She just took Victoria in the baby holder, strapped it to her body with Victoria's back to her and went gathering berries. As she gathered the berries, she put them directly in the mouth of Victoria. Victoria was a very lively child, she turned her head all the time. This way, her mother did not always get her mouth, so Victoria ended up with all her face covered with red and blue from the berries she was eating.

Valerie also spoke a lot with her daughter, even if her daughter could not speak back to her very well yet. Valerie was sure Victoria understood her. Victoria understood her while she was still inside her tummy, why wouldn't she understand her now? Valerie always felt Victoria was a little angel sent to her by God to help her overcome all the difficulties in her life.

A little angel with an old, wise soul, who always understood things deeper than anybody else. Victoria said more and more words and in November she made her first step on her own. Valerie was sitting on a chair and Victoria was standing up, holding on to her mom. Valerie stood up and told Victoria to hold on to the chair. Then she went to the bed, which was two steps away from the chair and called her little daughter to her:

"*Come to mama, little angel. Come on. Come on, my treasure.*"

So, Victoria let go the chair and one step, two steps, she was next the bed, in her mother arms.

"*Wow, way to go, bravo, my love.*" Valerie said, happy and proud of her little treasure. These two little steps were the most important, after these more and more steps were following, and look! Her little girl learned how to walk!

Whenever her mom was very excited about a success of hers, Victoria used to repeat:

"*Com'measure, com'measure*"

Valerie did not understand what her daughter was telling her. « *What does she want? She wants me to measure her? Or what?*"

Victoria saw her mother did not get it so she repeated:

"*Com'measure, com'measure*".

Valerie did not understand this for weeks, until one day she picked up her daughter in her arms and said:

"*Come on, my treasure.*"

Victoria repeated happily:

"*Com'measure, com'measure*"

"*Oh! That's what you are telling me, my precious little one: come on my treasure! Oh, you are mammy's little smart angel.*" And she kissed her daughter happily.

Another thing Victoria learned to say pretty soon was: "*Go-way, go-way.*" She used to say this to her grandfather, Camil, and went to him and pushed him out with her little hands whenever he came in front of the room where they were. Camil did not get angry. After all, little Victoria learned this from him: whenever she was little and went on all four all over the house until the door of his room, he sent her away by telling her: "*Go away from here, go away.*" Now he was just getting it back.

Valerie was a happy mom, even if at her job she did not feel appreciated and her marriage was as if it did not exist. Alan threatened to divorce during her entire pregnancy, but did not actually divorce. He brought Valerie home to her parents and continued to live his own life in Steville. He spent 24 hours a month with his wife and daughter and that was it. In the beginning, Valerie was terrified he wanted to divorce, because she depended on him both sentimentally and materially. She has suffered a lot, many times she had to call him on the phone at his work and beg him to send the monthly allowance, as she literally has no money to live. Now, when she got her job, she was so happy not to depend on him materially anymore, that she did not have to call him anymore. When he called they spoke, and nothing in rest. She did not waste energy to try to understand what happened with their marriage, she just focused on her child, trying to be mother and father for Victoria in the same time. She was still in survival mode – hardly being able to keep the job that allowed her the absolute minimum for her and her daughter.

Valerie avoided to call him. She could only call him at his job. Once, Alan's parents called to tell her Alan's grandmother died and he had to go home for the funeral. They could not reach him and asked her to announce him. Valerie called him at the office. After several minutes of waiting and being passed from one extension to another, a male colleague of Alan answered and Valerie said:

"*Hello, I am Valerie. I would like to speak with Alan please.*"

"*Who is calling?*" the man at the other end of the line asked.

"*I'm his wife.*"

"*His wife from Steville or his wife from Mineville?*"

"*His wife from Mineville. Could I please speak with him? I have a very urgent and important message for him.*"

"*Yes, OK, I'll call him on the phone.*"

This experience made her feel humiliated and hurt. She promised herself she'll not bother him again. If he wanted something, he will call her.

For the winter holidays, Valerie stayed home with her daughter. She bought presents for Victoria and her parents, and as usual she did not receive anything. But despite of this, she was happy. She did not have to spend Christmas looking out the window, crying, and waiting for her husband to come home.

She heard her colleagues speaking how they go skiing with their husbands and for New Year's Eve how they go to party at fancy restaurants. She did not have that kind of money or husband. So she spent more time with the treasure she had: Victoria. The walks they had and the time spent together meant more than any holiday in a ski resort.

Right next to the Institute there was the Mining University. As a student, Valerie made some money by compiling her colleagues' projects. She pretty much could write an essay about anything if she had the right bibliography. So she started asking around in the Institute if anybody knew students who needed their project done by somebody. Eventually, she found some customers. She asked for the theme, the requirements of the project and the right books that were treating the subject and off she went! She compiled several projects and she made a little more money, besides the salary. At night she was working on projects, at day she was going to her regular job.

A usual day began for Valerie at 5,30 in the morning. First of all, she changed and fed her baby. Then she spent a few minutes with her, while she drank her coffee. She could not eat in the morning, she just prepared herself a sandwich to take to work. Then she made a shower, dressed up and went to work. She started work at 7 o'clock in the morning. The Institute was very close to her house, she got there by foot in 5 minutes. She worked until 3 p.m. Sometimes, when the weather was good, Eva came with little Victoria to wait for Valerie in front of the Institute and they walked back home together. After getting home, Valerie ate and took Victoria out for a longer walk. During this longer walk, Valerie also bought whatever she needed for the little then. Back then, in Mineville there were many stores that sold fruit, coffee, soda, cigarettes and many other things at windows, right by the footway. You could just stop at a window and buy whatever you needed. For Valerie this was very convenient, as she was afraid to leave her daughter in front of the shop and go in. With the bags in her hands and pushing the buggy, Valerie went back home, climbed up to the second floor with the buggy, the child and the bags. Then she undressed the little one, changed her and fed her and went to the bathroom to wash the diapers with her hands. Eva used the washing machine only once or twice a week for the regular cloths. As the diapers were many every day, Valerie washed them by hand with hot water and homemade soap and rinsed them three times with cold water. Then she cooked something for the little one, she cleaned the house and did whatever else was necessary. At nine o'clock in the evening, Valerie put Victoria to sleep. The little one did not fall asleep immediately. It took at least half an hour until she finally fell asleep. If she heard any noise, she woke up again. Nobody was quiet in the house especially for this. Valerie wanted little Victoria to be able to sleep in any noisy conditions. She had to be used to hear the normal noises of the house and still sleep. Just that the noises prolonged the falling asleep process. Then, Valerie started the work on her projects. She continued until 1 or 2 a.m. At least this way she was awake when the little one got up. Victoria wasn't a troublesome child, but she woke up several times during the night and Valerie woke up too. Sometimes, Victoria was crying so loud that even Eva and Camil heard her. Valerie went to her crib and checked if there was anything wrong. If she was wet, she got changed. But if everything was OK, Valerie did not pick her up in her arms. She just stayed around and waited until the little one calmed down.

Once Eva came in their room. Camil was annoyed by the baby's cry and Eva wanted to take Victoria in her arms. Valerie reacted immediately:

"If you take her in your arms now, you'll sleep with her from now on. I don't care, I could use a good night uninterrupted sleep. Just make up your mind: if you want to teach her to cry whenever she wants to be taken in our arms, then pick her up and you'll continue doing it. I will not do it."

Eva just turned around and went out of the room. Valerie felt good, she liked being so determined that her parents listened to her. But at least, if she was going to be totally responsible for the little one, she had to have the control over the raising process. She used to tell Alan and her parents:

"I take full responsibility for Victoria: for the bad things, and also for the good things. I have to raise her without her father, OK, I'll do that, but on my own terms. You cannot set the rules and the decisions, and then hold me responsible for the outcome. Either I take the decisions and set the rules and I'm responsible, or you take the decisions and set the rules and you're responsible."

Valerie was very grateful she had somebody to leave her child with while she was at work. Even though this seemed a little annoying for her parents. Besides the eight hours she was at work, Valerie was at home taking care of her child. Sometimes it happened she had to go to the bathroom for a few minutes. Victoria started to cry, so Camil came to the bathroom door and shouted:

"The child is crying. Can't you hear?"

"I'm in the bathroom. Can't you ask mom to see what's wrong with her, just a minute until I'm out?"

"No, I can't. Your mother has taken care of her for eight hours. That's a full job, you know. And she does not even get paid for it. Take care of your child. It's enough we take care of her for the eight hours while you are at work."

So Valerie went out and took Victoria with her in bathroom. And this went on several times. Valerie could not take a bath, she could not go in town to the bank for an hour without her father telling her to take care of her child. So she took little Victoria with her wherever she went. To the toilet. Into the bath tub. To the bank or to church. Anywhere she went, she always took her daughter with her. This way, she hoped she did not disturb anybody. Of course, in this case she was criticized that she was too close to her daughter, that she was smothering her. But, hey, nobody is perfect. Like they say "People's mouth only shuts up when it is covered by earth".

The economical situation was still not so good in that period. The old communist plants were almost totally closed down all over the country. It was still very hard to find a job. The mines in Mineville closed down. Nobody invested anything for decades in them and by then, the state noticed they are not profitable. Instead of investing and making them profitable, the rich oligarchy stole whatever they could steal and closed the mines down. It didn't matter that thousands of families remained without income. All that mattered for the oligarchy was for them get even more richer. With the mines closed down, the Institute was also reducing drastically its activity. The research orders of the Institute were all from the mines, so it remained almost without activity.

After the local mining was destroyed, an Australian guy appeared who said he wanted to buy all the depleted ore from Mineville area. During the communist regime, gold and copper was extracted from the ores beneath the mountains surrounding Mineville. The depleted ore was than deposited in huge piles all over the city, respecting no environmental rules whatsoever. They said it was not profitable to extract the minerals remained in these depleted ore. No vegetation grew on these ores, except the acacias. Many times, during the heavy rains, these piles just went down and destroyed everything in their way. Now, this Australian investor said he had the technology to process these ores and that they still contained a lot very valuable minerals. He was going to dismantle a factory of his from Australia, bring it into the country by sea and build it in Mineville. He was looking for trained personnel for this venture and he was headhunting also in the Institute. He had some collaboration with the team in which Valerie was working, but Valerie knew she had no chance to get to him. He wanted to collaborate with her boss and her assistant, Valerie was used only as translator and interpreter in this process.

The worse the Institute's activity was, the more they promised the employees they will get more contracts, so needed for its survival. More meetings were held between the highest management and all the employees filled with bla-bla that should have strengthen the trust of the employees. After one of these meetings, Valerie returned in her office and found the walking papers on her desk. The Institute was firing her. Of course, they did not call it firing they said "rendering available" like in rendering the person available for a new, wonderful job. It wasn't enough the person lost probably the only income he or she had, they had to be cynical too. They didn't even call her and told this to her face. They just put the papers on her desk, without saying anything. Valerie called immediately home and told her father the bad news. He reacted unexpectedly great:

"*Don't worry about a thing. We'll get by. It's not your fault, you gave them no reason to fire you. Don't worry, you'll find something else. Just come home and we'll figure something out.*" Camil told her on the phone.

Valerie turned around quickly from the shock. What was she going to do? She had to start again insisting with Alin to give her money for the child? No way, she could not go through that again! She had to find a new job as soon as possible. The Institute was giving her some redundancy payments, plus she was going to get the unemployment aid from the state. Of course, these were not much, but they were something and she had to manage to live somehow out of them until she found a new job.

She wasn't the only one in this situation. Many persons were "rendered available" in the beginning of the 90's. What Valerie did not understand how could they all accept this situation without protesting! Many of them were quite happy for being laid off, because they received those redundancy payments. As soon as they received the money they spent it foolishly for home appliances, food, cigarettes and booze and then remained with nothing. They hardly found new jobs most of them, especially the miners, they had almost no education. Thousands and thousands of families remained almost dying of hunger and nobody did anything for them.

Eduard was in a pretty desperate situation too. He did not have a job. He just worked unregistered in a couple of places for a few weeks. He was totally relying on his married lover.

Eduard lived in his one room apartment, up on the fourth floor. He had no heating, the window and the door did not close well. During winter, the temperature in the house went down to 0^0C and in summer it could up above 30^0C. The walls were black with damp. It was heartbreaking to see him living in those conditions. Eva insisted with him many times:

"*Eduard, come back home and live with us. You can have back your own room. I'll stay with Valerie and Victoria in a different room from you. At least our place is heated and you can eat with us, it will not cost you anything. What do you say?*"

"*I don't want to come home. You tormented me enough while I was a child. What do you think, I want to listen to Camil while he is babbling incoherently drunk? I don't need this shit.*" answered always aggressively Eduard.

"*Come on now, don't be like that. He doesn't drink so much now that he's old. And he doesn't beat me anymore. And if all three of us are home, he cannot hurt us. Come on, come home with us.*" pleaded Eva.

"*I will not come home. I hate to stay with you. It's all your fault, you know. You should have divorced him. Then we could have lived in peace. But no, you chose him over me and Valerie. So now stay with him. I'm better off without you.*" replied Eduard.

Valerie knew Eva was very hurt by these replies. Why did her brother treat their mom so bad? And who did he think she was fooling? Both Eva and Valerie knew that the only reason Eduard did not come home was so that he could just live the way he wanted to. Valerie went crazy with all these thoughts in her head. Many times she forced herself to stop thinking of all these complicated problems of her family and focus on what she had to do for the best interest of her child. She was not going to focus on the present and on the past, but only on the future, on the best future for Victoria.

Valerie registered again at the Unemployment Office. The huge queues were still in place. Strangely, she got back her stomach aches staying in those queues, just like she had after finishing the faculty. The Unemployment Office decided she was not trained enough, the prestigious university she graduated was not enough. The country did not need chemical engineers, so she had to be re-*conversed* (sic!) professionally. There were a few courses she could choose from, but she necessarily had to chose one, otherwise she could not get the unemployment aid. Valerie chose the accountancy course.

Alan got suddenly interested of her faith. He spoke with his mother about getting a job for Valerie in Streamtown. Valerie did not rely on his promises, she just went on with the courses and the searching of a new job. If she would have known he was serious this time, maybe she would have opposed it from day one.

After less than two months, she got the call from Alan:

"*Well, it's solved.*" said Alan by the phone.

"*What is?"* asked Valerie.

"*My mom, she solved the whole thing.*"

"*What thing?"*

"*Well, with the job and everything. At the company she works, there is a job opening. She said you can go work there. Of course, there will be a competition for the job, but she can get you the bibliography and all. You will stay at my parents house with Victoria.*"

"*What about you?*" asked Valerie.

"*What about me?"* answered Alan.

"*Where will you stay? You work and stay in Steville and I will work and stay in Streamtown?* "asked Valerie.

"*Yes, what's your problem? Of course, I will come also to Streamtown after a while. Until then, you can work at my mom's company. Or you don't want to work?*" asked Alan.

"*Yes, I want to work, But staying at your parents house without you? With your sister and all?*"

CHAPTER 5

Three years after she graduated as a chemical engineer, Valerie has got her first registered job in a research institute. But after 1 year and 9 months of working there she was fired as the activity was drastically downsized. She went back to being unemployed. After less than 2 months of being unemployed, her mother-in-law found her a job at the company she was working. Alan took her to live in Streamtown with his parents and sister, while he was still living in Steville. For Valerie it was a tough decision. It did not seem natural for her to go live with those total strangers without her husband. Why did he want her to do this? First he said he wanted a divorce. Then, when they were in Steville with him he was never home. After she came to Mineville, he hardly came to visit his daughter. When she gave birth to his child, he said he got no day off from work and he could not stay with them more than 24 hours in one weekend. Why does he ask now us to go to his parents? Soon enough, Valerie stopped herself from thinking to these things. She had to do what was best for her daughter. If they remained in Mineville, it was pretty much clear how their marriage will end. Victoria will never have a father. On the other hand, if they went to Streamtown, maybe in a few years he will come there too. With her heart broken, Valerie decided to go to Streamtown with her three years old daughter.

Alan and his father came for them once again to Mineville. Valerie took a few cloths and off they went. Valerie was able to save a little money while she worked. She forced herself to put aside a small amount every month in the bank, she thought you never know when you might need some money, and then who is going to lend it to you? She always liked to have some backup plan, some money put aside, even if her family and Alan laughed at her for this and took advantage of her. He even used to say:

"This is why however cold it is in the room, you always have to stick out a foot from the blanket. Because you always have to have a backup plan, an insurance of some kind."

"So what is wrong with that? Is it a bad quality to be prepared for the worst?" asked back Valerie wondering what her big sin was in this case.

"Nothing wrong in it, I'm just saying. I've never seen anybody like this. It's strange."

For Valerie it wasn't strange, it was perfectly normal. After becoming a mother, this quality got stronger in her. She thought ahead and tried to be prepared for what she thought could happen. Of course there were always events she could not foresee, but the minimum precautions have to be taken, especially when you are a parent and you are responsible for your children.

Alan's family welcomed her very nicely, at least this part went by OK. After she arrived, she started immediately studying for the competition for the job. They gave a room to her and her daughter. The house consisted of four rooms and it was type wagon, that is you entered in the house at one end, there was the room of Alan's parents with access to the bathroom. This was the kitchen too. Then, from this room you entered into the second room. From the second room you entered in the third room and from there into the fourth room. This fourth room was where Valerie and Victoria was going to stay. They called it the front room. It had windows towards the street and toward the courtyard. All the houses in the country had a front room, Valerie used to call it the "room of the dead" because when somebody died in the family, this is where there they put them on the catafalque.

Living in the front room had its advantages and disadvantages. The advantages were that it was the most secluded room in the house, rarely somebody from the family came there to see what they were doing. The disadvantage was that if they wanted to get out the house or wanted to go to the bathroom, they had to pass through each and every room and they had to disturb the whole house.

After a few days, the competition for the position in the state company took place. As with all these jobs in state companies, where the salary was low but there was not much work to do, there were a lot of competitors. Valerie studied hard for the competition, she took it very seriously. Most of the competitors relied on the insiders they knew in the company. Valerie however, even if she already knew somebody – her mother-in-law- she studied consciously all the bibliography. In a few days, Valerie got the result. She got the job. So, here she was, in Streamtown, with her daughter, working in a state company and living with her in-laws, while Alan, her husband was living in Steville, 100 km away from her and their daughter.

Her company was around 6 km away from the house. Her program started at 7 o'clock in the morning and ended at 3 p.m. She had to go by bus. At home, Valerie felt she was obligated to help with all the works were done. After all, she was living there with her daughter and they were not paying anything as rent, utilities or food.

Soon after they moved there, Alan's sister started to prepare for his wedding. All the family was in the middle of the preparations, except for Alan who was in Steville minding his own business. Valerie was unemployed for about two months between the job in Mineville and the job in Streamtown. She did not get yet the unemployment aid and she has already found a new job. When she went to the Unemployment Office to ask about the money, they said:

"*Well, it takes some time until we process all the documents. Usually, the first payment comes a little late, then the next ones come every month precisely. Plus, people don't get new jobs so fast like you do.*"

Having received this intelligent explication, Valerie waited patiently to receive the unemployment aid. About one month after she got her new job, she finally got the unemployment aid and it was the sum for three months received at once. She had also a small amount from the redundancy payments. She saved carefully all these amounts.

Many times, Valerie thought about the money they received at their wedding. They were managed by her mother in law. She put them all to buy a car, a new locally produced car. Then, after the years of strong depreciation of the local currency, she took the money back from the car factory and deposited it to a bank that she trusted. This was a bank founded in Steville and one of her brothers was a branch manager. She said:

"*At least, if something goes wrong, he will warn us to take out the money, not to lose it all.*"

Well, the bank had gone soon bankrupt and her brother never told them one word. Valerie complained loudly:

"How come your brother did not warn us?"

"He did not know. It was a political thing."

"How could he not know? He was a branch manager. He wasn't the damn janitor."

"You don't understand these things. He just did not know. It was a big conspiracy. Nobody knew."

"Nobody knew, but the bank's managers knew."

"Why are you making this big scene now? You'll get back the money. The state guarantees this."

"Yeah, we'll get the money back, after a few more years. In the end, maybe we shall buy a couple of ice creams with the entire amount of 70.000 crowns, which in 1990 was enough to buy a new car!"

After a few months, they got the money back. Now followed the final stroke from her mother in law: she deposited all the remaining money into a pyramidal scheme, that functioned in Steville for a couple of years. The scheme went bankrupt in the end and they never got back a penny even.

Finally, in a pathetic attempt to hush the whole mess up, Alan's parents finally bought them a used car, an old local car. Victoria commented they did not need a car. They had nothing, no place of their own, nothing.

Valerie asked:

"OK, we get a car, but who will use it. Me, here, to go to work? You know, my office is 10 km away from the house."

Alan said:

"You cannot get the car. You don't even have a driving license. Of course, I will use the car. Besides, I will be able to come home more often if I have a car."

"*Yeah, right.*" mumbled Valerie.

"Look, if you get your driving license, I will give you the car too. One week at me, one week at you. What do you say?"

"OK, I'll get the driving license too."

Alan thought « *She'll never get her driving license. She is not capable of driving.*» Actually his whole family was convinced Valerie was not capable to get the driving license. Well, maybe, after several examinations and failed trials, but she will not drive ever. They thought she just did not have it in her blood. Only they had this natural talent.

Alan's sister was preparing to get married. Valerie asked Alan:

"What on earth will you wear at the wedding?"

"I can wear my suit from our wedding." answered Alan.

"But that suit is old. Everybody will be very elegant, it's your sister's wedding." said Valerie.

"I don't care what people say about me. You know that. Plus I don't have money to buy a new suit."

"Yes, I know, but I don't want them to comment about you. I don't want them to say you're the poorest of the family. We'll go and buy you a new suit." decided Valerie.

"What about you? Do you have anything to wear? "asked her Alan.

"Don't worry about me. Everybody knows I'm poor anyway. I don't care about their opinion. We'll see. If I remain with some money, I'll buy myself too something."

Valerie always thought about her loved ones before thinking of herself. She thought this is the normal way to be. Putting her loved ones first made her feel happy.

This behavior convinced Alan one more time that he could take her for granted. He thought she will be there for him forever, no matter what he did, even if he did not give her anything in return – a decent home, a normal married life, a father for their child, love, protection, money. Furthermore, he could live happily on his own in Steville, while she will stay in his parents' home and will raise their child all by herself. How could he divorce? His life could not get better than this!

The wedding preparations were going on. One day, Alan's mother approached Valerie:

"Valerie, I have to speak something with you. Let's go into the front room."

«Oh my God, what did I do? It cannot be good news» thought Valerie.

"Look Valerie, you know we are a lot of us living in this house. There are a lot of expenses."

"I know" replied Valerie, thinking *«Where is this going? She asks money from me? Surely Alan told her I have some money in the bank.»*

"You know I don't ask money from you for anything. But it is very hard for us, for me and father. Many times I don't even have money to buy bread!"

«Good thing you have money for cigarettes, that's what matters.» thought Valerie, but she replied just:

"I know."

"You know, Victoria drinks four liters of milk every day. We have milk,

it's not a problem. But did you know that Alan's grandmother was asking us to pay for the milk our children were drinking back then? She had cows, we did not have the cows back then."

«*Four liters of milk a day? I don't think so. Anyway, could you cut to the chase? It's really getting boring now.*» thought Valerie, just looking at her and saying:

"*I know.*"

"*Now I have to prepare everything for the wedding. Could you lend me some money? Of course, I will pay you back after things settle down.*"

Valerie was processing at light speed all the variants. She could not refuse. On the other hand she could not say she did not have money, Alan knew about her money and she surely told his mother.

"*Of course, I will lend you the money if you need it. How much do you need?*"

"*Whatever you have.*"

"*Alright, but the money is in the bank. I don't have it on me.*"

"*It's not a problem. We shall take you tomorrow to the bank with the car and you can take it out.*"

Valerie thought « *Now that is weird. When I gave birth to a girl, instead of a boy, I was not worthy to be brought home with their car. Now I'm worthy to be taken with their car. Weird, very weird.*»

"*OK, I can give you this amount. I don't have more.*" of course this time, Valerie lied. She knew that whatever amount she told her mother in law she has, she will take it all away and never give it back. She did not want to remain with absolutely nothing.

"*It's alright. If only that is what you have.*"

So the next day, Valerie was taken to the bank with the family car and she gave them the part of the money she saved of her little salary from her first job.

One month before the wedding, Alan came to pay his monthly visit to his child and wife. He left Sunday morning as usual, he never could stay at least until Sunday afternoon. Steville was 100 km away, it took maximum 2 hours to get there by car. Every Sunday morning he left, Valerie could hardly stop herself from crying. Victoria felt her mother's pain. They just had breakfast together and not longer after that, Alan started the explanations and the reasons he had to go back to Steville. Valerie packed him some food. It all took place quite fast. Then he drove his car out of his parents courtyard. Victoria asked her mom to pick her up in her arms. So, Valerie picked her up and they went out, in front of the gate. Alan got out of the car and said goodbye. The two girls were almost crying. He was at peace. He just looked at them, his beautiful young wife holding that gorgeous little girl in her arms, both waving goodbye with tears in their eyes, trying to smile underneath the tears, and he got into his car and drove away. This scene, that broke Valerie's and Victoria's heart had no effect on his heart whatsoever. He was eager to get to his other family, in Steville.

On one particular Sunday, a few hours after he left, Valerie received a phone call from Alan:

"*Hey, Valerie. Please don't get alarmed.*"

"*What happened?*" she asked.

"*I had a car accident.*"

"*What happened?*"

"*Don't worry, nothing happened to me, but the car is destroyed.*" Alan said from the other end of the line.

"*What do you mean you're OK but the car is destroyed?*"

"*I ran into a tree, the frontal half of the car is smashed but I'm fine. I just have a little bump on my head and contusion on my right leg, because of the speed changer. That's all. Don't worry.*"

"*Do you need help? Is there anybody to help you? Do you want me to come to you?*"

"*No, don't come, I'm fine. The police came, they will take me to a hospital to check everything and then I have to go to give some declarations. It happened before the entrance to Steville, I made a wrong overtaking and I ran into a tree. Can you please pass me my father?*"

"*Yes, of course, here he is.*"

Alan's father went to Alan. They did not take Valerie with them. The official reason was she should not see the state of the car because she would get alarmed. This did not ring true to her. She never ever felt any compassion whatsoever from Alan or his family since she got pregnant with his child. Where did this compassion come from now all of the sudden?

Alan remained in Steville, they brought home the car wrecked. The next day, the mother in law:

"*Valerie, you know the car is destroyed. All the front half has to be replaced. Fortunately, the motor is not destroyed, but many parts have to replaced. We don't have the money now for this."*

"What about Alan, he uses the car, right? Why doesn't he pay for the repair?"

"He doesn't have the money. You know how expensive it is to live in Steville with no help from anybody? He hardly has money for the gas to come home every month." answered Alan's mother.

"He is not obliged to come. Nobody puts a gun to his head. If he cannot come once a month home to see his child, he should just remain in Steville."

"I didn't mean that. Why do you have to be so mean always? I just said he does not have the money and neither do we with the wedding and all. So, if you want the car fixed, you'll have to pay. That's all."

So Valerie paid again and as soon as the car was repaired, Alan was able to come home! To take the car back with him, of course.

Valerie told him on a neutral tone:

"Next time when you want to kill yourself, just jump off a tall building. Don't try to kill yourself with the car. I'll just have to pay some more to repair it and I really ran out of money."

Alan was very hurt by what she said. He replied:

"I thought I come home to you and you will comfort me. Instead I get this from you."

"Well, I got married to you and I had your child thinking you will be my husband and a father to our child. Instead I did not get any of this. So, what can I say? Life is a bitch. We don't always get what we expect."

The discussion ended here, Alan always avoided the discussions as he knew they could lead to the serious issues he did not want to confront. But besides these petty discussions between them, Valerie knew her marriage was not headed into the right direction. She felt she could not feel any compassion or love for Alan and worst of all, she could not trust him anymore.

At least Victoria was feeling fine in the house of her paternal grandparents. They had a big yard and garden and a lot of animals around the house. Valerie taught her to get as close as possible to the animals. She took her out into the garden and on long walks by the river was flowing nearby.

Alan's parents had jobs and Alan's sister was at school.

Finding a place in a kindergarten was a big challenge. There were not enough places, not even in the private ones, even though the private ones were quite expensive. Valerie searched a lot and finally found a kindergarten for her daughter. It was very close to where they lived. Victoria could spend time and socialize with other kids of her age.

"*Mammy will take you to a kindergarten, Victoria.*"

"*What's a kindergarten, mammy?*" asked Victoria.

"*Kindergarten is a place where all the children go from morning till afternoon, when their parents come home from work.*" answered Valerie.

"*And what do they do there all day long, mammy?*"

"*Ooh, they do a lot of nice things. They play together wonderful new games. They learn poems.*"

"*Ohh, that's great, mom. You and I will play wonderfully there!*" said gladly Victoria.

"*No dear, mammy cannot stay there with you. I have to go to work. If I don't go to work, I will not receive salary and then we shall have no money to buy food and cloths and everything we need. Do you understand my love?*"

"*Yes, mom, I know we need the money, but can't you stay with me and play and just get the money?*"

"*No, my love. It does not work that way. You have to work to get the money, nobody will give you money for doing nothing.*"

"*Alright, if you have to....*" answered Victoria.

"*Mammy will take you to kindergarten and leave you there. Then I go to work and at 4 o'clock in the afternoon I will come to take you home. The time will go by so fast!*"

Valerie was a bit nervous, she knew her daughter will cry and will not want to remain there without her, but she really had to do it. Victoria had to learn to behave among other kids, had to learn to stand up for herself. She could not grow and develop under her mother's wings.

She spoke with Victoria many times about it before the first day so that she could get used to the idea. Then, on the first day, Valerie dressed Victoria up nicely and they went to the kindergarten. It was not far away from the house they were living, so they could make a nice walk and speak a little more:

"*What time are you going to take me home, mammy?*"

"*Well even if it is a place for children there is a certain schedule you have to follow there. Mammy has a certain schedule at work: from seven a.m. to three p.m. In the same way, you have a certain schedule: from seven to three. The only problem is I have to go to work too, so I will have to leave you a little earlier there and pick you up a little later than 3 p.m. Do you understand my love?"*

"I understand, but can you come quickly to pick me up, mammy?"

"Yes my love, I will come as fast as I can. I promise you." answered Valerie, with her heart pounding out of her chest. She knew Victoria will cry when she will leave her there.

So, they arrived at the kindergarten and entered the front door. The room where the children were staying was at the first floor and they had to climb some stairs to get there. The walls of the staircase were painted beautiful. It was a scene from a fairy tale. «*Oh my God!*» Valerie noticed the scene was from Little Red Riding Hood and of course there was the big bad wolf. Valerie thought for herself « *Oh God, please don't let her see the wolf, please!* » But Victoria noticed it and the scene started right away:

"Mammy, mammy, look, there the big bad wolf! I don't like him. Tell him to go away!"

"It's just a picture dear. There is no wolf here."

"I don't want to remain here, the wolf will come and eat me."

Valerie thought it was quite strange that her daughter was afraid of the wolf. She knew she was afraid of the wolf when she was little, but also Victoria was very afraid of it, even if she never frightened her with it like other parents do. The only thing little Victoria knew was this story and maybe some scenes from TV. And still she was afraid of the wolf. This had to be an ancestral fear, that we people inherit from our forefathers. The howling of a wolf tells us we are in danger…

Valerie left Victoria crying there. Her heart was breaking, she felt terribly sorry for the suffering of her daughter and terribly ashamed she put the personnel from the kindergarten to go through this with her child. But she had no choice. Even if she could find somebody to stay with Victoria home when she was at work, she did not want to do it. Victoria had to learn to cope with other children, with society. If she did not get used now, she will be forced to get used later. The later this process took place, the harder it was. The two of them, mother and daughter, had to go over it now.

When she left her there, Victoria was crying with all her strength. The women working there were trying to convince her not to cry, because she will learn a lot of new things and they will play games and so on. After ten-twenty minutes of convincing, Victoria looked at them with her eyes filled with tears and asked:

"*Don't you understand I cannot remain here without mammy?*"

Valerie could hardly wait 3 p.m. She rushed away from work and practically ran to take her daughter from the kindergarten. She ran up the stairs, looked at the wolf and thought « *Now look mister, you caused us a lot of trouble this morning. Don't you have some other place to go?* » Then, she smiled «*Oh my God, I'm speaking with wolfs painted on the walls*». She entered slowly the room and she saw her daughter. The governess was sitting on her chair and Victoria was sitting in her lap, looking down with some superiority to the other children who were playing and running around the room. Valerie started to laugh happily. It looked like Victoria has adjusted quite nicely.

"*Hello Mrs.Governess. I came to take Victoria home.*"

As soon as she saw her mom, the little one jumped out of the governess arms and ran to her mom and hold her tightly around her legs, like a little monkey that hangs on to her mom.

"*Hello Ma'am. You already came for her?*" answered the governess.

"*Yes, I came as fast as I could. How did she behave?*"

"*Of, she is a wonderful child. She did not cause any problems whatsoever.*"

"*I'm relieved. I was so worried that she'll cry all the time and annoy you. I know you have a lot of children and all.*"

"*No, no, nonsense. She is one the quietest children we have here. We named her the sunflower.*"

"*Why did you do that?*" asked Valerie.

"*Well, in the morning when you left, I was not here. You left her with the caretakers. Then, at 8 when I arrived, I presented myself, I said I will be in charge and after that she practically followed me wherever I went. If she could not come after me physically, then she followed me with her eyes. If I went around the room, she was turning around to see me in every moment. Like a sun flower turns after the sun, you know?*"

"*That's nice.*" said Valerie. "*But didn't she bother you?*" asked Valerie.

"*No, no, she is a wonderful little girl. So well behaved. She knows so many things, you can discuss with her like with a ten years old child. She understands and listens, she does not cause any trouble at all. I am looking forward to see you both tomorrow!"*

"*Thank you Madame. Thank you so much. We'll see you tomorrow! Bye!*"

"*Good-bye Madame*" said also little Victoria, who learned early on from her mom that she has to greet people whenever she left some place.

Valerie was happy this important step was over. She was very proud of her daughter, about the way she coped in this situation.

Step by step, Victoria was developing from every point of view. She started to eat more kinds of food. As a little baby, she did not eat very well, preferring only milk and some fruit. This was always a great source of stress for Valerie. First thing Valerie did was that she never ate sweets in front of her daughter. She never bought sweets and she never had sweets in the house. She thought: "*If the child does not sweets exist, she cannot crave for them.*" And right she was. Victoria grew up without eating sweets, without even liking sweets. Then, Valerie was very careful with the portions she served her little one. Many times she saw other parents serving huge portions of food in big plates to children who barely ate something. Poor children, who were already scared of the idea of eating, knowing also the fighting that will take place if they did not eat, found themselves in front of the huge frightening portions and panicked. The result was that they ended up not eating anything. Valerie solved this in a different way: she bought a few plates and a cup that were only for Victoria. Small sized, especially designed for children. Then, she served tiny little portions of food, specially prepared for her when it was possible, very nicely arranged on the plate so that Victoria enjoyed looking at them. This way, Victoria started to enjoy food more and more. It's not that Valerie wanted to make a food minded out of her, she never fed her daughter with unhealthy, fat food or sweets. The reason was that she believed a young body and mind that were growing and developing so much day by day needed various nutrients that were offered by very various types of food. Her little daughter needed the goodness of every food to build up a smart mind and a strong body and she was going to make sure she provided this to her.

After a couple of months of work, Valerie's working hours at job have changed. She worked 24 hours, then she was free for 72 hours. Free is just a manner of speaking, because in her free time she worked harder at her in-law than she worked at the office. Alan's parents lived in a house in a little town, but they had like a regular farm on their hands. They had garden, a huge field to work, also a few cows, chickens, rabbits many times, sometimes ducks. It was a lot of work around the house. Valerie was not used to such hard work. At her parents' house they did not work so hard outside the house. First of all they lived in a block of flats, they had no garden or animals to care for. Secondly, their parents' only interest was to eat and live the current day. They never tried to work more to make more money, or buy a bigger house or buy a car. They just survived of their salary from one month to the other. For Valerie it was very hard to get used to this new life style. She wanted to help with all that work, no matter how hard it was. She considered that if she and her daughter were living there and were not paying a rent, she had to work and help Alan's parents with everything.

Valerie cooked for them. Of course Alan's sister was always commenting that her food was not as good as their mother's cooking, but the food was eaten after all. Alan's mother washed the laundry with her hands for the entire family, it has been like that since the beginning. The poor woman spent hours to wash so many cloths. Valerie washed her cloths and her daughter's cloths, but she felt very sorry for her mother in law. As often as she could she washed all the laundry for her. The cleaning of the house was another routine, every week. It usually took place on Saturday, after working all day out on the field or in the garden. Valerie felt like she was ran over by the train after a day like this. When they got back in the house, they all looked at her like at a strange animal:

"*What's the matter with her? Why does she have to put on this face? We did not work that much.*" They were speaking among themselves. Valerie felt their disapproval, but she was so tired, she could hardly stand on her feet. Many times, she retired to her room and lied directly down on the floor and just cried desperately. Little Victoria always came after her and consoled her:

"*Don't cry mammy, I love you. Please don't cry.*" caressing her mother forehead and she started to cry too.

Valerie could not bear to see her daughter crying, she just could not bear it. No matter how hard it was for her, she wiped her tears and consoled back her little girl:

"Hey, my little angel. Don't cry. Don't cry, mammy is fine. I just have a head ache, that's all. But if you give me a kiss, it will pass."

"I give you a kiss, but I don't want you to die, mammy. Please don't cry anymore." answered little Victoria, understanding more than a little girl her age should understand.

"I will not die, my love. Now, let's go and help to clean the house. What do you say? And after that we can play a little bit together." continued Valerie.

"Can't we just stay here and play mammy?" asked Victoria.

"We have to help to clean the house my little one. They let us stay here, we have to do something in return. It is not our house, you know, they just let us stay here."

"Why don't we have our own house mammy? If we would have our own house, we could do whatever we want all the time, couldn't we? You would just go to work so that we have money and at home we would just play."

"We don't have our own house because mammy does not have so much money to buy one. One day maybe we shall have a house of our own. But right now, we don't have enough money for that. One day, my love, one day…."

"Alright, mammy, let's go."

So they went out and asked how could they help. So the sisters instructed Valerie what she had to do. And instructed her how to do it. For example, if she had to take out the rug and beat it, she could not fold it in the direction she wanted, she had to fold it in the direction they told her to. Otherwise, they started to criticize her and explain that the only good way to fold a rug was their way.

Valerie was not convinced it mattered so much how the carpet was folded as long as it was taken out of somebody, beat and cleaned and then put back in the house. She would have just be happy if somebody did this for her, like she was doing it for them. But they were not happy. They were very dissatisfied with what she did and how she did it.

Then her father in law was the top. He repeated several times every day, every single day:

"You don't work enough to earn the water you are drinking. Not to mention the lodging, the food and everything."

Valerie felt very uncomfortable with this. She knew they just let her stay there. If she annoyed them so much, why did Alan call her there? Why did her mother in lay tell her about the job in her company? She could have remained in Mineville, she did not ask to come to Streamtown. She had to get out of there! The sooner the better. She will save every penny until she will have enough to buy a little apartment, no matter how small and in what area, just to be enough for her and her little girl. Just like the Japanese said: "*by enduring the unendurable and suffering what is unsufferable*" ["Text of Hirohito's Radio Rescript", *The New York Times*, 15 August 1945, p. 3, retrieved 8 August 2015].

She had no money whatsoever again. She came with a little amount from Mineville. First, her mother in law asked her a loan for the wedding of Alan's sister. Then, there was Alan's car accident, Valerie had to pay for the repairs, even if she was not the one actually using the car. Finally, Eduard asked her money. A law came out that everybody who was living in an apartment received during the communist regime could buy the respective apartment by paying a fair amount of money. Much less than the prices on the free market, but still an amount of money. It could be paid also in several installments, but it had to be paid. Eduard had no money whatsoever. He was not working. All the money he received from his lover went for food and booze. Now, desperately, he asked help from his sister and her sister to pay the apartment he was living in. Eva sold everything she could without Camil knowing it and Valerie sent Eduard all the money she still had in her bank account. Fortunately, Eduard was able to buy in this way the little apartment on the last floor of that wretched block. So Valerie continued to save money. She never bought any new cloths, if she needed something, she bought it from the second hand shops. She never went to a beauty parlor. She did not buy even an ice cream or a soda for herself, absolutely nothing.

Alan however bought himself whatever he liked and he wanted. Always the best cigarettes and the best coffee; expensive soap and shampoo; good, new cloths, even if not elegant, but as expensive as possible. Valerie did not know how to cut more on her expenses, he just lived his life and bought whatever he desired. His salary was three times Valerie's salary. He was not saving any money, she saved every penny she could and in the meantime she was also raising Victoria.

Valerie felt lonely and unhappy in the house of her in-laws. She was mentally in a very dangerous situation. She was living in a hostile environment, nobody had a good word towards her. She worked like a slave from dusk to dawn, all she got in return was criticism and malicious comments. In this state of mind, a person is in the most vulnerable position of all. If anyone would have come close to her and told her one single good word, one single friendly remark, her heart would have melted completely. She felt this and tried very hard to isolate herself from everybody, because she did not want to be an easy target. She felt the only important thing was the best interest of her child. Her internal loneliness, her desperate need for a little bit of love and attention had to be covered up, as deep as possible inside her heart.

All she did was work at her job, then she came home and worked some more. Besides this, she spoke a lot with her daughter, teaching her all that was important. Also, she taught her daughter the other little things, like riding a bicycle or swimming.

She went to work by bus. As she worked 24 hours, then she was free for 72 hours, her working hours could be on any day, no matter if it was a working day or a holiday. Her turn to work could be on Christmas day, or Easter day or New Year's day. She did not mind that she had to work on holidays, she felt much better at work than it that house. The only problem was that on holidays the buses were not circulating. Her colleagues went to work by cars, if they did not have a car, some family member or friend took them to work. In Valerie's case, the situation was different. Her father in law always told her:

"*Look, Valerie, if you want, we can take you to work with our car, but you have to pay for the gas.*"

Valerie answered:

"*If I have to pay anyway, I will take a taxi. Thank you though.*"

Of course she never took a taxi, she saved her money. Therefore, in these days she went to work by foot. It took her one and a half hour to get there. During spring or summer it was not so bad. But during winter, it was pretty hard. The road on which she walked crossed over the field in a particular area and it was very dark. There were a lot of stray dogs there and there was no footway. She could be hit by any passing car. Many times in winter the snow was big and not cleaned from the road so early in the morning. She could hardly walk. She cried almost all the way to work, she only wiped her tears when she arrived there, so that others will not see that she was crying.

When she finished work and it was holiday, she walked home. She enjoyed how all the town was looking at her, they were all gossiping:

"Look at her, she is walking all that way by foot. In that house where she lives there are three cars in the backyard, isn't there anybody to come and pick her up?"

After one of these trips home, on a very snowy winter morning, Valerie arrived home absolutely beat. Little Victoria was on holiday and she was playing quietly in the room. Valerie laid down on the bed and fell immediately in a deep sleep.

After less than 30 minutes, her mother in law came into their room and woke her up:

"*Valerie, wake up.*"

"*What? What is going on?*" asked Valerie still sleepy.

"*Wake up. Come on, wake up. Dress up and come outside.*"

"*What for?*" asked Valerie still not understanding what she had to do.

"*You have to come out and clean the snow. It has snowed a lot and you have to clean the snow, otherwise we shall not be able to walk through the backyard. Come on. I'll wait for you outside.*"

Valerie woke up immediately. Now she understood what she had to do. She dressed up and went out to clean the snow, after 24 hours of work and one trip by foot until home.

On many occasions like this, her colleagues and acquaintances saw her working all day long right after she came out of her shift. Everybody saw what was going on.

During spring and summer time, she had to go out on the field as soon as she arrived home. There was no rest, she had to work. After all, they were allowing her to live there and gave her and Victoria food, right?

One of the hardest things for Valerie was when she had to go on the field with the herd of cows. In that particular area where her in-laws were living, many families had cows and they all gathered them during the day and one person took them to pasture on the field. Every family's turn came one after the other. When their turn came, they sent out Valerie with the cows. It's not that it was hard work or anything, because it was not a work, but she had to be very careful not to lose any of the cows. There were around 40 cows in the herd. Most of them minded their own business and stayed calm, but there were some of them who just started to wander away.

Plus, you had to gather them on the street from each and every house, cross a busy street with them, get on the field, than at noon go with them to the river to drink water, then back to the field, back across the busy street and home to every house. Valerie ran around them all day long, calling back the ones that wanted to get away. Running like this, once she jumped over a puddle and put her foot down in a wrong position, so her ankle went out. It hurt and she could not step on it. She stayed with the cows limping all day long. When she got home, her ankle has swollen and it was quite red. She told them:

"I jumped over a puddle today and I put my foot down wrong. Now my ankle is swollen and it hurts very much."

"Oh, dear, that's a shame."

"Can I stay home tomorrow maybe, I cannot step on it, I'm limping."

"Tomorrow no, it's still our turn with the cows. We have to go 2 days with them, as we have 4 cows. For one cow everybody has to stay half of a day. 4 cows means 2 complete days. So you have to go tomorrow with the herd too."

"But I cannot walk, I cannot step on my foot. What happens if one of the cows walks away, I cannot run after it."

"Now, now, you always have to make such a big drama. No cow will go away. And at 4 p.m. I'll come from work and take your place, OK? Are you satisfied now?" her mother in law asked her with her usual despiteful face.

Valerie went the next day again with the cows. All day long out on the field she cried. She hoped somebody will come and rescue her from there. Just like she saw in the movies, a car will stop by and she will get on it, go home, take her daughter and run off into the big wide world. Nobody came to rescue her, but out there, all alone on the field, she felt closer to God than ever. She knew God saw what she was going through. She knew He did not forget about her and things will turn for the better. She just had to hold on. If she could not walk on proudly, with her head held up high, she had to go forward on her two knees. If that was not possible either, she had to crawl forward, but no matter what, she could not to give up. For sure, things will turn for the better.

Eating was also an interesting venture. In the evening, all the family had to eat together. Alan's father was always mad because his family was not working enough and at dinner he found the opportunity to express all his dissatisfaction in this regard. Even after he finally stopped sharing his feelings, nobody dared to speak, they just sat quietly and eat as fast as they could, just to get over it. Valerie preferred many times to declare she and Victoria were not hungry than to stay for a few minutes in that environment. She took her little girl into their room and they ate an apple with some biscuits and that was all. Other times she tried to eat at different hours than the family, but he was watching every move they made and when he saw they were at the table he came and shared his feelings with them while they were eating. Valerie's stomach was aching and she could hardly swallow listening to him. Once she actually had the courage and asked him:

"*Why do you always tell us these things when we are eating?*"

"*Because it's the only time you are in one place, willing to listen.*" her father in law replied.

This wasn't even true, Valerie always listened to Alan's parents if they were speaking, she never treated them with disrespect.

The food wasn't either like at her parents. Back home, if they were eating chicken for example, Eva would cook two or three chickens for the four members of the family. It's true, they were small chickens, what they found in the store, but anyway, there was enough for everybody. Alan's mother cooked one chicken for all family members. Of course she was bragging that it was a farm chicken and so on, but it was just one chicken divided to all of them. Always the same persons got the drumsticks and these persons were not Valerie or Victoria. Valerie never said anything to them, she just told once Alan:

"*Your mother never gives us the drumsticks when she divides the chicken. But don't worry, we'll get our drumsticks, God will provide for it. Don't worry.*"

Valerie got very thin, even the food she was eating made her more harm than good. She got into a point when she could hardly swallow the food in the presence of her in-laws. At night, she was dreaming about food. One night she dreamt she was walking with her mom in her mom's garden. It was spring and they walking among the blooming trees. Valerie looked at the branches of the trees and she saw there were pieces of food hanging off the branches! Pieces of meat balls and schnitzels, just like her mom used to cook for her!

Valerie had a condition because of which every night she had to go out to the bathroom. In her in-laws house, this was torture. Valerie and Victoria slept in the front room. The bathroom was in the other end of the house. To get from her room to the bathroom, Valerie had to cross three rooms, and in each and every one of these rooms somebody was sleeping. If she went through all the rooms, she did it as quietly as she could, but in the morning she heard the comments:

"*You know, I am OK with it, but father is disturbed by your night trips to the bathroom. He wakes up and cannot go back to sleep.*" her sister-in-law told her.

"*You know, I am OK with it, but your sister-in-law is disturbed by your night trips to the bathroom. She wakes up and cannot go back to sleep.*" her father-in-law told her.

Valerie heard these comments a few times, then she decided she rather went to the outhouse. The problem with the outhouse was that it was full of rats and spiders. There was no light there and you had to go through the barn to get there. The barn was also very scary at night. As there was no light, Valerie bought herself a lantern. Even so, all the darkness scared her terribly. The worst was in winter, when the temperature dropped much under zero Celsius degrees. Woken up from the warm bed, Valerie had to dress up and go out to the outhouse. No matter how thick the clothes were on her, she was so cold when she went out that she trembled uncontrollably and her jaws clinched. She used to think in these moments: «*This is bad cold, bad cold*». For Valerie this was bad cold. The good cold was when she felt it, but she did not start to tremble. Valerie did not mind the good cold, but she hated the bad cold. It took her more than fifteen minutes, back in bed, to stop trembling. Sometimes she trembled so hard, Victoria woke up and asked her what was wrong. Valerie just answered her:

"*Nothing, my love. I'm just cold. I'm fine. Go back to sleep.*"

Even so, she was hoping Alan will come finally to Streamtown and live with her and their daughter. A multinational company was founded in Streamtown and Valerie found out they were hiring engineers. She thought Alan's eternal reason not to come home was his job of Steville. What if he found a job in Streamtown? Wouldn't that solve the problem? Of course, he never actually searched for a job in Streamtown, so what chances could he have for finding one? But what if she found him a job? Will he take it? Maybe, maybe not, but she will arrange an interview for him anyway, and if he refuses to come, at least she will know where they stand. Valerie spoke with Alan first of all:

"Look Alan, this new multinational company is hiring engineers right now. Wouldn't you like to try to get a job there?"

"I don't know. I heard they are not very serious."

"What do you mean they are not serious?"

"Well I heard they hire you and then they fire you and you remain on the streets."

"I didn't hear that. I heard they give good salaries too. Well, possible they fired some persons, but what company doesn't? Professionally speaking you are an asset, I'm sure they will not fire you with no real reason."

"If you say so…"

"So, what do you say? Give it a shot?"

"I don't have time for this. I have to make my resumé, bring it to them in a working day. You want me to stay away from my current job for one day for this?"

"No, no, I'll arrange everything. You should just come to the interview. Would you do that if they call you?"

"Yeah, OK, whatever."

Valerie wrote his curriculum vitae and forwarded it to the human resources department of that company. Then, she waited patiently.

After a few days, her mother in law approached Valerie:

"Hey Valerie, guess what?"

"*What?*" Valerie thought «*I hope it's a good thing*».

"That multinational called on the phone today. They wanted to set an interview with Alan."

"Wow, great! I'm very glad. So when is the interview?"

"They said on Tuesday, 14th at 16.00 hours."

"Oh, great. Alan should have time to arrange everything and come to the interview. Did you call him?"

"Yes, yes, I called him at work and told him about the interview. He said he'll come."

"Great! Oh, God help us! I hope they will hire him!"

Valerie put her hopes very high. If Alan came home, things would have changed. Whenever he came home, her in-laws treated her better. Imagine how things would have changed if he would have come home for good!

They could buy a house of their own! Have a real family! Victoria would have finally a father!

Valerie was counting the days until the day of interview. In the respective morning, Alan came to Streamtown with his car. Valerie went with him to the company and waited until he went in. In about 5 minutes, Alan came out:

"*What happened? How come you came out already?* "asked Valerie

"*The interview was on Friday, the 10th. Not today.*"

"*What? I can't believe this.*"

"*This is what she told me.*"

"*Who told you?*"

"*The lady from human resources. She said the interview was on Friday the 10th. They waited for me, I didn't show up, so they hired somebody else.*"

"*I can't believe this! Your mother said it was on Tuesday the 14th!*"

"*Yes, this is what she told me too!*"

"*I don't understand! Does she do this on purpose?*"

"*What! You think she did this on purpose?*"

"*Yeah, I think she did this on purpose. It's not the first time she screws us. Didn't it happen that time she promised she would wait for us at the railway station when we told her come home and then she said she thought it was on another day? Don't you remember?*"

"*Yes, I remember, but it was an honest mistake.*"

"*Honest mistake my foot. She does this on purpose. Alright, never mind. Go back to Steville.*"

"*I have to go back, I have to go work. I'm sorry.*"

"*Yeah, yeah, you have to go to work.*"

Alan went to Steville, Valerie went back to the house of her in-laws.

"*So? How did it go?*" asked her mother-in –law.

"*It didn't go. Alan was there on Tuesday the 14th at 16 hours, just like you said.*"

"*And?*"

"*And the lady from human resources told him the interview was on Friday, not today. She said she told you the interview was scheduled for Friday and you said you will give the message to Alan.*"

"*What? That woman is stupid! She said the interview is on Tuesday the 14th! I remember it very well! She is lying!*"

"She is lying? Why would she lie? If she didn't not want to call Alan to the interview, she just wouldn't have called him. Why would she call him on a wrong day?"

"I don't know why, but this is the way it is! She told me the interview is on Friday!"

"Yeah, OK, whatever. Alan went back to Steville."

Valerie just could not let this be. After a couple of days, she decided to call personally the human resources lady from the company. Even if it was very intimidating to call her and she felt like an idiot because her husband could not show up at a certain date and time, she still wanted to speak with that lady. «*What could happen worse than this?*» thought Valerie. «*By now she already figured out we're just a bunch of idiots. In the worst case, she will refuse to speak with me.*»

Valerie went to a public phone and dialed the number. Unlike in state companies, somebody actually picked up in a couple of seconds. A very nice voice asked her who was she looking for. She said she wanted to speak with the head of human resources. The person on the other end of the line connected her immediately and the lady from human resources answered after a few seconds. «*Hey, these guys are OK*» thought Valerie. «*If I would have called a state company and asked to speak with the head of human resources, they would have kept me hanging on the line for minutes, then told me the person is not available for the moment and that I should call back later. These guys are OK, I like them. They are very professional. Why does everybody tell frightening stories about them?* » wondered Valerie.

"Hello, I am Valerie. My husband had to come to an interview a few days ago. Alan is his name."

"Hello, yes, I remember. He came on a wrong day, however. What happened?"

"Well, when you called the phone number I wrote on the application, my mother-in-law answered. She took the message from you and she told him when to come."

"Alright, you are right, I did not speak with you or him, I spoke to another lady."

"Well, I wrote my in-laws phone number on the application because we have no other phone, it's the only way to contact us. Alan is working in Steville, he does not have a phone there. Anyway, my mother-in-law told us

that you said the interview is on Tuesday the 14th, when in fact the interview was on Friday the 10th. I don't believe her and I called you to thank you for the opportunity you gave us and apologize for what happened."

"Well, yes, I did not understand what happened. First of all, we wanted very much to speak with him. If he would have come to the interview, he would have spoken directly with the general manager. We were disappointed he did not show up. You know, there are many persons who can hardly wait to get a job in our company."

"I know."

"If he didn't come, we hired somebody else. Then, on Tuesday, she shows up and asks for me, saying he came for the interview. It was quite strange."

"Yes, it was, This is why I called you now. Sorry for taking your time, I know you are very busy. But I just had to explain to you what happened."

"Thank you for calling, you are not taking my time. But she said I told her the interview was on Tuesday? This is just not true! I called around 10 persons to the interview that day and I told all of them the interview is on Friday. They all came, except for your husband."

"Well, I know, I'm sorry. This is what happened. Anyway, thank you anyway and sorry for all the story."

"No problem, no problem. Maybe the next time. There will be other job openings, perhaps next time will be better."

"Yes, thank you so much. Bye!"

"Bye!"

Valerie decided she would follow the announcements of this company and at their next interviewing, she will get Alan in no matter what. She will call personally to confirm the interview date and hour.

Victoria was growing to be a very friendly and well adjusted girl. Valerie always felt guilty she could not provide a normal family, or a home of their own for her child. She felt guilty she could not keep her father with them. On the other hand, Victoria did not look as she was missing her father. She grew up seeing him 24 hours a month, she never asked for more.

After a couple of years spent in the first kindergarten, Valerie started asking around at her acquaintances which was the best kindergarten in the town. She wanted her daughter to go to the best kindergarten there was, so that when she starts school she will be well prepared. Finally, she found out. Then, Valerie started to ask around who knows somebody at that kindergarten so that she could get in. There were more children than places and you had to know somebody, so that you could get your child in. Furthermore, this best kindergarten was farther away the house they were living, but this did not stop Valerie to register her child there. So what if it was farther? They will walk there every day, she could not chose the most comfortable variant when it came to the best interest of her daughter.

Valerie registered Victoria where she wanted to. There were two variants: she could take her daughter there from 9 o'clock to 12 o'clock, just for the activities for children and not pay anything. The second variant was to take her daughter as early in the morning as she wanted and let her there until at least 3 p.m. In this way, the child received breakfast, at noon she received lunch and then between 1 and 3 p.m. children had to sleep. For this, Valerie had to pay a fee for each day Victoria spent there. Valerie chose the second variant. She thought this way she had several advantages: first of all, Victoria ate breakfast and lunch cooked in a very clean kitchen, at specific hours, together with other children. At her in-laws house, Valerie could not provide this. They always ate in the "company" of her father-in-law, who was lecturing them while they were swallowing the food. Every time they ate, several persons of the family passed by them and looked what they eating and so on. Even if Victoria was a very picky eater, Valerie was sure that in the presence of other children, she will be ashamed to comment so much and she will eat whatever they served her. Second of all, this way Victoria slept at noon two hours, again, just because all the children did this. At home, she always fought her mom for this. Thirdly, Victoria will socialize with other children. Playing, eating, sleeping together with other children will help her be a more sociable person than she already was.

Of course, Alan and his family disapproved Valerie's decision.

"*It's stupid to pay for the kindergarten of Victoria. She could take her only from 9 to 12 and not pay anything. She does not know how to manage her money.*"

«*Yeah, and you know how to manage money. Let's just look what you did with the money from our wedding.*» thought Valerie every time she heard them, but she did not say anything. It was just a loss of time to reason with them, they did not see eye to eye in several issues. But at least, they respected Valerie's decisions. Like at home with her parents, Valerie told her in-laws:

"I take full responsibility for Victoria. For the good things and for the bad things. I shall not allow anybody to interfere in my decisions. If you want to interfere in my decisions, you will take over her completely, and I shall not interfere."

The only person Valerie wanted to contribute in the decisions regarding her daughter was Alan, but he couldn't care less. So that was it, Valerie was on her own.

Only a few weeks after the first "attempt" of interview, Valerie saw an ad in the local newspaper. The company was hiring again. This time, Valerie was determined to take the matter in her hands. She forwarded again the updated CV of Alan. Then, waited patiently for them to call. After her mother-in-law said they called for an interview, Valerie called immediately back to confirm the date and hour. She also made sure Alan came to the interview. She accompanied him there and made sure he went in at the right hour, exactly fifteen minutes before the scheduled hour.

After almost an hour, Alan came out.

"*So, how was it?*" asked Valerie.

"*It was OK. I think I did OK.*" answered Alan, not as excited as she was.

"*What is it? It's not good it went OK?*" asked Valerie.

"*No, no, it's OK. Everything is fine. Now, let's see what they say. They said they will call in a few days to tell us their decision.*"

"*Great, great! I'm looking forward to it.*" said Valerie, really glad and hopeful.

In a few days the company called. This time, Valerie picked up the phone. They wanted to hire Alan and he was supposed to come and discuss the specific details about it. Valerie was happy about this. She called Alan immediately and told him the good news.

Alan came to the scheduled meeting. Valerie was waiting for him outside. When it was over, he came out.

Valerie jumped happily on him:

"*Well? What did they say? Will they hire you?*"

"*Yes, they said they wanted to hire me. They will send the transfer request directly to where work now. They said they want me to start right away.*"

"*So, what did you say?*"

"I said OK, I told them I have to go back and discuss at my current workplace."

"So, what's the matter? I see you're not very pleased..."

"No, no, I'm pleased, I'm pleased. Look, I have to back to Steville now, I'll call when it's all settled, alright?"

"OK, fine. I'll wait for your call."

After a few days, Alan came to his parents' house unannounced. He sat on his parents' bed and called Valerie for a discussion. His parents were assisting.

Alan started:

"Look, Valerie, I went to my current job and told them I found a new job here in Streamtown."

Valerie thought «*Why did he call me here to discuss? And his parents are present. This is not good. I wonder what is he up to.*»

"So, what did they say?" asked Valerie, curious where this discussion was headed to.

"They said they don't want me to go. They said they give me raise if I stay."

"So, what's your decision, Alan?"

"I haven't decided yet. I came to discuss with you first."

"You wanted to discuss with me first? Don't you know what I want? Didn't I make it clear until now? Why do you think I went through all the trouble to bring you to the interview?"

"So, you say I should accept this new job."

"Of course I say you should accept this new job. I'm amazed you don't know this and you have to ask me."

"Yes, I know, but they offered me a raise at the old job. You understand? They really appreciate me. They don't want me to leave. As for this new company from Streamtown. I heard they are not very serious. And they are not friendly, they are firing people easily and capriciously."

"They are friendlier than many people from here from Streamtown. And they invested millions to build up this huge factory. You think they did all this for an activity of a few months? Don't you see the size of this factory? And did you think about Victoria and me? That we are here and you are in Steville and we see you once a month? Did you consider this?"

"Look Valerie, I will do whatever you want me to do. You decide. What

do you want me to do? You want me to give up my safe job in Steville or you want me to come here and work in this factory?"

Valerie could not understand him. «*Why is he hesitating? What is keeping him in Steville? And why doesn't he say out loud he doesn't want to come home? He's just like my father. He doesn't even have the guts to decide something, he always passes this responsibility to someone else, so that if anything goes wrong, he will not be held accountable.*»

"*Well, Valerie? What do you want me to do?"* insisted Alan.

"*Stay in Steville Alan if that's what you want. Just stay in Steville.*" said Valerie and she walked out of the house.

CHAPTER 6

Valerie has come to Streamtown, in the house of her husband's parents, hoping after a while he will come too. He didn't come. His reason was always his job from Steville. Valerie arranged two interviews for him in Streamtown in a huge multinational company. He never went to the first interview, his mother noted the wrong date and he came in another day. He went to the second interview and the company offered him a job. Alan refused, saying the company where he worked in Steville offered him a raise just to stay with them.

Valerie was going insane trying to figure out what was on her husband's mind. «*It's obvious he doesn't want to come to stay with us in Streamtown. But then why did he bring us here? Why did his mother tell me about this job at her company? I was unemployed in Mineville and desperate for a job, it's true, but I was going to find a new job. I never asked them to bring me here. So why, why did he bring me here? And to his parents' house? He brought me here, and he continues to stay in Steville? What kind of a life is this? I'm going crazy in this house, they treat me like a piece of dirt. And for what?*"

Valerie did not have any friend, she had nobody to talk about her concerns with. Even if some persons were friendly with her and invited her to their house for example, she couldn't have invited anybody where she lived. She lived in her in-laws' house. They were always giving her the black looks. Nothing she said or did was right. They always criticized what she or her daughter did. Alan's family was perfect and knew always what was the best of everything. Valerie and her daughter were the humble and stupid little servants, allowed to live in their home on sufferance.

The connection between Valerie and Victoria grew stronger and stronger every day. Victoria saw and understood much more a little girl should see and understand. She saw her mother cry desperately many times, hidden in their room, after everybody went to sleep. She always consoled her mother and in her little child innocence and good faith knew that the sun will shine on their street too. She just went to her mammy and told her:

"*Mammy, look at me. Don't cry. Mammy smile.*"

"*Oh my dear one, mammy is a little upset no, but I'll be fine, don't worry.*"

"*Mammy smile. Just smile. It'll all pass, you'll see. I love you, don't worry about anything else.*"

Victoria always made Valerie stop crying. She thought «*You know what? Victoria is right. She is a few years old, but she is absolutely right. I shouldn't care what they think about me. All that matters is what my daughter thinks of me and my daughter loves me. So what do I care about them? So what if they don't like me? What if Alan doesn't want me anymore? If my daughter loves me and she is my ally I'll get through this.*»

Victoria went to the best kindergarten there was in Streamtown. Her governess was absolutely thrilled about her. When Valerie was in her free 72 hours, she took Victoria to kindergarten and she went for her. In the days, she was at work, her brother-in-law did this. Valerie and Victoria would walk there and back and this way they had time to talk a lot about everything. Once, the governess stopped Valerie just when she was leaving with Victoria.

"*Hello, wait a little bit Madame Valerie, I want to talk you.*" said the governess.

"*Oh, hello! You want to talk with me? Yes, of course, please. I'm listening.*"

"*You know you have an amazing little girl there. You did a great job raising her.*"

Valerie looked back instinctively and made two steps aside, as wanting to get away between two persons that were talking with each other. She unconsciously knew no good word, no praise could have been addressed to her. Alan's family managed very well in convincing her she was worthless. But the governess insisted.

"*Come on now, Madame Valerie, I'm talking to you. Don't act like I'm talking with somebody else.*"

Indeed surprised Valerie stopped and looked at the governess.

"*Now, don't tell me you don't know what daughter you have there. She is smart, ambitious, extremely dependable for her age.*" continued the governess.

"Well, yeas, I know what daughter I have, it's just that..." Valerie never finished her sentence. What was she going to say? That she never got credit for her achievements? That all the people surrounding her, except for her daughter, thought very little of her and she started to think very little of herself too?

"Thank you Madame governess. I admit, I try my best with Victoria. What you tell me now makes me believe I'm on the right track with her."

"Yes, you are on the right track with her. Keep it up like this. By the way, did you ever think where will you take her to school? It's not so far off, you know."

"I know. I have been thinking about it. Which do you say would be the best school for her?" asked Valerie.

"Now, truly, the school closest to the house you live is not the best choice, for Victoria I mean."

"It's not a problem. Just tell me which would be the best school for her."

"I know a different school, it's right on the end of the street you live on, it's just that it's a very long street. There I know a schoolmistress that selects very rigorously her pupils. If you want to, I can talk with her and you can register Victoria right away. Usually, before the start of school, she has no more free places in her class. So it's better to register right now. What do you say?"

"Yes, yes, please talk with her. As soon as she says yes, I will go and register Victoria in her class. Thank you, Madame governess"

"Oh, you're welcome. I'll speak with her and let you know."

"Alright, we'll keep in touch."

No matter how trapped and hopeless she felt in her marriage, Valerie did not want to give up on her daughter. She knew she could not afford a break-down or a depression while her daughter was growing up and needed her. Especially because Victoria did not have a father either and she wasn't close to her grandparents either. The closest Victoria felt to, after her mom of course, was Eva. But Eva was far away and they went only once every few months to Mineville.

Valerie was obsessed thinking what she should do with her marriage. The conclusion she reached was that she had to get away as soon as possible, but materially speaking she was not yet in the position to become independent. Furthermore, Victoria was still too young to be left alone for 24 hours when she was at work, so she had to endure a little more. Save money, be prepared, and endure a little more. The opportunity was going to appear, she just had to be prepared psychologically and had to save as much money as possible and until then she had to give the best education possible to her daughter, as these growing up years of her daughter were not going to come back later. This was the time to raise her daughter right.

One of the best ways Valerie found to educate her daughter was to take long trips with her, only the two of them. Not expensive ones, just in the frame of their budget.

First, there were little trips, like going out on a field nearby and gather herbs or mushrooms. Valerie put some sandwiches, boiled eggs, a couple of apples and some lemon tea and a blanket and off they went. Victoria also carried something in a little backpack, a little toy, a book to read, maybe a camera to take some pictures. They went for a couple of kilometers by foot and spoke about all kind of things. Valerie confided in her daughter like in a best friend. She did not have a best friend, Victoria was her best friend. This caused Victoria to grow up mentally much more than other kids of her age, but Valerie never considered this a bad thing. She always thought Victoria was an old and wise soul, despite her young age.

Then, there were a little longer trips. At these ones they went a little farther, with raw meat in their bag and Valerie was starting up a fire and she fried the meat right out there, in a forest or by the river. People were giving them the black look. Valerie tried to understand what was bothering them? They never left any trash behind, always put out the fire when they left, they did not listen to loud music, never made a lot of noise. They were used from Alan's family's house not to make much noise so they don't bother anyone. What bothered those people? The fact that a woman and a girl, with no man with them were able to go out and have a good time, start up a fire on they own and then leave quietly without causing any problem?

The longest trips they took together was going to the seaside. Valerie found private houses for lodging, were they had access also to a kitchen and she could cook some food for her daughter. This variant was cheaper than going to a normal hotel where they could eat. Valerie packed the baggage very carefully, it could not be enormous but in the same time she had to make sure everything was packed in. They went to the seaside by train. To get to the railway station, there was no one to take them with the car, even though Alan's family had several cars at their disposal. Valerie called for a cab and they got on the train. Usually, they had to change several trains, as there was no direct train from Streamtown to the seaside. For Valerie, these trips were extremely tiresome. Not so much because of the work and carrying of the bags involved, but especially because she was stressed out of worrying too much. What if something bad happened with them? What if the persons with whom she talked will not have the room available like they promised? What if somebody stole their money and they would not have money to return home? Usual mother's worries. Then she calmed herself down «*Everything is going to be just fine. We'll be fine. God is protecting us, He will look out for us. He always protected us, why would He let us down now?* » For Victoria however, these all were great ventures which remained in her memory associated with joy and love for her mom. The way they were walking on the empty streets of the town, at 3 or 4 o'clock in the morning to get to an early train or bus. How they were laughing and going on the middle of the road, knowing no car will pass. The way they ate out on picnic or right on the train, the way Valerie unfolded the table napkin and put it down between them, how she prepared everything, the boiled eggs, the tomatoes, the peppers, the sandwiches and how they ate together. Then the lemon tea her mom prepared home, from herbs they gathered together, prepared with honey and freshly squeezed lemon juice.

These trips proved Victoria her mother could do absolutely anything she put her mind to and she was very capable to succeed in any venture on her own, without the help of a man. Yes, maybe sometimes they needed some help, but she always kept her composure and reason and knew how to ask for help. Even though Valerie felt guilty because Victoria grew up without a father, Victoria remained with nice memories about her childhood and never complained for missing her father.

Victoria still has not started school when Valerie got a strange invitation from her husband. Alan invited Valerie for a couple of days to Steville, without Victoria. He said he wanted to spend two days with her, just the two of them. Honestly Valerie was very suspicious as this had never happened before. What was he up to? Valerie accepted, mostly out of curiosity. So, she went to Steville on a Friday afternoon and planned to stay until Sunday.

She arrived in Steville and of course Alan could not wait for her, he was at work. Valerie went to where he lived. As soon as Alan got employed at the company where he was working, he got a room in a hostel that belonged to the company. It was a building on four levels, with twenty rooms on a level and in every room lived a family of an employee. There were common bathrooms on every floor with showers and toilets and no common kitchen, so everybody was cooking in the room. These types of hostels remained since the communist age. Whenever the dictator built a factory, he built also places for the people to live in. The regime that came after him, so called democratic regime, left the people for a while to continue to live in these hostels, then they were taken over by the smart guys of the day and the people was thrown out on the street. Sorry, they were released to find themselves better living conditions, by renting an apartment. Problem is that with a normal salary in Steville you could never find anything decent to rent, it has always been a very crowded and expensive and hostile city.

As soon as she arrived in Alan's room, Valerie started to clean up the place. She watered and cleaned the plants she had brought him. Then, when it was all done, she went out to the store nearby and bought some meat to cook for dinner. She went to the market and bought some fresh vegetables for a salad. She saw also a guy selling cassettes with music. Valerie was tempted to buy a cassette with Guns'N'Roses. She stopped and thought: «*No, I shouldn't buy it. I have to save my money.*» She made a few steps away from the music stand, but stopped and thought: «Oh, just this once. I love this album. I'll buy it. Just this once I'll indulge myself."

For cooking, Alan had, as everybody, a sink in the room and an electric plate. This electric plate was used also for heating, so everybody used a pretty powerful one. The problem was that its power could not be reduced and as a result, the food was always burnt on it. Valerie did the best she could in the given conditions. She cooked the meat with water so it did not burn. She made some mashed potatoes and a salad. She thought it would be nice to make also some desert, so she bought a sachet a pudding powder and she made some pudding. She bought also some apples, as Alan liked them and she sat down for a minute, waiting for her husband to come home from work.

Late in the afternoon he arrived home. They ate and he actually told her:

"*The dinner was very good. You've outdone yourself.*"

"*Well, I'm happy you enjoyed it.*" answered Valerie thinking «*Wow, it's very hard what he wants to tell me, otherwise he never praises me for anything*» She continued:

"*How about the music? Like it? I just love Guns'N'Roses. 'Don't cry' is my absolute favorite. Isn't this song great? I just wanted this to be a special evening, just for the two of us.*"

"*Yes, great. Look Valerie, the reason why I called you to Steville...*"

"*Is because you missed me and you wanted to spend some quality time with me, right*?" asked Valerie smiling, still trying to believe nothing bad will happen.

"*Yes, that too.*" continued Alan.

"*Ohhhh, I knew it.*"

"*And also because I wanted to tell you something.*"

"*So, what is it. I'm listening.*" said Valerie.

"*I have a child with another woman.*" said Alan.

"*What?*" asked Valerie, not understanding, even though she heard the words.

"*I have a child with another woman.*" repeated Alan imperturbably.

Valerie remained mute. She could not articulate one word. She always became mute and paralyzed after a shock. All the years of abuse in her life, every time she was suffering she was not allowed to express her feelings, because she was a drama queen. As a child she was not allowed to cry because: "*Your father has just fallen asleep. Don't wake him up.*" As a grown up "*Why do you have to make such a scene for anything? Can't you control yourself?*" Now, her mind received this information like a blow in her head with a sledge hammer and totally paralyzed her entire being.

"*I just wanted you to know to learn it from me.*" said Alan and looked at her.

Valerie was looking back at him helplessly and trying to process somehow what he had to say.

"*You know, you always told me that if something happens, we have to tell each other. You told me you don't want to learn from others if something happens.*"

Valerie's gaze turned from expressing the shock to expressing the pain.

"*You see how much I love you? How I listen to you?*" continued Alan.

In this phase, Valerie gaze turned into disapproval and rejection. Just like she used to look at her father as a child, back home, when he was walking drunk through the house. Her father was always annoyed by this look of hers. Alan also was annoyed. Men do not stand women from their pack to disapprove them. No matter how much they hurt them, the women are not allowed to look at them without the smile on their face. No matter what, women must smile back at them and submit. Even though men are the predators and they hurt the women, only they have the right to get mad, women don't have this right, no matter how much they suffered. Eva, Valerie's mother always used to tell Camil: "*Please* ***forgive me*** *because* ***you hurt me***." This was very, very true. Maybe this was a reminiscence from the Dark Ages, when the men were the masters of the family, only they provided for the family and only them were allowed to get mad or angry, the women always had to be sweet and smiley and submissive.

Valerie still could not say anything. She tried to move her arms, but she couldn't. Alan laid her down on the bed and had a sexual intercourse with her. Valerie wanted to fight back, but she could not say one word or do one gesture. This intercourse was in her mind a rape. Maybe legally it was not a rape, because it was not a constraint and penetration, but it was lack of approval or lack of strength to fight back and penetration. Isn't that still rape? She could not fight back because she was raised to submit to the abuser. Whenever her father abused her, if she looked at him otherwise than submissive, if she ever tried to fight back or cry, she was abused even more. This happened even in her nightmares: she was dreaming that she was stalked or hurt by an evil man and she could not move or scream for help. An intelligent man knows sex is much better when a woman cooperates. Only a stupid man can rape a woman. Valerie always thought Alan was an intelligent man, but slowly she started to understand he was not intelligent at all.

After it was all over, Alan went to sleep. Valerie could not sleep. She went to the bathroom and threw up, then she took a shower. She came back in the room and tried to sleep. She could not. She could not even cry, still could not process the event. Then again she went to throw up and again she took a shower. The only thought in her mind was to get away from there. She decided she will turn to Streamtown, next morning, even if it was only Saturday morning. She has told back home that she will return on Sunday, but there will be no problem. Victoria will be happy she came home sooner. And her in-laws did not care if she was home or not. Of course they were annoyed by her presence, but they could not care less, they did not ask for explanations.

Valerie came back to Streamtown on Saturday morning. Victoria ran to her and jumped into her arms:

"Mammy, mammy, I'm so happy you came home earlier. I dreamt you would come home today. Then I woke up and I told grandma what I dreamt, but she told me I have to sleep one more time until you come home. And look, you're home, mammy!"

Valerie was holding her daughter in her arms and they were both crying. Once again, Valerie felt safe holding her daughter. She just enjoyed the moment, the embrace of her daughter was like a balm to her aching soul.

Valerie never told one word to anyone about what has happened. As the days went by, she started to analyze what she found out and the pieces of the puzzle were falling into place. She understood why Alan drifted away from her while she was pregnant. He probably started his relationship with the other woman in that period. This is why he wanted to divorce. This is why he came home so rarely. This is why he refused to come to Streamtown and why he did not want Valerie to go to Steville.

But then why did he bring her to Streamtown, to live in his parents' house? It's true, Valerie always wanted to get away from Camil, but he should have left her there if he was involved with another woman. And who is she? What's her name? When is the child born? What's the child's name?

Valerie was preparing the questions she will ask Alan when he came home again. Of course, he will answer monosyllabically as always and will avoid the discussion. But he's not going to get away with it this time.

The first time Alan came home, Valerie asked for details:

"So, who is she?"

"It's not relevant. You don't know her."

"How could you cheat on me like this? And how could you get pregnant another woman while you are still married to me?"

"I did not do it purpose. I just had an affair with her."

"You wanted to divorce when I got pregnant with Victoria, but you were too weak and coward to go through with it. So now you are going to leave me for her?"

"No, no, it's you I love. I have never loved her, I just slept with her and she got pregnant."

"She got pregnant? Just like that? By accident, right?"

"Yes, she got pregnant by accident and she does not want to get an abortion. Just like you."

"Please don't compare me with her. Don't compare me with her, or I swear to God I'll crack your head open, don't you dare compare me with her."

"So what do you want me to do? You want me to kill myself? I made a mistake, I cannot undo it. What do you want me to do?"

"There's nothing you can do now. But you could not have cheated on me in the first place and then none of this would have happened."

"Nothing bad happened. Why do you have to make such a big drama over this? So she has my child. So what?"

"So what? You really are that stupid, aren't you? And when I think I accepted to marry you and to have a child with you because I thought you are smart. But you are stupid, you are just a stupid idiot. SHE DID IT ON PURPOSE YOU STUPID IDIOT! She did it because she knew this way she can take you away from your family, from your child. Don't you understand it?"

"No, she didn't. She just wanted to have a child. She was never married and she did not want to grow old and remain alone. All she wanted was a child."

"So why didn't she have a child with an unmarried man? Why did she want a child with you? Aaah, right, sorry, because you're some kind of a genius and she wanted to have a genius child, right?"

"You don't have to be ironic."

"I'll be any way I want to be. You will not tell me how to be."

"Whatever."

Valerie did not take it this way at the moment, but this final blow was the best thing that could happen to her. She wasted all her youth hoping Alan will come back to her. She was blocked in this relationship. Alan was holding her back, like a big grindstone tied to her leg. She could not advance one step. She lost all her self confidence. She became convinced she is worthless and ugly. Valerie decided she will leave Alan. After all, what was she about to lose? She never had a husband. Her child never had a father. They never had a home. She had nothing out of this marriage.

She only had her daughter, who was a gift from God. She will take her daughter and they will leave Alan and that house. When and how was a totally different story. But the first step was done: Valerie and Victoria decided to get out of there.

In that particular moment of her life, Valerie was still working at a state company from Streamtown. Her salary was little over the minimum wage and she has managed to save some money, but not so much. With her salary no bank gave her a loan to buy an apartment and she did not have enough money to pay the advance payment of the loan. She lent money to her brother, never got it back. She lent money to her mother in law, never got it back. She paid for the repair of Alan's car, never got back the money. She needed more money, much more money. For this she needed to cut even more on her expenses which were only for Victoria anyway and she needed a better paying job. She needed to save more. She also needed a second job. The best thing she could do was related to the knowledge of English. She thought she could teach English hours and she could become a translator.

Her working hours were 24 hours of work and then 72 hours off. This had its advantages, but considering that Victoria was still pre-school, this was not an advantage. If they moved out of there, she had to hire a baby-sitter for Victoria, but she could not afford one from her salary. Again, she understood she needed another job, with 8 hours working hours in the morning, then in the afternoon and at night she could stay with Victoria. Until then however she had to remain in her in-laws house.

As for her personal life, Victoria reached the conclusion that she totally lost her confidence in her husband. What good was it to go on? It was obvious he did not want to spend time with her. He had absolutely no interest in his daughter. Since Valerie got pregnant, they drifted away, little by little. Valerie felt sorry for Victoria, for the way she grew up without a father. But even if she remained married with Alan, Victoria still would not have a father. What was the object of her marriage then? Why remain married to him? Just because he was to coward to divorce himself? He threatened her all the nine months of pregnancy that he wanted a divorce and he did not go through with it. Now Valerie decided she will leave him. If he did not have the guts to do it, she will do this. Valerie knew however she could not go through with the divorce while she was still living in his parents' house. She was sure his parents will oppose this, even though the marriage was not working anymore. So first she had to move out and then she was going to divorce.

Thinking everything over, Valerie decided that first of all she had to find a new job and then she had to work something as second job. For this she started immediately to ask around if anybody needed an English teacher for private lessons. She started to ask around how to become an authorized translator.

Victoria was getting close to the start of school. Following the advice from her governess, Valerie registered Victoria months in advance to school. She bought Victoria well in advance a desk, a modern chair and a little bookstand. She found a little corner in the room where they were living and organized this way a little space for her daughter. She also bought Victoria her first computer. It was an old desktop, with a huge old monitor, but enough for Victoria to learn how to use the computer.

On the first day of school, Valerie was a little nervous. She was afraid Victoria will cry when she leaves her there. And so it was. As soon as the ceremony was over and Valerie wanted to leave, Victoria looked desperately to her mom and started to cry. Valerie consoled her daughter:

"*My dearest, don't cry. Mom will go to work and you remain here in school. Here you will learn a lot of exciting, new things. Don't cry my love.*"

Then she turned to the schoolmistress and told her:

"*I'm terribly sorry Madame.*"

"*Don't worry, I know how it is. I have a boy that starts today school, only in a different class and he cries too. So, I know exactly how you feel.*"

Valerie felt a lot better after this. She kissed her daughter and left peacefully.

Valerie started to ask around how she could become an authorized translator. Nobody knew. So she went to a public notary.

"*Hello.*"

"*Hello. How can we help you?*"

"*My name is Valerie. I wonder if you could spare a few minutes for me? I would like to ask you something if that is possible.*"

"*Of course. Please ask.*"

"*I would like to become an authorized translator. Do you know what do I have to do for this?*"

"Well, we don't know exactly how you can get it, but we know that you need to have an authorization for that, issued by the Ministry of Justice."

"But how do I get the authorization?"

"You should call the Ministry, surely they will explain it to you. Most likely you will have to sustain a language knowledge test."

"Alright, I can get that. I will obtain it and come back right to you. Thank you."

Valerie did not graduate from a philology faculty, she graduated from a technical university. The good marks she had in English were not enough. What could she do?

She searched the phone number of the Philology Faculty from the University of Steville and she called them. She asked if they have some official testing of language knowledge. They told them they had such tests. They were called "Tests for English knowledge for non-philological graduates". She had to go to Steville to register personally to the testing.

Valerie never went to Steville without speaking with Alan first. She did not want to find him in some awkward situation. So she called Alan and asked:

"Alan, I have to come to Steville. Is it a problem for you?"

"Hmmm. No problem. You can come. What business do you have here?"

"I have to go to the university for something. I'll explain you when I'm there."

"When are you going to come?"

"I'll come on Thursday evening. On Friday I go to the University and on Friday afternoon I will return to Streamtown. If that's OK with you."

"Yeah, OK, whatever." mumbled Alan.

With this 'welcoming' attitude of Alan, Valerie was not very keen to go to visit him, but she had to go to Stevilleto solve her problem.

On Thursday evening she went to Steville as promised. Alan came home late from work as usual. She cooked something for him and went right to sleep. He played on the computer until late at night, Valerie pretended she was asleep. Next day early in the morning Alan went to work. Valerie woke up right after he left. She drank her coffee alone, looking out on the window in the cold morning. The smell and the noises of Steville were bringing back all her bad memories. The nights when she was waiting him to come home. The night when he told him he had a child with another woman. Valerie thought «*He never gave me details about this other child. Who's his mother? When is the boy born? Does he wear his surname?*» Every time she thought about this, she got more and more angry. If she thought about it in the evening, she could sleep all night. If she thought about it in the morning, her whole day was ruined. She knew the more details she found out, the unhappier she will be, but the curiosity was too big. There were no places where he kept documents, so she started to search in his wardrobe. She turned around every piece of clothing and finally she found what she was looking for. There they were: a copy of the child's birth certificate and some pictures with him and his son. The birth certificate was quite interesting. The child had Alan's surname and his name was Samuel. This meant he legally recognized his son. The boy's mother was somebody Valerie knew. She was working with Alan. Valerie heard him speaking about her. Isabella this, Isabella that. Aa, she was his boss! He spoke several times about her, she was his boss! Alan was having an affair and a child from his boss from work! Valerie's mind was chasing back in time. All those things that happened. All the things he said. And when was the child born? Valerie searched the birth day on the certificate. The boy was born nine months after Victoria. Was this correct? Valerie's heart started to race. «*Calm down, just calm down*» she thought.

«*So, when is the boy born? Think, damn it, think! Now count back nine months.... Yes, the boy is born nine months after Victoria. What kind of an animal is he? How could he cheat on me on very days I was giving birth to his daughter?*»

Valerie was looking at the birth certificate, recalculating over and over the child's birth.

«*It's correct, it's true. The boy is born nine months after my daughter. But why? How could he do this? Did I drive him away from me? Maybe I wasn't a good wife... But I behave nicely with him during my pregnancy. I never rejected him. It was him, he was the one who rejected me. He rejected me right after I told him I was pregnant. I understand now. He was already having the affair with her when I got pregnant. And he took me to Mineville to give birth he said, but he just took me out of his way. He wanted to be with Isabella, me and my child were standing in his way. And he still has the nerve to say he loves me... Well, if he loves me and did this to me, imagine what he would have done if he did not love me! He would have probably beat me up or kill me! Actually, I am quite fortunate!*» finished Valerie her thought with a bitter smile on her face.

She gathered the few things she had with her and left. She went to the Philology University and registered to the language exam. She wrote down carefully the date and hour when it was scheduled. Then she went to the station and took the bus back to Streamtown.

Not long after she started looking, she found two children who wanted to take private English lessons from her. She prepared carefully the lessons and she did her best to teach the children how to be able to use English in a specific situation, not only doing theoretical grammar exercises. Valerie had no training as teacher, but she tried to respond to the need of the children taking the hours. What did they want? They wanted to be able to use English in a conversation or in a written communication. So this is what she taught them.

On the scheduled date, Valerie had the English examination in Steville. This time she didn't actually go to meet Alan. She started to have a very hard time to get close to him physically. She felt a deep physical repulsion in his presence. If he did not get within 2 meters of her, she was OK, but as soon as he got closer than this she was feeling very uncomfortable. Especially if he got close to her from her back and she could not see him. She felt his presence like she wolf felt a danger comes from her back and the muscles of her back contracted involuntarily forcing her to turn around and face the attack.

Valerie passed the exam very well and got a diploma that said she knew English very well. After she got this diploma, she phoned to the Ministry of Justice to ask how could she get the translator authorization. She waited several minutes on the line. They passed her from one office to the other. None of the persons she spoke with was responsible for authorized translators and could not give her more details. Finally, she was passed back to the secretary she first spoke with and she told her she should ask locally, at the notary what she has to do. Valerie replied:

"*But I spoke with the notary and he told me to ask you!*"

"*Well, I'm just the secretary. Have a nice day!*"

And she hung up the phone.

Valerie did not know what to do. How could she find out? «*So, the notary does not know how I can get the authorization. He tells me to call the ministry. I call the ministry, they tell me to ask locally. OK. Who else is part of the ministry of justice locally? The courthouse! I will ask at the courthouse! And not even in Streamtown. I hate this little town. Everybody knows me and they want to know all about me. Not to help me in any way, but only to gossip. I'll go to the courthouse of Julestown! Yeah, there nobody knows me!*»

The very next day, Valerie took the local bus and went to Julestown. She got to the courthouse and looked around in the building. Where should she go? There were a lot of busy people, everybody in a hurry. What if she asked the secretary? She went to the door on which "SECRETARY" was written and knocked on the door. «*What is the worst that can happen? She'll tell me she doesn't know and go to hell.*» Valerie thought.

Nobody answered, so Valerie opened fearfully the door. For most persons to approach a state entity was extremely intimidating. The state employees were terribly arrogant and spoke ugly to the people. You could not complain anywhere about it and if you spoke back to them in the same way, you never got your problem solved. The only way you could get good will and help from these state employees was to bribe them or maybe know somebody who knew them. Valerie did not have any money to bribe and she knew nobody. The only thing she could do was speak nicely.

"*Hello Madam, I was wondering if you could help me.*"

"*Hello, please, do tell.*"

"*I was wondering is there anybody who could give more details about authorized translators?*"

"*What do you want to know?*"

"*I was asking around about the procedure of becoming an authorized translator. I asked at the notary, he told me to ask at the ministry. Then I called the ministry on the phone, they said I should ask locally. I don't know where to ask anymore.*"

"*Actually, you might have luck this time.*" said the secretary. "*I have a very good friend who is an authorized translator. Let me just call her and I will tell you.*"

Valerie waited patiently. When the secretary finished speaking, she explained Valerie:

"*This is what you should do. You have to go to the Public Library, here in Julestown. There you have to ask for the procedure for getting the translation authorization. They receive in February or March every year the procedure for the current year. In that procedure you will find all the information you need."*

"*Thank you Madam, thank you very much! You were very kind!*"

"*You're welcome!*"

Valerie was indeed very grateful She has searched for weeks to find this information and now this lady out of nowhere gave it to her. Valerie went to the nearest florist, bought a nice bunch of flowers and at a little store nearby bought a chocolate and returned to the lady that helped her.

"*Here you go Madam. Please accept this from me. You cannot imagine how much I needed this information. Thank you very much once again!*" said Valerie.

"*Ohh, thank you! You didn't have to go through all this trouble. It just happened that this friend of mine is an authorized translator, so that I could help you. That is all.*"

"*Yes, but it was really nice of you to help me. Thank you once again!*"

Valerie went straight to the Public Library of Julestown. She asked for the procedure and got it right away. She copied in her notebook everything she needed to know: dates, documents needed, registration period, phone numbers. Valerie went then home knowing all she had to know about it.

The exams were organized only two times a year, in the capital. The registrations were done months in advance. She could go and register personally or she could send the needed documents by registered post. She chose the second modality and asked for the receipt confirmation. Then she called and asked again if the documents were alright and they confirmed her everything was OK. Valerie was a little bit nervous of going to the capital all by herself. Victoria was too small to accompany her and there was nobody else who could go with her. She bought her two way train tickets in due time and prepared a minimum baggage. On the scheduled date, she was on her way to the capital. A little bit nervous, a little bit scared of the unknown city she was going to see. She was well prepared, she asked about the buses she had to take, the address where she had to go and she took money with her.

The exam was pretty expensive and if you failed, you did not get your money back. Also, you could have on you a dictionary, but no other means to help you. Valerie thought this was a good investment. She paid the fee and bought herself the best dictionaries she could find in the capital in that moment. She attended two exams: one for translator from her mother tongue to English and the other from English to her mother tongue. Fortunately, her exams were scheduled one after the other, so she had to stay in the capital only one day. The exams were very difficult. She got one page of legal text that she had to translate only by using the dictionary in one hour. There were many persons attending the exams and they all had a hard time translating those difficult texts. Valerie looked around her a few times, but she could not lose much time looking to other, as she wanted to finish her translation in the hour she had at her disposal.

After the exam, she went straight to the railway station. She bought some little gift for Victoria, but nothing else. She never spent any money foolishly. She never bought herself a soda, or an ice cream or anything. She has brought herself some sandwiches from home and a bottle of water, so she settled with those. She was aware that every little penny she saved, brought her closer to her freedom. If she could save the money necessary for the advance payment and if she could find a better paying job, she could get a loan and buy herself an apartment of her own. The trip back home with the train seemed much shorter. A heavy weight was lifted off her shoulders, she felt relieved. She was looking forward to hold her daughter in her arms. She arrived in Streamtown early in the morning, tired and dirty and hungry. Nobody was waiting for her in the railway station. She went home by foot and took a shower and laid down by her daughter, who was still sleeping. Her daughter turned around and felt her and jumped up happy:

"Mammy, mammy, you're home!"

"Yes my love, I'm home!"

"Oh, mammy, I missed you so much. Don't you ever go away again."

"I will not go away again, my love, but this time I had to go. I had to go to the capital for the exam, you know that. I told you all about it. If I get this authorization, I will be able to make some money and maybe we shall be able to buy a place of our own. I went away only for this my love. You know I wouldn't leave you for the world."

"OK, mammy, but when shall we buy a place of our own?"

"I hope soon, my love. We don't have enough money yet, but I promise you, I'll do everything in my power to buy it soon. I'll work more, I'll work harder and finally we shall be able to buy it. I love you, my dear."

"I love you too, mammy."

"I'm sorry your father does not stay with us and I'm sorry we don't have a home like every other family. You should have a father and a mother like every child."

"Don't worry mammy, I don't need a father, I only need you. And I would like it very much if we could have a place of our own. But mammy, when we shall have our place, shall I have my own room?"

"Yes, my dear, you'll have your own room."

On the date scheduled, Valerie called the ministry where she had the exams to ask about the mark she got.

"Hello, I called to ask about the results of the language exam."

"Name please."

Valerie gave her name and waited a few seconds.

"You passed the exams, both of them"

"I did? Wow, that's great. So, what do I have to do next?"

"We shall send you the diploma by post. You have to go with the diploma and a few more documents to the Ministry of Justice and they will issue the authorization."

"Great, thank you! Thank you so much! I'll wait for the diploma by post then. Bye bye!"

"Bye."

Valerie was quite happy. This was another little victory that made her feel good about herself, despite of all the mess in her life.

CHAPTER 7

In a couple of months and after another trip to the capital, Valerie managed to obtain her translator authorization. She started to find some customers for translations. Even though there were also other translators in Streamtown, she still got some extra money from this, besides the money she got from the private lessons she taught. As a minimal investment for her translator activity, she bought a printer and the stationary she needed.

Victoria has always been a very wise little girl. Valerie always felt Victoria was "an old and wise soul". Valerie invested in her daughter what was the very best of her: all her love, all her spare time, she bought Victoria all she considered was absolutely necessary for her development. Valerie helped her with her homework. She involved her daughter in everything she did around the house. Even if many times she felt she did not have the patience and the energy to explain over and over again to her daughter how she had to clean for example, or to wash the laundry, or to cook, Valerie forced herself to involve Victoria. How else could little Victoria learn to do anything? If Victoria did something by herself, Valerie praised her. Even if it wasn't always a perfect result, she praised her daughter and encouraged her to continue doing it.

"Mammy, I'm sorry, my pudding did not turn out so well. Are you mad at me?"

"No, my love. Why should I get mad with you? Because you made the pudding for me, so that I did not have to work so much?"

"Mammy, but it has a funny taste. It's burnt."

"It's burnt because the fire was too strong. You know, the pudding is made with milk and milk has this property: it does not like strong direct fire."

"So the milk has given that burnt taste?"

"Yes, my love. This is why we have that special milk cooker. So that the

milk does not burn. But don't worry, my love, next time it will turn out just fine. Learning is about perseverance my love."

"What is perseverance mammy?"

"To persevere means not to give up if something does not turn out perfect when you first try. You have to look back and understand what you did wrong. Then you have to do it again. Second time you do it, it will be better. If again it does not turn out perfect, no sweat. Try it over and over again. Eventually, you'll obtain the result you want. This means perseverance."

Valerie felt there were only the two of them in the whole wide world. She confided in Victoria and totally trusted her. Victoria was the strongest ally Valerie ever had. Valerie wanted her daughter to become a strong independent woman. And the greatest power she could ever have was faith in God. Valerie grew up with contradictory signals. Her mother told her to believe in God. Her brother told her there was no God. She found God all by herself after the train accident that almost cost her life. But she did not want her daughter to grow up like this. She wanted her daughter growing up with the belief that the only thing she can be sure of was that God loves her and that He is the only one who will never leave her.

"My love, the only one who will never leave you is the good Lord above. You know you never had a father. For this, when I was pregnant with you I have asked Jesus to be your father. I asked Him to take care of you. And He did. All along. He watched over us. And he is the strongest father anybody can ever have! My dearest, mammy can die any day."

"I don't want you to die, mammy!"

"I am not going to die, my love, don't take it like that. You know I take care of myself and don't risk anything, but it's just possible. You know, it can happen. Even if this would happen, Jesus will remain with you and will continue to take care of you. You can lose everything in life: you can lose all your money, or your home, or your job. Your husband can leave you for another woman. Your parents will eventually die. But Jesus will always love you and He will never leave you."

"OK mammy, but don't die."

"I will not die, my love."

On Sunday morning, when the church bell was tolling, Valerie always told Victoria:

"Listen, God is calling us to go to His house."

"Which is God's house, mammy?"

"God is everywhere my love, but His house is the church. And when you hear the bell toll, you have to know God is calling us to His house. And you know how in some houses you feel that you are not welcome, even though they don't say it straight to your face?"

"Yes, mammy, like we are not welcome here, at grandpa's?"

"Exactly, my love. But you are always welcome in the house of God. Always. He is always happy when you go there."

"Let's go to the church mammy."

"We'll go my dear. We'll dress up with our best cloths and we shall go. We shall pray and He will help us get out of here. He will always take care of us."

Alan was a total stranger to her daughter. Once a month when he came to see them, he could hardly communicate with Victoria. They needed Valerie between them to be able to communicate. Once he had the idea of taking Victoria with him to Steville for one week, without Valerie. Valerie did not agree. Her entire being told her to be against this idea. She could not trust Alan, she could not trust his judgement. He did not fight this decision too much. The little time they were together, Alan received phone calls from his mistress. Valerie's heart was breaking when she saw him answering. She thought: «*What kind of a woman calls a man up, intentionally, a married man, when she knows he is with his family? What kind of a woman is that?*» She looked at Alan how he talked with her right in her presence.

With one occasion, Valerie asked him:

"Look, it's obvious you cannot live one without the other. Why don't you divorce me, so that you can be with her and your child?"

"I don't want to divorce. It's you that I love." These words, this cynicism hurt Valerie more than any bad word and worst of all, made her lose her faith in love.

"I think you don't divorce because you are weak and coward. You want to get rid of me, but you don't have the balls to go through with a divorce. Remember how you treated me when I was pregnant? Remember how you tried to break me down? Do you understand that you were so weak that you could not defeat a pregnant, defenseless woman?"

No answer from Alan.

Valerie thought for herself: «*Actually, I could not imagine a better punishment for him than to be with that woman and I could not imagine a better punishment for that woman than to be with him.»*

Victoria saw and felt what her mother went through. She was soul and body on her mother's side. Only the two of them, against the whole world. Also, she was her mother's biggest fan. She was the only one who had faith in Valerie. Valerie did not dress nicely. Even if now she could afford some better cloths, she was saving money for their freedom. She never went to a beauty parlor. She had bad teeth and all this gave her a bad image. Alan's family considered she was also stupid, and this just because she was different from them. Valerie didn't mind this. She never needed their approval, all she needed was her daughter's approval and admiration. On the other hand, she liked it if Alan's family, the enemy as she called them, underestimated her. She knew this was a big advantage for her. It was better if they never saw her coming. The more unexpected her breakthrough, the bigger impact it will have over them.

Victoria was a good pupil in school. Valerie helped her as much as she could, but Victoria was a very serious and ambitious girl, she needed no extra push to learn. Her main motivation was that she did not want to disappoint her mom and Valerie knew this motivation was not good, as this was too much pressure on her child, but she never could change this.

"My love, you know I love you. You're my treasure. I trust you. There's nothing you can do to disappoint me."

"I know mom, but when I see how much you work so that I can have all that I need, I must learn. I want you to be proud of me."

"I am proud of you my love. You're a great child. You're a golden child. You cannot disappoint me. But you must understand you don't have to learn to please me. You have to learn for yourself. So that you can become a better person. So that you can have a better life. If you don't learn, you get a worse job with less money. If you learn and work seriously, you will get a good job, where people respect you. This is why you have to learn, not for me."

"What about those wise guys who never learned in their life and have a lot of money?"

"Don't worry about them my love. Life has a funny way of putting all things and all men into their place. Don't worry about their money, they'll lose it. Eventually, they will fall. And the ones that are serious and hard working and perseverant will rise eventually. You'll see."

Valerie was searching for a better job. Back then, there were not so many possibilities to have very good job, unless you got one at the multinational company Alan was for interview. She sent them several times applications, but they never called her back. She was determined however to continue trying. She was determined to wait for her chance. She believed everybody gets a chance, the most important thing is to be alert and prepared, so that when your chance appears, you grab it with both hands.

In anticipation for her future interview, Valerie bought herself a nice suit and some good looking shoes. She also found a dentist and went several months for treatment. Her parents never took her to a dentist. She was two times for some checking, at the school dentist, but that was all. Her teeth got worse and worse in time. By the time she was in university, she suffered terribly of tooth ache. Regularly her face swelled up because of the dental abscesses. Giving her teeth a nice appearance gave her a lot of confidence.

Another thing that gave her confidence was getting a driver's license. She fought many time with Alan on this theme:

"How come the car is always with you? How come when the reparation has to be paid, it is our car, that is I have to pay, because you don't have the money? But when I have to go to work by foot, it's your car. How is this?"

"So what do you want me to do? Do you want me to leave the car here?"

"Yes, I want you to leave the car here. You know I go to work by foot when the bus does not go? Your father has a car, your sister has a car and I walk for miles and miles to get to work? After all the money I paid to repair that bloody car?"

"I would leave the car here, but you have no driving license. What are you going to do with it?"

"I don't know. I'll put it on fire or I'll toss it into the river. What does it matter?"

"Look, if you get the driving license, I'll leave you the car. It will stay here for one month and I will stay with me in Steville for one month. OK?"

"What, you think I still believe your lies? First you said we have to buy a car because this way you'll come home more often. Before the car, you came once per month. After the car, you come home once a month. Now you are trying to fool me with this? You really think I'm stupid, don't you?"

"No, I don't think you're stupid."

«*Yes you do*», thought Valerie, « *but this is only in my advantage*».

While still learning to drive, Alan's family were making comments like this:

"*She'll never get her driving license. She has no technical sense.*"

"*Or even if she will get it finally, she will pass the exam the tenth time.*"

And they were laughing and laughing.

Valerie learned very diligently for the driving exam. She was really afraid to drive a car. She kept having a dream where she was at the steering wheel of a car and she did not know how to drive it. She looked down at her feet and saw the three pedals and she did not know which one is the break. After a few driving hours though, she was not so terrified anymore. Plus she was extremely motivated to learn it, especially because they were so convinced.

Valerie succeeded to get her driving license at her first exam. After this, a new type of comments appeared:

"*I cannot believe she passed the exam. She is not capable of driving.*"

"*Wonder how she passed the exam. She probably 'arranged' it with somebody.*"

Alan let her drive for a few miles once and they got into a big fight. He was not pleased at all by her driving style.

"*What the hell are you doing?*"

"*I'm driving. What's your problem?*"

"*Slow down, slow down, don't take that curb so fast.*"

"*You take the curbs even faster. What's the matter with you?*"

"*When I take the curb, the wheels don't squeak. They squeak when you take the curb.*"

"*So what?*"

"*It's not OK. And why do you slow down now? We are starting to climb the hill and you reduce the acceleration? The car will not be able to go up the slope!*"

"*Will you shut up already?*"

"*No, I will not shut up. How on earth did they give the license? You have no idea about driving!*"

"*I slept with the instructor and the policeman too. That's why they gave me the license. Are you satisfied now?*"

"*You are a menace. You shouldn't be driving.*"

"*You know what, I won't drive anymore with you in the car.*"

"*What do you mean?*"

"*I mean I'll stop the car and get off right now.*"

"*Don't stop, are you crazy?*"

"*Yes I am. I'm getting off.*"

"*How will you get home?*"

"*I'll hitchhike. I don't care, I can't listen to you anymore.*"

Valerie actually did get off the car and went home hitchhiking. She never drove again with Alan in the car. Of course, he never left her the car, he always took it with him in Steville. Moreover, many times when he came home, he complained he did not have money for gas to go back to Steville. Valerie did not buy it. But with one occasion she was not home and Alan complained to his mother that he did not have money. So his mother went to the wardrobe where she knew Valerie kept her money, took money from there and gave it to Alan.

Alan didn't want to take it at first:

"*Come on Alan, I'll give you money from her. I know where she keeps her money.*"

"*No, mom, don't take her money. She'll be furious.*"

"*No, no, she won't mind. I take money from her all the time.*"

"*And she doesn't say anything?*"

"*No, never. Don't worry. Just take it and get some gas. I'll give it back to her.*"

Alan's mother was right. Valerie never said anything bad to her. Valerie respected Alan's parents. In the beginning, she tried to love them. She thought: «*If they brought to the world the man I love most in the world, there must be something good in them, even if I don't see it.*» After she moved in with them, it was harder and harder to love them, then to like them, then even to tolerate them. Finally, Valerie could hardly stand them, she could hardly stand their presence, she could not eat in their presence anymore. But she never fought with them, never criticized them. She considered that she was the one who has adapt to them as long as she was living in their house and not the other way around. She taught Victoria the same principle: as long as you are living in somebody else's house, you have to adapt to them. When you cannot stand them anymore, you move out. You cannot expect them to adapt to what you like.

Indeed, Valerie did not say anything to her mother in law when she told her she took her money. But the first time Alan called her on the phone, she shared her feelings with him:

"How could you do that to me? How could you?"

"I did not want to take money from you. I asked from mom and she did not have any."

"Your mother never has money. All I hear is that she doesn't even have money to buy bread. On the other hand, she has a good job, your father has a good job, they live in a big house, they have the land and the animals. She insults my intelligence if she thinks I believe this bullshit."

"So don't believe it. But believe me I did not want to take money from you. She said that she can take, because you won't mind."

"What kind of a man takes money from the woman that raises his child? It's not just that you don't contribute anything to the education of this child, you actually have the nerve to take money from me? How low can you sink?"

"I'll give you back the money, calm down."

"You'll never give me back the money, you know that. But how could you take it from me? Did I take anything of yours without asking you?"

"Whatever. I'll give you back the money, don't worry."

Valerie never kept her money in that house again. She saved anyway the most as she could and the money she needed for the daily expenses were only with her, in her purse.

Still searching a new, better paying job, Valerie knew that her looks did not help her a lot. Her clothes were always from second hand, her hair was just left to grow long, she never went to arrange it a little bit, but the thing that bothered her the most was the state of her teeth. Besides the tooth aches that tormented her for years, they did not look good either. Valerie was also terrified to go to the dentist. The mere thought that she had to go to a dentist made her heart pound. She knew though that she had to do it so she started to ask around for a good dentist. Finally, someone from her office indicated her a dentist and he called for a programming.

A few days later, Valerie started her visits to the dentist that lasted for months and cost her a lot of money. Her dentist was professionally speaking alright, but he wasn't a very friendly guy and hardly spoke a word. Valerie was terrified anyway, but given also his attitude, she felt like she was going to the torture chamber. The dentist had to extract several of her teeth. Then he tried to recover a couple of them and finally he filled her front teeth. The end result was much better then Valerie ever expected. After many years, Valerie was able to smile again, not fearing that her decayed teeth will show.

In this point of her life, Valerie was prepared to step up. She gained some self-confidence. She was able to save some money, even if it still was not enough for the advance payment for the apartment. Unlike when she was twenty years old, now she knew exactly what she wanted. First of all, she wanted the best for her daughter. Secondly, she wanted to break free. For both things she wanted, she needed more money. And the money started to come slowly.

Valerie had constantly customers for English private lessons and for translations. Eventually, she received an order for a translation from the multinational company Alan had turned down. She had been waiting for a long time for this chance. She left everything aside and made the translation impeccably in a couple of hours and called back the person who contacted her saying that the job is done. The person who gave her the order was very pleased and praised her, saying she will receive more work from them in the future.

After a few months of collaboration with this company, Valerie was contacted by them for private lessons of English for one foreign employee of them. She accepted gladly. They made a contract with her. Now she had two working contracts and she worked also besides these whenever she had the chance.

With Victoria, the expenses were higher and higher as she grew. Alan was not contributing at all. Valerie knew that if she divorced, at least he will pay the alimony. He was no husband to her, no father for Victoria, he was just a stranger who didn't pay anything. Well, she was determined to make him a stranger that will have to pay!

Valerie went to teach the private lessons for several months. One day, she finally got the call she was expecting: the company asked her if she would be interested in a position at the sales department. Valerie jumped up with joy. They called her to an interview.

"Hello, I am the general manager of the company."

"Hello, I am Valerie."

"I know who you are, I heard a lot about you. We all speak of you as the English teacher."

"*I know you do.*" replied Valerie smiling.

"*Soooo....*" and the general manager looked very attentively to her. Valerie just looked right back at him, straight into his eyes, with a friendly smile on her face. She was surprised that she was not nervous at all. "*I understand you are interested in the opening position we have at the sales department.*"

"*Yes, I am. I would love to work in your company.*"

"*I'm sure you would. So, tell me, do you have any experience in sales?*"

"*No, I don't have experience in sales, but I would really like to learn sales if you give me the chance.*"

"*Well, we have a girl now in sales and you will learn from her. We need another person because the sales volume will increase in the near future. For us it's important to hire somebody we know, somebody we trust. Do you understand that?*"

"*Yes, I do, Sir. I'm honored you gave me a chance and called me to this interview.*"

"*OK. I like you. And your students speak very highly of you. So, what is your current salary?*"

"*I currently have a salary of 3 million crowns.*"

"*OK, we'll give you the same salary for starters.*"

"*With all due respect Sir, for the same salary it's not worth all the trouble of changing my job. The reason why I look for a new job is because my daughter is growing up and the expenses with her are higher and higher. I need more money.*"

"*Are you married?*"

"*Yes, I am Sir, but my husband lives in Steville and he does not contribute at all to our expenses. I can't count on him.*"

"*Alright. You are not a young girl, who just finished school. We'll give you 3 and a half million crowns. Is that OK?*"

"*It's perfect Sir.*"

"*One more thing: if you are good, we'll raise your salary. If you are not good, we'll fire you. Do you understand that?*"

"*Yes, I do. I am good, you'll see.*"

"*Alright, you're hired. Welcome aboard.*"

"*Thank you Sir.*"

Valerie was in seventh heaven.

Professionally she felt she stepped up a whole lot. This multinational company was totally different from the two state companies she has worked until then. The state companies were depressing for Valerie. First of all, the activity was in slow motion. Whatever you wanted with them, it took place very slowly. She always thought this was not a very good sign for business. Than the state of the buildings: old buildings, with parts of wall fallen down, not painted, some of the windows broken. The offices dirty, the bathrooms in a very poor state. Old technology, missing materials. That old aroma that reminded her how her mother's office smelled. Here however it was a totally different story. The buildings looked very good. In the offices, everybody had a desk and a computer. There was a printer in every office. There were no broken windows. In the winter it was warm and in the summer it was warm in the offices. The bathrooms were clean and smelled good. There always running hot water. If something broke down, it was immediately repaired.

People were also different. The basic principle in the state companies was: 'We pretend we are working, they pretend they are paying us'. They were not necessarily kinder people, but at least they were bathed and they used deodorant, they washed their teeth and they combed their hair. The discussions were on a much higher level and much less chatter. There were very strict rules: you were not allowed to eat on your desk. You were not allowed to keep any personal items on it, no coffee, no water. If you needed anything, you have to go to the kitchen and take it from there.

Valerie adjusted very quickly to all of this. It's always easy to adjust from bad working conditions to better working conditions! She adjusted much harder though was the highly refined wickedness of the people. Valerie had no experience in this swimming with sharks yet. But she was about to learn.

At home also things have changed a little bit. Valerie went to work in the morning and arrived home late in the afternoon. They could not work her so hard anymore. In the evening, she prepared dinner for her and her daughter. Victoria was still a very picky eater. Even though Alan's mother called her to eat lunch with them, she always replied that she was not hungry. She ate only with her mom. Then they went into their room and Valerie spoke with her about school and helped her with homework if it was necessary. Usually, Victoria did not need help with the studying.

She was a very ambitious little girl. She learned by herself, with no push from anywhere.

The two of them were already making plans for the future.

"Mom, when do you think we shall have our own home?"

"I don't know yet my love. Mom is saving money. You know, you should not tell anyone about our money, OK? If your father and his folks find out about our money, they'll ask a loan from us and never give it back to us."

"I know, mom, I don't tell. If they ask me, I say I don't know. I don't know about your salary, nothing."

"Yes, my love. That's the spirit. Well, the good news is I receive much more money know. Not only my salary has increased, but they also pay for the extra hours, you know? That's why mammy has to stay so late in the afternoon."

"But other moms stay only until 3 o'clock at work and they stay in beautiful big houses of their own. Why can't we do the same?"

"My dear, most of them have inherited the land or even the entire house. Then, they have husbands who worked for that house. Your father does not give us any money, but other fathers support their families and build homes for their family. Do you understand?"

"Yes mom I understand."

"I'm sorry things did not turn out good for you. It's my fault, I could not keep your father with us. I could not motivate him to become a good father for you."

"It's not your fault mom, it's his fault because he's a loser."

"Well, he's still your father. Don't you ever forget that. Even if I will divorce him eventually, he will always remain your father. The blood ties are eternal and it is not good to fight against them."

"I cannot get close to him. He never reached out to me."

"I know that and I don't ask you to reach out to him. I just tell you should not hate him. If you hate him, he will not be touched in any way by your hatred, but only you will get sick of your own hatred. Just like I have to forgive my father, you have to forgive your father my love."

"OK mom."

"I love you my treasure."

"I love you too mom. I love you more than anything in this world."

"Me too my dear."

"But mom, when we have our own place, shall I have my own room, only mine?"

"Yes my love, if we shall have two rooms, one of them will be yours. I don't know what I will be able to afford. I went to the bank the other day in my lunch break. Just like that, you know, to ask information about loans for housing. They asked me my salary. When I told them, they said they cannot give me a credit with my salary. I felt like an idiot there."

"Don't worry mom. Things will change for the better, you'll see."

"Yes, my love, I know that."

Valerie analyzed herself many times. Why most of the women she knew had good husbands, who took care of their families and she didn't have? What did she do wrong? She loved Alan, she took care of him. She never saw a woman to pamper her husband like she did, except her mother. So what went so wrong?

Analyzing this over and over, Valerie reached some conclusions. Men don't want to be with a woman smarter than them. They need to be with a woman which is less than them, so that they can feel superior.

Men always say they like a strong, independent woman. But it's not true. A strong, independent woman who is capable of getting by without any man is psychologically castrating for a man.

When choosing their partner, men's first choice is a less intelligent woman, so that they can fell smarter in comparison with her. If she is not so stupid, she has to be evil, so that in comparison with her, he can feel so good at heart. She has to have some flaw, something that lowers her in his eyes. This is the only way they can feel good about themselves. In any case, she has to be as shallow as possible too, they don't need an insightful judge in their bed. Valerie saw the strongest bonds between a man and his wife only in the cases she was really sick or mentally ill or an alcoholic or an evil person or a stupid woman. Men need to come in first in the competition with their woman companions, they need to feel superior when they compare themselves with the woman by their side.

At work, Valerie saw all these have-it-all women and always wondered looking at them. She did not envy them, it was not envy. She just tried to understand what she did wrong. Valerie accepted everything in life provided that she found an explanation for it. The explanation could be spiritual, karmic, religious, logical, whatever, but it had to be an explanation. Valerie was looking and listening to these women and wondered. They saw she was unhappy, she was poorly dressed, she had no home of her own, no car, nothing. They were bragging and bragging about what they had: they had a good husband, who did all the work in the house, cooked, made shopping, repaired the car, Valerie was married but had no husband at all. Checked. They had a huge house, with a garden, and the furniture, that was so expensive, and the grass cut by the husband. Valerie did not have even a one room apartment. Checked. The car, the foreign, expensive car they had and how they went for lunch break in town and they had lunch in a fancy restaurant. And how Valerie only brought to work a sandwich and ate it in the kitchen. Checked. By when it came down to the children, Valerie had the audacity to say a good word about her daughter. She could say finally there was an aspect in her life she could be proud of. This was the moment when she saw the envy in the rich colleagues eyes. Valerie wondered how could they envy her for anything? They were so great, so beautiful, so rich, so beloved, so, so, so? Still they envied Valerie? And immediately started in a forensic attack to speak how their kids were so great, and how well they learned, and how they took private lessons for painting and piano and German and what not. God forbid Valerie had one issue she was better in! They could not stand that! They had to be better than her in every aspect and they had to make this very clear to her!

Valerie was aware they would never treat her as an equal. In her eyes, Valerie was an inferior person, who was not able to get a good husband, who was not able to have a house of her own or a decent car. They did not dig into the reasons, they did not analyze what happened to her or how much she worked and suffered just to survive. Valerie just did not rise to their standards. Valerie was aware of this, but still she fought for a place of hers in that multinational company. She tried at least make them accept her, tolerate her, because she needed the wages, she needed to provide the best upbringing for her daughter.

At home, Valerie's in-laws did not treat her as an equal. She was kind of the Cinderella in the house. But Valerie had to accept this too until she found a better variant for her and daughter.

Valerie thought these things over and over. Even though she worked hard from morning to the evening at the company, than at home she continued the work, her mind still searched obsessively the way out from the mess she was in. Many times she felt psychologically as she was walking on sand that was slipping away under her feet. Many times she felt she just wanted to give it all up. In these moments, when she almost lost it completely, her mind had an extraordinary ability to stop as from a bad dream and reason very clearly and ruthlessly. «*What's the matter with you? You want to give it all up? What will happen with your daughter?*» Then she just started to analyze what were exactly the very things that were bothering her. Usually, all the web woven around her came down to two or three things that were holding her down. After founding these two or three things, she thought of the best solutions for those things to be solved. Finally, she applied the solutions to her problems and this way she could get out the web that was blocking her.

In that moment of her life, Valerie got the job she wanted, she got the translator authorization, she got her driver license. She needed to save more money for the apartment and this was going on well.

Things at work were going very well. Unlike the bosses from her two first jobs, now Valerie had a great boss. He always spoke to her with respect. Sometimes, he praised her work. He showed her that he relied on her, that she was very important for the work she was doing. Valerie was the kind of person that liked these kinds of things. She needed to be treated with respect, especially because she never got respect at home. She needed a little pat on her back every now and then. She needed somebody to tell her how important her work is. This boss knew these things. Valerie was aware that he did all this to get better results from her, to have her working more, of course she knew it. But everybody wanted her to work more, everybody wanted to use her, at least this man did it in an intelligent way.

He knew how to treat her. He always asked her how Victoria was. If Victoria came to the company in her mammy's lunch break, she stood out in front of the gate. Children were not allowed inside, people said that one of the highest managers, the economic manager, hated children. Valerie was called to come out to her daughter, they spoke for a few minutes, than Victoria went home. In one such occasion, when coming back to work from his lunch break, Valerie's boss saw Victoria waiting for her mom outside the gate. He took her by the hand and just went with her right into her mom's office. Valerie admired him very much for this gesture, for his courage to bring in the company a child, even though it was forbidden.

One of Valerie's tasks was to receive the checks from the customers. She had to find what invoices were they for, than she had to make copies of the respective invoices, attach the corresponding check and take them to the financial department.

In this particular company where she worked it was not allowed to have any food or drink on the desk. No water, no coffee, nothing. If you wanted water, you had to keep it in your closet. No plants were allowed in the offices.

One day, Valerie received a lot of checks from the customers, they were all in a big pile on her desk. Of course, she was drinking heavily coffee and her coffee cup was on the table. Actually, the only one from whom she had to be afraid was the financial manager, an evil guy who hated children. When he came, Valerie hid her coffee cup, but otherwise she kept it on the desk, just like everybody else. Valerie received a lot of phone calls and she was very caught up as usual and she accidentally overturned her coffee cup. The coffee spilled over the pile of checks. In a different company, Valerie would have been afraid she was going to be fired. In this particular company, Valerie felt they will not even fire her for this, they will kill her on the spot. Especially that financial manager. «*Oh my God, he is going to kill me. Lord have mercy!*» Valerie thought. She actually saw her entire life flashing in front of her eyes and felt the cold pipe of the shotgun stuck to her temple, that's how afraid she got. She absorbed quickly the coffee of them with a napkin. She put them on the radiator to dry them. The checks got all crumpled. So she pressed them down under a pile of paper. After this, there was nothing left to do. Se took them and went to her colleague cashier who used to take the checks to the bank.

"*Hey, Maria, I did the most stupid thing.*"

"*Hey Valerie. What is it?*"

"*I spilt some coffee on the checks. What should I do? I have to go to the child hater and confess, right? He's gonna kill me, I know it.*"

"*Hmmm, now this is going to be a problem. Let me think. I know, I know. I'll take them to the bank. After all, the writing is not wiped out. If they accept them like that, it's all over. If not, I'm very sorry, but I'll have to inform the child hater. What do you think?*"

"*It's perfect. There's nothing else to do. Thank you so very much!*"

"*Hey, it's OK, it can happen to anyone.*"

"*Thank you.*"

Maria went to the bank with the checks and fortunately, the bank accepted them. They accepted them because the writing was not wiped out.

Valerie did at work whatever they asked her to. She was volunteering for any job had to be done. Most colleagues of her did not see this with good eyes, but even so, Valerie did not change her style. As long as she and her daughter lived only based on this salary, she felt she had to give something back to the company in return. Besides her particular job, she did also other chorus if it was necessary. She translated hundreds of pages, even though they did not pay her extra for it.

Valerie's boss also cared if Valerie was sick. If she didn't feel good, he sent her home. Never in her life, Valerie was not excused from school or work, no matter how bad she felt. She got used to this. And now, this man, this total stranger cared for her health? He was the only one Valerie told about her cyst. He reacted quite loudly.

"*So, what are you going to do about it?*"

"*Nothing. The doctor said I have to undergo an operation. I should miss from work three weeks, a month. I cannot afford that. I'll lose my job.*"

"*Are you crazy? You have to do something about it. You have to go to the doctor and operate it. How do know it's not cancer?*"

"*I don't know. Nobody knows. The doctor said the cyst has to be taken out and analyzed, that's the only way to see if it's cancer or not.*"

So, what are you waiting for?"

"*Nobody cares if I live or die. My husband is looking forward to get rid of me. Why bother?*"

"*Do you hear what you're saying? What about your daughter? What will happen to your daughter? Who will take care of her? She doesn't have a father, now you want to leave her without a mother too?*"

"*What about my job?*"

"*Don't worry about that. I'll speak here with everybody, you just take care of the papers that are needed.*"

Valerie had to undergo surgery. Valerie had severe pain in her tummy since an early age. She went for the first time in her life to a gynecologist when she got pregnant with Victoria. Back then, the doctor told her she had a huge cyst but he also told her that the cyst will be reabsorbed during the pregnancy. The pain never stopped for Valerie after she gave birth. She had also severe blood loss that lasted for months after the birth and she still did not go to the doctor. The severe pains came back and tormented her over and over again. She never told anybody about it. Victoria would have only worried. Alan couldn't care less. Who else cared what happened with her? Absolutely nobody. She always thought that if she died, at least she will make Alan happy. This way, he got rid of her and remained with Victoria. After years and years of thinking like this, in this awaking moment Valerie understood fully the risks she put herself to and she decided to go to the best doctor there was and undergo the surgery before it was too late. Also, she got to a point when she did not want to do anymore what Alan wanted from her, now she wanted to do exactly the opposite of what he wanted. So, if he wanted her to wear red hair, she would die her hair black. If he wanted her to wear short hair, she will leave her hair grow long. If he wanted her out of his life in the most comfortable way possible for him, that is by her dying, she will get out of his life in the most complicated way possible for him: by divorce. He never did for her what she needed, what she wanted. Why would she do what he wanted?

Next step was finding the doctor. The best doctors were in Steville. Of course, there were doctors all over the country, in every little town, but if you wanted the best treatment possible and if you had the money of course, you went to Steville. Going to a doctor to Steville was not so easy though. You had to know somebody who knew the doctor and who asked him nicely to accept to see you. Even though you were the customer and you was the one paying him money, you had to know somebody who introduced you to him or her. Valerie asked around at work about a good gynecologist. Finally, a colleague of hers told her she too was operated and knew the doctor very well. She promised she will speak with him. So she did and the doctor from Steville accepted to see Valerie. Valerie called him and made an appointment. This happened in March.

"*Hello. Sit down please. What is the problem, Madam?*"

"*Hello Doctor. I came for a check-up.*"

"*What seems to be bothering you?*"

"*Well, I had severe pains in my tummy all my life. Irregular cycles, severe blood losses. When I got pregnant, my doctor told me I had a big cyst. I just want to see how things are now.*"

"*OK, I see. Please lie down on the sofa by that monitor, roll up your blouse and open a little bit your pants. I just have to put a little bit of gel. This is necessary for the echography. It's a little cold, I know."*

Valerie lied down and looked at the monitor. The doctor started the procedure. A few seconds later:

"Madam, you have a huge cyst. It has to be operated immediately."

Valerie did not answer.

"Do you see? It's so big it does not fit on the screen. For how long did you have this cyst?"

"I don't know for how long. Last time I was at a gynecologist when I was pregnant."

"How old is your daughter Madam?"

"Nine years old."

"Well, this is not good. It is not good at all. Do you know that a cyst so big like this can be very dangerous?"

"I know."

"So why didn't you do anything about it? I see you are an educated person. Do you know the risk involved?"

"Nobody cares if I die."

"Are you married Madam?"

"Yes I am."

"Where is your husband? Can I speak with him?"

"He's not here. He doesn't stay with us. He couldn't care less."

"What about your daughter? You think she doesn't need you? Especially because her father doesn't care for her!"

"Well, my daughter is the reason I finally came to see you. Only because she needs me."

"Alright then. Tomorrow you will have to be admitted in the hospital, we'll run some testes and in a couple of days you will undergo surgery."

"I cannot be admitted tomorrow in the hospital. I have to ask permission from my boss first. I have to arrange proper conditions for my daughter. I cannot tomorrow."

"I'm warning you, it's very dangerous. If you remain like this, you might end up in emergency room."

"I understand that, but I cannot do this now. I'll come back to you in summer. I promise."

"When in summer?"

"Right after my daughter gets her holiday. I will come right after that."

"Alright. Please make sure you'll call my assistant couple of weeks before your admission to the hospital. You can arrange it with her."

"Alright Doctor. Thank you very much."

"You're welcome. See you soon."

Valerie got out from the doctor. Victoria was waiting for her in the waiting room. Alan had no time to come with her.

"So, mammy, what did the doctor tell you?"

"He told me I have a little bit of a problem. You know how my tummy hurts many times."

"I know mom."

"Well, it seems I have cyst. You know, I had a cyst also when I was pregnant with you my love. But that disappeared during the pregnancy."

"Yes, mammy you told me about it. So now you have another one."

"Yes, my love."

"And this also will disappear in time?"

"No, my love, this time I have to operate it. Mammy will have to undergo surgery here in Steville."

"Will anything wrong happen to you during surgery?"

"No, my love, this doctor is one of the best doctors in our country. He operated hundreds of women. He knows what he is doing."

"OK, mammy, if you have to do it, then do it."

"I have to do it my love. I love you."

"I love you too mammy."

Valerie acted very cool and composed and explained calmly everything to Victoria, but in her mind her old fears reappeared. What if something will go wrong during the surgery? What if she will never wake up after the anesthesia? What if after the surgery the doctor will tell her it was cancer?

CHAPTER 8

After many years of postponing her gynecological problems, Valerie made up her mind finally and went for a check up to a doctor. The doctor told Valerie her condition was very serious and she should undergo surgery as soon as possible. Valerie decided to do this in the summer of the same year.

Valerie was very afraid of this surgery. For no apparent reason, she seemed to relive the terror she went through during her pregnancy, when her husband told her he wanted to divorce and to take their daughter away from her. Only that this time she had her daughter's support, even though she could not be totally honest with Victoria. She did not want to frighten little Victoria. After days and days of obsessive and irrational fear, Valerie just woke up of it. She decided she will not be afraid of the event anymore. Her life was in God's hands, as always. If she was scared, the operation will go better? No. If she worried, the operation will go better? No. So why be afraid? Better yet, she had to be best prepared and she had to arrange everything carefully. First of all, what was best for Victoria? If something bad happened to her, Valerie could not leave Victoria at her in-laws. Alan didn't care about his daughter. So Victoria will have to go to Mineville, to Eva and Camil. After Victoria will take the summer vacation, Valerie was going to take her to Mineville and leave her there. Then she will return to Steville and undergo the surgery. Then, after the surgery she will go to Mineville too. Valerie had to speak with her boss. She had to tell him that she will be missing from work probably a whole month. Valerie hoped she will not lose her job because of this. In their country, if a woman had to miss from work a longer period because she was giving birth to a child or because she was ill, she was risking her job. She would have no job when she got back and there was no authority to protect her against the abuses of the employer. Valerie was aware of the situation and of the risks she was taking. She was going to ask permission from her boss well in advance. If he agrees, she will go to operation. If not, she won't go. This was the best she could come up with. Furthermore, Valerie decided not to tell neither Victoria, nor her parents about the operation. Victoria knew that her mom had to do the operation, but she did not have to know when she was going to do it. Eva and Camil would have been worrying too much, so Valerie decided to tell them only after it was all over.

Having decided all this, Valerie continued her life not telling anything to anybody. She was thinking Victoria needed to become a strong and independent woman. Whenever they had a chance, mother and daughter spoke about all kind of things.

"*You know, my little one, you have to grow up to be a strong woman. Never rely on anybody but yourself and the good Lord above. Of course, if someone wants to help you, accept and thank him or her. But never rely on that. The only one in whom you can have faith is Jesus Christ, your Father from above. He will always be there for you, never let you down. You can lose everything in life, but you cannot lose Him.*"

"*I know mommy. I know God is taking care of me.*"

"*Until you are child, you have to study seriously. What you learn, nobody can take away from you. In life, seriousness and perseverance cannot be defeated. Live a healthy life. God has given you a very healthy and strong little body. Take care of it. You have to eat healthy food, you have to rest, you have to spend as much time as possible out in the fresh air, practice a sport whenever possible.*"

"*What sport do you think I should do mommy?*"

"*I think the best sport you can practice is martial arts. The most important is that it will teach you defend yourself. It's very important to be strong and to know how to defend yourself. You should never attack anyone. But when you're attacked – and believe me, in life everyone gets attacked – you have to stand up and defend yourself. And the fact that you know how to defend yourself will give you self-confidence. The predators never attack you if you have self-confidence. They attack you if they see that you are weak and afraid and vulnerable. Generally speaking, in our country especially, it's better to avoid to be a victim. In our country, the laws are made so that they punish the victims and let the offenders and thieves get away. It's better not be a victim, because our state, and the state means police, county police, government, you name it, will not lift a finger to defend you or to take care of you. You must learn to defend yourself. You must learn and have a profession and take care of yourself. What you know and your profession cannot be stolen from you. Avoid all kind of risky and dangerous situations. If you spot one, just walk away. Keep in mind that if you get near it and something will happen to you, nobody will jump into the fire to save you. Better not to get into the fire. Do you understand what I'm telling you?"*

"*Yes, mommy. I know what you mean.*"

Valerie asked around about some martial arts lessons. She heard about a teacher who was training several children. It was in the evening, downtown. It cost a lot of money too. She registered Victoria anyway. Every evening, after she got home from work, Valerie and Victoria went to the gym. Valerie waited until she finished and then they went back home. By foot, in the dark town. Valerie did not get taxi for saving money. Victoria did not complain, she liked to walk and speak with her mom any chance she had.

Three months later, Victoria finished school and got her vacation. Valerie called the doctor's assistant and made the appointment and then prepared for the trip to Mineville. She did not want to tell anything to her in-laws, they did not care if she lived or died anyway. But she thought it over and realized it was safer if she told them. She had to go away from there for while and maybe they will get some wild idea and called Eva somehow and blew her cover this way. So one hour before they left, Valerie told only her mother-in-law:

"*Look, I have to tell you something. I am going to leave Victoria in Mineville. Then I shall return to Steville and undergo surgery. So we shall be missing for a longer time. I just wanted you to know.*"

"*Alright. Whatever.*" her mother-in-law replied.

To go from Streamtown to Mineville was a real adventure. If you went by train, you had to exchange three trains: one from Streamtown to Julestown, another from Julestown to Teaville and then another from Teaville to Mineville. Direct bus was only one. It came from the capital in the evening and in the middle of the night it arrived to Mineville. Valerie decided to go by bus this time. She made reservations weeks before the trip. Of course, when they got on the bus, it was full. There was no free seat for her and her daughter, with reservations and tickets bought and everything.

This was a very normal situation. All the transport companies were doing this. They picked up as many persons as possible, much more than the maximum number of persons for which the car was built. Nobody checked them ever. If you as passenger complaint, the state authority that called itself the authority for the protection of the consumer made a superficial checking at the respective transport company, the transport company's owner said that it was a special situation, and his other car had a technical problem that particular time and that it happened only then and that was it. It did not matter that it happened over and over again, at almost every transport, they always got away with it. Many times Valerie and Victoria went for the 380 km trip between Streamtown and Mineville sitting down on the lane between the seats, but this time the bus was so crowded, that also the lane was full of sitting persons. They had to travel standing up all the way. It was warm, the air conditioning was not working, the bus was dirty and smelly, all kinds of people drinking and eating all kinds of stuff. Fortunately, Victoria was not sick, there was not even place to throw up!

This horrible trip convinced Valerie she was doing the right thing. She noticed along the way that whenever she was dedicated to accomplish something serious and big, all kind of adversities appeared along the way and she went over each and every one of them. It was like from a certain point, the harder it seemed to achieve something, the more determined she was to continue the work and struggle towards that achievement. At least, if she was going to give up something, she will give it up because she decided to do so, and not because some difficulties appeared along the way.

In Mineville they spent a beautiful weekend. Valerie could be a very good actress when she wanted to be. She did not tell them a word about the surgery. She told Victoria she was going back to Streamtown to work and that she will call her whenever she had the chance.

On Sunday evening, Valerie went to Steville. She went to Alan's rented apartment. She has brought from Mineville a little food as she knew Alan's fridge was going to be empty. Valerie looked around, washed her hands and prepared a little dinner for the two of them. Alan went straight to the room and started to play on the computer. Valerie was used to this. He never helped her with anything. It wasn't enough that he came only rarely to see her and their daughter, whenever he came he went out to help his parents in the field or in the garden, and then started to play on the computer. He never helped Valerie with Victoria. When Victoria was still little, never took her out for the daily walk, never changed her, never fed her. When dinner was ready, Valerie called him.

"Dinner's ready. Come to eat."

Alan said:

"Just a minute".

Victoria waited patiently. This was another of his MO's. After she called him to eat, he spent several more minutes playing, while she was waiting for him with the food on the table.

"So, what are we eating?"

"I made some roast and mashed potatoes and I brought some pickles from home. OK?"

"Yeah, whatever."

They started eating without telling each other anything. Valerie always had a very good appetite and ate too fast and sometimes a little drop of food remained on her chin or on her lip.

"Wipe yourself up. You have food on your chin. Can't you feel that?"

"Oh, sorry, I'll wipe myself." defended herself Valerie.

"I don't understand how you can eat like that."

"Well I'm sorry. I'll try to be more careful."

Alan usually criticized each and every one of her move. After these criticisms Valeria usually cut her finger or burnt herself by accident or spilled something. More and more criticisms followed from Alan. This time, she tipped over her glass of milk from table. It poured on the whole table, soaking the bread and the dishes.

"Dear, why can't you be more attentive?" jumped Alan up from his chair.

"I'm sorry, I'm terribly sorry." Valerie jumped up her chair too and started to clean up the mess she made. Valerie thought for herself «*Why is he so annoyed? He doesn't clean it up anyway. Well, don't worry, dear, there has been a lot of pain, little has left.*»

"I can't understand you. You always eat like this. What is the matter with you?"

"Nothing's the matter with me. I'm just sloppy. OK? I'm sorry to tell you, but your wife is a sloppy, stupid, dirty person. I'm sorry you picked such a woman to marry."

"I didn't say that."

"No, you didn't say that, but you think that all the time."

"How do you know what I think?"

"Oh, dear, I know exactly what you think. But don't worry about a thing. Everything will be fixed some way or another. All of us will get what we deserve. OK?"

"OK, whatever. I don't know why you are making such a big case out of it. I just asked you nicely to be more careful not to tip over things. It can be dangerous. That's all."

"No, that it's not all. Because you always ask me kindly to be careful how I eat. To be careful how I speak and what I say. To be careful how I walk. To be careful how I drive. Is there anything I do correctly from your point of view?"

Alan looked back at her and said:

"Actually, yes, there is one thing."

Valerie looked back at him. She could not believe her eyes, but yes, he was meaning sex. «*It's amazing. He treats me like this and then he expects me to sleep with him?*»

"Well, that is the one thing you will not get from me anymore."

Valerie turned her back on him and went into the room. He changed into her pajamas and went right to sleep, turned towards the wall and pretended to sleep

Next day, on Monday morning Alan went to work as usual. What reason would he have had not go? What, that his wife was going to be admitted in the hospital and that she had to carry with her a lot of stuff? Or that she was scared to death and maybe she needed a soul to speak to while she was waiting for hours on the halls of the hospital? This was no reason for him not to go to work. Valerie took all the things she needed, and those things were: pajamas, slippers, towels, soap, shampoo, comb, a little radio, books to read, pain killers, underwear, it was whole list. All these things went into one big bag which she took on her shoulder, went to the bus station, took the bus and at a quarter to eight she was in front of the doctor's surgery.

The doctor had his visiting hours. Even though they had the appointment at 8 o'clock, he arrived only after 9 o'clock to his surgery. This was a very common thing, not only at the doctors, but generally. Nobody respected the agreed appointment hour ever. If you had your birthday and invited ten friends over at 8 o'clock in the evening, five of them came at 7 and five of them came at 9. Valerie could not understand this, no matter how hard she tried. If she complained, she was considered aggressive and they came up with all kind of dramatic excuses like they could not find the place or their car broke down, or they hadn't eaten all day long and if they did not go first to buy a pretzel, they would have had the blood sugar drop. Well, at the doctor she did not complain. Her life was in his hands.

Valerie went into his surgery with her heart pounding. There was the doctor, his assistant and also a young resident doctor, an incredibly beautiful young woman. The doctor asked the resident to consult Valerie, but without the echograph and tell him what was wrong with her. Valerie had to lay down on the gynecological chair and the consulted her. She told the doctor:

"*Mrs. Valerie has a cyst as big as a goose egg.*"

"*Mrs.Valerie has a cyst as big as a newborn's head! What's the matter with you*?" almost shouted the doctor back to her.

"*Uhh, I didn't ...*" tried the resident to defend herself.

"*You didn't what? Suppose a woman comes to you with a cyst like this and you don't have the ultrasound, what do you do? You send her home saying her cyst is as big as a goose egg, and her belly is almost bursting out so huge her cyst is!*"

The doctor was so mean to her that Valerie felt ashamed. The resident turned red, but she carried on like nothing happened. After that, the doctor wrote down all the analyses Valerie had to do and then she sent her to the admission office of the hospital.

Valerie waited a little bit in the admission office. She left there her clothes and received the hospital pajama. These hospital pajamas were actually rags, nobody wore them. Everybody was bringing from home some decent pajamas and slippers. From here, Valerie was directed to the hospital ward in which she was going to stay. The hospital was an old building, with two floors. The wards were very big, there were eight beds in one ward. All the persons from one floor were using one common bathroom, situated at the end of the corridor.

In Valerie's ward there were all kinds of women.

There was a sixty years old, simple and nice woman, with cancer. Her hair has fallen off due to chemotherapy. She was a kind person. It seemed unfair that such a kind, smiling, friendly person has cancer. Valerie's 'understanding mechanism', the one that helped her accept anything as long as it had an explanation of whatever nature, was struggling to find the reason. Why does cancer strike a good person? Shouldn't it only strike bad persons?

There was a sixty five years old woman who was a little weird. Everybody said she was crazy. She did not speak with anybody. She had a little radio with battery and she was listening to it all day and all night, no matter what anybody told her. Valerie personally did not feel disturbed neither by this woman, nor by her radio. The sound of a radio always lifted Valerie's spirit. When she gave birth to Victoria, she was so scared, so afraid of Alan leaving her and taking away her baby, so afraid she will not have money to bring up her daughter. The radio was the only thing that said to her 'Everything is OK. It will be OK. Life goes on. Day, evening, night, morning. Same routine. News, music, advertising. So on, so on. This is the rhythm of life, it goes on and on.'

There was a rich forty years old woman. She had a great job, a good husband, a big house. Perfect in every sense. She worked for the gas company. She was admitted for a cyst operation. Very popular, otherwise she knew everything and everybody. She liked to ask Valerie all kind of personal questions. Valerie was an honest, open person. She answered all these questions honestly and with the due discretion. Valerie always attracted this kind of rich women with their perfect lives. They liked to ask her all these personal questions, then she would answer them and each and every one of her answers proved them once again how much better they compared with her, how much more they had compared with her, what a good husband they had compared to her. These dialogues made them feel good about themselves. Valerie understood this situation very well. She understood only some weak persons could draw joy out of someone else's misery. When they finished their "friendly" chat, Valerie always thought *«I would like to see what would you have done in my situation, given the conditions I had started in. I would like to see what you would have done.»*

There was a thirty year old woman, also married. She had a very serious husband, who never smiled. He was a stern man. Valerie did not like stern men. Alan was a stern man. Always so serious. When she met him, Valerie thought he is so serious, so stern, because of the serious thoughts and ideals and projects he had. But no. This was not the case. He was serious and stern just so that nobody could read him correctly. This was just a mask that hid something, usually the fact that he was just a cheater and a liar. Valerie was sure this particular man also cheated on his wife, who was due to be operated for a cyst. Poor woman, she felt something was not right. Valerie did not know if she knew for sure that her husband is cheating on her or she only guessed, but the woman clearly suffered. Valerie could feel her pain, even though they hardly exchanged a few words. Valerie understood that she suffered and why she suffered, but she could not understand why doesn't she cry out loud her pain? Why doesn't she fight back? Why does she hide it? Who does she think she's fooling?

There was a thirty five year old woman. She was a doctor and was also due to operate a cyst. Valerie became good friends with her in the few days they spent together. Valerie could speak with her as if they were good old friends. This woman was married with a man who had lost his first wife to cancer. Now as she had this cyst, her husband was terrified that he could lose her too. Valerie admired very much this relationship between them, she thought it was nice that a husband cared what was going on with his wife.

Alan wasn't very concerned what was going on with his wife. He didn't speak with Valerie's doctor. He came in the afternoon, stayed for about fifteen minutes, looking at his watch every thirty seconds, until Valerie erupted:

"*Why are you looking at your watch all the time?*"

"*I want to know what the time is. Is it anything wrong with it?*"

"*Do you have to go somewhere?*"

"*No, I just want to see what the time is.*"

"*So, did you see what the time is?*"

"*Yes, I did.*"

"*This means you don't have to look at your watch anymore, right?*"

"*Whatever you say love.*"

Valerie looked at him. They did not have anything to talk about. Even two complete strangers could speak about something if they tried to. Not them, they were just sitting in the yard of the hospital, Alan anxious to get away from there, Valerie just wondering how she ended up with this man.

"*Look, it's obvious you don't have time to stay. You're a very busy man. So please, go, I don't want to retain you anymore.*"

"*Whatever you say love.*"

"*I say go, just go.*"

"*OK. I'll come tomorrow again.*"

"*Whatever you say love.*"

"*Do you need anything?*"

"*No, thank you. I'm fine.*"

Alan could hardly wait this moment. He went away from the hospital as fast as he could. Valerie also felt better after he left. She preferred to be without him, than to be with an absent man, always thinking about another woman.

Valerie's surgery was scheduled for Wednesday morning. The night before that, she called her parents and Victoria on the phone.

"*Hello mom. How are you?*"

"*Oh, we are fine. Just fine.*" Eva answered.

"*Great. How's Victoria?*"

"*She's a great kid. She's just great. Such a good child. She helps me every day with the house work. We go in the morning to the market. You know she likes to come with me to the market. You raised her very well.*"

"*I know, she always me how she likes to go with you to the market. That's because you took her with you since she was a little girl. Remember?*"

"*Yeah, she was so sweet. We went to the bus station few minutes earlier. We were waiting a little while for the bus. Then, when it finally came, Victoria always shouted «Great, grandma, the bus is coming.» She shouted so loud, all the old ladies from the bus station turned and looked at us and smiled. Yeah, those were the days. Well, I'll pass you Victoria.*"

And Eva shouted:

"*Victoria, come over to the phone. It's mammy.*"

Victoria came running, she could hardly wait for her mammy to call.

"*Hello mammy. How are you?*"

"*I'm fine my love. I love so much. How are you? Do you like your vacation in Mineville?*"

"*I love you too mom. And I miss you so much. I like it here, I help grandma every day in the house. We cook together, I wash the dished, I help her clean.*"

"*You're a very good little girl. You have to help grandma, and grandpa too. They need help now as they are growing old. You know?*"

"I know mom. I like to help them. And I like when they tell me old stories about their work and the times you were little."

"Good, good, my love. I'm glad you have good time. I wanted to tell you that in the next couple of days I will be very busy at work."

Valerie was calling from the hospital corridor. It was a warm summer evening, the window was wide open. She had the best signal on her mobile phone in the window. The birds were singing out on the trees from behind the hospital. A lot of women were walking along the corridor, some of them speaking loudly. Victoria heard all these noises and they seemed strange to her. So she asked Valerie:

"Mammy, what are those noises? Where are you?"

"I'm home, where can I be at this hour. Why are you asking?"

"I hear all those birds and all those voices. Who are you with?"

"Oh, I came to the garden. Grandma is here with your aunt and they are speaking with the neighbor. There are a lot of birds here too, I think they are glad it's not so warm anymore."

Victoria bought this explanation. She was a very smart girl, she felt something was not right, but on the other hand she totally trusted her mom. If Valerie told her she's in the garden and the birds are there, she bought it.

"OK, mom. When are you coming home?"

"I'll come at the end of next week. But until then, I will call you again. I'll call you again in a few days, OK?"

"OK mammy but I miss you so much."

"I know my love, I miss you too. But I also know you are a very strong little girl and you will be OK in any situation. Because you are brave and smart and adaptable."

"Yes, mammy, but please come as soon as you can."

"I'll come my love. I'll come. I love you. I have to leave now. Bye."

"Bye, mammy, bye. I love you."

"I love you too."

Valerie was nervous waiting for the surgery of next day. She prayed the evening before for the operation to go well. She put all her faith in God. Whenever fear crawled into her mind, she just thought «*God, please take care of me. My little daughter needs me. She doesn't have a father, she only has me. Please God don't let anything bad happen to me. I know I am bad many times and I don't deserve Your help, but I'm begging You, don't let anything bad happen to me.»*

God always helped her and always took care of her. Many times in her life Valerie felt His divine intervention and His protection. And she always was grateful for this. Even after the danger passed away. As she analyzed herself many times, she noticed she tended to think more of God and to pray whenever she was in danger or whenever she had very hard times. Then, after the situation passed or it was solved, her mind slipped away in the daily routine forgetting who she called for help and who helped her. This seemed to her a very ungrateful way of living. Why do people call God only when they are in a great trouble? Only after a serious accident? Only after losing a loved one? They never think of Him otherwise, after they are helped by God they never think back one second to thank Him. Thinking of all this over and over again, she decided she will always be grateful to God. She will always think of Him, in good times and in bad times. She will always go to church, not only for baptisms and funerals.

Valerie could not sleep all night long. She could hardly wait for the morning to come. She wanted to be over with it. She closed her mobile phone, as she was not allowed to go into surgery with it. Actually to surgery she was allowed to go only with a torn gown given to her by the hospital, that was all. Pretty final she thought.

Right as scheduled, at nine o'clock, the person with the stretcher came to pick her up from the ward. She stood up from the bed and lied on the stretcher. The operating room was a few feet away from her ward. In there, they transferred her on the operating bed. The assistant started to disinfect her tummy. She chatted with the doctor, in the mean time the doctor was looking straight into Valerie's eyes. Valerie was glad the doctor looked into her eyes, she felt more comfortable this way. A few seconds later the anesthesiologist came. He sat near Valerie's head, in order to see him Valerie had to look above her head. He told Valerie:

"I will put this mask on your face. You have to breathe in deep, after which you will soon fall asleep. Usually, after a few breathes, you should become unconscious."

Valerie did not say one word. She just looked into his eyes. The anesthesiologist had big brown warm eyes. He put the mask on Valerie's face. She breathed in as deep as she could, thinking of God « *My Lord, I put my life into your hands."* This was her last thought. After her second breath in she passed out.

"Mrs. Valerie! Mrs. Valerie!"

"What? What?"

"Mrs. Valerie, wake up! You have to open your eyes, you have to wake up!"

An assistant from intensive care was waking up Valerie. The operation was over and Valerie was transferred here for the following days.

"I'm up, I'm up! Don't shout anymore!"

The assistant smiled, happy that Valerie reacted and answered her.

"Are you alright? Do you know where you are?"

"I know, I know, I have been operated. Now I believe I'm in intensive care."

"It's true. The operation is over, now you have to rest. Go to sleep now."

Valerie did indeed fell right back into a deep sleep. She woke up a few times just to turn to the other side.

In the afternoon Alan came to visit her. She was glad to see a familiar face, also she was a little surprised he came. She took advantage he came and asked him to help her to stand up. Even though she felt very weak and woozy, her instinct told her she has to stand up and walk. As she did not feel capable to stand up on her own, she asked Alan to help her. He did help her and somehow she stood up from the bed. A few seconds later, the nurse saw her.

"What are you doing? You are not supposed to stand up. You have been operated today."

"I just wanted to make a few steps..." Valerie defended herself.

"You cannot do that. It's very dangerous. You are weak, you can fall down and injure yourself. Please, go right back to bed."

"Alright, I'll go back to bed..." answered Valerie disappointed.

"Until you are intensive care you are not allowed to stand up and walk without our assistance. After you will be taken back into your ward, then you'll be able to walk."

So Valerie went back to her bed. Alan went away after a few minutes, not much longer after that she fell back asleep.

Next morning she woke up feeling much better. Moreover, when she turned with her face towards the bed next to her, she saw the lady doctor from her ward. Valerie was really happy. She was isolated there for a few days in intensive care and she was facing one of the few persons who really liked in the hospital.

The two women chatted away all the time they were there. They couldn't do anything else, so they took advantage of this time and told each other the story of their lives.

"*What I don't understand how could come to the hospital for such a serious operation and not tell anything your parents.*"

"*I did not want them to worry.*" explained Valerie.

"*Yes, but do you know how many persons do not wake up of total anesthesia? What if you didn't wake up?*"

"*I know, I know. But I didn't want to put them on the road. Even if they came to Steville, where would they have slept? What about Victoria? She would have wanted to stay with me and help me and it is not allowed. I didn't want to cause all that that trouble…*"

"*You're reckless. It's not fair what you did in their confronts, you know that?*"

"*I know, but look, now it's all over. I woke up and when I will go home to them, it will be all over.*" Valerie looked at her roommate and smiled.

The women in intensive care were discussing when will they going to be sent back into their ward. Everybody was looking forward to go back into their ward.

They asked also the nurse about this. The nurse explained them:

"*You will be sent back into your ward as soon as your intestines start to work.*"

"*How do we know they started to work?*"

"*Well, you know they started to work because you feel the winds.*"

«*The winds?*» thought Valerie smiling. «*This is nice.*»

Valerie heard the other women speaking that they were there for four or five days already. Valerie thought «*I cannot stay here so much. I need to go back to my ward to call my daughter. She will be worried.*»

The woman doctor from the bed next to her told her:

"*Wouldn't you like to drink a coffee?*"

"*I would kill for a cup of coffee.*" answered Valerie. Valerie liked coffee very much. It was the only vice she never could give up. Every morning of her life, the first cup of coffee was the thing that put her into motion. No matter how tired, no matter how scared, no matter how depressed. That first cup of coffee made the morning worth waking up for…

"*They don't let us drink coffee.*" continued Valerie.

"*Yeah, yeah, but I told my mom to bring us some coffee tomorrow when she comes to me. You know they don't allow many persons to visit us, but one person can visit us. In my case, that person is my mom and she is going to smuggle in some coffee for us.*"

They both giggled happily. Like two school girls doing something forbidden, but so nice to do.

Next day, they got coffee. The doctor's mom managed to bring it still warm and nobody noticed it. When all the nurses went out, Valerie and the woman doctor from the next bed drank it with great pleasure in just a few minutes. It was great. They felt much better after this. Plus they remained with a great story to remember afterwards.

Forty eight hours after she was operated, Valerie was ready to be transferred back to her ward. Nobody was transferred back so quickly after such a difficult operation. Valerie thought «*I'm a she wolf. I really am. It's amazing how I can regenerate after each and every blow I get from life, after each and every illness. It's just amazing how God takes care of me all the time. How can I still have so little faith? How can I still worry about everything, after He has proven me so many times that He takes care of me, no matter what?*»

First thing Valerie did after she got into her ward was to call her daughter up.

"*Hello, mom. How are you?*"

"*We're fine, we're fine. And you? You did not call for the last few days. Everything OK?*"

"*Yeas, I'm fine. I was really busy at work. How's Victoria? Is she alright?*"

"*Yes, she is fine. A very good kid. She caused no problem, she behaves very well. Even your father said she's a very good kid.*"

"*I'm glad she did not cause any problems. Can you pass her on the phone?*"

"*Of course. Victoria, come to the phone, it's mammy.*"

"*Hi, mammy. How are you?*" said Victoria happy she can finally speak with her mom.

"*I'm fine, my sweet child. I miss you so much. How are you? How's your holiday in Mineville?*"

"It's great. I was at the market with grandma. I also was on trips with her on the mountain. We went with the bus until its last station, and then we went by foot up to that place she used to take you too. Remember?"

"Of course I remember."

"We made the fire there and ate and we found some wild strawberries and blueberries. And we drank water from a spring."

"Oh, that sounds great. I miss those trips. I'm sorry I wasn't there with you."

"So, what have you been doing, mom?"

"You know me, work at work and work at home. Same old story. Nothing interesting."

"When are you coming home mommy? I miss you so much."

"Well, if everything goes well, in a few days I will be able to come. I don't know exactly the date yet, but when I know I'll tell you. Will you come to the train station to wait for me?"

"Of course I will. I'm looking forward to it."

"Alright my dear. I gotta go now. Be good and help your grandma, OK?"

"Alright, mammy. I can hardly wait for you to come."

"Yes, me too, my love. I love you. Bye!"

"I love you too. Bye!"

Valerie recovered after the operation very well. Fortunately, she did not get an infection. Actually she never got infections. She had a good flesh, as they used to say. She dressed back into her pajamas, which were with short sleeves and short trousers. She used to sit cross legged in her bed and read for hours. She took with her in the hospital ten books written by Agatha Christie. She never had the time to read them, so now, in the hospital, as she had time, she read them all. Valerie did not look as an operated woman at all and she didn't behave like one. There was a doctor who saw her once sitting on the bed and reading and he joked:

"Now look at this lady, she looks like she came on holiday, not in the hospital."

"Well, I can never sleep and rest back home, so now it's true, I am holiday."

"Good for you that you rest, that's the spirit."

Of course, all the other women who came back from the operation were acting like they were totally destroyed. They felt weak, they could not eat, they could not go to the bathroom by themselves. Valerie didn't feel great either but she had nobody to help her, she didn't have anybody to complain to, just like when she was pregnant and when Victoria was born, so she managed by herself as she could. After all, the operation was over, it went alright, what was bad, was over, right? Valerie was hungry, she was hungrier than before the operation because she did not worry anymore. Valerie went to the bathroom on her own, she walked a lot every day, she helped the other women stand up or went to buy and bring back things and food for them. She knew there was nobody there to help her. She had to stand up, if she waited for help from Alan, she knew she was never going to get it.

Alan continued to visit her and he actually brought her food once. Valerie was surprised he went through that trouble.

After the operation, Valerie discussed with the doctor:

"*Hello doctor, I'm sorry I disturb you.*"

"*You don't disturb me. I wanted to speak with you anyway.*"

"*I wanted to ask you about the cyst.*"

"*Yes, well, at a visual check it looked that it only contained clot.*"

"*Oh, that's good. It's good it wasn't something else.*"

"*Yes, but still. We sent a sample for analysis.*"

"*When will the result come back?*"

"*It takes almost a month for the result to come. You can go home in a couple of days, you're healing very well. Tomorrow morning I will take out the stitches. At seven o'clock please come to my cabinet.*"

"*OK, I'll be there.*"

"*One more thing. After you get out of hospital, you will have to start to take a hormonal treatment. This will prevent you to develop more cysts. You will actually take contraceptives.*"

"*For how long will I have to take them?*"

"*Well, you'll have to take them as long as you live. You also will have to come at least once per year for physical examination. We'll see how things evolve. You have to be very careful, if we have to operate you once again for another cyst, we'll have to perform a total hysterectomy. Do you understand?*"

"*Yes doctor, I do. Thank you very much for everything.*"

"*You're welcome. You're very welcome. See you tomorrow.*"

"*Thank you. Bye.*"

Next morning, the doctor took out Valerie's stitches personally. She couldn't even feel it, he had very mild hands. Also, he told her the exact day when she could check out from the hospital.

Valerie planned immediately what she was going to do. The checking out was around noon. She had to go to the post to send to work the hospital discharge note, they needed it right away. Then she was going to buy the train ticket. The very next day, she could go to Mineville.

First of all, she called her daughter and told her the day she was coming home. Victoria was very happy, she wanted to go with Camil to the train station to wait for her mom. Then, Valerie spoke with Alan:

"Alan, the day after tomorrow I'm checking out. Can you please come take me home?"

"I can't come, you know that. I cannot miss from work. What time should this happen?"

"Why do you ask what time if you cannot come anyway?"

"I'm just asking..."

"Around noon, OK? Everybody checks out around noon. And everybody has somebody to help. I have to take all my things, the slippers, the pajamas, the books and so on. You really could come to help me."

"I'm sorry, but I can't come. They won't let me miss from work."

"Alright, so if you cannot come, then don't come."

Valerie got very angry he didn't want to come, but she did not fight with him. She just thought: « *Stay calm, just stay calm. Be patient a little more. It will soon be all over. I'll file for divorce as soon as possible, it will all be over soon.*»

On the day of discharge from the hospital, Valerie woke up earlier, she was nervous, she hoped everything will go alright. The only thing she was afraid of was that she will faint on the street. She thought she should take a taxi. But she had to go first to a postal office, then to the travel agency to buy her train ticket and then to Alan's place. They will charge her a fortune. No, she was going to go by foot to the post and to the agency, then she will take a tram to Alan's place. Right after the doctor's visit, she went down. Behind the hospital there was a little booth where they sold coffee and sweets and biscuits. She bought a large coffee and biscuits. Usually, when she was worried or nervous and had some big project going on, her blood sugar dropped and she felt weak. Drinking the coffee and eating the biscuits prevented that.

Valerie packed all her stuff, then, with the discharge note from the doctor she went down to the hospital admission office where she gave back the gown they gave her and she got back her clothes and shoes. It was all over at noon. She got out on the street. Steville has always been a very busy city. It seemed more busy and noisy now, after all those days of isolation and silence. She thought « *Just take it easy. One step at the time. Don't hurry. You have all the time in the world. Just go slowly. If these aggressive persons from Steville are annoyed by my presence as usual, it's their problem. If they are in a hurry, then they can pass me by. I cannot walk faster.*»

Valerie set her pace and kept on going slowly and steadily. The postal office was around 500 meters away from the hospital. When she got there, she saw there was a queue. Well, she stood at the end of the queue and waited patiently. It went very slowly, but at least she did not have to walk, she could put her stuff down and it wasn't so noisy and sunny and dusty like outside.

After half an hour it was her turn. She made a copy of the discharge note and kept it and she sent the original to the company where she worked. After this was solved, she went to the travel agency. Here another queue. This time longer, but at least it went faster. She bought herself a ticket to Mineville for the next day.

Then, still by foot, she went to the tram station. Physically she felt very tired, but psychologically she was much better as these two issues were solved. The tram came quickly, but it was very crowded. She got up on it. She found no place to sit down. The tram shook everybody as it went on. Valerie held herself to a bar and in her other hand she held her baggage from the hospital. She was pale, it was obvious she did not feel very well. But, no matter how weak you felt, no matter how tired you looked or how much baggage did you carry, there was always a person in Steville that was extremely annoyed if you lost your balance on their horrible public transportation means. God forbid one of them offered to help you. No way. They were extremely bothered by the presence of any person from outside of Steville. Valerie knew this and she made huge efforts not to lose her balance, but the tram shook her so hard that eventually she lost it anyway. So she got the comment from the person next to her:

"Hey, what are you doing? Pay attention!"

"I'm sorry. I'm terribly sorry."

"It's not enough to be sorry. You have to take care not to step or fall on somebody."

Valerie did not want to continue this discussion. She did not step on anybody and she did not fall on anybody, but it made no sense to get into a polemic now. So she just repeated:

"I'm sorry."

Finally, she got to Alan's place. When she got in the house, she felt so grateful nothing wrong happened to her. She burst into tears. This happened many times with her. When caught up in a critical situation, she handled everything courageously and efficiently. But when it was all over and she was finally alone, she burst into tears and thanked God for getting her out of that mess. This time, again, she fell on her knees and thanked God for everything. And she cried and cried.

Eventually she got up back on her feet and looked around. Alan's place was a typical bachelor place. Obviously Isabella was not cooking and cleaning for him. Well, at least not here. Valerie was not able to clean for him this time. She usually cleaned his place when she came to Steville, but now she felt too tired. She looked into his fridge. Empty, totally empty. She took her purse and went to the little shop in the neighborhood and bought some food. Then she came back and cooked a simple dinner. When Alan came home from work, the food was ready and still warm.

Valerie looked at his face, trying to read it. Alan always had an impenetrable poker face, he never showed his feelings. Something like Keanu Reeves. Valerie remembered «*God, how I liked this once. I loved it that he never expressed his feelings. Well, after my father and his feelings and how he always showed us violently his feelings, I found it very calming that Alan was not showing anything violently. But unfortunately, instead of choosing a man who controls himself and his feelings, I chose a man <u>with no feelings</u>, a man totally empty inside.*» It seemed he was pleased she prepared dinner. «*This is good.*» continued Valerie to think. «*He does not have to know about my intention to divorce. He does not have to be prepared for it. He will not know what hit him.*»

They slept together, as it was only one room and one bed, but fortunately he didn't get any ideas, as Valerie has just been operated. She couldn't stand him touching or holding her anymore. Her body could not relax in bed with him, she just crouched on her side of the bed and hoped they don't even touch during the night.

Next day Valerie went alone to the railway station and got to the train to Mineville. The train was slow and dirty and smelled bad as usual, but Valerie did not pay attention to these minor details. She could hardly wait to hold her daughter in her arms. She wanted to get home to her daughter so fast, that she felt she could just stretch out her wings and fly. But the train did not take into consideration these feelings of her. He just went on in his rhythm. Finally, after three and a half hour it arrived to Mineville.

Victoria was waiting for her mom with her grandfather. Valerie's heart almost jumped out of her chest when she saw her little girl. After she got down from the train, her daughter jumped on her. Valerie was visibly thinner and she was also very pale. Camil and Victoria noticed this immediately. Camil asked:

"*What happened?*"

"*I have just been operated, but I'm fine. Please don't worry. I am quite alright. I'll tell you all about it at home.*"

They went by foot home. It was a twenty minutes walk from the railway station to their block. Camil and Victoria took all her bags, so it was easier for Valerie to walk. Compared to Steville, here existed somebody who helped her.

At home, Eva held her in her arms for minutes. Valerie ate while Victoria, Eva and Camil stood in the kitchen and they were all chatting about all kind of things. Valerie felt happy and grateful, this was really her family.

After they ate, they all went to Eva's room. Eva started:

"*Alright, now tell us everything.*"

"*Well, you know I had a cyst. You remember I had one when I was pregnant with Victoria. The doctor told me back then that it will disappear during the pregnancy. And it probably did disappear. Many years after Victoria was born, I did not go to a doctor. I suffered a lot, I had terrible pains because of this problem of mine. Anyway, I was speaking with my boss about this, as I have felt very bad several times at work too. So he convinced me to go to a doctor. The doctor said I have to undergo surgery and so I did.*"

"*Very well, you did very well. What did the doctor say, it's everything OK now?*" asked Camil.

"*Well it looks as if everything is OK. But I will get the final result only in a month, after the laboratory tests are done.*"

"*OK, perfect. You did well. And I am glad you brought Valerie here to us.*" continued Camil.

Valerie wanted to say: «*I wanted Victoria to be with you if anything bad happened to me.*» But she thought this will lead to further discussions and Camil will tell her that she should have gone earlier to the doctor and so on, so Valerie re-phrased:

"*I trust you more with Victoria than the other grandparents. Also, Victoria likes it better with you than with them, so I decided to bring her here while I'm in hospital.*"

"*But you should have told us that you are going to the operation.*" continued Camil.

"*I didn't want you to worry and I did not want you to come to Steville and so on. I managed OK and for me it was a great help to know Victoria is very well taken care of.*"

"*OK, than I'm glad everything turned out well. And I'm glad you are here now.*" ended Camil the discussion and wanted to go in his room.

"*Dad, wait a little more. I want to tell you and mom some other thing.*"

"*Tell us, what is it?* "asked Camil.

"*I want to get a divorce.*"

"*It's your decision. You do however you think it's best.*" said Camil.

"*Are you sure about this? I mean after fourteen years? After all you have done for him and all the money you spent for him and all you worked in your in-laws house?*" asked Eva.

"*It's a dead end marriage, mom. This marriage of mine does not go anywhere. It's like a big communist factory that loses money every month. Of course you invested a lot, of course if you give it up you lose all the money you invested, but the best solution is to give it up immediately. At least, if you give it up you don't lose any more money, right?*" explained Valerie her point of view.

"*What about Victoria?*" asked Eva.

"*What about her? She never had a father. Since she was born, she spent 24 hours a month with him. What will she lose if I divorce?*"

Valerie waited a few seconds, than she continued:

"*If I divorce, maybe the judge will grant my child and alimony and at least he will give me some money for his child. Now he does not give me any money for the child. He has bigger salary than I have but he never has money. Sometimes, he actually expects me to give money to him. What kind of a man is the one that takes money from the woman who raises his child?"*

"Oh, and when I think back how much you loved him. We told you he was no good for you..."

"Yes, you told me and yes I loved him, but I don't love him anymore. I have stayed with my in-laws for seven years now, hoping he will come and stay with me and Victoria. He never came and he has no intention to come. In all this time, he stayed in Steville, living his life and I worked for his parents trying to compensate somehow the fact they let me live there and eat there. Well, I'm sick and tired of this. I don't want to continue anymore. I drew the line and made my calculations. It's all been a big loss and I have to end it immediately."

"If you decided this, we are right behind you." said Camil.

"Of course we are behind you" said Eva too.

Victoria came to her mother and kissed her and hugged her.

CHAPTER 9

After years of not caring for her health issues, Valerie has finally operated her ovarian cyst. She felt good after the operation, she was recovering very well. She stayed in Mineville for a couple of weeks, until she had to return to work.

Two days before her sick leave was over Valerie returned with Victoria to Streamtown. A couple of hours after they arrived to her in-laws house, Alan's mother told Valerie:

"*It rained a lot lately, the weeds have grown like crazy.*" said Alan's mother.

"*But… I don't know if… The doctor said I shouldn't make any efforts for a while…*"

"*What? The operation? Don't worry about it. You will just heal faster if you work a little bit. Go on, it will be alright.*" her mother-in-law insisted.

Valerie did not say another word, she went to the garden and started to pull out the weeds. Then she helped with any other chorus her mother in law gave her, she could not refuse. After all, she and her daughter were living in that house. By this time, Valerie was not even surprised anymore at their total lack of compassion. She got used to it, so she just executed what she had to do and waited patiently the day when she was going to be free again.

A month after the operation she went to Steville to her doctor and he confirmed the cyst taken out of her was only clothed blood, the analysis did not reveal any cancer cells. Valerie was relieved to hear this. She only told her parents, Alan did not care anyway and she thought probably he would have been happier if she had cancer.

Valerie wanted to take Victoria a week to the seaside. Since Victoria was four years old, every year, in the end of May and beginning of June she made an asthmatic bronchitis episode. One time the episode was so severe, that she could hardly breathe. Every time Valerie worried sick about this, but the doctor knew exactly what to administrate the little one to solve the issue. He always prescribed an antiallergic medicine and it passed. Valerie asked the doctor:

"What could I do about this? Can I do anything to avoid these episodes?"

"Well, it's obvious she is allergic to something with which she is in contact only this time of the year. It could be the pollen of a flower that blooms now or who knows what else. You could go to Steville to find out exactly what is allergic to, but I don't think this is absolutely necessary. I mean, in order to find out what she allergic to, they will sting her with several allergens and they will see which ones swallows up. This will not be pleasant for her at all. Then they will tell you what is she allergic to, but what if you cannot isolate her from the respective allergen? What if it's something in the air?"

"Yeah, you're right. She would not like those stings. But what can we do? Is there anything we can do to avoid this?"

"What you can do is to strengthen her immune system. It would help a lot if you would take her to the seaside."

"To the seaside?"

"Yes. That salty air is very good to cure this condition of hers. It would be good to make long walks with her early in the morning or late at night so that she breathes that air. Also, you will see, she will grow faster and she will have a better appetite."

"Well this sounds good. She is a very picky eater. And how many times do I have to take her to the seaside?"

"It would be good to take her there every year for at least six years in a row. I know it will be hard and also costly, but in time you will see the result."

"Alright doctor, we shall do so."

Valerie did so. She took Victoria to the seaside every year and she took her also in the year she was operated. Valerie asked her doctor if it was alright to go to the seaside so soon after she was operated. He said it was alright, the only thing she had to take care of not to expose her operation to the sun.

Valerie was a little bit worried about this particular trip to the seaside. She felt she lost some strength with the operation. How will she be able to carry all those bags? Up and down the train? Then at the seaside she always went by foot to the house where she had lodging. The taxis were driven by all kind of wise guys who charged foreigners as much as they wanted, with no control over them. Valerie preferred to walk a couple of kilometers than to be these guys' sucker.

Valerie felt however that all this worry, the fatigue and the expenses were worthwhile. The joy of Victoria being at the seaside, all those long baths in the sea, the walks right on the beach, in the soft sand, just so the waves touched them on their bare feet. All these were sheer heaven for the girl.

Valerie taught Victoria how to swim, just as she taught her how to ride the bicycle. Victoria did not have to feel his father absence, she had the right to develop as a normal child. For this Valerie was her mother and her father in the same time.

After the vacation was over they came back to Streamtown. Valerie went back to work, Victoria was still on holiday. Victoria was a friendly and popular girl, she always had good friends to play with. She was sociable and mannered. Valerie always told her:

"*You must have friends and play with other children of your age. I know you like to spend time with me, but I'm a grown-up and you are a child. You must spend time with other children of your age. Only 'competing' with them for your toy, actually for your place under the sun, will make you strong and adaptable and resourceful. Go out and play with children. You must go out into the fresh air and get dirty. Run and play with the ball and ride your bicycle.*"

Valerie made a small party every year for her birthday. Victoria invited over around ten children and Valerie prepared sandwiches, egg rolls, schnitzels and a nice big cake. She could make a very big fuss, as they were still living in the in-laws' house, but they still did a small celebration every year. Victoria was happy and they made a lot of pictures. Valerie was stressed before these events, as she wanted everything to turn out perfectly for Victoria, but in the meantime she did not want to disturb the in-laws. Quietly, with no help from anybody, she planned carefully and prepared the meals. She was so stressed that she always dreamt before Victoria's birthday that the children came and the food was not ready yet. In reality everything turned out just great and Valerie was pleased she made her daughter a joy every time.

Valerie and Victoria had a secret they did not tell anyone. Valerie was looking for a rented apartment. As soon as she found it, she was going to file for divorce. She couldn't divorce while she was staying in that house. Finding a place to live seemed easier than it actually was. With Valerie's salary, it was hard to find a decent 1 room apartment that fit her budget. She didn't look for luxury, but she had to find an apartment with decent heating, running hot water, windows and doors that closed well. Valerie looked for months for a rented apartment. She visited several. The owners were out of their mind. They asked enormous prices, which Valerie could not afford. Streamtown area developed very much after the multinational company was open. The price in the area grew exponentially. This happened in the end of 2003, the real estate field was growing out of control.

In December 2003 Valerie received for the first time in her life a Christmas bonus. It was an impressive amount, at least for her, who was not used to having much money. From the money she got, she bought a TV set to have when she and her daughter moved out.

For the winter holidays, Valerie and Victoria went to Mineville as they used to do. Except for the trips to the seaside, made for the health of Victoria, whenever she had some days off, Valerie took Victoria and they went to Mineville. Alan was always very busy, he never could come with them, but they were already used to this.

Right after the winter holidays, Valerie found out that some friends of a person working the next office of hers had an apartment to rent. Valerie spoke with her and got the phone number of the owners. She called them and set up a meeting to visit the apartment.

The owners were a young couple. He was working, she was a student. They got the apartment from his parents. His mother was involved in the renting process, she was helping them out.

The apartment was very close to the company. It was in a block of flats, on the third floor. The apartment had a room, a kitchen, a bathroom and a small balcony. Important thing: it was heated and it had hot running water. The next step was the price. The residence area was the poorest from the town, therefore the owner did not ask for very much. They were willing to rent it for 65 euro per month. Valerie made her calculations fast. She had a salary of around 165 euro. After she paid the rent, she remained with half of her salary to pay the utilities, buy food, clothes for her daughter. Hopefully, after the divorce, Victoria got alimony from her father. This wasn't one hundred percent sure. Valerie was aware this was not one hundred percent sure. It was possible that Alan will not grant her the divorce. Even though he did not stay with them, it was possible that he decided not to divorce, just because Valerie wanted to. In this case, Victoria got no alimony. Then, it was possible Alan arranged a certificate where it was stated he had no income, then Victoria got no alimony. Then, it was possible the state decided Victoria did not deserve an alimony. Valerie thought of all possibilities. But even with no help from anywhere, she felt she could get by with this rent. So she told the owners:

"*Well, it's a little steep. I have to think about it. I have one more question. For how long do you want to rent it out?*"

"*For long term. We want to find a serious family to rent it out for a long time. You see we are not asking that much. But we want to rent it out to somebody trustworthy.*"

"*I'm asking you because I want to get divorced in a couple of weeks. I have a ten years old daughter. I will bring over some furniture. I don't want to move out in a couple of months.*"

"*Don't worry about that.*" said the young man. "*My wife is a student in Polville. She rents and apartment there. We thought to rent this apartment out and use the money for her rent. In the meantime I will live with my parents. At least until she's a student, you can live in this apartment. That means at least three years.*"

"*Alright then. I will take the apartment.*"

"*OK, we are glad. You can move in immediately.*" said the young man.

"*I will move in on the 1st of February. I will pay you now the rent for the first month and the security deposit.*"

"*OK, it's fine with us. So, we meet here on the 1st of next month?*"

"*Yes, sometimes in the afternoon. I will call you one day before that. Then we shall write down the gas, electricity and water meter. You think we should make a little contract?*" asked Valerie.

"*For us it is not necessary.*"

"*OK, then we shall just go on trust.*" concluded Valerie.

Valerie had to organize carefully everything. Victoria was too small to pack or carry things, so Valerie had to do everything by herself. First of all, she spoke with the boss of a transport company with whom she had a good collaboration. The man said he will help her gladly, of course Valerie specified from the beginning that she will pay the normal fee. They agreed on the date and hour when the truck had to come to her in-laws to load all her stuff. She did not have that much really, but when it came down to packing it was quite some baggage. There were all her clothes and her daughter's clothes. The toys of her daughter. Her books, her notebooks, school supplies. Victoria had a bookshelf, a desk and a modern chair since she began school. She had a desktop computer. Valerie had also a printer for her translation activity. Valerie had some books of her own, plus all the huge dictionaries. They had some pots, pans and dishes. In the end, there was quite some stuff to carry. Fortunately, she just had to take it out from the house and put in the car that will come in front of the house. Valerie planned everything carefully and started to pack right away.

Next she had to communicate to the in-laws that after seven years of living with them, she was moving out. The most she feared to tell this to her father-in-law. She was sure he will have quite a reaction, he was always yelling at her for everything. If his son, Alan, was not coming home more often, he yelled at Valerie. If he did not take care of Victoria, he was yelling at Valerie. If he came home and did not work enough, he yelled at Valerie. Several times he asked for money from her, money that he never gave her back. Of course he did not want her there, nobody wanted Valerie and Victoria in that house, but Valerie was sure that they will blame her for giving up on the "great" marriage she and Alan had so far and they will be very concerned "*What will our acquaintances say?*"

By the time Valerie was preparing to move out, Alan's sister was married. Valerie noticed every day that the husband of Alan's sister was treated with respect, unlike her. Their children were considered little princes, when they were sleeping for example, you had to take care not to breathe to loudly, because you would have disturbed the little sleeping prince. Unlike Victoria was treated back when she was very little. Victoria was always treated rudely, loudly and with a constant dose of hostility. Valerie was treated in the same way, but Valerie was a grown up. She was not so bothered by the fact they treated <u>her</u> like that, but she was quite upset they treated <u>Victoria</u> like that, she was just a child and could not be blamed things turned out so bad between her mother and her father. Even so, Victoria was always polite, always behaved well, both at school and at home and she learned very well. For Valerie, the seven years spent at her in-laws were seven years of misery. She tried her best to provide Victoria with all that she needed, but she always felt guilty because Victoria did not have a father, because they did not have a place of their own, because they were treated as so poorly in that house. But for all those seven years, there was nothing Valerie could do based on her financial resources. Only now, Valerie got into a point when she had saved the amount she needed for the down payment of the cheapest apartment in Streamtown and she could finally afford to rent an apartment until she could buy one her own. She also told Alan that she was moving out, of course he had no reaction.

Finally, the day came when she had to tell her in-laws she was moving out. God helped Valerie one more time: her father-in-law was not home, he was in Steville, in the hospital. Valerie was relieved. She only had to tell her mother-in-law and she was pretty much like Alan: no reaction whatsoever, all she said was:

"*You don't want to stay with us anymore?*"

"*Well, it doesn't make sense without Alan.*"

That was it.

Valerie could not miss one day from work. Ever since she was a little girl, she never was allowed to miss one day from school, then later when she grew up she never missed a day from work. Did not matter if she sick, if she felt bad, if she had fever. She went to work. Now she had to move, but she could not miss from work for this. Therefore, she asked for the truck to come on a Saturday morning. All her things were packed. She woke up Victoria at around seven o'clock. She gave Victoria breakfast, they washed, combed their hair and brushed their teeth. In the house, nobody cared about them. Nobody addressed them one word. Some of them were still sleeping, some were around the house, but nobody asked them if they needed some help or anything. Valerie could not care less. She had everything ready. When the truck came, she started to laugh. A huge truck came for them, he blocked down the whole street parking in front of the house. Valerie started to carry her things out of the house. Victoria was eager to help, but Valerie only let her help with the light stuff. She could carry the desk along to the back door of the truck and with the help of the driver, she put it on the truck. Then the bookshelf, being empty it was not that heavy. Then Victoria's chair. The next heavier thing was the TV. After all these heavy things were loaded, only the lighter things came: the toys, the clothes, the books, the shoes, their pillows, a blanket, some dishes they had. In a couple of hours, everything was loaded. Valerie was trembling from the huge effort. And the hard part was just beginning. Their rented apartment was on the third floor and there was no elevator.

Few minutes later, the truck arrived with the girls in front of the block where they rented. They unloaded everything. The driver had been instructed to help Valerie carry up the stuff. Valerie only let the driver help her with the desk and the bookshelf. She left the rest of the stuff down, in front of the block and sent the driver away. Victoria waited for her upstairs, in the apartment. Slowly, Valerie carried everything upstairs all by herself. It took her several hours, when she finished she was totally finished.

The feeling they had after having all the stuff in and closing the door was priceless: they turned on the TV loud, on their favorite music channel. They left everything on the ground, Valerie did not have the power to put them into their place and Victoria had to learn. But they felt absolutely great. Valerie prepared a list with what they did not have: a quilt, a pot, some glasses and mugs and so on. They were chatting and laughing and making plans for the future.

Valerie's first wish was to divorce. A few days after she moved out, she went and discussed with a lawyer. She knew it took some time anyway, so it was better if she started as soon as possible. She gave the lawyer all the information and documents needed. For the first time in her life, Valerie told someone all what she went through in her marriage. The lawyer promised her she will forward the file and she will inform her as soon as the first hearing was scheduled. Also, she explained Valerie:

"*The duration of a divorce depends very much. If you get quickly to an agreement with your husband, it can go very fast. Do you have many assets to split by divorce?*"

"*We have nothing, so it will be easy. Actually he has a car, but I don't want that piece of junk. I want the child and I want to keep my name after marriage. It will be better if my last name is the same as my daughter's and I will not have to change all the documents I already have: driving license, identity card, translator authorization and so on.*"

"*You can keep his name only if he agrees.*"

"*Right, only if he agrees.*"

"Regarding the child, there will be a social investigation, but it will be more a formality. In 99% percent of the cases, the child remains with the mother. You will have to bring two witnesses to the trial. Think whom you can call. Also, you will have to discuss with a social worker and you will have to present the living conditions you provide for the child."

"Well, I will fight with all my power for the child."

"Did you discuss with him? Will he fight for the child too?"

"He's a strange man. I cannot discuss with him anything seriously. Honestly, I don't know how he will react. He might refuse my claims, just to make my life miserable. When it comes to him, I am always prepared for what's worst."

"OK, we shall be prepared. I need his address, he will receive the citation to the trial."

"Well, he stays in Steville, in a rented apartment."

"What about his stable address, from the identity card?"

"That is his parents' house, his stable address is still there."

"Alright then, the citation will be sent to his parents' house."

"Yeah, it's better like that." concluded Valerie.

The first step was done. Valerie couldn't help think back to the time she was pregnant. When she told Alan she was pregnant, he told her he wanted to divorce and he continued to say this during her entire pregnancy. She was so stressed because of this. And he never actually did it. Valerie thought « *Why was I so stressed? I should have no known he was to weak and coward to do such thing. How could I misjudged him so much?* » And now it was she who filed for divorce, the difference was that she never told him she was going to divorce, she just did it.

A couple of weeks after Valerie filed for divorce, Alan came to Streamtown for his monthly visit of his child. He went and worked at his parents', at night however he came to sleep with Valerie and Victoria. Again, this was very strange, after fourteen years of marriage Valerie was not able to understand her husband. All the three of them slept in the single bed there was in the apartment.

In the morning, Valerie made the coffee and made the breakfast for the three of them. After they ate, she told Alan:

"I filed for divorce."

"I was expecting this." said Alan.

"Really? You did?"

"Yes, I knew it since you moved out from our house that this is what you were going to do." and Alan's eyes actually got filled with tears.

Valerie wanted to ask him «*And why didn't you do anything about it if you knew I was going to divorce? Why didn't you do anything? Why didn't you say anything?"*» But no word came out of her mouth, she was speechless. She remained speechless seeing how cynical Alan was, to cry after the way he treated her all those years. He reminded Valerie about her father. Camil also used to cry after he beat up Eva real good. After he abused and aggressed his wife, he was crying because his heart was broken by her.

Valerie just looked at Alan, she did not say anything else, he did not say anything else. But rarely did she see a more disgusting image. The abuser crying after the abuse...

Valerie changed the subject, Alan left very soon and she was not going to see him soon. Another strange thing for Valerie was how Alan's sister was looking at her after she moved out. She noticed she was looking very insistently to her belly. At first, Valerie did not understand why. Then, it hit her: she thought she was pregnant. She thought she was pregnant and that's why she moved out and divorced! Valerie laughed and laughed when she understood this. Her divorce did not take place for something like this. She planned and waited for the divorce for years and years. And she did it now because she finally saved the money she needed for the down payment for an apartment. Of course, she could have first bought the apartment and then divorce, but then she had to split the apartment with Alan. If she went out into a rented apartment, divorced and only after that bought the apartment, he could not have any claim.

Valerie needed a lot of things in her rented apartment. First thing she did was to buy a four liter pot in which she could cook. Then a colleague of hers offered to take her to Sibiu, to Metro with her boyfriend and his car, there she could find everything she needed. Valerie bought glasses, a clothes drier, a quilt, food for her and for Victoria. Victoria was very happy they went to Sibiu, she adored to shop with her mom, as her mom could never say no to her. After they finished shopping, they went to McDonalds. Victoria did not like the food there, but she liked the toy she got with the Happy Meal. Then they got home and unpacked everything they have bought.

Valerie could never invite friends over. While she was a girl at Mineville,

Camil did not like it too much. While she was a student, Alan was not a particularly hospitable person. While she was staying at her in-laws, it was out of the question. Now, when she finally was in a place rented by her, she could finally invite someone over. She invited her boss for dinner. Valerie was grateful to him. He always treated her with respect, appreciated her work, cared for her and for her health, unlike her own husband. She knew he liked very much tripe soup and cabbage rolls, so this was what she cooked for him.

It turned out to be a very nice quiet dinner, only Valerie, Victoria and her boss. Victoria acted very naturally in his presence. Valerie was a little afraid her little girl will behave awkwardly in the presence of men, as she never had a father, but fortunately this was not the case. She showed him the old family pictures, the old pictures of her mom and could not help saying:

"*Isn't my mom beautiful?*" asked Victoria with all her sincerity.

"*Yes, she is beautiful.*"

"*She is the most beautiful in the world, right?*"

"*Well, I don't know about that.*"

"*What do you mean? Who is more beautiful than my mom?*"

"*Well, you cannot compare your mom with Brigitte Bardot for example. It is like to compare a local car with a Porsche.*"

Valerie did not enjoy especially this comment of her boss. She knew she wasn't well dressed, she never wore make-up, she never went to a hair dresser, but her boss could have humored her a little bit. The situation was saved by Victoria who immediately asked:

"*Who was Brigitte Bardot mom? And what is a Porsche?*"

"*Well, Brigitte Bardot was a famous French actress, one of the most beautiful women in the world. And Porsche is a very expensive German car.*"

Valerie's mind was still processing the comparison of her boss «*Well, poor little local car, maybe it's not snazzy like those German cars, but you can solve your problems with it. You can carry many stuff with it. You can bring home your crops and your hay from the field with it. It carried us so many times. At least you can use it for heavy works, in all kind of conditions and on any kind of road and it is cheap and not hard to upkeep. Hmmm, actually I am like a local car. I don't need much money to survive, I am good to be used for heavy works. Yeah, I really am a local car, he's right! This is why I attract a certain type of men. I attract the ones that want to get as much as possible from woman with whom they don't have to spend a dime!»*

The evening ended nicely and quietly, Valerie felt pleased she was able to put together this small dinner for her boss, as poor as she was, in the one room of her little apartment.

Victoria seemed to be fine with the idea of the divorce. However, her schoolmistress noticed she changed a bit in time. This was quite normal, but still. She told Valerie this and the two women promised one another they will speak with Victoria and keep each other informed.

"My dear girl, we did not speak yet about the divorce. How do you feel about it?"

"I'm fine mom. I'm OK."

"Do you miss your father?"

"No, I've always seen him once a month all my life, I continue to see him once a month, so what changed?"

"Do you want us to talk about it? You seem a little quiet lately ..."

"No mammy, I'm fine. I was just thinking..." and her beautiful little eyes filled with tears.

"Yes my love?"

"I was thinking my colleagues live in big houses. And they have a father and a mother, they go together on holidays. You know..."

"I know my love, and I'm sorry. It's not your fault. You are innocent. It's my fault, I just did not know how to choose the right man and so you ended up without a father. I thought it did not make sense to remain with him. We never lived with him, we had no family, no home together. This is why I ended it. If we are alone, at least we know why we are alone. Can you forgive me my love?"

"I'm not mad at you mom. I was just wondering how come some children have everything and others..."

"I know my love, but this is how life is. But eventually it all turns out as it has to turn out. You know? The Universe has a funny way of putting all things and all men into their places."

"I know mom, but others have so much..."

"It's not about the amount of resources you have at your disposal, it's about how you manage them. Give a stupid man a big wealth, he will destroy it. Give a smart man one grain of wheat and he will grow a fortune out of it. We all have resources within, it's all about how we manage them. We all are given

chances and opportunities in life, it's all about how we grab them and use them for our advantage. Do you understand my love? In our situation, we can cry on each other shoulder or we can fight for our place under the sun. We're on our own now my love. It's all within our power. You are a very good, strong, smart and beautiful little girl. I am so proud of you and I trust you totally and love you more than anything. We'll be fine my love."

"*I know mammy. I love you.*"

"*Do you promise me something? Do you promise me you'll always tell me whatever bothers you? If it will be about me, I will change it. If it's something I cannot change, at least we acknowledge it and we discuss it and finally we find a solution. Promise my love?*"

"*Yes, mammy, I promise.*"

Wiping of her tears, Victoria continued:

"*You know, mammy, sometimes my friends ask me if I miss my father.*"

"*So, what do you tell them?*"

"*I ask them "Hey, have you ever eaten a mango?" "No, I haven't." Do you miss it?" "No, I don't, I don't even know what it is." "Well, it's the same way with me and missing my father.*"

This was a joke, Victoria told it to her mother to cheer her up and Valerie managed to put a smile on her face, but her heart was broken.

Valerie prayed for her little girl every day. She begged God to take care of her daughter, to give her the strength to overcome everything and provide the best for her daughter.

Not long after they moved, Eva decided to come to live with them for while. Fortunately, Camil agreed, so Eva came to Streamtown. She knew her daughter did not have much, so she carried a lot of things for her: dishes, kitchen appliances, blankets, pillows and of course food. Even though they could buy food in Streamtown too, the food from Mineville always seemed to taste better. Eva did not have a direct transportation from Mineville to Streamtown. The easiest way for her was to travel by train from Mineville to Teaville and then from Teaville to Streamtown she had to come by bus or by a car. It was a trip of about 30 kilometers and there was not a direct bus between the two small towns, you had to take a bus from Teaville to Julestown, and then another bus from Julestown to Streamtown. Considering the large amount of baggage brought by Eva, Valerie decided to take a taxi for this. So she and Victoria got on a taxi and went to the railway station of Teaville, picked up Eva and the baggage and returned with the same taxi. It cost a lot of money, but there was no other way to solve the issue.

Eva coming to stay with them had a very good effect on their moral. Eva cooked for them and she was always home. It was heartwarming for Victoria to come home from school and find a warm lunch on the table. On the other hand, Valerie was peaceful her little daughter did not stay alone at home until the evening when she arrived home. Finally, Eva was happy too as she was taking a break from Camil.

With the arrival of Eva though, another problem arose. In the room there was only one bed. Eva said she did not mind to sleep on the floor. Of course, Valerie could not accept this situation for more than a couple of days. She spoke with her boss about this and he said she could go on a lunch break to town, buy the folding armchair and take it home, then return to work.

"*With whom shall I carry it from the store home?*" wondered Valerie.

"*Why don't you speak with our colleague from transport, surely he knows some guy with a little pick up van.*" answered her boss.

"*You think he will accept?*"

"*Just tell him I asked him to do this. He'll accept.*"

"*Thank you very much for your help!*"

"*Don't forget to tell him to come with another man, so that they can carry it up to the third floor. I hope you'll not carry it up by yourself!*"

"*I can't carry it up three floors carrying it by myself. It's an armchair that can be folded out to a bed. My mom came to us and she has no bed to sleep on, you know...*"

"*It's a good idea to buy one of those.*"

"*Thank you again.*"

Valerie spoke with the guy from transport and told him the next day in the lunch break she wanted to solve this problem. They agreed and the next day Valerie went to a furniture store in Streamtown. She found a nice, robust armchair which could be opened and turned into a nice, one person bed. She bought it, called the guy with the car. He came with a helper, they went to Valerie's block and carried up the armchair. Valerie paid them and was very happy Eva had a bed to sleep on.

The three girls were very happy together, they loved each other and felt free. Eva woke up first every morning. She woke up around four o'clock. Even though she was retired for fourteen years now, she still kept her habit to wake up at four, just like she used to do when she was working. She made the coffee. Then Valerie woke up at six o'clock and prepared to go to work. They drank their coffee together, Valerie adored drinking coffee with her mom, they could speak about all kind of stuff. Valerie woke up fifteen minutes earlier just to enjoy every morning these chats. Valerie woke up Victoria at a quarter to seven. Valerie thought the way a person is woken up was very important. She went near her daughter, kissed her very gently and whispered:

"*Victoria, my love, it's time to wake up.*"

No reaction.

"*My little one, it's time to wake up.*"

Victoria just mumbled:

"*Hmmm, what?*"

"*You have to wake up my love.*"

"*What? Why?*"

"*Because you have to go to school.*"

"*Yeah, yeah, can I sleep five more minutes?*"

"*Yes, my love, I'll let you sleep five more minutes.*"

After five minutes, Valerie came again.

"*Victoria, my dear, it's time to wake up.*"

"*Oh, again? I don't want to wake up!*"

"*You have to wake up.*"

"*But why?*"

"*You have to go to school.*"

"*But I don't want to go to school.*"

"*You have to go to school, all children go to school.*"

"I don't care what all the children do. Don't you always tell me I'm not like other children?"

"*Yes, I tell you, but for this one you have to be like all the other children.*"

Finally, Victoria woke up and went to the bathroom. By when she got out, she was smiling and in a good mood. She started to prepare for school. Valerie left to work at a quarter past seven, then at half past seven Victoria left to school, with a sandwich and apple, as unfortunately they never ate in the morning. Victoria, just like all children, had to carry a very heavy schoolbag. They usually had six classes every day and they had to carry several notebooks and books with them. They had no places arranged in the school where they could leave some of their things. If they had also sport or drawing class, they had to carry an additional package. This heavy baggage, combined with the continuously decreasing number of sport classes led to generations and generations of children with back problems. Valerie raised the subject once at school, just as she raised the subject of sexual education for children. Of course the answer was invariably for both issues that it was not in the official school program, so nothing could be done in the matter. Valerie did not see anything extraordinary in explaining her daughter about sex. Whenever her daughter asked her about this, she explained her calmly and naturally. Valerie could not understand why for a parent it's such a taboo to speak of these things with his or her child. If the child is curious, he or she was going to find out anyway, especially nowadays when the media and the internet bombs us with all kind of aggressive information. Isn't it better if the child finds out about the matters of sex from a normal, clean person? Why should a child remain with the impression that sex means what in a pornographic films happens, when he or she can remain with the impression that sex is what happens between two persons that love each other? Why shouldn't a child know how he or she can protect himself or herself? Why all that guilt and shame and hiding?

When Victoria was still very little, many times there were acquaintances that asked her:

"*Do you want the stork to bring you a little brother?*"

"*No, I want my mother to give birth to a little girl.*" She was raised since she was a little girl that there is nothing extraordinary in conceiving or giving birth to a child. It is just as normal as any other human function.

Eva was happy to remain alone for a few hours after the girls left. She and Camil have retired in 1990. In 1990, one year after the Revolution, most of the state companies were closed. Hundreds of thousands of persons had to be sent home. Those who fulfilled the conditions for retirement, have retired. The others became unemployed. Since then, they have been at home together all the time. Eva has been abused by him for decades. She did not divorce him, but she found it harder and harder to live with him. Camil was a very violent and difficult man. The only good thing about him was that as he was getting older, he could not drink so much anymore and when he did not drink, he was almost bearable. But he was still drinking from time to time, in spite Eva's pleads to stop. He got into a point when he drank so much, that he turned blue and fell unconsciously on the floor. Eva picked him up and called emergency and he was saved. When she told him about it, he said she was lying. He just did not understand that drinking could kill him. After all their rocky marriage of over forty years now, Eva was grateful to have a few hours on her own.

One day, before Victoria came home from school. Eva got a visit from Valerie's mother-in-law. She said she came to see her, but Eva understood why she came. She wanted to see how bad things were going for Valerie after she went away from them. After about one hour of gossip, she prepared to leave. Just before she went, speaking about her daughter, she told Eva:

"Can you imagine? What did my daughter get after her two years of marriage?"

"What did Valerie get after fourteen years of marriage to your son? After cooking for all of you, after washing the laundry for the six of you with her hands, after cleaning the house for you, after working in the field like an animal for you, after carrying cement and bricks for the renovation of your bathroom and replacing the tiles on the roof and so on and so forth, after giving your son money so many times, after changing her name, her religion, after leaving her family for your son, what did Valerie get after all this?" replied Eva. But she got no answer to this one. This question remained unanswered by Alan's mother, even though she usually had an answer for everything.

Victoria visited once in a great while her grandparents from her father's side, but quite rarely. Alan's mother was always asking her:

"What should I give you? Are you hungry?"

"No, no, thanks. I have everything I need."

"Come on, at least some fruit? You know, the grapes are ripe. Want some?"

"No, grandma, thank you. Mom bought me grapes."

"I know your mother buys you grapes, but these are from me."

"Thank you, grandma, but I don't want any."

Valerie never taught Victoria to act like this, but she was proud about the way her daughter behaved.

Valerie and Victoria were very grateful to have Eva with them. When they came home, lunch was ready and warm, the dishes were washed.

Victoria could just eat and start doing her homework. Victoria has always been a very diligent little girl. She did not need to be pushed by her mother to study. Valerie repeated her over and over again:

"You don't study for me, you study for yourself. If you study and get a university degree, you will be able to get a better job. If you don't study, you'll end up working hard for just a little money. It's your choice, Nobody forces you to study. You are not obliged to go to school either. You can be a shepherd. You don't need education to become a shepherd."

"I know mom about the shepherd, you already told me. I got it."

"If you got it, you'd better study harder. Because I know you've got the brains for it. You got what it takes, you just have to work harder. The hard work is what makes the difference."

On Saturday morning, they all went to the supermarket to buy what they needed for the following week. Then in the afternoon Valerie and Victoria cleaned up the house, Valerie washed the laundry with her hands, as they had no washing machine. She used a plastic tub to soak and wash the laundry, then the bathtub to rinse them. Fortunately, they had a very small balcony where she could dry the laundry.

On Sunday morning, Valerie and Victoria went to church. At noon they came home and all three of them had lunch together. They were in harmony, chatting peacefully. No aggressor with them. These lunches, full of love and peace, were the best food for their souls. After lunch, they watched some TV, or took a nap or just chatted.

The peace of one Sunday afternoon was interrupted by a strong knock on the door. Valerie went to open the door. The owners were at the door. The young pair and his mother and a couple of people Valerie did not know.

"*Hello. Are we disturbing?*" asked the young man owner.

"*Hello.*" answered Valerie almost as a question. She could not understand what they wanted on a Sunday afternoon from her, without a phone call to warn her, nothing.

"*We would like to visit the apartment if it's OK with you.*"

"*What can I say…*" answered Valerie and opened widely the front door.

All five of them came into the house. Looked at everything. Even in the saucepan that was on the stove. In the bathroom. They came into the room where Victoria and Eva were. They looked at them. Valerie was wondering what did they want to see, the apartment or their faces?

When the visit was over, the young man explained Valerie:

"*I'll come tomorrow to discuss with you about this.*"

"*I don't understand. What is this about?*"

"*We'll speak tomorrow.*"

Valerie started trembling after they left. She was panicked. What was she going to do? It took her months to find this place, if they forced her to leave, where was she going to move now? With the divorce, and Victoria and all? Eva and Victoria felt how scared she was and they tried to give her courage. Victoria was the sweetest of all:

"*Don't worry mammy, we'll figure this out. Isn't this what you always tell me? No matter what problem we have, if we sit down and discuss it, we can find a solution. I know that you are the smartest and strongest mom in the world, I am sure you'll find the best solution for this.*"

Valerie kissed Victoria on her forehead. She did not feel smart or strong, she felt lost and helpless. But her daughter's love and trust meant the worlds to her, she could not give up, she could not disappoint her daughter.

The next day, after she came home from work, the young couple of owners came to discuss with her. He was doing all the talking.

"*I am sorry to tell you, but you will have to move out.*" he said.

"*What?*" asked Valerie.

"*You have to move out. We found some people who want to buy this apartment.*"

"*How come you found them? You rented the apartment out. I told you I wanted to rent on the long term. And now after two months you are kicking me out?*"

"*We are not kicking you out. Please try to understand me. They offered me 400 million crowns for this apartment. I could not get so much on it in a million years. You would do the same if you were me.*"

"*No, I wouldn't. If I were you, I would not try to sell the apartment after I rented it out.*"

"*For this amount of money you would.*"

"*No, I wouldn't. And I told you I wanted it for long term. I am in the middle of a divorce. I brought here some pieces of furniture.*" Valerie looked at him showing all that she felt in that moment.

"*Don't look at me like that.*"

«*Wow, he doesn't like how I look at him. Just like Camil. No matter how bad a man treats you, he expects you to look at him smiling and obedient, otherwise he is disturbed*» thought Valerie.

"*I will look at you as I like. So, when do I have to move out?*"

"*This weekend.*"

"*What? This weekend?*"

"*Yes, they give me the money only if they can move in on Monday.*"

"*This is not fair. It's unheard of.*"

"*Look, I want to help you.*"

"*Really…*"

"*Yes, really. Please don't be ironic. We have some friends that have an empty apartment. You can move there if you want. Of course, the rent is 150 euro a month.*"

"*Well, this is all very nice.*" concluded Valerie. She continued: "*I will let you know the exact day when I can turn you over the apartment and we can settle our scores. OK?*"

"*Yes, thank you.*" and the owners left.

CHAPTER 10

Two months after she rented her first apartment, right in the middle of her divorce, Valerie got notice from her landlords that she had to leave the apartment in a few days. Valerie thought it over. She could not find another apartment so fast, not with her salary. It took her months to find a decent apartment with the 65 euro she could pay for the rent. And now she had only a few days to move out. Of course, she could find a cheap apartment to live in, but those were in terrible condition. She was not concerned about herself, her concern was her daughter. She could not take her daughter just in any place, she needed to have heating and windows that closed and at least a stove in the kitchen, especially now when the divorce was ongoing and she was going to be visited by a social worker to see the living conditions of the child.

Valerie could not risk to lose her child after all she's been through. She was starting to believe she was not capable to get by on her own. So she decided to go back to her parents, to Mineville. She will come a few times more to Streamtown until the divorce was over and that was it. Victoria will move to a school to Mineville and she will find another job in Mineville. Under the pressure and the deadline she was subjected to, this was the best solution she could find.

Next day, Valerie went to work and told her boss she had to speak something with him.

"Yes, Valerie, what is this about?"

"I have to tell something. I have to quit."

"What? Why?"

"Well, you know the rented apartment where I live."

"Yes, what about it?"

"Well, yesterday evening the owners came and told me I have to move out, because they want to sell it."

"OK, you have to move out. So?"

"I have to move out until Sunday. I cannot find another apartment until Sunday. It took me months until I found this place. The rents are expensive in Streamtown. I cannot find something decent so fast with my salary."

"Alright, did you start to search?"

"No, I did not start to search. I'm taking my child and I go home to Mineville. Therefore, I have to quit. I'm sorry it's at such short notice, but I don't know what else to do."

"Alright, alright, don't push the panic button. Let me think."

"There's nothing to think about. This is the situation."

"Yes, there is to think about. What's the matter with you? Alright, so your landlord kicks you out, so what? It happens all the time."

"Yes, but the agreement between us was that I rent for long term."

"Did you sign a contract?"

"No, I didn't. They said they trusted me."

"Of course they said so. And in the meantime, they were searching for somebody else. Most likely they found somebody who is willing to pay them more for the rent. It happens all the time. So what, kid? This is the way life goes! And what stupid decision did you take? To go to Mineville. I mean where did you come up from with this idea? Clearly, you didn't think it over! Is it worth to lose your job because that guy is an asshole? After all you've worked here?"

"It's not worth it, but tell me, where am I going to go?"

"Let me give a couple of phone calls, alright? Give me a couple of hours. We'll figure something out."

"Alright, if you say so."

"Of course I say so. Now go back to work, let me do the thinking."

"*Alright.*" Valerie smiled gratefully. "*Thank you.*"

"*OK, OK, kid.*" her boss smiled back at her.

Valerie was aware this was the best boss she was ever going to have. She had a great relationship with him. She loved him like a brother. She could tell him anything, he listened to her, appreciated her and valued a lot the hard work she was putting in.

After a few hours, her boss called her back into his office.

"Look, I've spoken with a couple of people. There is a place to rent and

it's free. The only problem would be that it is not 65 euro, but 75 euro. What do you say?"

"*I say it's great! When can I see it?*"

"*Write down the phone number and call them.*"

"*OK, I will. Thank you for your help!*"

"*It's fine, kid, you're welcome. Call them and go solve your problem.*"

Valerie went the same evening to see the apartment. It also had only one room, but it was larger than the first one, with a beautiful balcony that had a table and two armchairs. It was downtown, in a very good location. It was on the first floor. It was perfect for her. She proposed to the owners to make a little contract. They agreed. The price was 75 euro. She could move in immediately.

Valerie went home and gave the good news to her mom and her daughter:

"*Hey, girls, I have good news!*"

"*What is it mammy? What?*"

"*I found another apartment. We're moving on Saturday!*"

"*This means we don't go to Mineville? I don't have to change school?*"

"*Yes, my love, this means you don't have to change the school. It is spring, I hope they'll let us stay there until summer when you finish school. Then we'll see what we'll do.*"

"*Oh, mammy, I'm so glad. I told you you'll solve this. I knew it.*"

"*Actually, I did not solve it, my boss did.*"

"*Well, that's very nice of him.*" Eva concluded.

The girls started packing. It was Wednesday and on Saturday they had to move out. Valerie spoke with some other guys to help her move. They promised her they will help her with the car and the pieces of furniture she had. The rest of the stuff: the clothes, the books, the dishes, pots and pans she had to carry on her own. Victoria was still too little to carry and Eva was over sixty years, so she had to do it by herself.

She called the owner on Friday evening and told him on Saturday morning she was moving out, so he had to come to take over the apartment. He did not come, he sent his wife. The young woman tried to mumble some apologies, but Valerie did not have patience for that. She just gave her the paid invoices, read together with her the water, gas and electricity counters, showed her the calculations and asked back for the deposit money and for the one month rent paid in advance, as she was kicked out after she paid for the three months, but she lived there only two months. The moving guys came and carried down the furniture pieces. They came with a smaller car this time, they loaded on it all that was possible and left the rest of the stuff in front of the block. Valerie brought down from the apartment all the other things and waited for them to return. She had sent Eva and Victoria to the new apartment before it all started, so that they could open the door for the moving guys with the furniture. They went by foot, holding each other hands.

Valerie waited for almost two hours for them to return for her, in front of the block, with all her stuff there. People were looking at her, but she didn't care. All she wanted was to be over with it.

The three girls cleaned up the new apartment and put all the stuff in place real fast.

Valerie's divorce was finalized after two months. It was easier than she expected. At the first hearing, the judge presented the case and read the requests of the plaintiff, that was Valerie. Alan agreed with all she asked. The judge said the social investigation will follow and that there will be a second and last hearing. After they came out from the first hearing, Valerie actually jumped happy at Alan and kissed him.

"*What was that for?*" asked Alan.

"*Thank you for not causing any trouble. Thank you.*"

For the social investigation, a social worker came to Valerie's apartment to check out the living conditions of her and child. It all went well. Another social worker visited Alan in Stevilleand asked him all kind of questions. He did not know the answer to all of the questions, for example he did not know exactly in what grade his daughter is. This made the social worker think. Then, when she heard that he visited his daughter once a month, it all became very clear to her. The results of these investigations were presented at the second hearing at the court house. Valerie also had to bring two witnesses. One of the witnesses was her mother and the other one was one of her colleagues. Alan did not even show up at this second hearing and nobody from his family showed up, even though the trial took place in Streamtown. The judge ruled in favor of Valerie. She got Victoria after the divorce, she could keep Alan's last name and Alan had to pay a monthly alimony of 2,5 million crowns.

Valerie was free. Now she had to take a credit and buy a place of her own, so that the apartment owners will not throw her out again whenever they wish. She started to search for something to buy that fit her budget. The situation did not look very well. In that year, 2004, the prices of the apartments doubled in Streamtown. She thought she had enough money for the advance payment for the credit, but by the time she was divorced, this money was not enough anymore. Since she moved out from her in-laws she could not save anymore, as half of her salary went for her rent. Valerie resigned herself, she decided to go on as she could, trusting things will turn for the best. Her motto was: if you cannot walk forward, then crawl. But don't ever give up. Don't ever stop.

At the company where she worked, things were transforming too. The owner of the company sold it to his biggest competitor from Europe. The new owner came with totally new ideas and new rules. Everything had to be changed, even if it was working OK. They changed the huge logos, painted on the outer walls. They painted everything with the new company's colors. They changed the rules and the working principles. After one month the new owner came to see the factory. He entered the receiving room and his eyes fell on the huge clock that was hung there. They forgot to change that clock and it had on it the logo of the old owner. He got very upset and made a big case out of it.

Before the previous owner left, the ex-economic manager, the child hater, promised Valerie he will pay all the translations Valerie did for the company. Of course, he never did. Then, the ex-managers threw a big party where all employees could come and order whatever food they wanted. «*Wow*» thought Valerie. «*I am so damn impressed. Before they leave, they throw us a piece of bone, after they got rich here on our work and our nerves and our personal lives sacrificed.* » Valerie refused to go to this party. Her colleagues could not understand her.

"*Why don't you come? We can order anything.*"

"*I can afford to eat whatever I want, I don't need their pity.*"

"*Why don't you come? We can take advantage of them. Come, and we'll order all kind of stuff even if we don't eat it.*"

"*You go and take advantage of them. I'm sick of them. They should have done this before, not now. They cannot buy me off with this. We work here and accept all the shit from them because we need the salary, we have to put food on the table for our children and we have to pay our credits. This is why we accept everything without comment. Do they consider we are stupid because we don't say anything? If they think they can buy my friendship with a free meal, they insult my intelligence.*"

The previous general manager, the one who hired Valerie, also heard she did not want to come.

"*Valerie*"

"*Yes, Sir.*"

"*I heard you're not coming to the party.*"

"*You heard correctly.*"

"*Don't you want a free meal?*"

"*I want respect, not a free meal, Sir.*"

After the take-over, Valerie's boss was one of the first ones that announced his resignation. As soon as he announced it, they started to look for a new person to take over his job. Valerie spoke with her boss:

"*You know, they want to hire someone for your position.*"

"*I know. I couldn't care less.*"

"*You know what I was thinking? What if I applied for it? Of course, they will never give me the job, I am aware of it. But I'm very curious what will they tell me.*"

"*Yeah, I like your idea. Go for it.*"

And she did. Valerie applied for his boss's position. As soon as he found out, the new general manager called her in his office:

"*Hello Valerie. Please sit down.*"

"*Thank you. What did you want to speak with me about?*"

"*I was informed that you applied for the new position.*"

"*Yes, it's true. I have the experience for it. I have been my boss's assistant for one and a half year now. Every time he was away, I have coordinated the office. I consider I am the best choice for it.*"

"*Well, we are honored that you are interested in it. But unfortunately...*"

"*I cannot have it, right?*" Valerie continued.

"*No, you can't. You see, you are so good in your position of coordinator of the office, we don't want to take you out of that position. We'll ruin the entire equilibrium, you understand?*"

"*Of course. Thank you for your time.*"

"Anytime. Really, anytime you wish to discuss with me, my door is open for you, Valerie. We appreciate the work you are doing."

Valerie went to her boss and told him the whole story. They had a good laugh.

"*Well, you have to admit he is a smart guy and classy too.*" her boss told her laughing.

After the discussion with Valerie, the general manager went to Valerie's boss and told him:

"Are you aware that Valerie has applied for your position? Did you know about it?"

He was convinced Valerie did not tell anything to his boss, that she just wanted to take his place.

"*Yes, I know.*"

"*You do?*" asked the general manager surprised. "*How do you know?*"

"*Because she came and told me she wants to apply for the job and asked my opinion about it.*"

"And what did you tell her?"

"*I told her to go for it. And honestly, I think she would be very good for it, but of course, it is your decision, not mine.*"

"*I like you two. You have a great relationship. Hmmm...*" and he left.

The new owner of the company brought his own managers. These were young people with no experience whatsoever in managing such a big production company as this was. They did not trust any of the employees they found there and treated them accordingly. Valerie did not feel comfortable in the new situation. She has worked very hard in the last one and a half year and now they treated her like this? Like everything she did was wrong? Like whatever she did she was trying to steal from them? She hoped to find a job in a different company. Her salary was not so great either, she could not save one penny.

Valerie's boss soon moved to a different company, also located in Streamtown. He promised her he will inform her as soon as there will be an opening position for her.

After he left, for around three months, nobody was hired for his position. Valerie coordinated the office by herself. When the decisions were above her responsibility she went straight to the general manager. Finally, on the 1st of September, a new guy was hired as her boss. Now, when this new guy became boss, first thing he wanted to do was to demonstrate everybody that he is the boss. Especially to Valerie of course. He found her there, unofficially the leader of the department, clearly capable to manage it well on her own for long term, she had to be put in her place. Valerie had no problem with this, she needed the job and she did not have a better alternative yet. Valerie never jeopardized her position, unless her back was covered. Her first concern was the material welfare of her child, the other issues came in after this.

Victoria got over her parents' divorce pretty soon. Valerie spoke with her every day and encouraged her to say out loud whatever bothered her. Victoria was close to finish the fourth grade in school. She could continue going to the same primary school until eighth grade or she could go to a very good high school that was in Streamtown. Normally, the high schools did not have children between fifth and eighth grade, but this particular high school had two classes of children they prepared with teachers from the high school. It was very hard to get in these two classes, there was an admission examination to get in, then it was very hard to study in those two classes, because the standards of the teachers were very high, but the children who studied in these classes were very well prepared and had no problem when they started high school.

"Vicky, I want to discuss with you where you will go for the fifth grade."

"Yes, mammy."

"I was thinking you should go to the high school for the fifth grade. It is hard to get in one of those classes, you'll have to take an exam. Then, it is a little far from our home, further than the school you go to now and you'll have to go by foot every day. The teachers are very exigent there, you'll have to study very hard, otherwise you'll fail. What do you say?"

"I was thinking about the same thing too. I want to go there. They are the best classes in town. Only the best children go there."

"Yeah, I heard, the best children and the richest children. You know that, my dear. You are very smart, but we are not rich. There you will see children that have it all. Can you handle it?"

"Yes, mammy, I'm fine with it."

"I want you to go to that school because there you can get the best education and they will prepare you for anything you decide to do in your life."

"I have already decided what I want to do in life. I want to become a doctor."

"Well, we'll see about that. There is still time to decide. Maybe you'll change your mind."

"No, mammy, I'll not change my mind. That is what I want to do since I was a little girl. Remember when you bought me that kit for little doctors, with those plastic instruments?"

"Yes, I remember." And Valerie smiled. Victoria's childhood was always a very pleasant memory for both of them.

"I think that is when I decided inside that I will become a doctor."

"OK my love, you'll become a doctor. But first you have to finish school. You still have eight years until you start university. It will be hard work and a lot of sacrifices. Other children will play and have fun and you will have to stay indoors and study. Are you OK with that?"

"Yes, mammy, I'm fine."

"OK then. I will start asking around what is necessary for the registration. You think you need some private lessons?"

"No mammy, I'm OK. I will also ask my colleagues and my teachers to get some info about the examination, but I think I'll pass it with no problems."

The preparations for this project of them started. Valerie searched for the phone number of the high school and called them up. Asked about all the details about the registration and examination. She prepared the necessary papers and registered Victoria for the upcoming examination.

The examination was on a summer morning. Valerie was at work as always, she could not go with Victoria. Eva went with her. Fortunately, there were some benches in front of the high school and Eva could sit down and wait for Victoria as long as it was necessary. The examination lasted for about two hours. Victoria came out smiling, this meant everything was OK.

"Well, how was it?" Eva asked her.

"It was hard, but I think I did OK. At point two, there was something I did not know..."

"Oh, don't worry about it. You'll pass it. I'm sure you'll pass it. You are exactly like me: smart, beautiful and very resourceful."

"Yes, grandma, I know I'm just like you." answered Victoria smiling.

Eva took her granddaughter by her hand and they walked slowly home together. Victoria felt very well having her grandma with them. Grandma was cooking for them every day. She was always at home, waited for her to come home from school with warm lunch on the table. Even with the little money they had left after paying the rent and utilities, the three girls got by very fine. There was always healthy home cooked food in the house, they never spent money on those unhealthy snacks or sodas from the supermarkets. Valerie never bought those and since Victoria did not grow up with them, she never asked for them. The only luxury they afforded were fruit and those were plenty in the house.

Victoria passed the admission examination to the one of the two best classes in Streamtown. After the examination, her holiday started, so she went to Mineville with Eva for a few weeks. While Eva was in Streamtown with the girls, Camil lived alone in Mineville. He said he did not mind, but the truth was he felt very lonely without his wife. Victoria liked to go to Mineville. It was a totally different life style here than at home. The best thing was that she was on holiday. Then, she spent a lot of time with Eduard. Eduard took her to the movies, to the public libraries and they discussed a lot about all kind of subjects. Even though Eduard was not like Valerie at all, he was not permissive and had totally different views about life, he really loved Victoria.

Valerie wanted Victoria to be in contact with different types of life styles and different type of adults and children. She thought one of the best qualities one can have in the modern world was adaptability and in order to be adaptable, one has to be used to be in all kinds of situations and to interact with all kinds of persons. Most of the parents kept their children 'protected' all their childhood. When the children were small, they kept them home. "*If they go to the kindergarten, they get sick immediately.*" So they did not take them to the kindergarten. Valerie considered this was not the right way, she considered the right way was to take them to the kindergarten, but strengthen their immune system, so that they get used to being exposed to germs and not get sick. "*If I let him/her play with those children, he/she will learn only bad things from them.*" So they did not let them play with other children. Valerie considered the right way to let them play with other children, but teach them to distinguish what is right and what is wrong and explain them what happens if they did the right thing and what happens if they did the wrong thing. "*If I send him/*

her to the grandparents/ aunt/ uncle they don't treat them as I do at home." Valerie considered the child has to go every now and then in different environments, so that he/she gets used to it, he/she learns to get by in every environment and every situation. All these 'trainings' of the child did not mean the parent had to let the child on his/her own, to do whatever they wanted. A parent must always keep a close eye on the child, but firmly and discretely, so that the child does not feel neither controlled, nor neglected. The child has to feel he/she is master of his/her own life, but with the deepest love and total support of his/her parents.

As a result, Victoria turned out to be a very sociable, popular girl, appreciated by the other children as well as by the adults she got in contact in. Of course there were some that treated her with hostility, out of envy mostly. But Victoria discussed it with her mom and just like her mom, after she understood what the adversity was about, she just got over it.

"Mom, I have to tell you what happened today in school."

"Tell me my love."

"I was at class and at a certain point I yawned. I did not mean to do it, it just happened, I did not even realize it until my mouth was already doing it."

"So what? I also yawned in school many times, I don't know why. I don't even think it's because you're bored, I think it's mostly because of lack of oxygen."

"Yes, but the teacher saw me. She told me I was rude and that I did not get my basic education from my parents."

"Well, she's the teacher. You have to respect her, even if you think she overreacts. First of all, she is older and you have to respect that and secondly she attended school so many years, so you have to be polite with her. You understand my love?"

"I understand mom, but she told me I have to read the "Code of good manners", that book, you know?"

Valerie thought it was a little exaggerated. Victoria wasn't at all the rudest child in class. On the contrary. So what was the problem with this teacher? Well, whatever the problem was, Valerie was not that kind of parent that told her child that he or she was right no matter what and that the teacher was a stupid idiot, she always said surely the teacher had some reason to act like this and that the child had to adapt to the teacher, not the other way around. Valerie knew already how the real life was. After you get married, your husband's family will not adapt to you, you will have to adapt to them. After you get a job, the company and your boss, will not adapt to you, you will have to adapt to them. If you wait to the real world adapt to you, you will get excluded. The world does not wait for you, it just moves forward, it's you who has to keep up with it, not the other way around. So she answered her daughter:

"Victoria, I think her reaction was exaggerated, but if she said you have to read the book, you will read it. It's good for you to read that book, I also read it when I was you age, you learn interesting things from there. Who knows what's the matter with your teacher? Maybe she was angry for something. You have to be more careful at her classes, that is all. You'll get read of her sooner or later, until than try to cope with it."

"Alright mom."

Things were not rosy at all at Valerie's job. Her new boss acted like a jerk. There were all kinds of decisions that were taken before his arrival and the department acted according to those decisions. Whenever he found out about them, he made a great deal about it, shouted at Valerie like a mad man. Valerie tried to explain him the decision was taken by the general manager before his arrival, it wasn't her decision, what was her fault? Then he went to the general manager to complain about Valerie and the general manager confirmed him the decision was taken by him, not by Valerie and this happened in the months when there was no department manager. So he calmed down for a period, until the next situation appeared. Valerie's life was very hard at work. She could hardly resist there, but she could not leave, she had no other job to go to and she needed the money. Who will support her and her daughter? Alan was not paying alimony, even though the judge ruled he had to pay every month. He explained Valerie that he had some financial difficulties, he had to change his job, Valerie did not understand exactly if he quit his job or if he was fired. The thing was he did not give them any money. Valerie felt trapped and totally desperate. At work she could not cry, she wouldn't give that satisfaction to her boss. At home she could not cry, her daughter would have seen her. So many times, she cried while she was going home by foot from work. She just walked on the street and cried. People were looking at her, but she couldn't care less. She cried many times since she came to Streamtown, also back when she was married, and mostly out on the street or when they sent her out on the field to work. Nobody ever stuck out a hand to help her. They just gossiped satisfied with her misery. So why would she have minded what they thought of her?

In November, she finally got the call she expected so much from her former boss.

"Hey Valerie, how are you?"

"I'm fine, how about you? It's nice to hear you!"

"How are things at work?"

"They are terrible, absolutely terrible. This guy is an asshole. It's not enough he is stupid, he does not have any experience either. Do you know what he did before he came here? He was a busboy! A busboy! And now he is a department manager and he is annoyed that I know more than him. But I have been working here for more than two years already! Anyway... Tell me? How are things going with you?"

"Well, you know after I left from there, I got a job at another factory here in Streamtown. They were just building the factory back then, but now it's finished and they want to start to manufacture and sell. They start now the hiring and they need somebody in the position you are in now. What do you say? Are you interested?"

"Are you kidding me? Of course I'm interested! Whom should I send my CV and letter of intent?"

"Send it to me. I'll forward it to the right person and then you will be contacted by the person from human resources."

"Alright, I'll send it tonight. Thank you so very much for thinking about me!"

"It's OK, kid, we'll keep in touch. Take care."

"Yes, you too, thank you!"

Valerie was happy about this news. She wasn't eager to change her job, changing the job and moving was always a very stressful experience for her. But there was no way she could remain where she was. Her new boss was driving her crazy. She did not want to end up a total wreck, her daughter needed her sane. So she sent her CV to her boss and waited to be called to the interview.

Victoria has just started her fifth grade. It was hard for her. The teachers were very exacting. Children were at school from eight a.m. to two p.m. They had to carry those heavy backpacks to school and back.

Then, at home, they had so much homework to do for next day, that they could hardly finish it even if that was all they did all afternoon until late at night. Victoria was a smart and diligent girl, but even she had a hard time to keep up with this rhythm. Many times, in the evening, she broke down in tears. Valerie saw her and her heart was breaking, but she could not help her child. It was frustrating. Many parents would like to take over the hardships of their children, but that is not the way to help a child. The way to help a child is to teach him to overcome the hardships, always knowing you're right there for them. Valerie sat by her daughter's side on the bed and tried to lift her spirit.

"Mammy, I started to do my homework as soon as I got home. I started to do Math homework and I still did not finish it. I still have to write a composition and tomorrow we'll have a test in Geography. Look, it's already seven o'clock in the evening. What am I going to do? When shall I finish all this?"

"My dear, you'll finish. Just don't panic. Tell me: how can I help you?"

"You can't help me. You can't write my homework. You can't study for me. Are you going to give the test in my place tomorrow?"

"I can't give the test in your place tomorrow my love. But don't panic, don't give up. You'll finish."

"And this Math teacher, I think she's nuts. You know how many exercises she gave us for homework. Fifty! She's crazy! How can anybody do so much homework in one afternoon. And it's like this every day! Every single day!"

"Alright I understand. How do your colleagues cope? Did you ask them? How do they finish the homework? You are not more stupid than any of them. Did you ask them how they manage?"

"Well, yeah, we speak about this. Most of them don't finish their homework. Or they do only the Math homework, and not do the others."

"You see? If it is so much and so hard, nobody can do it. You just have to do the best you can."

"Yes, but I don't want to come home with a poor grade, mom. I don't want to disappoint you, mammy." and she cried even harder.

"My dearest, you don't disappoint me. You don't have to worry about disappointing me. There isn't anything you can do that could disappoint me. I know you do your best, I know you work hard. You don't cheat, you don't lie and you don't steal. There is no way you can disappoint me. Now, let me wipe

up your tears. Come one, my love. Oh, my dearest, dearest child." and Valerie hugged and kissed her daughter. "*Let's see. Give me a piece of paper and a pencil. We'll write down all you have to do and prioritize.*"

"*What does prioritize mean, mom?*"

"*To prioritize means to establish which are the most important tasks from a list of chorus you have to do. Come on, I'll show you.*" and Valerie took the paper and pencil and started to write. "*So, you have to finish your Math exercises. OK, then what? You have to write a composition. And you will take a test in Geography. Right?*"

"*Yes, well, I had some other homework too, but I already finished it.*"

"*OK. For Math. Ho many exercises do you have to do in total?*"

"*Fifty. Well, forty eight as a matter of fact.*"

"*OK. How many did you do already?*"

"*Thirty two.*"

"*OK, you stop doing Math. I take full responsibility. If tomorrow the teacher says something about you not doing all the fifty exercises, you tell her I told you so. OK?*"

"*Alright mom.*"

"*My opinion is let's go out on the balcony, sit comfortably in the armchair and after a short break I'll help you learn for Geography. You said you have to learn because you have a test tomorrow. You are already tired, later you will be even more tired and you will not able to memorize anything. This is priority one. Then, when we finish that, we'll write the composition. This is priority two. After that, you will go to sleep. This is priority three. It makes no sense to go to sleep very late, because tomorrow you will be tired and you will not remember what you learned today. Here's a tip: whenever you have to learn, to memorize, make sure you sleep enough. During sleep, your brain is sorting and putting in place the information it gets during day time. You have to let it time to sort and put in place the information, otherwise, when your brain will need, them, it will not find them. You know? It's like at home. If all the things are not in their place, you cannot find them. Even though you bought them and you know you have them, it is a total mess in your house and you cannot find anything. So, what good to have them? Well, your brain is cleaning and arranging information during sleep. You have to sleep when you study. OK, my love?*"

"*Yes, mom.*"

Victoria did as her mom told her to. Next day, Victoria woke up earlier as usual and made some more exercises for Math. In the end she did thirty eight exercises. Most of the other children didn't do even half of them. In the end, it all turned out just fine.

Two weeks after she sent her CV to her former boss, she as called for an interview. Valerie did good there and they agreed to hire her. Moreover, she got a bigger salary. They said they needed her right away, but she could not come to the new job right away. She had to give the notice at the current job and then wait to see when they let her go away.

The very next morning, Valerie gave the notice and informed her current boss she was quitting. He acted very surprised and talked nicely to her. He even called her out from the office into a meeting her and discussed at a very personal level. Like he wanted to understand why she was leaving. Valerie was not impressed at all and she would have loved to give him a taste of the hurt she experienced because of him. But she calculated in her mind «*I still need him to sign me the papers so that I can leave. If I am honest with him no, he will get mad with me and as stupid as he is, maybe he'll cause me trouble. Not because he really wants me to stay, he hates my guts, just like I hate him. Just to give me a hard time. So, I will act nicely with him, not say anything. I will be nice until I get from him what I need. The signature on my papers to leave. Then he can go straight to hell. Idiot, stupid asshole.*»

"*So, can we make you change your mind?*" her boss asked her trying to be the good boss that keeps the employees around him.

"*Well, you know, it's nice of you. But I really have to go. I go to a company where my former boss is. You know, we were very close and now I'm going to work with him again.*" said Valerie. She thought «*Oh, he will like this reason. As stupid as he is, he will interpret the wrong way that I was close to my boss. We were not close in that sense, we just worked very well together. Unlike with him. At least, he will let me go more easily when he hears this.*»

Valerie's reason worked. Her boss finished this so called convincing her to stay conversation immediately and let her go.

Working for a few months with a boss like this, Valerie reached the conclusion she was worthless in the company. Now, that she wanted to leave, she found she wasn't worthless at all. Two high level managers also called her for private discussions and insisted with her to stay. «*Well, it certainly looks they appreciate me. And they tell me now, after I decided to leave. Actually, I decided a long time ago to leave, it's just that now I have got the opportunity and I don't want to miss it. But if they appreciated me, why didn't they show this to me while I was still here? Why am I valuable only now when I found something else? And why did they let this asshole be my boss and treat me so bad? How could they even let this asshole be the manager of such a key department like ours?»*

This all happened in the beginning of December 2004. The company was organizing the Christmas party. The general manager had two secretaries. One blonde and one red. Nobody knew why he needed two secretaries. Word was that the reason was that one spoke English and the other spoke German. Well, the blonde one was inviting people to the Christmas party and when she got in Valerie's office, she looked at Valerie and said:

"*Oh, I almost invited you to the Christmas party. But you leave the company, so you're not invited.*"

"*Whatever.*" said Valerie. She did not intend to go to the Christmas party anyway. She did not spend any money on clothes on herself, she wouldn't even have a dress to wear.

When the general manager found out the incident however, he got very angry and scolded her:

"*Who told you not to invite her?*"

"*Nobody, but considering...*"

"*Considering what? Didn't I tell you to invite everybody? Isn't this what I said?*"

"*Yes, you did, but I thought...*"

"*You shouldn't have thought, you should have invited everybody as I told you. Valerie worked hard in this company since the beginning of this year. Now go to her and invite her to the Christmas party.*"

So the over-paid, arrogant blonde, wearing kilos of make-up and dressed up with clothes that were probably hundreds of euro worth, just like Valerie's salary, came to Valerie and invited her to the Christmas part. Valerie turned her down looking totally indifferent, but inside she felt just great.

Nobody could convince Valerie to stay. On the last day the general manager of the company she was leaving called her up on the office phone.

"*Hello. I'm the general manager.*"

"Hello, Valerie speaking."

"I'm glad I still found you. When do you leave?"

"Well, actually it's my last day here."

"We could not convince you to stay, could we?"

"No, it's not about convincing, it's just that I decided to leave for personal reasons."

"Alright, I respect that. I am sorry I am not in the company to tell you in person what I am about to say."

"I'm listening."

"I want to thank you for all that you've done in the company. I want to thank you for your strength and the hard work you've put in. We certainly are going to miss you."

"Thank you. Your words mean more to me than you can imagine. Thank you."

Valerie did not expect this, but it certainly did very good for her self esteem.

Valerie needed a lot of self esteem and moreover she needed a lot of strength as she was about to change her job again.

CHAPTER 11

Valerie started to work in the new company in the middle of December 2004, with no pause between jobs. Most of the persons took long holidays when they changed jobs, but not Valerie. Her culture of work would not have allowed this. Plus, if she went away from a company and she still had not effected holiday days, they were paid, so this way she could get some more money.

Valerie needed the money as she wanted to buy an apartment for her and her daughter as soon as possible. The plan was that she buys something as soon as she divorced. The problem however was that in the year following her divorce the prices of apartments have increased by 100%, it was the greatest boom in the real estate market. She searched and searched something to fit her budget, but with no success. Having to pay for the rent and also supporting now three persons from her salary (herself, her daughter and now her mother too who stayed with them), left her with nothing at the end of the month. Valerie translated and she also gave private lessons to make some more money. Now her salary also raised a little bit, so she hoped she could save some money, at least a little bit every month.

Alan was still in difficulty and still did not pay any alimony. Valerie was upset because of this and raised the subject several times when she spoke on the phone with him. All she got were promises.

Valerie came to this new company at the recommendation of her former boss. In this company he was the general manager and he had a totally different attitude, towards her and towards everything. Valerie was wondering where was that warm person with whom I could talk like with a good friend. She asked him upfront too, once. He explained that now he wasn't just a department manager fighting for his team, now he was a general manager and he had to think about cutting expenses and this kind of stuff. Valerie did not comment anything, but she didn't agree with this explanation. Wasn't the company just a bigger team? It wasn't a very large company either. In total, there were about 150 employees, compared with the previous company where she worked and where there were about 1.000 employees. The truth was that her boss did not feel comfortable here at all, things did not turn out as he expected. He did not see eye to eye with the owners and after a few months he left this company too, without as much as a word of goodbye to Valerie. Fortunately, the years of marriage and the years spent in her in-laws house made her strong and hard as a rock, maybe as insensitive as a rock too, but this was the reverse of her years of misery.

Valerie stood her ground in her position and did her job as good as she could. On the other hand, she searched frantically an apartment to buy. The prices were so high, she could not even get close. She just phoned, they told her the price, she thanked them and hung up. Just like in the times when she was pregnant and looking for a rent in Steville. One day however, she saw a notice for sale written by hand on a piece of paper stuck on the window of an old, abandoned little shop, in cheapest neighborhood of Streamtown. She wrote down the phone number and called. They told her the apartment was still for sale and the price was 450 million crowns. Valerie made some calculations and found that this was almost affordable for her. She established a meeting with the owners and went with Victoria to see it.

The apartment was in a block in a good state, compared to most of the blocks from this neighborhood. This part of town was the cheapest. Here stayed all the persons who did not have money. Most of them got their apartment from the state after the revolution. Some of them remained there as they could not afford something in a nicer area. Others managed to get out and now they wanted to sell the apartments from here and they were asking astronomical prices. They explained that this was the market, as it was a boom the real estate market, they were sure they could sell the apartments no matter how much they were asking for them. This was the case with the apartment visited now by Valerie. It belonged to the mother of the lady owner. The mother died and she inherited it. So now she wanted to sell it. It was on the fourth floor of a four floor block of flats. This was a problem, because the roofs of the blocks were in a horrible state and whenever it rained the water was pouring into the house. This caused mold and dampness and that typical smell of wet, unhealthy apartments. Of course there was no lift, so who stayed on the fourth floor had to carry up everything in their hands. These apartments were the cheapest and of course those from the ground floor, where other issues caused troubles and people avoided them too. Valerie would have liked to avoid these two floors too, but unfortunately she could not afford a place on a decent floor.

The apartment was full of ancient furniture and all kinds of old drapes and blankets. It all smelt like old stuff. There was also a refrigerator and a stove, old and dirty. There was no central heating. In those days, everybody had to install a central heating device if they wanted to have hot water and heating in the apartment. Before the revolution, in these neighborhoods of blocks there were central heating installations that provided heat and hot water for all the surrounding blocks. Of course, after the revolution, they were all abandoned and people remained some years with no civilized mean of heating and the old installations were taken over by wise guys who used them for their own personal benefits. The installation of central heating in an apartment was very costly for an average family. For a small apartment it cost around 1000 euro. Considering Valerie's income was around 180 euro per month at this stage, it was a great financial effort. On the other hand, the apartment was big, it had 26 sqm which was big for a one room apartment and had a nice balcony.

"*So, what would be the price for this place?*" started Valerie.

"*You know the prices now. Everything is going sky rocket in the real estate market.*"

"*I know. How much?*"

"*The apartment is clean as you can see. My mother lived here and it is very important for us to sell it to a decent person, like yourself. We wanted to ask more, but we are willing to let it for 450 million crowns.*"

«*Fortunately I'm a decent person.*» thought Valerie. «*Otherwise who knows how much they would ask for this dump.*»

"*Well, 450 million is a little over my possibilities. Can you let it go for 400 million crowns?*"

"*No, no way. Absolutely no. We've got offers for 500 million but we did not like the persons who were offering. Bear in mind that the block is a nice, quiet one. And you have everything, you can just move right in.*"

"Well, I don't know if I will be able to raise all that money at once. I have to talk with the bank to see how much credit they can give me. According to my calculations, 400 million crowns is as far as I can go."

"The price is 450 million lei, not a penny less. If you cannot raise all the amount at once, we are willing to wait. We are reasonable people."

"OK, then I'll discuss with the bank and I will get back to you. If you a reasonable, I think we can work something out."

Valerie did talk with the bank. She calculated everything carefully and she decided to go for it. She called the owners and told them she would like to buy the place, even though the price was a bit high for her. They repeated that they understand and that they were willing to wait as long as it was necessary. They all went to a notary to make a pre-contract. This was necessary to get the credit from the bank. Valerie got together all the documents necessary for the bank and applied for the credit. It took a few days until they called her to the bank and presented her all the payments she will have to make and the amount of the down payment she will have to make. Valerie was shocked. It was much, much more than initially promised in their advertisements. And she still had to give around 50 million crowns to the owner, as the credit from the bank was only 400 million crowns. Then, if she got the credit, she had to start paying installments. She could not continue to stay in the rented apartment, she had to move into the bought apartment and that was in deplorable state. It had to be renewed. Everything had to be thrown out and new furniture had to be bought. Central heating had to be installed. The roof was leaking for God sake. Valerie just tossed and turned all night in her bed. In the morning she decided to call up the owners and tell them they will receive the 400 million crowns as soon as she gets the credit from the bank and the rest of 50 million crowns in a couple of months. They said they were willing to wait. She could not do better than this.

"Hello, this is Valerie."

"Hello. How are you?"

"I am fine, thank you. Well, I have applied for the credit and they told me what I expected. The maximum amount I can get is 400 million crowns. This means I still have to give you 50 million crowns and unfortunately I don't have them just now. I have to pay the down payment and a lot of other expenses for the credit, plus what I will have to pay at the notary. My question is, if you

receive now the 400 million crowns, could you wait a couple of months for the rest of 50 million crowns?"

"That is out of the question. The price is 450 million crowns. We told you this and you agreed."

"Yes, I know the price is 450 million. It's just that I don't have now the whole amount. You receive now the 400 million and 50 million in a couple of months. You said you were willing to wait and that you are reasonable."

"We are reasonable and we shall wait until you get the amount from the bank, but we have to receive all the 450 million crowns at once, when you get the credit from the bank."

"Well, I cannot do that. In this case, I have to call off the whole thing."

"What? We made a pre-contract at the notary!"

"Well, we'll have to cancel it. See you at the notary tomorrow at 12 o'clock to cancel the pre-contract. Good-bye."

"Good-bye."

Next day Valerie met the two owners at the notary. The owners probably said a lot of things until Valerie arrived, but at least in front of the notary they did not say anything. It was the notary's turn to speak his mind.

"*Well, you changed your mind regarding the purchase of the apartment?*"

"*Yes. I did not mean to cause any trouble, but I really don't have all the money and it's better if I give up.*"

"*Well, she should pay a cancellation fee, right?*" said the notary turning to the owners.

"*There was no such provision in the pre-contract.*" said Valerie, very composed and cold hearted. «*What an asshole*» she thought.

"*No, there was no such provision in the pre-contract. We don't want any cancellation fee, we just want to make a paper that cancels the pre-contract.*" answered the owners.

"*It's not nice to change your mind like this. These people trusted you.*" continued the notary, turning back to Valerie.

"*I did not mean to break their trust. I just don't have enough money.*" answered Valerie.

"*Well, it is a fact of life*" continued the notary, turning again to the owners. "*The seller is serious, the buyer is not serious. The person who rents out the apartment is serious, the person who takes the apartment in rent is not serious. We should have thought of this and make a provision with cancellation fee in the pre-contract.*" continued the notary, speaking with the owners.

«*How easy for you to speak. You are the famous notary, with your nice office right downtown, with all your money and your big house and your big car. How easy is for you to speak. Ohh, and how serious the apartment owners are, really... I guess it's true what they say. The man who is full will never believe the man who is hungry.*» Valerie thought. But she did not say anything else, she just waited for the whole deal to be over.

Valerie continued searching for an apartment to buy after this story was over. Eva was still with them, but Camil was not doing so well. He did not complain about anything, but living alone affected him. He started having blackouts, when he collapsed and fell right down, no matter where he was. It happened out on the street and it happened in the house too. Once he fell near the balcony door and he broke it with his head. After he got up, he never remembered anything. If this would have happened after he drank, he wouldn't have been surprised. But it happened when he was sober. Eva discussed with Valerie and decided she had to return to Mineville. Of course, she would come to stay with them every once in a while, but not permanently.

Once Eva came back home, Camil went to several doctors to find out what was wrong with him. Finally, a cardiologist told him his heart stopped beating for a minute or two and that is why he had those blackouts. The only thing to solve this was for him to get a pacemaker. Camil discussed this with Eva and with Valerie over the phone. He was not so convinced he should get the pacemaker. It was expensive and he could get it only in Steville, no doctor in Mineville could put him a pacemaker.

"*Of course you'll get a pacemaker, dad.*"

"*I don't know. I mean it's so expensive and we have that kind of money.*"

"*I don't care it's expensive. I'll give you the money.*"

"*I don't know, I have to think about it.*"

"*It's nothing to think about. You'll go to Steville and you'll get a pacemaker. I'll ask around for a doctor in Steville who does this. And I'll give you the money. That's all.*"

"*Wait, wait, don't speak with anybody yet. Let me speak with my doctor first.*"

"What is there to speak? He told you what's the problem and he told you what you have to do. So, we'll do it."

"No, no, I promised him I'll think about it and inform him. The day after tomorrow I go and speak with him. I'll call you after that. OK?"

"OK, dad. I'll let you until the day after tomorrow. Then we'll go right ahead with the pacemaker. Hear you afterwards."

"Alright. Take care of yourselves."

"OK, dad, you too. Bye."

Two days later Valerie called her father again.

"Hey, dad, how are you?"

"I'm fine. And you? Are you OK? Victoria is OK?"

"Yes, dad, we are both fine. So, what did your doctor say?"

"He told me I am lucky. He told a team of doctors come from Steville with two pacemakers for two persons that have been waiting for them for a long time. And one of them changed his mind so a pacemaker remains not taken sort of speaking. He said I could get that remaining pacemaker. The best thing I don't even have to pay for it as it is covered by health insurance and since I am retired, I can get it for free."

"Hey, that's great. So you get it in Mineville, right? You don't have to go to Steville?"

"No, I don't. The doctors from Steville are coming here. I just have to check in the hospital on Friday. They will do all my analyses and On Monday I go into surgery."

"That's great dad, I'm very glad, this is great news. In weekend I'll come home."

"You don't have to come. We're fine, we'll get by with your mother."

"No, no, I'll come. See you on Saturday, dad. Bye."

"Bye, little one."

Valerie has always been close to her mother. With her father, the relationship was very complicated. Although she has been protected by most of the abuse and the violence that went on in the family while she was at home, she still knew what was going on. Many times she accused her father in her heart for all the wrong that went on in the family. But the older she grew, her heart changed a lot in regard of her parents. Her marriage falling apart, the hostility of the strangers amongst whom she was living, all their judgment and prejudice whispered obsessively into her heart «*Your true family are your parents and your child. Blood connections are sacred. They are the ones that will always stay by your side, no matter what.*» She thought back of her life and understood that her parents did not mean to hurt her, did not mean to deprive her of anything. They did what they could to the best of their knowledge. Detaching herself from them, living so many years far from them and struggling so hard to get by on her own, Valerie grew to love more and more her parents and forgave them from the bottom of her heart for the things from her childhood which hurt her.

She took out money from her bank account and in the same weekend she went to Mineville. Victoria was the happiest of all. She adored these adventures with her mom, when they went by foot to the railway station as nobody took them with a car and Valerie did not want to spend for a taxi. When they ate on the filthy, stinking train the sandwiches and fruit Valerie packed for the trip and they drank the tea with lemon and honey she made for the occasion. When they had to exchange three trains and travel for almost 10 hours to make a trip of 280 kilometers from Streamtown to Mineville.

Valerie had to go to work on Friday. She never missed from work, except for the holidays which were rare. On Saturday morning they arrived in Mineville. Together with Eva, they went to the hospital and visited Camil. His moral was fine, truly he was happy they came to visit him, even though he did not express it loudly. They stayed with him for a couple of hours, after which they went home. Valerie gave her mother a nice amount of money which she did not want to accept. Valerie insisted:

"*Take it, you need the money. There will be a lot of expenses with the operation. Believe me, I know. Please take it.*"

"*Alright, if you insist. Thank you. Are you OK if you give us this amount?*" Eva asked her.

"*Yes, I am fine. Don't worry about me.*"

Valerie and Victoria cleaned the house as well as they could. Eva cooked something for Camil and prepared some things he needed in the hospital. On Sunday she was going to visit him again. Valerie and Victoria went back to Streamtown on Sunday morning. On the way back, Victoria fell asleep on the train. She was tired. Valerie was tired too, but she could not sleep. She was thinking about her father. She was praying for the operation to go well. She was thinking about Eduard too. Eduard surely was not praying for his father. He always affirmed loudly that he did not love his father. That he wished he was dead. Eduard seemed to be stuck in the past. He hated his father when he was child at his parents' house. He still hated him now. He could not forgive him, no matter what. He drank, just to annoy him. He drank to punish her mother who was not strong enough to leave him, even though he knew how much he hurt all of them. He never kept a job on the long term, knowing this will annoy her parents. They were mean to her while he was little, they hurt him and abused him, now was payback time. But who was he punishing in fact? Wasn't he really punishing his own self? Who did he annoy in fact? Who could he not forgive no matter what?

Valerie felt that forgiving her parents, she healed her very own soul. Not forgiving her parents did not affect her parents. They could go on living without her forgiveness. Valerie felt that not forgiving her parents affected her, not them. It made her sick literally, not them. If she hated her parents, she actually hated a part of her. Wasn't she the result of the combination of a cell from her mother and a cell of her father? How could she hate a part of herself? Of course, when she was a child many times she thought she hated them. She wanted to get away from home. She considered them guilty because her childhood was not as she wanted it to be. But then she grew up. She went away into the great wide world. She saw the strangers were no way better than her parents. She saw there were no persons more honest than her parents. At least they did not try to act as they were somebody else than they really were. At least they did not steal and then go to church and act like saints. If Camil drank, he put the bottle and the glass on the table and he drank in front of the family. He did not drink hidden in the cellar and then did not claim that he hasn't been drinking for ten years, while everybody saw he was drunk. At least the meals were decent meals. Everybody could eat as much as they wanted, they did not have one chicken for six persons, they had four chickens for four persons. When they could afford it, of course. When they could not afford it, they ate bread with lard and onions and that was it. But they always stood up full from the table. At least her father did not abandon the family. He was bad to them so many times because he was always jealous, but the love for his family was beyond question. He never cheated on his wife and he was happy both times his wife told him she was pregnant. He did not tell her he wanted to divorce. No strangers she met could convince Valerie they were better than her parents.

Valerie felt good. She felt she did the right thing going home and visiting her father in the hospital and giving her parents some money for the operation and cleaning a little her parents' house. She really felt good.

Camil was operated and he got a pacemaker. He recovered very well and fast after the operation. In Mineville, things went back to normal. Valerie called her parents every other day and asked them how they were doing. Victoria was doing better and better in school. She was getting used to the high standards and coped with them better every day.

Valerie was cooking every evening after work. She did not want her daughter to eat any junk food. She did not even buy junk food, or sweets or soda, so there were no temptations in the house. Growing up like this, Victoria was not even tempted when she saw her friend eating such things. Valerie tried new recipes all the time. She always went a step forward and presented the food so that her picky daughter will eat it. For example, Victoria did not want to eat meatballs. So Valerie made her hamburger. She took the minced meat, made some larger meatballs out of it, but flattened. She fried it on both sides. Then put it in a bun with vegetables and that was it. Hamburger sounded much better than meatballs and Victoria liked it. In the weekends, they cleaned the house together. Twice a week Valerie washed the laundry with her hands. There was no washing machine in their rented apartment. The two girls were very happy and grateful for everything they had, for their freedom and for being together. And for all the little things they had. For the TV set, for the computer, for the radio set. For the clothes and the dishes. On Saturdays, they went shopping. On Sundays they went to church. Then they had lunch and went for a walk in the park nearby, for a picnic and also they took water from a spring there. Valerie was grateful she did not have to go to any outhouse. The bathroom was in the apartment and she did not disturb anybody when she went at night. Money was short, but Victoria did not miss anything. She had nice clothes, everything she needed for school and she ate healthy food. Valerie cut all the possible expenses for herself. It was not hard, as all of her life she was a very "*low maintenance*", inexpensive woman. She used to think probably this was the most appealing for Alan. He read her right, he saw he will not have to spend much with her.

One Sunday, after the girls ate, there was a knock on the door. Exactly like in the previous rent, the owner came unannounced with some people who wanted to see the apartment. They were interested to buy it. Valerie let them in, they looked at everything, even to what was on the cooker stove. When the owners were getting out on the door, Valerie asked them:

"Are you selling the apartment?"

"We don't know yet. We are thinking about it. We are very short on money."

"And you don't tell me about it? I have to find out like this?"

"We have not decided anything yet."

Valerie understood exactly what this meant. It meant they did not get the amount of money they were asking for yet, but as soon as they got it, they were going to sell the place. It wasn't an ultimatum yet, but there was no time to wait for the ultimatum.

Valerie started the search for another apartment right away. This time without any help. She asked around for weeks but she could not find anything she could afford.

She could not show this in front of Victoria, but she lost all her courage and confidence. «*What did I do wrong? Clearly there is a lesson here that I have to learn. This happens exactly like one and a half year ago. I need to learn something from here, but what? What? I was too brave? So what, I have to be more coward? I was too hardworking? So what, I have to be lazier? I was too honest? So what, I have to a liar? I was too proud? Hmmm, well, yes, I was proud. I was proud that I had the power to get away from it all. I was proud I had the strength to leave my husband. I was proud I was able to get by on my own. That's it, I was too proud. This means it's the humility lesson I have to learn. Alright, what is the thing that would humiliate me the most? Going back to my in-laws house. Yeah, absolutely, that's the thing that would teach my pride the hardest lesson. Oh my God, the very thought of it makes me faint. It's the greatest punishment ever. But I should look at the bright side. I still have my daughter. I still have my job. This is what's important. I'll go and ask my in-laws if they accept to have me back. This is the lowest I can go. At least, if I reach my lowest point, I cannot go lower than that. I can only go up from there."*

After weeks of searching for a new rent, Valerie decided to go back to her in-laws until she found something suitable or went away to Mineville for good. It was a heart-breaking decision for her. She stepped on her own pride and felt totally humiliated and defeated to do this. But as she analyzed more and more these feelings of her, she thought maybe this is what God wanted from her. Maybe He was teaching her a lesson of humbleness this way.

Valerie went to her in-laws on a lunch break from work. Only they were at home, Alan's sister was at work. She asked them very directly:

"*Look, I have some problems. The apartment where I stay with rent. They want to sell it. Hey all are going crazy with the selling of their houses. I looked and looked for something else, but I did not find anything to fit my budget. I wanted to ask you if I could come back here in rent? Could you let me stay with Victoria in one of your rooms and I will pay you rent?*"

"*We never sent you away from here*" her mother-in-law said.

"*I know you didn't. But if Alan did not want to come to stay with us...*" and in this point Valerie burst into tears without wanting it.

Her mother-in-law answered:

"*Yes, you can come back. And you don't have to pay any rent. You just have to pay for your share of utilities.*"

"*OK, thank you so very much. Could we move in on Saturday morning?*"

"*Yes, of course.*"

After she left from them, Valerie called up Alan and his sister to ask them if they would be disturbed if she moved back. They said they wouldn't be disturbed, so that was it. In the same evening she started packing.

On the following Saturday, Valerie and Victoria moved back to her in-laws house. Valerie decided not to analyze the situation very deeply, just take one day at a time. And search for an apartment to buy, no matter how small and bad, so that she could move out as soon as possible.

Valerie and Victoria moved back to her in-laws in August 2005. The next month, Valerie found a small, one-room apartment. It was quite small, only 20 square meters. It had a room, a kitchen and a bathroom and a 1 square meter little entrance. It was on the ground floor in a block that did not look so bad in the outside, in the cheap neighborhood of Streamtown. Valerie met with a woman who showed her the apartment. It was in a horrible state. The door and windows were very old, they did not close very well. The bathroom had no bath tub and the toilet and the sink were horrifying. Under the sink, some black, stinking black fluid oozed from somewhere. In the kitchen there was only an old, horribly dirt sink and nothing else. No stove cooker, nothing. The room was empty, with an old, musty parquet. In the rest of the house there was the original, green ceramic tiles. At least there was electricity and running water and hopefully also gas. The woman showing the apartment said the price was 400 million crowns, but Valerie had to go discuss with the owner about it.

Valerie called the owners and set up a meeting. The owners were living in a good neighborhood of the town, in a nice big house. They have got this little apartment for free from the state and now they wanted to sell it with more than 10.000 euro, without investing in it one single penny. This is the way things were going.

The negotiation did not take long. Valerie started:

"*So, how much is the apartment?*"

"*We want 400 million lei for it.*"

"*I can give you 380 million lei. What do you say?*"

"*390 million lei and that is the lowest we can go. And we shall not pay for any taxes at the notary or anything. This is the net amount we have to receive. You see, the apartment belongs actually to my son, who is working in Spain and wants to buy an apartment there. He needs the money for the down payment.*"

«*Wow, that's a nice story.*» thought Valerie.

"*Alright, 390 million lei it is. I must tell you I will have to get a mortgage credit to buy this. I don't have the money.*"

"*Well, I would prefer to receive all the money cash, without going to the bank and so on.*" said the old lady. "*But I will speak with my son about it. I will let you know.*"

"*OK, I wait to hear from you.*"

The very next day, Valerie was called up by the old lady and she told her son agreed to sell it to Valerie. He had nothing against the mortgage credit, he was getting one too in Spain. Valerie was glad to hear this. The very next day she went to a bank. To a different bank this time. At her first attempt to get a mortgage credit, the bank clerk told her their long boring story which hid exactly the most important things she should have known. Like the real cost she will have to pay from the beginning to the end. This time, Valerie had done her homework. She knew exactly what she had to ask. The bank clerk saw she knew what she was talking about, so he treated automatically with more respect. This was the banking market in the country. Like the entire country, it was a jungle. The tough ones, the fit ones got by. The others were coned in every possible way. There was no authority to defend the simple people's rights. The institution called The Office for the Consumer's Protection was just like the state it was representing: false, superficial, coward, ineffective, demagogical. Even if you asked their help, nothing was solved. They just sent you a cold answer which did not say anything.

Valerie brought to the bank as fast as she could all the necessary documents. Now, she had to wait for the approval of the credit. This of course was not done in Streamtown, it was done in the capital. They explained it could take a few weeks. Like somebody on a horseback had to ride to the capital with the application, wait for the approval and then ride back with the result to Streamtown. Well, it was understandable. It could take some weeks. Come on! In the era of IT and internet! How hard is it to check and application and send an email? She called the old lady and told her this. Of course the old lady told her she did not want to wait too much. And that she would have preferred to receive all the money at once, like she got it for the other apartment. She told Valerie again the story with the buyer of the other apartment, who came with all the money in his bag and just put it on her table. Valerie excused herself for not being able to do this. Not that she did not want to, but she just did not have all that money.

Valerie applied for a credit in euro. This way her apartment cost 11.111 euro. Many got credits in euro because the interest rates were lower. The only risk was that euro could go up like crazy, while the salaries in crowns stayed the same.

The approval of her application came in a few days after all. The bank clerk told her she could come on Tuesday with the owner. Valerie was happy she was so close to buying her little place. She called up the old lady and told her they had to go on Tuesday to the bank. Instead of saying thank you or something, the old lady got very upset and told Valerie she had different plans for Tuesday. She planned to go to Sibiu that day. And now all her plans were all upside down because of Valerie and her mortgage credit. Why didn't she have all the amount of money? She told her son to wait for someone who had all the money, but he said to sell it now, with this damn mortgage credit. Valerie could not believe her ears. The old lady yelled at her for fifteen minutes on the phone. Finally, she agreed to meet with Valerie on Tuesday at the bank.

Valerie thought there had to be an easier way to get by in life. She never heard of a case like this when the seller of an apartment actually yells dissatisfied to the buyer on the phone. But this was just an adversity. Valerie knew that anytime she was about to accomplish something big, something nobody believed she was capable of, she had go over some terrible adversities, adversities that came in all shapes and sizes. This time, the adversity was this mean, old, bitter woman. At least she did not have to live in the same house with her for years. After the day of the transaction, Valerie did not have to see her ever again in her life.

At the bank, the old woman made another scene. The procedure was that first she had to sign the sales contract, then all the documents were arranged at the bank and at the notary and only after a couple of hours she actually got the money. Well, she did not agree to sign the documents. How could she sign the documents if she did not get the money? The bank clerk had to call the bank manager who personally guaranteed her that she will get the money, in cash, into her hands, but first she had to sign the contract. Finally, the old lady was convinced and in the end she got her money. She did not pay any taxes, not at the bank, not at the notary. And she acted like an old bitch, the whole time. But in the end, it was all over. She got her money and left the bank. So did Valerie with the keys of her tiny and ugly little place.

First thing Valerie did was to take Victoria there and show her the apartment. It seemed even smaller than it initially seemed. It had only 20 square meters, the room was only 9 square meters. But it was theirs. From here nobody could kick them out. Nobody could come on a Sunday afternoon to visit the apartment and look what they have in the pot on the stove. Victoria was just happy. It was theirs. Of course, she would have liked to have her own room, but she did not say one word. She was just thrilled to see her mom so happy. She could not ruin this.

Valerie started immediately to plan the renovation of the apartment. The good thing she moved back to her in-laws was that she did not have to pay any rent. All that money saved this was, she was going to use to renew her apartment.

First thing Valerie did was to change the entrance door. She wanted to buy a nice door from a great department store, but there was no such thing in Streamtown. With the transport and all, it would have cost her a lot. So she went into a store in Streamtown. She found a nice door, very robust, made of medium density fiber boards. The lady from the store also said that if she wanted, they could send two men to mount the door the same evening. Valerie agreed. She paid for the door and in the evening she was waiting for the men to mount the door. In a couple of hours, it was all solved. The door was quite good. It insulated very well, both thermally and phonically.

The old parquet she took out by herself. It was relatively easy to take out, the only issue was the dust that resulted. With the help of Victoria. Victoria held up the sack and Valerie put the pieces of parquet into the sack. They removed all the old parquet, put it into big raffia sacks and then on a little hand cart and carried it to her in-laws house. They could use it as fire wood, as it was very dry wood. After this operation was finished, Valerie bought a nice Samsung vacuum cleaner, little and strong, and she tried to collect all the dust that remained, as she did not want to reactivate Victoria's allergic bronchitis.

Now Valerie needed somebody to help her. She had to replace the window, the interior doors, the plumbing. She asked around at work. One of her collaborators said there was a guy who could help her with all these three tasks. He did not ask for a lot of money for his work, the only problem was that he did not have so much time, so the works could last longer. Valerie accepted gladly. She thought, at least for the moment, she had a place to live, so there was no such big rush. And she could continue save money for everything she needed to do. Valerie called Vali, the handy man:

"Hello, I am Valerie. Mr.Vali?"

"Hello. Yes, I am Vali."

"I am Valerie. Mr.Frank gave me you number."

"Yes."

"I need some works done in my apartment. He told me you could help me with them."

"What is about?"

"Well, I would like to replace the windows, the interior doors and the plumbing."

"OK, yes, I can do all these works, but I don't have very much time. Probably Mr.Frank told you."

"Yes, he told me."

"I have my job and I also have some different works I still have to finish."

"OK, I understand. So, can you help me or not?"

"Yes, of course, I will help you, you'll just have to be patient."

"I'll be patient. I have no other choice, at least for now. So, how do we start this?"

"Well, first of all, I have to see the apartment. I need to get an idea about what we are talking about."

"OK, the apartment is on Broken Street. Could you come this evening? Or tomorrow evening?"

"Let's make it tomorrow evening. OK? Seven o'clock?"

"OK, tomorrow evening at seven o'clock. I'll wait for you in the taxi station. OK?"

"OK, I'll see you tomorrow."

"Thank you, bye."

They met the next evening. The handy man looked very disappointed of what he saw.

"Oooh, it's on the ground floor." he said going into the little room.

"Yes, it's on the ground floor."

"Well, this means a lot of moisture. How is the basement? If it is flooded basement, the moisture will kill you. What was here? Parquet? It was all damp, right? Smelled bad?"

"Yes, it was parquet, but I removed it."

"Well, I don't even recommend parquet. With all this moisture, it would be better to put on the floor ceramic tiles."

"How can I put ceramic tiles on the floor in the room? » wondered Valerie. She did not say anything. Vali, the handy man was going on and on.

"For the windows. What do you want?"

"I would like insulating glass."

"With what joinery? Wood, metal, plastic?"

"Well, I would like wood."

"Wood is no good. It works in time and it bends. Then, you will have problems with the windows. Plus, it is more expensive."

"Well, then..."

"The metal joinery is not nice, it looks ugly."

Valerie thought «*Why does he ask me what joinery I want? Then he tells me wood and metal is not good.*»

"*Oh, my God!*" said Vali looking out the window.

"*What happened?*" asked Valerie.

"Did you see that? The sewer is a few meters away. Do you know what that means? Rats. Huge rats, as big as cats."

"Do you see now rats?" asked Valerie.

"Now I don't see them, but you will see them, there a lot of rats in the sewers and they come out to search for food."

"*Well…*"

"So what else do you want to do in the room, besides the window?"

"The paint from the walls must be scrapped down totally. Who knows how many layers of paint are there. Then we can paint."

"Yes, well, OK. On the floor I recommend ceramic tiles. With all this moisture."

"We'll put parquet, not ceramic tiles."

"*What else?*"

"I want to replace the room door."

"What's wrong with the door? We can repair it, paint it a little and that's all."

"I want to replace it."

"*Why?*"

"I don't like it."

"OK. What about the bathroom? Oh dear. You have no bath tub. Well, we can put a shower cabin. And what is this filth here under the sink? Here we have a big problem. We shall have to break the mask under the sink and check out what is oozing. Then, you know what is the problem at the ground floor? People throw all kind of things into the toilet. Tampons, rags, all kind of stuff. Then, the pipe gets clogs up and it flows out at you. Why did you buy this apartment? It's so small. And this neighborhood is terrible. Plus, the ground floor. You'll have great problems with the dampness….."

Valerie's ears were aching already. «*Is this guy normal? I bought this apartment because I could not afford a better one. He thinks I don't know about all the problems? What was I to do? To remain in my in-laws house until they throw me out on the street? And what the damn does he care? I called him to do a job for which he will get paid. I did not need his opinion. I did not call him to chat. If II needed somebody to chat with, I wouldn't have chosen him. That's all.*» Valerie stopped his speech:

"*So, what do you say? Can you help me? I want to change all the plumbing, put ceramic tiles on the ground, except for the room, put new interior doors.*"

"*Yes, I can help you.*"

"*Until when do you think you could finish this job and how much will it cost.*"

"*Well, I don't have much time. I told you this. I will come on some Saturdays, whenever I can.*"

"*But can you at least estimate?*"

"*I can't. I don't know how much time the works will take. By the way, do you want to put new windows? Because there is a warehouse where they sell second hand windows with insulated glass. Do you want me to check if we find something?*"

"*Yes, please. If they are good, why not? I think they are less expensive than the new ones. The new ones are around 500 euro. I have asked already.*"

"*Yes, the new ones are very expensive.*"

"*OK, then I will go to search for the window. I'll call you.*"

Valerie expected the call in the next days, but Vali never called her. She went to her apartment every night, hoping that one day she will see the works started. But nothing. After a week, she called him. He told her a long story, the conclusion of which was that he did nothing. Because he did not have time. He said from the beginning he does not have much time. The next week the same story, week after week the same story.

Finally, the windows were replaced after two months. He found second hand windows, but with the dimensions slightly different from the old ones. He had to break a part of the wall to be able to mount them. But finally, the windows were installed.

At home, Alan's mother was asking Valerie almost every day how the works were going. Valerie knew she was not interested of this for Valerie's welfare. She had no place to live there. She never had place to live there, not even when she was married with Alan. Now, when she was divorced even the less. Valerie felt very uncomfortable, she was waiting to hear every day that she has to move out with her child.

At least Victoria was not affected by all this. She continued learning very well, she had great results in school. And she totally trusted her mom will arrange everything in time.

After almost one year, Val the handy man was able to replace the windows and take out the old interior doors. That was it. Valerie lost her patience. She found a plumber willing to exchange all the plumbing and put ceramic tiles and she hired her. Then she told Val she did not need his services anymore.

The new plumber started the work right way. First, he broke the old ceramic tiles floor of the entrance hall, bathroom and kitchen. Then he dismounted the old sinks and the old toilet. Valerie was at work until 6 p.m. every day. She always came to the apartment to see the situation. She was so happy to see some work has been done. She saw all the broken tiles and the dismantled stuff on the floor. She carried it all out to the dumpster. The dumpster was around 200 meters away from her block and she had to make twelve trips to carry it all out. She carried everything in her hands or with two buckets. She cleaned nicely everything up, the next day the plumber could continue his work.

In almost three weeks, the job was done. All the pipes from the house were replaced and installed into the walls. Ceramic tiles were mounted on the walls and on the floors in the bathroom and the kitchen. There was a place prepared for the automatic machine, with water inlet and outlet. Also, the pipes for the central heating were prepared. New sinks were installed. There was no shower cabin, but the place for shower was covered with ceramic tiles. The pipe that was oozing under the sink was replaced. It was all done.

Valerie was happy to see this big step. She paid the plumber around 300 euro. All the material cost around 500 euro.

This took place in summer. Valerie went with Victoria to the seaside, as they went every year, to cure Victoria's allergic bronchitis. They went by train and tried to spend as little money as possible.

After one week at the seaside, they went one week to Mineville.

They returned on Sunday to Streamtown. Alan's mother told Valerie repeatedly she wanted to renovate the whole house. Now, she started to do it. For this, she took out all the things from Valerie's room. Absolutely all of them. She put everything in big sacks and took them into the barn. After the long, difficult trip from Mineville to Streamtown, Valerie had a big surprise. She opened the door of the room where they were sleeping and she saw it empty. The bed on which she slept with her daughter was not there either. It was quite a clear message Valerie and Victoria were not wanted there anymore. Alan's mother was not home, actually only Alan's father was home, the others were away visiting a relative.

Valerie did not even unpack her bags after the two weeks of holiday. She asked her father-in-law if she could take a shower. He agreed. Valerie took a shower. Then she took her bags from the trip and her daughter and went to their apartment. It was time for her to move out for good from her in-laws. Her little apartment was not ready yet. There was no hot water. No room door. The room had nothing on the floor, it was not painted yet. There was no table, no tables and no chairs in the house. There was no cooker stove. No refrigerator. No furniture. There was only Valerie's unfolding armchair, a chair and a desk.

CHAPTER 12

In August 2006 Valerie and her daughter moved into her apartment. The small 20 square meter apartment was still in a bad condition. But they moved there so soon because they had no choice.

In the room, there was only one unfolding armchair on which mother and daughter were sleeping. It was room for only one person on it, but they held each other in their arms and it was fine. The funny part was when they needed to turn over. They were like Laurel and Hardy: they had to turn over in the same time. The room had good windows, but no door. It was not painted yet and there was nothing on the floor, just concrete.

In the bathroom, the plumbing was new, everything was clean. The only problem was that they had no hot water yet. They had a little small plastic tub and a plastic basin. Also in the bathroom Valerie put their clothes in raffia sacks, as they still had no furniture.

In the kitchen there was only the sink, the plumbing prepared for the central heating and the washing machine. There was Victoria's desk and her chair, the ones Valerie bought when she started school. They had an electric plate for cooking and for warning up the water to wash themselves.

This was pretty much it. Most of their things were still in the barn of her in-laws. To bring them home, Valerie went every day and brought on her back and in her hands as much as she could. She did not want to spend money on taxis or cars, as she knew there will be a lot of expenses.

First thing Valerie wanted to do was to paint the room, put down the parquet on the floor and buy an unfolding sofa and the furniture. Every evening Valerie climbed up on a chair and scrapped the old paintings from the room walls. She wanted to clean it as well as she could. The room was very small, but when it came down to scrapping it, this work just never ended. It was a hard job that generated a lot of dust.

Fortunately, Victoria was still on holiday. She played and listened to music and enjoyed herself. Valerie watched over her very carefully, but the 12 years old girl did not display any signs of psychological discomfort. The worst part was the washing of her long, blond hair. Valerie warmed up 10 liters of water two times to be able to wash and rinse properly her beautiful hair.

Valerie finished the scrapping of the walls in six evenings. Then she painted in another two evenings. She did these works only in the evening, because she could not miss from work. It was very hard to get a day off from work. Whenever she asked for a day off, there were only risen eyebrows. No help, not even slight understanding or help. But it was fine. She was happy to have a job. Her personal works could be done in the evening.

Valerie finished the painting of the room on a Friday evening. When she still had to paint half of the room, the handle of her paintbrush broke. She could not go and buy a new one, as the shops were already closed. Next morning Valerie wanted desperately to buy a sofa, as she was tired of sleeping on the armchair with her daughter. So she definitely had to finish the painting that evening. She grabbed the brush directly with her hand and continued painting. In certain positions, her hand touched the wall and in combination with the lime she got some serious wounds on her hands and they were bleeding. Some of her blood actually got on the walls but it could not be seen as she painted the walls orange. At around midnight, she could not feel her hands and her feet anymore, so tired she was. But she did not give up, she finished the painting the same night. She hardly had power to take a cold shower. Fortunately, Victoria was lifting her spirit, she was very happy the next day they were going to sleep in a decent bed. The next morning, she called a carpenter to put the parquet. He suggested to put on the floor melamine chipboard, which was much less expensive than the parquet. Valerie agreed and in a couple of hours they were able to fix it to the floor. This being done, Valerie and the carpenter went to the furniture from the neighborhood and bought an unfolding sofa, for two persons. The furniture store was 200 meters away from Valerie's block. The two of them brought the sofa home in their hands and got it into the room through the window. It was easier through the window than through the long, narrow block corridor.

This was a huge victory for the two girls. Now they could sleep comfortably throughout the night. Even so, many times they remembered how they slept holding each other tight on the armchair and it always made them smile.

Valerie drew the furniture she calculated would be the best for the tiny room. She thought of a modular furniture, on the wall opposite with the sofa. This furniture had to contain the desk for Victoria, spaces for clothes, for books and also for the TV. The armchair was going to be on the wall opposite to the wall with the window and there was going to be a shelf near it and this was pretty much it. She spoke with the carpenter, he understood what she wanted and started to work on her furniture.

Meanwhile, Valerie asked around for somebody to mount the central heating. Now this was a big expense. She had to buy the station itself, three radiators, one for the room, one for the bathroom and one for the kitchen and the copper pipes. Even if the house was so small, it all cost around 1000 euro. Valerie had the money. She found two men who were willing to do it right away. It was not too much time left until the school was starting and she wanted her daughter to have decent conditions to learn.

After all the materials were bought, the installation of the central heating took two days. Late at night, the two men finished the job. Valerie asked them:

"*So, you say I can start the hot water? I actually have hot water at the tap?*"

"*Yes, you do. Try it.*"

Valerie went to the shower and turned the hot water on. As she turned it on, some cold water gushed out of the tap and sprinkled Valerie from head to toe. She couldn't help letting out a scream. Right after that, they all started to laugh.

"*What happened? What was that?*" asked Valerie.

"*Oh, let me check. It's just that the plumber forgot to place a gasket at the hot water tap. As you did not use it until now, there was no way to know. But we'll put one right now.*"

This problem was also solved. Valerie paid the men the entire amount for their labor and they left. That evening, the two girls took their first hot shower in their own apartment.

After this, Valerie still had around 1000 euro left. She went to a household appliances store in Streamtown and she bought a refrigerator, a cooker stove, a cooker hood and a washing machine. The store sent all of them to her house. A truck arrived with the appliances in front of Valerie's block. The truck driver got out of the truck and asked Valerie:

"*Where is your man? Call him, we have to unload the stuff.*"

"*I have no man. The store said the transport to my home is free.*" answered Valerie.

"*Well, yes, we bring it to your home, but we don't take it into your house. I will unload everything, but that is it. I will leave everything right here in front of your block.*"

Valerie started to think whom she could call to help bring everything in. Victoria could not help her, the appliances were very heavy and big. She remembered the carpenter was living in the block next to him. Maybe he will agree to come and help her if she paid him. Valerie called him up and explained what help she needed. He agreed to come and brought another man with him. It took them several hours to bring everything in. The hardest thing to bring in was the refrigerator. Valerie bought the biggest refrigerator form the store. As she had no pantry, she needed a place to keep all her food. It was 2 meters high and 60 centimeters wide. They could hardly bring it in through the front door, only tilted they could bring it in.

There was one thing left to do. Valerie called an authorized person from the gas company. He checked central heating and installed the cooker stove. And it was all done. School was just starting and Valerie was a little calmed down. All that was still missing was the furniture.

In about another week she got her furniture too. Valerie brought the furniture in through the window, together with the carpenter. After this, she could put all the clothes into the wardrobe. Victoria could arrange her little corner, where she had a few shelves, a desk and a chair.

Valerie's apartment became a decent place to live in. Of course, it still needed a lot of things. First, the entrance hall, the bathroom and the kitchen had to be painted. She needed a carpet, a luster and curtains in the room. For now, she had just a big piece of textile hanging on the window, so that people don't see in. She needed cable TV and internet. But the most important thing of all is that she could live in her own place, a place from which nobody could kick her out, a place where nobody could come on a Sunday afternoon to look in the pot she had on the cooker stove, a place where nobody could count how many bites of food she swallowed.

Victoria started to speak with her mom about what she wanted to study in university. She was a smart girl, very serious. Valerie felt Victoria was too serious for her age. But how could she be anything less? She has always been her mom's best friend. Her mom's only friend. Her mom's only help. Victoria wanted to become a medical doctor. She wanted to help people, to ease their suffering. Especially women, her soft spot was the suffering of women. Seeing her mom struggling all by herself, crying herself to sleep so many nights made her feel a deep and warm feeling of understanding towards women. And it also made her believe with all her heart and mind that there was nothing a woman cannot do. No matter how hard, no matter how complicated, no matter how courageous. Victoria became convinced that a single mom can achieve anything.

In the summer of 2008, Valerie grew more and more concerned about the future of the company she was working in. When they hired Valerie, back in 2004, there were around 50 employees there. In the beginning, there was the investment phase. There was money to spend and some wise guys took advantage of this. Some bonuses got also to the employees and everybody was happy. After a few months, the first general manager, who was Valerie's former boss quit. He did not get along well with the owners, so he left the company. The owners were foreigners, they did not live in the country, just came visiting from time to time, so they needed somebody trustworthy to take care of the company. Of course they did not trust any locals, so they brought somebody from their country. The expenses were still growing like crazy and in a certain point, the company started to have some cash in-flow problems. The owners asked explanations from the chief accountant, who explained very clearly what was going on. They concluded things could not continue like this, so they brought another general manager from their country. This actually was an intelligent man, a good leader. Valerie was already searching for a new job, these changes of management did not suggest her neither stability, nor trustworthiness of the company. She actually did find another job and forwarded her resignation to this man. Seeing this, he called her in his office.

"You wanted to see me, Sir?"

"Yes, Valerie, yes. Come in. Close the door please. Sit down."

"Yes, Sir."

"I saw your resignation."

"Well, yes."

"So, this means you don't like me?" asked the general manager smiling kindly.

"No, it's not that. It's not that at all. I have been searching for a long time and now I found something else. Unfortunately, it happened right now, when you are our boss."

"OK, so what can we do to convince you to stay?"

"Well, I'm concerned. Honestly, I am very concerned. What is with these changes? You know you are the fourth manager of the company?"

"I know, I know."

"What's wrong with these owners? And what is this impression of theirs that we don't work? That we don't do anything?"

"Listen to me. They are convinced that nobody does anything. Not you, not me, nobody. So it's not something against you, they are just like this."

"Well, what can I say. On the other hand, they trust the sales manager who is an idiot and the purchase manager who is a slot. Good, this is good, they trust right these two persons."

"I know, I know" the manager started to laugh loudly, he could not control himself.

"Really, I don't understand their logic."

"Neither do I, but now I want to convince you to stay. We need you here. You are serious and bright and hard working. What do you say?"

"Thank you for your appreciation, but you know, I'm a single mom. I have a credit to pay off."

"We'll give you a raise. What do you say?"

"How much?"

"25%. OK?"

"Great, thanks a lot. Fortunately, you are a great leader and I have the highest respect for you."

"Me too for you. Thank you, Valerie."

"Thank you, Sir."

The problem was that being intelligent, he did not stay for a long time either. After a few months, he quit too.

Valerie felt the company had potential and resources, but something was missing, a bond, a structure was not there. The management was weak. The top manager was changed every few months and the middle managers had no idea about management. Just like in the family. In a family, it is not a child who gives the tone and the attitude. It is the parent, well the parents actually, but Valerie was used to think always with the parent instead of the parents. The parent is the one who sets the calm assertive energy throughout the family. The children just adjust to this. You cannot except from a child to be balanced and calm and loving when he or she sees at his/her parents only aggression and fighting. And it is not a child's place to set the good energy in the family, it is the parent's place to do this. The same way, in a company, it is the manager's place to set the calm and balanced energies in his/her department. It's not the simple employee's place to do this. It's the manager who has to coordinate everything. The employees bring the ingredients, one brings the cooker stove, one brings the pot, one brings the water, another the salt, another the carrots and the meat. The manager is the one who arranges the soup to be served at the right temperature, in the right moment and in the right bowls. It's not easy, but it's the manager's job. The manager must make sure the bully is calmed down. The manager must make sure everybody understands the most important is the team. The manager must make sure everybody knows what they have to do and when. Valerie felt in the company she as working there was no coordination. Nobody seemed to know what the common goal was. The first year everybody was so enthusiastic and so much money was spent. Then, enthusiasm wore off. Some started to steal. Some continued to work hard, still believing in the company, even though they did not have the highest salaries. Continued to work hard, even if this disturbed the ones who were stealing.

A new general manager was brought to the company. Now this had a totally different approach. This one was sent to send home the thieves. He detected immediately that Valerie and the chief accountant were the only ones who did not steal, so he made friends first with these two. He invited first the chief accountant to dinner in one of the best restaurants in town. After that, he invited Valerie to dinner. Valerie was not used to this, she never went out. But with this man she went, she was the boss, now she had to try to maintain a good relationship with this man. They spent a couple of hours speaking about everybody from work. He wanted to know her opinion about everything and everybody. In a certain moment, in the restaurant a man approached them. Valerie did not understand at first who he was, but when he got closer, all smiling, she thought: «*Oh my*

God, it's the child hater. It's him! What the hell is he doing here? Why didn't he return in his own country? We locals were always thieves and idiots as far as he concerned.» As he was getting closer to their table, Valerie's boss asked her whispering:

"*Who is this guy? You know him?*"

"*Yes, I do. I'll tell you all about him after he's gone.*"

The guy got right next to their table and greeted them with exaggerated enthusiasm:

"*Hello, good evening. Hello Valerie, how are you?*"

"*I am fine, thank you. How are you?*" answered Valerie smiling also, but not so enthusiastically.

"*Oh, I'm fine, just fine. Oh, this gentleman does not know me.*"

"*Oh I'm sorry.*" said Valerie. "*Allow me to make the presentations. This gentleman here is the general manager of the company where I work now and this gentleman is the economic manager of the company where I worked before.*"

After this point, the child hater jumped right to Valerie's boss, in fact this was his target, he did not give a rat's ass on Valerie.

"*Hello, I am glad to meet you. Well, I heard you took over the company where Valerie works. It needed a strong, good leader. Well, actually, I am also looking for a job in the country. You know, after our previous company was taken over, we all went back to our country, but after a few months we returned here. I like it here. Valerie can tell you. I had a good report with the locals.*" At this point Valerie thought « *What is he talking about? He hated us!*» "*Oh, yes, those were the times, right Valerie?*" said he, turning to Valerie. As Valerie was not looking very convinced, he turned back to the boss: "*I would like to find a job here again, in a multinational company. I was the economic manager back in the other place. Valerie knows me, she can tell you how I was.*" «*I most certainly tell him how you are, you asshole.*» thought Valerie.

Valerie's boss let him finish his speech and said:

"*Well, right now we are re-organizing the company. But if something comes up, we'll let you know.*"

The enthusiastic child hater left. Valerie's boss turned to Valerie and said:

"*Story.*"

"The guy is an asshole. He hates our people. He thinks we're all thieves and idiots. And as long as I worked there, besides my daily job, I also translated a whole lot of documents for the company. He always promised me he would pay me for my extra work. I woke up at four o'clock in the morning and went to sleep at 12 o'clock at night when translations had to be done and they did not pay me a penny extra. Then, before he left he promised me he will pay for all my work and he didn't. He's a lying son of a bitch. A child hater. He could not stand the presence of any child in the company. Not even before Christmas, when in every company children were going to sing Christmas carols. Not there, he could not stand them. People said this was because he and his wife could not have children. That's no reason to hate children."

Valerie thought this was funny. Here it was, that powerful man, who treated her so arrogantly in the past, now he was asking for her approval. It was really funny.

After the dinner, a few weeks later, this new manager made some inappropriate proposals to Valerie. She turned him down, even though she was aware this could cost her job. Few months later, after he eliminated a lot of persons he did not like, mainly the ones who were stealing, he built up his own network for stealing. He could not touch the chief accountant. This lady knew everything. But Valerie, who turned him down and did not in any way help him steal, was really starting to annoy him.

Valerie became more and more concerned for her future there. She was speaking a lot of times with the chief accountant lady.

This was a rich lady, happily married, with a gorgeous great house, several cars. Her husband had a business of his own and loved her madly. Now, for Valerie, all this was science fiction. She often thought how it would have been to wake up in the morning next to your husband? How it would have been to have a man beside you to help you with the hard work around the house? How it would have been to cook for your husband and wash and iron his clothes? How it would have been to have a home for your family, where you can live with your child and your husband? Just as Victoria thought how it would have been to have a father? How it would have been to have your parents living together and sleeping together? How does it fell like to be protected and helped by your father?

Valerie had nothing in common with her, but felt this lady might have been her only ally in that company. She told her everything she noticed in the company, maybe somehow, when things will go bad, this lady will take her side. Even if this was the slightest chance, Valerie still felt obliged to maintain a close relationship with this lady.

The relationship between them became closer, but strictly at work. She was rich, Valerie was poor. No way they could meet ever outside the company. Valerie had rough times. Sometimes, she would have appreciated if somebody would have listened at least to her. When this chief lady asked her:

"Hey Valerie, how are you?"

"Oh, fine, fine. I'm just a little stressed as..." and this was about all Valerie could say. The chief lady interrupted her immediately:

"Oh, I know, I know!. I'm also totally stressed out. Well, not me, personally. You know, I can find a job whenever I want. I have several variants. It's just that I'm still weighing the possibilities. You know, I'm fine. But I'm stressed because of my god mother. With her cancer. You cannot imagine..."

And she went on and on for minutes. Valerie listened politely and nodded from time to time. There was no place for her to tell her story. And many times she would have preferred to turn around and leave her office and let her speak on for hours. She was speaking by herself anyway, right? But she could not do that. She was already on thin ice with her boss, she could not blow her relationship with this lady too.

Valerie was very careful what she did and what she signed in the company. On one occasion, her boss decided to sell one of the company's cars to one of his friends. The car was 8.000 euro worth, he sold it for 150 euro. Valerie had to issue the invoice, this was her job. Just that Valerie refused to do this. She went immediately in the chief accountant office and told her:

"Do you know what he wants to do?"

"What?"

"He wants to sell the Hyundai for 150 euro. To his friend."

"Well, you know, it's his decision."

"Yes, but do you agree? That car is worth 8.000 euro!"

"He's the administrator of the company. I will not be involved in any way in this."

"Of course you won't, it's my signature on the invoice, not yours."

"Actually, my signature does not appear anywhere" said the chief

accountant. "*He is responsible for the documents of the company, he is the administrator. I will not get involved in this.*"

Valerie thought «*Of course you won't get involved in this, you're not stupid to jeopardize your job, with your huge salary of 3.000 euro. How convenient your signature does not appear anywhere*»

"*Well, I will write the invoice, but I will not sign it. I don't care what he does. If he fires me, I will write to the owners themselves.*" said Valerie, thinking «*And you can go ahead tell him this*»

Valerie wrote the invoiced with the price her boss indicated, but then she said:

"*I wrote the invoice, but I will not sign it.*"

"*Why, why not?*" asked her boss.

"*I'm just a small clerk. This is a serious transaction for the company I don't want my name to appear on it.*"

"*Come on, don't be silly. Just sign it. It's fine.*"

"*I will not sign it. No way.*"

"*Alright, alright, I'll sign it.*" said the purchase manager.

"*Of course you'll sign it. You're in cahoots with him.*» thought Valerie.

"*Here it is. I wrote it 'cause it's my job. But I will not sing it. Now you can do whatever you want with it.*"

Valerie thought this was the end of her job. This was the last drop. Her boss yelled at her many times, to force her to say what he wanted to hear or to force her to do what he wanted to do. But this upfront mutiny. She came to work in the following days fearful she will be kicked out. She could not open her heart to her daughter. What will they do? How will she support her daughter? How will she pay the installments to the bank? There was nobody to comfort her. Except for good Lord above. She could tell Him everything. Valerie spoke with God in her soul and she heard Him answer back. In the evening, when she went home from work. On the street, where nobody could see her. Crying and praying.

«*My God, I know I have made a lot of sins. I know I am bad and many times I think bad thoughts. But please help me, please don't let me down. I'm afraid they'll fire me. Please help me not to lose my job.*»

And certainly God was listening to her prayers. Within the month, her boss and his beloved purchase manager were fired. The owners came with a new guy s general manager and actually said to Valerie:

"*Look, we know what you've been through. We know he treated you bad. But don't worry, now it's all over.*"

Valerie thought «*And where were you when I needed help? I almost got fired because I did not want to steal in cahoots with him and nobody helped me a little tiny bit.*» But she just said:

"*Your appreciation means a lot.*" It sounded more ironical than she meant it to sound. She looked at them. But they did not get the idea. What they said was just a formality. Well, Valerie answered back with a formality.

Unfortunately, things did not improve much after this new change of general manager. The new one did not steal, of course, but he was a complete idiot, with no idea about management. All she cared for to please the owners. They wanted to know the opinion of the workers. So Valerie had to go with him in the factory. He spoke personally with each and every one of the hundred workers. Valerie had to translate. She felt she was slowly getting and ulcer. He wanted to hire personnel, Valerie had to translate at the interview. The human resources department was subordinated to the chief accountant and she declared loud and clear that her subordinates have no time for this. So Valerie had to go to all the interviews. When the round of interviews was over, Valerie had to call the persons rejected to tell them that even though they were not hired, the company keeps them in its registry and they will contacted when the company will expand. Here they were, the company was going from bad to worse, and they were going around phoning people they kept them in their registry. Valerie really felt she was getting an ulcer. She felt physically she had to swallow tons and tons of bullshit and her stomach was just protesting.

After a year of torture for Valerie, the owners finally understood this new manager did not do any good to the company either. So, they decided to take over themselves the executive management of the company. The owner lady moved to the country. She lived right in the company, on the first floor, right above the offices. Now this was truly the end.

Valerie started to search frantically for a new job. The company went from bad to worse. The lady owner was terrible to deal with. She felt betrayed and robbed by everybody. And she took it out on the local employees, even though not the local employees robbed her. Her compatriots, the people who she brought and trusted robbed her. If the grass from the courtyard went yellow, she said somebody poured acid on it, so that her grass turn yellow instead of being green. Valerie told her the water consumption was too high. It was not normal that a company with 50 employees, that does not use water in the technological process, to have to pay for more 1.000 liters of water every month. She said the locals were stealing the water. How could somebody steal it? They are out on the field. Nobody was going home with big cans of water. Finally, the fact was researched and there was a leak of water at an underground pipe and the water kept accumulating underground. It combined with the groundwater and formed a giant water mattress under the office building. The building became unstable and the walls began to crack. Finally, the lady owner understood what was going on. She became angry. Wit Valerie of course, she could not get angry with the chief accountant who knew all her dirty secrets. So she took it out on Valerie:

"*Why didn't anybody inform me about this?*"

"*I informed you, Madam. I told you and I also wrote you on email the story, the history of the consumption, the conclusions of the people from the water company.*"

"*I didn't get this.*"

"*Yes, you did. Do you want me to forward you the email and call the chief accountant? She remembers the discussion.*"

"*No, no, I know you are all in cahoots. Alright, so you informed me, but you should have made me aware of what is going on. Do you know how many emails and information I get every day?*"

"*I tried to, Madam, you wouldn't listen. Remember, you said you don't care about the water consumption, it is used to water the grass.*"

"*Alright, you're dismissed. You're all just trying to screw me.*"

Valerie got out of her office, still perplex and not understanding what she did so wrong.

The suppliers were calling every five minutes to get their invoices paid. This company was never a very good payer of invoices towards the suppliers, but now, when the owner lady took over the payment situation became dramatic. They were threatening Valerie and the person in charge of acquisition continuously. There were already some law suits with a few important suppliers on this subject. One of them, who personally knew the lady owner, called her directly to ask for his money. He actually threatened her by the phone and the owner lady became furious. She called Valerie in her office:

"Do you know who called me today? Ovidiu, the driver."

"So, what did he have to say?"

"He told me I haven't paid his invoices for six months. And he threatened to sue. Me, he threatened me, can you imagine? Do you know the things he told me by the phone?"

"Oh Madam, if you knew the things the suppliers tell us on the phone, every day, every and each one of them."

"Yes, but I am the owner, he cannot speak like that with me."

Valerie thought «*Whatever*», she did not continue this discussion, she just got out of the office.

Even though the lady owner was convinced all locals do is betray her and steal from her, none of these issues were known to the persons outside the company. A proof of this was that CV's were still coming in by fax. One morning, Valerie arrived at work as usual and took out the faxes arrived since the previous day. In the hallway there were some workers from the factory and also the chief accountant, who got there a couple of minutes before. Valerie looked quickly over that particular CV and noticed the girl sending the CV was currently working at the company Valerie previously worked and now she was applying in this company. Valerie could not contain herself, so she started laughing loudly and said:

"Poor, stupid child. Look at her, she wants to quit her job in a serious company to come here! Poor little thing!"

The owner lady was not in the country on this particular occasion, but somebody from those who heard Valerie informed her about what she said. The lady owner spoke with the chief accountant on the phone every day about the daily business and one day she also told her:

"I am very angry with Valerie. Tell her when I get back we'll have a very serious discussion."

The chief accountant gave this message to Valerie. This was right before Easter and instead of having a few nice holidays, Valerie spent them afraid for her job. She knew this was it, this time she will not get away with it. But who told the lay owner what she said? And why? She wasn't even in the country at the time, why tell her about this short comment? What kind of *colleagues* were these?

Valerie has been already searching for a new job for months now, but she intensified her searches. When the lady owner came back, she called Valerie in her office and asked her to close the door.

"How could you say something like this? And in front of those workers? What will they now think? You know they respect your opinion! It is unacceptable what you did. After all that this company did for you. We have always treated you with respect and appreciation and you go out say things like this about our company? This comment of yours offended me personally Valerie, it hurt my feelings. You know how much I struggle here to make things work and you say something like this. This ruins our company's image, this ruins the respect the employees have for me and for the company ..."

And she went on and on for about 30 minutes. Finally, when it was over, Valerie felt nauseous. She got out of the lady owner's office trying to recall if she heard the words "You're fired." She did not recall hearing them, this meant she still had a few days left to find another job.

And right a few days later, a checque issued by the company bounced. It was a big issue in the small community of Streamtown, which still was a small town, even if a few multinational companies got built there. A highly placed influent person who knew Valerie from the previous company heard about the case and remembered Valerie came to work here at this company with the bounced checque. So, she called Valerie up:

"Hey, Valerie, Ana speaking. How are you?"

"Hi, Ana, I'm fine, thank you. And you?"

"I'm fine, just fine. Look, how are things going with you? Everything OK where you work?"

"Well, you know, usual things, there are some problems like everywhere."

"Hey, listen, I heard about the bounced check. So, you can tell me the truth. I know you have financial problems there."

"Oh my God, so the cat is out? We actually have a bounced check? I did not know about this. I know we don't pay our suppliers, but this, this is very serious, according to the law, right?"

"Yes, it is very serious. But never mind that, I want to see how you are. First of all, how's Victoria?"

"She's fine. She's a great kid. Learns well, quite well behaved. She's the only good thing in my life. And she's not even my merit, you know? God sent her to me as a gift. Without her, I would be lost."

"OK, I'm glad she's fine. What about you? Don't you want to get out of there? Things don't look so great, at least from the outside."

"Of course I want to get out. And I have been searching for something else for months now, but I could not find anything. So I keep on searching. I have to find something. My daughter depends on me."

"Listen, listen. I know a person, good friend of mine. He owns a serious company. It is not in Streamtown, it is 25 kilometers away, but there are several persons who work there. You can go with them by car to get to work. Do you want me to ask him if he has something suitable for you?"

"Of course, of course, please ask him."

"OK, I'll ask him. Do you prefer anything in particular?"

"No, no, I accept whatever he has. Now, you know my experience, but if he does not have a similar position for me, it's fine. I'll learn anything, I need to work. Should I send you a CV?"

"Well, yes, that would be great. Send me your CV, I'll send it to him and then I'll call him."

"Alright. Oh, thank you. Thank you so much!"

"You're welcome Valerie, hear you soon."

Valerie sent her CV and after a couple of days she called the owner of that company. They set up an interview. The interview went OK. Valerie got the job.

The interview was on Saturday. On Monday, Valerie went to the lady owner of the company she currently was working in.

"Good morning Madame. May I have a word with you?"

"Good morning Valerie. Yes, of course, come in. What is it?"

"I wanted to tell you that I want to quit. I'm leaving this company."

"I did not expect this. What happened?"

"Well, remember the last discussion we had. All those things you told me..."

"Everything I told you was perfectly rightful."

"Yes, yes, Madame, you're perfectly right. Exactly for that. You made me thinking ... you know..."

"I was under the impression that you are devoted to this company."

"Yeah, I was under the same impression. But obviously we both were wrong. You made it clear to me how totally wrong I am for this company. So now I will leave."

"Alright, if that is what you want to do."

"Yes, that is what I want to do."

"When do you want to leave?"

"As soon as possible."

"You will have to stay as long as it is required by the law. Call me the chief accountant."

"Right away, Madame."

The lady owner together with the chief accountant made all the calculations. Legally, they could not keep Valerie more than two weeks. She still had a lot of not-effected vacation days. These had to be paid according to the law. Valerie had to stay for another two and a half weeks. This meant until Thursday, the 31st of July 2008 inclusively. On the 4th of August she was starting to work at her new job.

Valerie put all her heart and her soul into the job until the very last day. She actually stayed over time the last day, so that she could leave everything in perfect order. She informed everybody about everything she worked, so that the one she took over after her knows everything. Most people did not do so when they were leaving. They thought they get back at the owner or at the boss if they leave behind a mess. Valerie however considered she was not getting back this way at the owner lady, she considered she was getting back to the colleagues she left behind. And that was something she did not want to do.

While she was working there, Valerie rarely could get any days off. The personnel have been cut with 70% and those who remained worked over-time and they were never allowed to take a day off. There was no flexibility in the working hours. For Valerie, this was very hard to deal with. Whatever problems she had to solve, she had to solve them herself and everything was open right when she was at work. Now, if she had a Friday off she decided to go to her parents, to Mineville.

Valerie felt tired. A tooth of hers has swollen and she was in a lot of pain. She was stressed because of the job changing. She could have used at least one weekend to rest. But she did not get it. When she arrived to Mineville, Eva started:

"So, when are you going to paint the big room?"

"I don't know yet, I stay for only two days. On Sunday we must go back. As soon as get one week of holiday, we'll paint the big room. Then the other

two rooms, and the kitchen, and the bathrooms and the hall. Victoria will help me, but we can do it only if I have a one week holiday."

"Alright, I understand that. But now I was asking at least arrange the window area of the room. This wallpaper you put with your brother twenty years ago looks terrible. This house looks like a dump. I'm saying this every day, nobody listens."

"What do you mean by arranging the window area?"

"I mean the wall with the window. Just take down the wallpaper and paint that wall. That's all I'm asking. All the appearance of the room will change."

"But I'm in terrible pain with my tooth..."

"Don't worry, it's not so much to do. Victoria can help you."

"OK, mom, I'll do it."

Valerie did what her mother asked her, with the help of Victoria. The more she moved and stressed herself, the worse her tooth ached. Whenever she remained alone, she just burst into tears, she felt she cannot take it anymore.

But she finished the job her mom asked her. On Sunday they went back to Streamtown for the next day she was going to start to work at her new job.

CHAPTER 13

In August 2008 Valerie was starting her fifth job. She had bought a very small, one room apartment with a mortgage credit. She was still paying installments to the bank. Victoria was 14 years old. Mother and daughter were independent and completely on their own.

Alan was living in Steville with his girlfriend Isabella and their child Samuel. He virtually never felt the need to see his daughter. Couple of times per year, when he had other business to attend to in Streamtown, he also came and visited Victoria, but that was all. He paid alimony when he could, but not every month as the judge ruled. He continued to claim he had financial difficulties. Valerie felt frustrated. There was nobody to protect her child's interest. Not the state anyway. She thought months and months about it and she thought she should sue him to claim her child's interest. Victoria ate every day. She needed clothes every day. She needed stationary and books for school every day. She needed a roof above her head and utilities every day. Not every two or three months like Alan considered. Valerie went to her lawyer and filed for a new law suit claiming the alimony to be paid every month by Alan. It was going to be hard, Valerie was aware of this. Alan was not working at the same company anymore. He started a little business of his own and probably it was not going to be possible to deduct the alimony from his salary every month. Even so, Valerie felt she had to go for it. At least she'll know she tried.

Valerie's lawyer filed for the lawsuit. After a few weeks, Alan got a summons. He had to send a declaration with his current income to the judge, then a hearing was going to be arranged. Alan did that. Valerie waited to be called to the hearing, but she just got a decision by mail. It basically said that the current income of Alan was lower than the income he had in the moment of the divorce, so the state dismissed Valerie's claim because the state considered her claim was not in the interest of her child. This was the great support the state gave a single mother, struggling to force the father of her child to pay child support. Valerie never wanted a higher amount of child support than the one decided at the divorce, all she wanted was that amount to be paid regularly, every month.

Typical resolution for the state. Shallow and stupid and with no logic whatsoever. First of all, how come Alan had a lower income than four years ago? Shouldn't there be a hearing to ask him some questions how is that possible? Secondly, shouldn't someone check his living expenses? How can he afford every year tours in Europe as a holiday, while having the minimum wage? Thirdly, did anyone check if what he declared was true? Did anyone ask for a bank statement to see how much money does he really receive a month and then give the ruling? No, none of these actions happened. There was just a judge sitting in an office, looking at a file and a piece of paper with a big lie on it who gave a despicable ruling. Valerie was left with a bad taste in her mouth after this decision, but she wasn't very surprised. She knew what the state was about. The state was about defending the liars, the thieves, the arrogant ones and punishing the innocents, the victims, the abused ones. There was nothing new for her.

Luckily, Valerie was a hard-worker and she could provide for her daughter and herself. They did not live in luxury, but her daughter had everything she needed. There was not much room in their apartment, so Valerie had to be very organized to keep it acceptable. Everything had its place and everything had to be put to its place. She cleaned the house thoroughly and Victoria helped her.

Every evening after work Valerie cooked a healthy meal for their dinner. She tried to feed as healthy as possible her daughter and in the mean time not to spend too much money. She liked to plan in advance their menu, so that she could buy only the necessary foods. There were no sweets in the house, but there was always milk, fresh fruit and a good homemade soup.

In the weekends Valerie did not rest too much. The only luxury she afforded was to sleep a little later than usual. Otherwise, she cooked, baked, washed and ironed more than on a normal day.

On one particular Sunday afternoon, Valerie was washing up the dishes after their meal. Victoria was on her computer, chatting on messenger with her friends. At a certain point, she came to her mom in the kitchen and told her:

"Mom, I'm chatting on messenger with dad."

"Really? Great."

"Do you want me to tell him anything?"

"No. What are you chatting about?"

"Nothing special. He asked me what we are doing. I told him we just ate. He asked me what goodies did you cook. I told him we ate broccoli with chicken cooked in the oven and he said that is yummy."

"Great."

"Um…."

"What is it my love?"

"I don't know. It's something strange about him."

"What do you mean?"

"I mean he doesn't use his usual words. You know?"

"I don't know why's that. Who knows?"

"OK, I go back, love you."

"Love you too darling."

A few minutes later, Victoria came back to the kitchen.

"Mammy, mammy. Do you know what he told me?"

"What my love?"

"Well, I asked him where he lives. You know, as he moved around so much. And you know what he told me? He told me he is living with his son in an apartment in Steville. Why did he say that?"

"Oh, my dear. There is something I never had the guts to tell you. I always thought you are too young to know about this and I kept postponing it."

"What is it? Tell me already!"

"Well, your father has a son with another woman."

"What?"

"Your father has a son with another woman. He was born nine months after you. I have known this for a long time but I did not have the courage to tell you."

"Why didn't you tell me mom?" Victoria burst into tears. *"You tell me everything else, don't you? Why didn't you tell me this? I wanted to know from you, not from him."*

"My love, I'm sorry. I'm terribly sorry. Please forgive me. Worst is that I

don't even think you found out from him on the internet. I think it's she who was chatting with you, connected on his user and everything."

"What? Which she?"

"The mother of his son, Isabella. I think she chatted with you posing as your father. You know you said he was not using his usual words..."

"How could she do something like this? And you, mom, you, how could you not tell me? I wanted to know from you!"

"I'm sorry my love, come on and give me a kiss."

Mother and daughter cried holding each other in the arms. On the other hand Isabella exulted «*Well, it seems that the relationship between mother and daughter is not so strong after all. She did not tell her daughter an important thing like this. Luckily I am smart and guessed this so I could inform her. How stupid this Valerie character must be. Taking Alan away from his family was like taking candy from a baby."*

"But mom, dad was staying alone when we were visiting him, right? When did he move in with her?" Victoria continued to ask her mother.

"Well, right after we were divorced. I know this, because I saw our things in the barn, at his parents. Well, in a certain point, I saw in the attic of the barn appeared some of the things we had with your father while we were in Steville together. Our radio, the TV antenna, some pots and pans, a bucket, some bowls, our mugs. We had them since we were students. He continued to use them after I went to Mineville and he remained in Steville. I did not understand at the time why they appeared and I did not think about it. We got divorced in April and in August they appeared there. This means he moved in with Isabella and their son four months after the divorce."

"So soon?"

"Well, yeah. He was looking forward to get rid of me. It's just that he did not have the courage to divorce himself, plus he did not want that aggravation. Me divorcing him was exactly what he and Isabella wanted. When he told me about his son, he said all Isabella wanted was a child, but I told him she wanted him, not the child. The child was meant to break us up. The child was meant to make me divorce him."

"Yes, mom, but so fast? So obvious?"

"Yes, yes, right upfront. This is how their family is. You know, I remember, after I got divorced, when I met his sister, she was always looking so suspiciously at me and especially to my belly. I think they thought I was pregnant with

another man and that is why I got divorced. I mean I was so happy with her brother, we had such a beautiful marriage and home, I would have to be crazy to give up such a winner, right? And in fact, it was the other way around. He wanted to get rid of me, he left me for another woman, he had a child with another woman, not me with another man."

"Yes, mom, I know. I'm sorry. Don't think about it anymore."

"Easier said than done."

"You know what else is strange?" Victoria continued.

"What my love?"

"He says he still loves you mom. He always says he still loves you."

"Yes, how fortunate of me. He loves me and he did all this to me. Imagine what he would have done if he didn't love me. He would have probably killed me. Yes, I am a fortunate woman."

"Are you being ironical mom?"

"Yes, my love, I am being ironical."

Valerie did not know how to avoid better the contact with Isabella. In Valerie's mind, Isabella was the impersonation of evil. Not because she had an affair with a married man. Valerie had an affair with a married man too. Not because she had a child with a married man. It happens. But because she conceived a child to destroy a marriage. To steal a father from his child.

Isabella, on the other hand, wanted to get in contact with Valerie. As she did not have the guts to approach Valerie directly, she approached Victoria. Victoria was the weak, defenseless child. Victoria had to be easier to hurt than Valerie. And if she hurt Victoria, Valerie would get even more angry. The way Victoria found out her father has a child with another woman was for Valerie one of the biggest failures in her life. Victoria should have found out about this from her mother, not from the impersonation of evil.

What Isabella did not know was how very smart Victoria was. How close Victoria was to her mother and how deep their love and their connection was. The two girls, abandoned by Alan for Isabella, passed over all this scheming quite easily. This wasn't by far as hard as living with Alan's family for eight years.

Isabella was waiting for some feedback from Alan. But Alan did not even find out about what happened. So Isabella continued scheming. The computer she had at home with Alan turned on automatically the messenger and skype. There was no need for her to write any password. One day she noticed Valerie was on skype so she started chatting with her, as if she was Alan. She was sure Valerie was so stupid, that she will not notice it's not Alan. In fact, Isabella showed just how stupid she was, if she thought a woman who has been his wife for fourteen years will not know she was not speaking with her husband. Valerie terminated the conversation immediately and removed Alan from the list of friends.

Victoria was doing very well at school. Valerie was able to explain her how important education was.

"*You have to learn for yourself. Not for me, I have already graduated university, I have my diplomas. And not because you don't want to disappoint me. You know I am proud of you and I trust you completely. But for yourself. So that you have a profession. What you learn, what you know, the job you are good at, nobody can take that away from you. Don't rely you get married and your husband will provide for you. Your husband can leave you anytime. Your money can be lost or stolen. Your house can burn down. Your car can get crashed in one second. But what you have in your little head, what you know how to do, your good sense, these are riches that nobody can take away from you. Rely as much as possible on yourself, not on others. I don't say not to have friends. You have to have friends. In life, no matter how independent you are, sometimes you need a little help from a friend. But don't rely on that, you should rely only on the Good Lord above and on yourself.*"

"*I rely on you, mom.*"

"*Yes, and I will be there for you as long as I live and even after I die, but don't rely on me. I can die today. You must only rely on yourself.*"

Valerie's latest job was the most unusual place to work. To Valerie, the things going on there seemed weird right from the beginning. The responsible from human resources presented the company like this:

"*Our schedule is not quite fix. You see most of us come from Polville or from Streamtown, or Julestown with our cars and we arrive around 8 o'clock in the morning. You should discuss with somebody to take you with them in the morning.*"

Valerie thought «*I should discuss? I don't know anybody around here! At the interview, the boss said transport is done by the company. This is what he meant? That now I have to go and ask somebody whom I don't know to take me with them?*»

"We don't leave home at a fix hour. Normally, the program ends at half past five in the afternoon, but, as we go home several persons in one car, we have to wait until the last one ends his or her job."

«Wow, that's great. I have some patience problems anyway, this is how God punishes me.»

"But the over time is paid, right?" dared Valerie to ask.

"It is not paid, but it is taken into consideration." the HR responsible answered.

«What the hell is that supposed to mean?» wondered Valerie.

"Umm, there is another thing."

"Yes?" asked curiously Valerie.

"Every other Saturday we all have to come to work. Usually we go home a little earlier than in a normal day, but that depends on how fast everybody who travels in the same car finished their work."

Valerie remained not only speechless, but also thoughtless.

The lady from HR went on.

"The official salary day is on the 18th of the month. But it is not a fix day. It can be the 25th, the 28th. It depends on the cash flow."

«Oh my God. What have I gotten myself into?»

"Do you have any questions?" finally the lady asked.

"No, not for now."

"OK, you can go now to your department. What did Mr.Siegfedge hire you for?"

"Well, he said sales. At least for the beginning."

"OK, this means you are in the right place. We are in the sales department."

Valerie looked around her. Of course, nobody had time for her. She was taken in a tour in all the offices and presented to everyone and that was all. Her entire being was telling her she has arrived to hell on earth. It was just like the feeling she had when she first entered on the street her in-laws lived. Her entire being told her to turn back and run away as fast as she could. But she did not run away. Back then, on her in-laws street she thought she was just imagining things. She loved Alan. She wanted to be with him. She had no intention to marry him, she just came to visit his parents. What bad could have happened? Now, at this company, she already trusted her instinct. But where could she have gone? She could not remain at the previous company. Many of her colleagues used to say "*Yes, it's bad here, but I don't leave. They'll have to throw me out.*" Valerie could not wait to be thrown out. She needed a secure job, her daughter's future was depending on her. They had no other income besides her salary. Now, she got this job with help of person with whom she worked in the past and she was very grateful. She needed this job badly. She could not run away.

Things were much worse than they seemed at first. Valerie has been indicated a few persons to talk to about the transportation from and to home. Most of them refused to accept her, as their cars were already full. They all told her they were using their personal cars and they had no obligation to take anyone and they did not understand why Mr.Siegfedge promised her transport is made by the company? The last person accepted Valerie somehow disgusted, but he told her there was no fix hour for coming to work and no fix hour to go home. This was very true. Valerie asked him at what hour should she wait in the waiting point. He told her an hour, but also told her not to worry, as he will call him when to get out of the house. Valerie saw his disgust and was afraid he will 'forget' to call her to get out of the house. So she went out at the established hour and waited and waited. Sometimes she had to wait for more than half an hour. The car never came on time. They left later from home many times, than the other parties were late and they waited for everyone. By the time they got to Valerie, it was half an hour later than agreed. This went one day after day for years. Valerie waited and waited outside, no matter what weather there was or how cold. Once even she was in the waiting point as usual and the car did not even stop. Valerie started to call desperately the driver and his wife, but they did not answer. The answer was the driver was angry that morning with Mr.Siegfedge and he decided not to take anybody with his personal car to work. Coming home from work was even worse. All the guys living towards Streamtown, where Valerie lived, were maintenance guys, they usually finished work at six, seven p.m., so all the persons travelling with their personal cars had to wait until then to go home. Valerie was going insane. This factory was somewhere between localities. The nearest train station was 5 km away and the nearest bus station was 6 km away. If she wanted to go home, she had to walk all this way to get to the station and then travel some more until Streamtown. As if this was not enough, Streamtown had back then one of the heaviest traffic in the country. Every entrance in Streamtown was blocked every single afternoon with traffic jams. Queues of 10, 15, even 20 km were waiting to go through the town, from Polville direction as well as from Huntown direction. All the traffic between the capital and the western exit from the country, as well as between the capital and Steville had to pass through Streamtown. This went on for years and years, neither the local authorities, nor the state could care less. Valerie and her colleagues had to stay for hours every afternoon in the jams.

Valerie arrived home every evening at seven, even eight o'clock. She still wanted her daughter to eat good healthy food. So she cooked every night dinner and she prepared the food for next morning. At noon Valerie ate at work, they received a warm meal. Victoria ate a bowl of soup, there was always good, nutritious, homemade food in the fridge. In the time remained until bed time, Valerie spoke with Victoria, tried to be as supportive as possible. Victoria, on the other hand, told Valerie everything. Just like she would have said to a good friend. Valerie felt sometimes it was hard to keep up with her teenager daughter, but this way she managed to remain alert and young.

Worst times were when something broke down in the house, especially their home computer. It was an old desktop, which had to be carried in a bag to the computer shop which repaired it. Now this computer had an interesting story. After the divorce, Alan proposed to Valerie to buy together a desktop computer for Victoria. He had already an offer. The computer was not new and it cost 14 million crowns. Alan promised to pay half of it and Valerie had to pay the other half. It was a big financial effort, but Valeria accepted, as her daughter needed it. The repair shop was in Julestown, she could not find a decent repair shop in Streamtown. Every time she took it to repair in Streamtown, when she brought home the computer it did not even start up. The computer shop in Julestown had open between 9 and 5 and of course they were closed on Saturday. In order to repair it, Valerie almost needed a day off, which was not seen well at her job. She had to take the big bag with the computer, to go by bus to Julestown and leave it there. Then she had to return to Streamtown by bus and then she had to hitchhike to work. When the repair was done, she had to do this all over again. She felt sick to her stomach every time the computer broke down. And it did break down frequently, every single month. Many years passed by until Valerie understood that she got impaled once again by Alan. It was he who made this computer, out of all kind of old spare parts. After he built it, he basically asked Valerie 7 million crowns for it, his expenses were in fact less than 1 million crowns. That is why he had no invoice, no guarantee, nothing for the computer. He told Valerie that he will come and repair it if it breaks down, but he never did. So Valerie was losing her mind every time she had to take it to be fixed.

Of course, when it happened, Victoria had to tell her mom about it and Valerie got angry every time. Victoria had a good strategy, she called her mom on the phone while she was at work, as she knew this way she could not react so loudly.

"*Hello mom. How are you?*"

"*Hello Victoria, I'm fine. And you? Are you home?*"

"*Yeah, I just got home. I wanted to turn on the computer but it does not start up. I'm sorry mom.*"

"*Hmmm, OK, we'll talk about it at home. I cannot talk right now. Otherwise everything OK? How was at school?*"

"*At school it was fine. We wrote the test at Math, I think I did good, we'll get the grades next week.*"

"*OK, my love. There is milk in the fridge and soup. Please eat something, OK? Then tonight I'll make something good to eat. OK?*"

"*OK, mom, love you.*"

"*Love you too.*"

Then, when Valerie arrived home, she started.

"*How come it does not start up. It started up yesterday, didn't it?*"

"*I don't know mom, yes, yesterday it worked.*"

"So, *if yesterday it worked and today it does not work, something must have happened in the meantime, right? So, tell me, what did you do with it Victoria? What did you do with it?*"

"*Don't call me Victoria.*"

"*So, what should I call you? Isn't that your name?*"

"*Yes, it is my name, but you only call me like that when you're angry. I want you to call me my love. It's not my fault it broke, mom. I did not do anything with it. You saw last night I turned it off and there was nothing wrong with it. Don't get angry with me, it's not my fault.*"

"*I know, it's nobody's fault, but as usual I have to solve it. You know what, it's my fault, everything is my fault. If would have been still born, none of this would have happened.*"

Then, after a few minutes, Valerie calmed down. She regretted terribly that she lost her patience. She did not want to take it out on Victoria, but just couldn't help herself. It was just too much. Always after she calmed down, she apologized to Victoria.

"*I'm sorry my love I got angry, but it's just so very complicated. Now I have to take it to Julestown to be repaired. You know these idiots in Streamtown do more wrong than good. Then I have to ask permission go away from work. You should see their faces and how they roll their eyes over every time I ask permission to leave for a few hours.*"

"*I know mom, I understand. It's OK.*"

"*Do you forgive me my love?*"

"*Of course, of course. I'm sorry it broke down again.*"

"*We'll fix it. It's not a good compute either. We should buy a new one. But they are so expensive. Hmmm. We'll see.*"

Poor Victoria has gotten into a point where she was afraid to turn it on. Whenever she turned on the computer, she said a little prayer «*God, please, let it work, please let it work.*»

The only thing Alan contributed with were advices for them if they asked, but never concrete help. Victoria did not mind him very much, but Valerie started to lose her patience with all of those who gave her advices. She needed badly a little bit of help, not advices. So they ended up never even telling Alan if something was wrong with the computer.

The more Valerie got involved in her new job, the more stressful it became. She began to think she was cursed, she always ended up in the most stressful company in the most stressful position. The truth was that since she was a person who always solved the issues handed to her, more and more issues were handed to her. In return, she got no respect, no appreciation, no thank you. Just more tasks, more stress and more criticism. The payment of the suppliers was even worse. In this company's case, the reason was that it was in expansion and a big credit was taken from the bank for this and there were never money. The salaries were paid always with delay, sometimes with two weeks delay. Always before the Christmas and Easter the salaries were smaller than usual. Valerie just could not understand why. But she dared not ask why, some employees dared to ask and they always got surreal explanations from HR and also a big squabble.

The biggest problem with Valerie was she did not take very much care of her looks. On the one hand, while being a child, Eva was not allowed to spend money on new cloths or anything to improve the looks of the children. Eduard took the matters in his own hands, and if he did not get what he wanted, he stole the money from his mother and still bought what he wanted. Valerie could not do such thing. She just got used to always wear old clothes, then bought her clothes from second hand shops. Then, while being an adult, she always had to save money. With no financial support from her parents or from her husband and having to raise her daughter, she took very good care of her money. Finally, when she started to have a little more money, she was already too used not to buy anything for herself. Victoria insisted very much with her mom on this subject. Victoria always knew what jewel hides under her mother's modest appearance and convinced her every day to build herself a more beautiful image.

Again Valerie could virtually never get some holiday. Her legal days of holiday kept accumulating, as it was not legal anymore to be paid. Once or twice a year she could take some days off. She went to Mineville to help her parents as much as she could. Victoria always insisted:

"Mom, why don't we go on a real holiday? To the seaside, or in the mountains? You never rest on holidays. You work more on your holidays than when you are at work!"

"I know my love, but I keep thinking maybe the next year my parents will not be here anymore, than whom shall we go to? I think we have to go to them as long as we have them. They are so happy when we visit them. Plus we can help them. It's that big apartment, it has to be renovated. We cannot leave them to live in a dirty house. I feel so sorry for all the old parents abandoned by their children. Their children whom they have raised with efforts and sacrifices. Then, their children never come home to them. They have no time and no money to clean or paint a little bit their parents' house. And you know what? The funniest thing: as soon as the old parents die, the children suddenly have enough money to renovate the old place, so that they can move in or sell it. I think it's despicable to treat your parents like this. And you know why? Because before you know it, you will grow old too and you will need a little help too, just like your parents did from you."

"Alright, mom, we'll do it your way."

"Thank you for helping me, my love."

Indeed the girls worked hard on their holidays in Mineville. In about five years, by working only one or two weeks per year, they painted the huge apartment of Eva and Camil. The rooms had also wallpaper and they had to scratch that down, then repair the wall and then paint it. Right in the year when they had to paint the biggest room, Valerie got a task from Mr.Siegfedge for her holiday. She had to translate for him a 200 pages book, during her holiday. She worked six hours to paint and clean, then she translated another 6 to 8 hours every day to finish the translation of the book. The reward for this task was again zero.

After around two years, Mr.Siegfedge, the owner, decided to bring a spiritual mentor to help his indirect employees. He wanted to build the team. The team was already strong however. Like any team led by a dictator, they we united and worked very well together. They needed more a decent treatment from Mr.Siegfedge, they needed him not to yell at them anymore, not a spiritual mentor. The offices could have used a little renovation, they were old and dirty. The money could have been invested there. But it was his company so it was he who decided in what to invest.

Valerie of course had to be the interpreter in the process, without any additional payment. So, she got pretty close to the spiritual mentor, who appreciated her sincerely and recommended her to Mr.Siegfedge. Following her recommendation, Valerie became manager. Truth was, Mr.Siegfedge did not need managers. He took all the decisions by himself. He did not respect the managers and humiliated them every time he had the chance. Not all of them, of course. He had couple of friends and a few relatives, of course those were treated with respect. But not Valerie. On the other hand, the unliked managers had absolutely no power. They had no power to reward or to punish a subordinate of theirs. They could not purchase a pen that cost 1 crown without the approval of Mr.Siegfedge.

Now in this company, the suppliers were not paid according to the due date on the invoices or according to the agreed payment terms. As the company was such a bad payer, they got into a point were no supplier accepted to dispatch any material to them without the payment of the previous invoice. Therefore, only the invoices of those suppliers were paid, from which the company needed to load materials. Valerie had to inform the financial department what materials she had to load next week, what incoming materials she had for which customs taxes had to be paid and give them exactly what invoices had to be paid. And this was not just a list sent to them. No. First, she had to go Mr. Siegfedge.

"Hello Mr.Siegfedge. I'm terribly sorry to disturb you, but I really need to speak to you about some payments."

"Alright, I don't have too much time. Can't you do anything by yourselves?"

«Of course we can asshole, but we need your approval for everything!» thought Valerie and just looked at him, not saying anything.

Mr.Siegfedge looked at her with his contemptuous and blasé look and said:

"OK, let's see. Come on."

"Well, it is about these four invoices. We have to pay them next week."

"Why?"

"Well, our stock of these particular materials will be over in two weeks from now. Therefore, next week I have to pick up the goods from them so that on next Monday we shall get the materials here."

"Hmmm, did you speak with them?"

"Yes, I speak with them every week. But they won't load anything for us until we don't pay the previous invoice."

"We shall not pay before the invoices are due."

"The invoices are well overdue."

"Hmmmm. But from you I expected a little more commitment."

Valerie did not say anything else. What commitment was he still expecting? Wasn't that enough that she worked tens of hours overtime without payment? All the translations and interpretations? All the negotiations with the suppliers and transport companies because the company did not pay in time?

"It's fine from my side, but you have to speak with my brother too."

"Yes, sir, I will. Thank you very much!"

Mr.Siegfedge's brother was working in the company too. He was the second man in the company. All decisions had to be approved by him too. So Valerie turned now to him, even though he had the same office as Mr.Siegfedge and they were fronting each other. He must have heard the entire conversation, but Valerie had to explain it again. She got the same contempt towards the suppliers, who were evil because they wanted the money and she was evil because she was not able to convince them to deliver them materials without money. And in the end:

"*OK, if there is no other way.*"

"*There is no other way.*" Valerie replied.

"*But you have to discuss with Flavia, the economic manager. She has to check with the cash flow.*"

"*Yes, I know, I go right to her.*"

Valerie went now to the economic manager.

"*Hello.*"

"*Yeah, hello. I hope you don't want money.*"

"*I don't want money. But we have to pay these suppliers next week.*"

"*Again? They are thick-skinned to ask for money all the time. Next week we also have to pay the salaries.*"

"*I have spoken with misters Siegfedge and they agreed and told me to speak with you.*"

"*Of course, they agreed but they did not tell you from where to get the money. That is my problem. If we shall not be able to pay the salaries next week it will be your fault, you know that?*"

"*I'm sorry, I don't want us not to pay the salaries, but we have to pay these suppliers, otherwise they don't agree to load us any materials and as a consequences the week after we shall have to stop production. I'm terribly sorry.*"

"*OK, fine. But you will have to discuss also with Amalia, the girls who makes the payments. Ask her to put these amounts in the cash flow. If we cash in something, we shall be able to pay. If not, not.*"

"*Alright, thank you. I will speak with her.*"

By the time Valerie got to the girl who made the payments, she was really pissed off. She started all over the begging. Finally, Amalia concluded:

"*You know Valerie, you tell what we have to pay and I put it in the list, and when I get to them, they refuse to sign, you know that? They promise you, but they don't actually sign the payments. And then you get upset with me, but it's not my fault, you know?*"

"*I know, I know, it's all my fault. It will be also my fault if we don't pay the salaries next week, I know, they explained me. And you know what? I think it is my fault. All this wouldn't have happened if I was still born. Nothing would have to be paid, nobody would have come to stress you all.*"

"Now you don't have to be sarcastic. I did not say that. I just told you the truth. You don't have to speak like that with me, I always help you."

"Yes, you are right. I'm sorry. It's just that..."

It was just that Valerie could not take it anymore. She had to go through all this for every invoice of a supplier or of a transport company. She had to listen to all the complaints from the suppliers, and sometimes, when they were not paid for months and months, they got quite angry. But there was nothing she could do. She had to accept all this. Right after she got the job in this company, the great crisis of 2008 began. There were no job openings anywhere. And she needed the money badly. Victoria depended on her.

At the next visit, the spiritual mentor, Rava, visited Valerie at her home to prepare some materials for the next day. She was quite shocked how small Valerie's apartment was. And after all, Valerie was a manager in a multinational company. She told Mr.Siegfedge that she knew that in the country the standard of living was low, but really was it that low? So she thought Valerie should get an apartment with the rent paid by the company. Valerie was pretty tired of the rented apartments. She has been kicked out several times and she did not trust the apartment owners. Plus she had to move again, all by herself, she had to find a truck to help her move, then to beg every month for the payment of the rent. Valerie did not need this trouble, she better off in her own small apartment. Mr.Siegfedge called her in his office. This time he was acting quite human, as he knew Valerie will tell the spiritual mentor what he said. Valerie was quite stunned to see what efforts he made to seem human and she thought «*Wow, he really thinks I buy this? He thinks if he speaks nicely with me this time BECAUSE SHE ASKED HIM TO I will be so stupid and believe he is a good person? He insults my intelligence. Anyway, let's see what he has to say...*»

"Hmmm, come on, sit down, Valerie."

"Yes, Mr.Siegfedge."

"Hmm, you know, I spoke with Rava about you."

"Yes."

"She thinks you should live in a nicer place. You and your daughter."

"Yes."

"So, find a nice apartment, we'll pay for the rent."

"OK, I'll start to search. Thank you!"

Valerie thought « *I'll tell him I searched but I found nothing that I liked. I don't want now to start all over with the moving in and out and so on.*» Unfortunately, Valerie did not get away with it so easily. Rava had left a precise task to Mr.Siegfedge, that by the time she comes again to the country, Valerie had to stay in a nice apartment. So Mr.Siegfedge found himself an apartment for Valerie. It was a huge apartment in a new block of flats, right down town in Streamtown. The rent was 200 euro per month and the contract was between the owners and the company.

Now Valerie had to move again. The rented apartment was empty, except for the kitchen, where there was furniture. The owners wanted to convince Valerie to buy this furniture.

"*It is quite new furniture, specially designed for this kitchen, as you can see.*"

"*Yes, I see.*"

"*If you want us to leave it here, you will have to buy it. It costs 300 euro.*"

"*I don't want you to leave it here.*"

"*If you don't buy it, we'll sell it somebody else.*"

"*I don't care. I don't want it.*"

"*Your kitchen will remain totally empty.*"

"*I don't care, I don't want it.*"

Valerie knew from her experience with apartment owners that she will not remain here for long. Surely in a few months they will find a buyer and they will want Valerie out of there. Then, she would have remained with the furniture that she bought, which was too big for her little kitchen in her own apartment and she already had furniture in her own kitchen. So no, she did not want to buy the furniture. The owners took it away and the apartment was handed over completely empty. Literally empty, they took even the mask under the sink from the kitchen and left the sink on the floor.

Valerie bought two metallic supports for the sink and she fixed them herself. There was no man to help her. So she bought herself a drill, made the whole herself and fixed back up the sink in the kitchen.

Fortunately, this time she was not pressed by time with the moving. She started carrying all the clothes and books with her hands. Every morning, before going to work she carried one back pack and two hand bags with stuff to the rented apartment, then she went to work.

Eduard also came from Mineville to help them move. He also carried some stuff during day time with Victoria. Victoria helped them with all her power, even though she was still a teenager. Sometimes, she worked so hard to help her mom, that her back went out and she could hardly move for a couple of days. When all of the small stuff was moved, Valerie called also a truck and some men for the furniture, the fridge and the washing machine. Now these ones came for money, but at least it all went quickly, as only the big furniture had to be moved.

After a week, Eduard returned to Mineville. Valerie was very grateful her brother came to help her. Even so, she found herself in that big apartment, almost empty. She did not have enough furniture to fill it and she did not want to buy new furniture for it as she knew soon she will get kicked out of there. So she just bought curtains and a carpet on the floors, they had a bed to sleep on, Valerie had her desk and her chair and that was it. It was enough.

Of course, after they moved here Valerie had to call the internet and TV provider to move their services from her apartment here. Now this was quite a nerve wrecking action. Victoria was asking her several times a day:

"*When will they come, mom? What did they say? Did you call them? When will they come?*"

Valerie had to call to a phone number and a robot said that her call was very important for them, but unfortunately now all the operators were busy, so she had to wait. And she waited and waited. Sometimes up to 30 minutes. That silly music playing. Valerie got into a point where she had a stomach ache only when she heard that music. The first phone call was not enough. After a couple of days, at the insistence of Victoria she had to call again. When finally they decided to come, there was always the time issue. They did not work on Saturdays and did not work in the evening. Only between 8 a.m. and 4 p.m. when everybody was at work. Plus, they never gave an exact hour when they will come, so in this company's view, if you needed their services you had to stay locked in your house for a month and wait for the second when they called and came to do their job. Even though the TV services provider and the internet services provider was one and the same company, you had to go through this procedure two times: once for the TV and once for the internet. As the TV guys could not do the internet guys job and vice versa. After three phone calls, one morning, a guy finally called Valerie up and told her in half an hour he could come. Valerie confirmed somebody will be home, as Victoria started school only at ten that day and she was at home. After she confirmed the guy, she started to call Victoria. And called her. And called her. Victoria did not answer. Valerie called her about thirty times, no answer from Victoria. Victoria went to bed very late the night before and of course she left her phone on silent. So Valerie could call as much as she wanted. Valerie almost had a stroke at the other end, as she knew if they will not be home when the TV guy came, she had to start all over the calling them and all. Fortunately, the guy came and knocked on the door pretty hard, Victoria woke up and let him in, but the stress Valerie went though could not be wiped so easily.

Valerie tried to do something useful for herself while she was in the rented apartment. She took advantage of the fact her own place was empty, so she painted the whole house. By herself. It wasn't big, but still there was a lot of work to do. After that she cleaned it nicely and went twice a week to her own place to see if everything was in order. Valerie loved very much this small place of hers. She had worked so much for the money to buy it and then so much to make it a pleasant place, that now she felt a little piece of her was in that small place.

At the first visit of Rava in the country, Valerie considered she should express her gratitude towards her for influencing Mr.Siegfedge to rent her this big apartment by inviting her to dinner one evening. Even though, Valerie would have preferred to remain in her small apartment, then to have to go once again through the stress of moving once again. Valerie always thought if you want to help a person, you should help him or her with what he or she needs, no with what is easy for you to give or with what you don't want or you don't like, then you dump it on them. Of course she never said it out loud. Whatever she received, she always said thank you and then maybe she used it, maybe not. She never offended anyone by refusing or commenting that she did not need the respective thing or help. Most of the people around her, including her family, took advantage of this. Whenever Eva or Eduard had something they did not like anymore or it was not quite good or functional, they dumped it on Valerie. Valerie accepted anything without comments just because she did not want to offend them. When her mother-in-law sacrificed the veal or the pig, Valerie and Alan got the bones or the pack with meat that already had green mold on it. Alan never said anything and Valerie always accepted anything, so why not dumping it on them?

Victoria however wanted to move into a bigger apartment. Valerie felt bad anyway she could not provide a separate room for her daughter. How could she have turned down now the opportunity to move into an apartment where Victoria could have her own room just because she did not want the stress of moving? The saddest part of it all for Valerie was to see how some rich lady who had it all and wanted to appear very helpful with Valerie asked her:

"I don't understand why are you so stressed by moving?"

"Well, I have to take tens of bags with clothes, the pans and pots, Victoria's books and notebooks and..." Valerie tried to continue that she had to find a car with men willing to help her with the furniture and fridge and washing machine, as there were no moving companies in Streamtown, but she did not get the chance, as the rich lady went on and on.

"I also had to move from our apartment to our house when it was ready and I just took a few clothes from the wardrobe on my arm, put it into the car and that was all, than I went with my husband to a nice restaurant."

«*This means I am an idiot*», Valerie thought, «*It takes me a few days until I transfer without a car all the stuff to the other. Clearly, I must be an idiot that for me it's so difficult and stressful.*»

In the new apartment, Valerie bought an unfolding table and some more chair and plates and she invited Rava over, together with Mr.Siegfedge and a couple of other managers. She prepared was much as she could the night before the dinner, she went to work, then in the evening they all came, so she just had to make the final preparations. She made some pasta, the tomato sauce was ready, just had to be warmed and the pasta to be cooked. For the second course she prepared some seafood with vegetables and for the third course she prepared pork knuckle with steamed cabbage. She thought this way there were international foods and also a local food. She finished the dinner with some cookies made by her personally. Everybody liked it and Valerie felt appreciated, one thing she did not feel very often.

Then Victoria's birthday came and Valerie was happy she finally could call over some of her friends. While they lived at her in-laws, they did not like it to have children over. Then, she moved into that small apartment.

The room was only three meters by three meters, plus the wardrobe and desk and sofa, there was hardly enough room for two persons. But now, being in this big apartment, they had room. Victoria invited around twelve friends to her birthday. Valerie did again her best and cooked for them all by herself and it turned out to be a great success.

Valerie liked cooking more and more. Deep down, inside, she was craving for appreciation. By cooking, she got the appreciation she needed so much. She started cooking when she was a student, for Alan. She got no appreciation in return. Then she cooked for Victoria. Victoria was a very picky eater as a child. Valerie always tried to cook something new, something different for her daughter, to make her eat a more types of food. She placed small portions of food on a nice plate, arranged with much care and as beautifully as possible. Valerie saw many times parents in despair their kids were not eating putting huge portions of food, just slapped on a big plate. Of course, the children, who did not like to eat anyway, got frightened of those huge portions of food and got even more disgusted by food. Valerie knew that her child had to eat good, healthy food, as varied as possible. So she tried her best and quite got specialized in cooking. Victoria turned out to be a healthy, smart child. She ate only healthy food and had perfect teeth. Valerie considered this one of her personal victories. The moments spent with her daughter, eating together, were some of the happiest moments for them. Eating is a social act most of all. We don't eat just to survive, we eat with the loved ones to enjoy life's simplest pleasures together. That is why Valerie could not eat in the presence of people she did not like. She preferred not to eat rather than to eat with somebody she did not like. One the other hand, sharing a simple apple with her beloved daughter, not only fed their body, not only appeased their thirst and hunger, but gave them a calm, deep feeling of love, togetherness and safety. No huge dinner, no expensive meal in a fancy restaurant, in the presence of all kind of stranger acquaintances could feed them like that one apple eaten together, at night, cuddling in front of a good movie they watched together, with nobody looking into their plates and counting the number of bites they take.

Valerie and Victoria have been living in this rented apartment for almost a year now. It was the Holy Week when Valerie received a phone call from the lady owner.

"Hello, Valerie. How are you?"

"I am fine."

"I called you because we need to talk about something. Well, we decided to sell the apartment."

"What, this apartment?"

"Yes, the one you live in. I'm sorry, but we need the money, You know with this crisis, things are not going so well and we have no other choice."

"Did you already find a buyer for it?"

"No, not yet, but we gave an ad at the local radio and at the local newspaper. I just wanted you to know."

"Alright, I understand. This means after you find a buyer I have at least two weeks to move out, right?"

"No way, you will have to move out in maximum one week."

"But that is impossible I cannot miss from work. I can only move out on Saturday. And every other Saturday I have to work…"

"Come one, your boss rented you this apartment. Why don't you ask him to buy it for you?"

"Just what do you think I am? A whore?"

"I don't care, if we find a buyer you'll have to move out and that's it."

"Well, OK, I see. Bye."

"Bye."

CHAPTER 14

For the third time in her life, Valerie got an ultimatum that she had to move out from the rented apartment where she lived. Even though this time it was not so dramatic for Valerie, as she had her own place, it was still a great stress and a great logistic challenge once again.

If it was for Valerie, she would have just moved back into her small apartment. But Rava has left Mr.Siegfedge the task to get Valerie a rented apartment, as hers was too small and Victoria wanted very much to have her own room. It didn't take him long either to find another apartment in Streamtown. This apartment was furnished, so she did not have to bring her furniture. Valerie had to organize this time a double moving: she had to take all the furniture, fridge, washing machine, TV and so on back to her own apartment and she had to take all the other stuff into the newly rented apartment. It took her two entire weeks, she had to speak with ten persons to help her and she also carried a lot of stuff by her own.

Valerie cleaned the apartment she left. Three weeks after the call of the owner Valerie called her and told her the apartment was empty and that she wanted to hand it over.

"Hello, I am Valerie."

"Hello, hello. How are you?"

"I am fine. I just wanted to tell you that I emptied the apartment. Please tell me when can we meet to hand it over to you."

"So soon? How come? I didn't find a buyer yet."

"I know you didn't find a buyer yet, but I did not want to wait until you find one. Then in one week I would have to be out. I wanted to leave on my terms, when I wanted, when it was convenient for me, not for you."

"OK, but you didn't have to do it so fast."

«*Yeah, right*» thought Valerie. « *I should have stayed a little longer and continue to pay you rent, right? Then, when you wanted me out, I would have be forced to move out in one week.*» but she just said:

"*So, when can we meet? This afternoon?*"

"*Yes, alright.*"

Valerie handed over the apartment that afternoon. In perfect condition and cleaned impeccably. After that, she went to clean the newly rented apartment, before she unpacked all the stuff. Here Victoria helped her with the cleaning and with the unpacking. Then Valerie had to start all over with the internet and TV provider.

Valerie's salary has increased after she became manager. Now she could afford much more things than before. In the meantime, Victoria was growing and the expenses with her were growing exponentially. Even if the job was not easy, at least this factory was still working. The factory where Valerie worked before has closed down because of the crisis of 2008. Valerie knew that God was the one who rescued her once again.

Valerie did her best because she was really grateful she had a job and she depended totally on her salary. Although her best was not good enough for Mr.Siegfedge. He lost his temper every day, several times. He used to shout at his employees and he got angry out of the blue for anything. Valerie did not want him to get angry, just like she did not want her father to get angry with her when she was a little child. But he got angry on her for things out of her control. Whenever Mr.Siegfedge shouted at her or at others in front of her, Valerie was afraid. This wasn't a rational fear, it was a fear that she felt in her guts. It wasn't rational, so she could not control it with her mind. She felt like this every time she saw a man losing his temper. Her instincts and her early childhood experiences told her the abuse was following.

Her other fear was that she was going to lose her job. Now this was a quiet, constant, always present fear. Every morning, after she finished preparing herself for work, Valerie brushed her teeth, put some moisturizing cream on her face and looked at herself into the mirror. The thing that crossed her mind was «*Oh my God, today he is going to fire me. He tells me almost every day that I am incompetent, that he does not need me, that he thought I was different and how I disappointed him. But today I can feel it. He is going to fire me.*» This went on every day. Every single day.

Valerie really tried not to give him reasons for this. She controlled the department for which she was responsible, but she could not control the external factors that were influencing it. She was responsible for bringing the raw materials and spare parts into the company. The suppliers did not dispatch them the material unless they paid the overdue invoices. These payments were made in the last minute, after days and weeks of escalations from her side. When they were finally paid, there was just a little time left to transport them into the company. She had to find the fastest transport for this. On the other hand, she was pressed continuously to buy the cheapest materials and find the cheapest transports to recue costs, but these transports were obviously not the fastest ones. God forbid after loading the materials something happened with these transports. Once, one of these trucks was stopped by the anti-drug police somewhere. Therefore, the truck had some delay. Valerie had to go and tell Mr.Siegfedge. He turned blue and black with anger. He made a scene quite in the middle of the factory. That the managers were totally useless. He had no use of them. He only needed three guys of his to run the company, who were his friends too by chance: the maintenance guy, the guy who planned production and the guy from sales. And the rest could all go home. And so on, and so forth. Valerie could not say a single word, as he was continuously shouting, while all the employees were looking at them. She was thinking «*Why is he bringing us spiritual mentors while he behaves like this us? Doesn't he know the Maslow hierarchy of needs? I fear I will lose my job and end up on the streets with my daughter, I feel my safety is jeopardized, and he brings me a spiritual mentor? If he fools anyone, it's only himself.*"

On the other hand, Valerie had to keep her department clean and orderly. All the incoming materials were her responsibility and most of them were on big heavy pallets. She had only two persons for whom she was responsible and of course they had no authorization to drive a forklift. Well, responsible in the sense that if they did something wrong, it was her fault. She could not decide anything in regards with their salary. She could not give them any bonuses. Therefore, she had no authority over them. The only boss in the company was Mr.Siegfedge. As all employees knew this, all of them knew only he had power of decision, all of them went directly to him if they needed something. Valerie tried her best to be a good boss for her subordinates. She spoke with them about their personal lives, brought little presents for them at holidays, tried to treat them as good as she could as she thought if a strong person wants to prove how tough she or he is, she or he should try this with who are stronger than her or him, not with those who are weaker than her or him and defenseless. Just like at home: if a man wants to prove how strong he is, he should fight with other men, not come home and beat up his wife and kids. A really strong person is good and kind with those below him or her and brave with those stronger and more powerful than him or her.

Even so, Valerie did not get much help from her subordinates. Honestly, she did not even expect very much from a person who has a salary of 200 euro per month. So she decided to clean and put everything in place on her own. She needed desperately the help of a forklift driver and there was no such authorized person in her department. Now in this particular company, the most powerful persons after Mr.Siegfedge were the forklift drivers. There were very few for such a big volume of goods incoming and outgoing on pallets and they were all close friends with Mr.Siegfedge. If Valerie asked them nicely to come and help her, they refused her upfront rudely. If Valerie then asked them less nicely, they went directly to Mr.Siegfedge and complained they were too busy and they don't have time to move the pallets as she wanted and if she doesn't leave them alone, they will leave everything and go home. And Mr.Siegfedge always decided in their favor. If trucks came with raw materials to unload, they were kept for hours and hours at the company and the forklift drivers refused to unload them because they did not have time. Then, the transport companies called Valerie to complaint their trucks were kept too much there. If Valerie called directly Mr.Siegfedge himself, he said:

"I am disappointed at you. I thought you were different. Isn't there anything you can solve by yourself? Go and speak with Nick and ask him to send you one of his forklift drivers!"

Valerie went and spoke with Nick from sales to ask for help, but he refused her directly:

"I'm sorry, I cannot help you. My guys have a lot of work to do. Mr.Siegfedge knows this. I don't understand why he sent you to me."

This went on every day. Valerie ended up cleaning and arranging the materials in the incoming materials warehouse by herself. Her colleagues just wondered:

"Valerie, you are a manager. You cannot clean and carry out the garbage and arrange the materials."

"I am not a manager. Until I don't have any decision power I am just a simple employee."

"Yes, but it is not appropriate for a manager to do such things."

"Yes, I know, but I have no other choice. I have to keep the warehouse clean, it is my responsibility. But with the two people I have in my department, it is impossible to do it. They work like animals all day long for 200 euro per month. In that horrible warehouse. In winters, they freeze there and at summer they boil there. Plus, I cannot get any forklift driver to help me, because I'm not friends with Mr.Siegfedge. So, what can I do? I don't care what people say of me. I only care what daughter says of me. I will do whatever I have to do because I need the salary." answered Valerie.

«*And as soon as I find something better, I am out of here.*» thought Valerie. And she was searching and searching. She spoke with all her acquaintances and asked them if they heard about something to tell her. But the economy was still recovering after the crisis of 2008 and it was very hard to find a decent job.

Rava, the spiritual mentor was coming two times per year to their company and one year she invited Valerie and Victoria to visit her in England for a whole week. She agreed to pay for the airplane tickets and to accept them in her home offering food and lodging without Valerie having to pay anything. Valerie thought this was an extraordinary gesture coming from a total stranger. Mr.Siegfedge never even thanked her even for all the translating and interpreting she did in the company, even if it was not her job and she did not have to do. So, in August 2010, Valerie and Victoria went and visited England.

Valerie got two weeks holidays that summer, so for the first week they went to Mineville and helped her parents and then they went to England. They went to Steville by bus on Sunday afternoon. Valerie booked a hotel room right next to the bus station in Steville. Valerie and Victoria slept very badly that night and in the morning at 3 o'clock they woke up. At 4 o'clock they had to be at the airport as the plane was leaving at 6 o'clock. They took a taxi to the airport and at 4 o'clock they were there. Rava had a house-keeper named Dina, co-national with Valeria, and she got in touch with Valerie explaining her how it was going to be in the airport. Also, she sent Valerie the airplane tickets by email and checked in online for them the previous day. This way, Valerie and Victoria did not have to stay in the long queue, they just had to hand over the check baggage. The flight was alright, except for the paranoia of the local airport workers. They were, let's say, almost aggressive, very impolite and snappy. Valerie just compared them with the workers from the English airport, who were very polite. In London, Dina's husband waited for them and drove them to Rava's house.

Rava lived in a beautiful, big house inhabited by several families. The windows were looking towards a beautiful scenery, with a small lake and a lot of green vegetation surrounding it. Valerie never seen anything so beautiful in her life, it really looked like a fairy tale scenery. There were also little ducklings on the lake and little rabbits were running around it. How different was this from the view she saw from her window. The dirty wrecked blocks, with the walls falling down, the grass below her window with the garbage thrown out by the neighbors right through the windows…

Valerie and Victoria were hungry. In their family, if somebody came to visit, especially from far away, it was customary to invite them to eat. This was the first thing. Valerie did not hear any such invitation, so she said herself:

"*Boy, are we hungry! Can we get something to eat?*"

"*No, I'm sorry. We cannot eat right now. We have very precise eating hours and I wouldn't want to ruin the boy's schedule.*"

«*Oh, my God, we've come to a convent.*» thought Valerie. «*How strange. We turn our lives upside down to please foreigners when they come to us. We learn their language, we try to adapt to them, just to make them feel welcome. Now, that we've come here, no intention from her side to adapt to us. This is going to be interesting.*»

Rava had a son, but she was separated from her husband.

Finally, the lunch hour came and Valerie and Victoria could finally eat. Again, they felt like in a convent, seeing the food and the eating habits. It wasn't proper how they ate and what they liked to eat. Fortunately, Dina cooked them some cauliflower with mayonnaise and there was bread, so the first lunch did not turn out so bad after all. Plus Valerie had some very bad eating habits. For example she took some jam out of a jar, put the spoon in her mouth, then took some more jam. Rava said now she will have to throw away the respective jar of jam, as it was ruined, as her saliva was now all over the jar and now the jam was infested. Valerie recognized this was correct, but she used to do this all the time at home. Also, back home, if several persons, friends actually, were invited to eat together, they were all taking salad for example from the same bowl and took the salad with theirs infested forks and nobody ever died of this. Or they all eating with their spoons from the same big piece of cake and it was OK. How sick and dirty they all were back home! And how Valerie wouldn't trade that sick and dirty habits of them with all this proper eating from England!

The other meals they had were quite healthy, let's put it this way. Rarely something actually cooked. No soups or anything. No English breakfast.

In England was not as hot as home. At home, in August, you did not need any warm clothes, you could get by only with t-shirts and some shorts. In England, they were cold with the clothes they brought. Rava took them every day to visit another place, so time went by pretty quickly. Whenever they met somebody, Rava presented them:

"*They are Valerie and Victoria. They are from Eastern Europe.*"

Valerie always felt it was too much emphasis on the fact they were from Eastern Europe. So what if they were from Eastern Europe? Were they inferior or dangerous or something if they were from Eastern Europe? Or did those people speak something bad about Eastern Europe every day, so Rava felt she had to warn them this time not to mention anything, as these two spies were here now?

Valerie always felt some day she will visit England, and there she was and it all came to her, she wasn't the one who pushed for this trip to England.

Besides the fact that they were hungry the whole time and that they felt like some peasants in the castle of a king, the trip was a great one. After a week, they went back home. The plane was again at six o'clock in the morning and they had to drive a very long way back from Rava's house to the airport. Very strangely for Valerie, Rava did not wake up in the morning to say good bye to them. She said the evening before they left:

"*I will say good bye to you now. Tomorrow I don't want to wake up so early, I like to wake up whenever I am rested, without an alarm clock. Otherwise I feel tired all the time. So please be quiet in the morning when you leave. Dina's husband knows how to close the door.*"

«How fortunate of her» thought Valerie. *«I go to sleep at midnight when I finish my chorus in the house and feed my child and wash the dishes and all and at 5 o'clock in the morning I have to wake up to go to work. I must be very stupid or very Eastern European to have such a hard life…»*

When they got on the plane in England, there were 13^{0}C. When they got off the plane in Steville, there were 38^{0}C, it was a hot August day. Again they took a cab to the bus station, they waited a few hours until they had a bus back to Streamtown. First thing they did when they arrived home was to eat bacon with bread and onion. Some original, peasant local food, as rustic and filling as possible.

Sometime after their trip to England, Valerie and Victoria met with Alan in Steville. Alan asked Valerie:

"*So, what did you think of England?*"

"*Why do you ask?*" asked Valerie, trying with all her strength not to fight with him. She still a very hard time not to fight with him whenever they spoke. She knew Victoria did not like her to fight with him and for the sake of her daughter Valerie struggled to control herself.

"*I just wanted to know your opinion.*"

Valerie thought *«You weren't there when we came to Steville. You live in Steville, but you could not take us to the airport or back. Nothing, nothing at all, even though you live here, you stupid idiot.»* but she just sad:

"*I thought England was a very sad country. I felt an overwhelming sadness there, alright?*"

"*Compared to what?*"

"*Compared to us. We are much more joyful I think. Even though we have no reason for it, we are very joyful. We live our lives. Barbecuing and holidays.*"

"*And where did you live while you were in England?*"

"*At a spiritual mentor.*"

Alan made an expression when he heard this.

"*Is there a problem?*"

"*No, no problem, I just was not expecting this answer.*"

"*So, please tell me then what answers you expect from me, so that I can give them to you.*" said Valerie.

"*Mom, calm down.*" said Victoria.

"*I am calm. I don't understand why your father asks for my opinion as he always is irritated by my opinions.*"

Valerie wanted to be able to forgive Alan. She knew her hatred towards him had no effect on him, it only made her sick. She knew that whenever we hate somebody and we are not able to forgive them we just cause our own diseases and unhappiness. While the object of our hatred remains untouched and not caring, we are just eaten up inside by what we feel. After all, she was able to forgive her father, she should have been able to forgive Alan too.

"*What did you visit in England?*" continued Alan. He found a strange sort of pleasure in provoking the ones who were violent and frightening to him. Just like his father was when he was a child. When his father beat him up badly, for his mistakes, but also for the mistakes of his sister, Alan did not withdraw, he did not close down like most children would have down. He always provoked him just a little bit more. He thought «*Now he beat me up, what worse could he do? He'll kill me? He would just do me a favor! Let's see who gives up first.*» Valerie liked this in the beginning. She thought Alan was courageous when he defied his father or another scaring authority. With the passing of the years though, she did not like this anymore. She understood this courage of him had no result, no resolution, it was pointing towards no direction. « *Maybe he should have used this courage of his to stick with his wife and daughter and try to survive as a family, out there alone in this cruel world.*»

"*We visited a museum where we saw the golden carriage of the queen of England. Now I ask you: where did the queen of England get that gold from? Does England have so many gold ores?*"

"*Well, I think it's nice to have a golden carriage...*" Alan continued.

"*Yes, it's great, while the majority of the world's population is starving. It's just great.*" Valerie concluded. "*Just for the record, I thought the English were terribly arrogant. They think they were superior compared with us. With all their castles and history and so on. I think it's easy to be so rich when you go and rob other of what they have. My people was in the way of the Russians and the Turks and kept them out of Europe, so that the English can build their beautiful castles. We hardly could build a little house, the looters came and burnt it down. How could we build something lasting in these conditions? You know how we, Eastern European are? We are like orphans. Nobody throughout history has ever protected us. And the worse part is that we have a rich country too. A poor orphan is not so vulnerable by far as a rich orphan. Everybody wants what we have, and we are weak and there is nobody to protect us. This is our problem. Rava asked me if I am proud of my people."*

"So, what did you answer her?"

"I mean she asked it as if there was nothing at my people to be proud of. And I see where she is coming from. We Eastern Europeans are ashamed of how we are. We try to be like others, instead of being ourselves and be proud of how we are."

"What did you answer her?"

"I told her I am very proud of my people. Of course she asked me why. Surely she thought even if I say I am proud, I will have no decent reason to give her. It's not enough I am Eastern European, I am stupid too. Anyway, I told her I was proud of my people because we never went to another country to rob them and kill them and try to enforce our power over them."

"I'm sure she liked it." concluded Alan smiling.

Valerie hated she always got carried away with certain subjects. And there were people who knew this and also knew with which subjects she got carried away, so they provoked her. Many times she controlled herself, but sometimes she just couldn't.

She was lucky she had Victoria at her side. Victoria turned out to be a very well behaved, intelligent, beautiful young lady. But her best quality was the social intelligence. Very popular in her school, excellent student, friendly and mannered with everybody, always proactive and involved in any activities she could help. Valerie tried to explain her that people are not perfect and many of them are even evil, but we cannot live isolated from them. She always encouraged her to have her group of friends, especially because they were all good children, well behaved, not causing any trouble ever. Victoria was strong opinioned, just like her mother. She had a very clear opinion about anything and everything. This came from the long discussion with her mother about all kind of stuff. These discussions also made her think over things thoroughly and try to look at things from a different angle too, not only from the usual angle.

She was much more rational than her mother. One year, Alan called her to congratulate for her birthday on a different day from her birthday. Valerie just lost her temper in situations like this. Victoria just treated her father with disregard.

Victoria was educated by her mother's personal example, not like

Valerie and Alan was, from the drunken lectures of their fathers. She saw her mother overcome all the hardships, all by herself. She learned that she is strong and independent and that she also can overcome all hardships. She saw her mother working hard from dusk to dawn. She learned that the only way in life is hard work. She saw her mother going to church and praying every time she had the chance. She learned that God is there for her all the time and everywhere, not only when tragedies happen. She learned that she has to thank God every day for all the blessings, not only turn to Him when she was in trouble.

Financially, Valerie was doing better and better every year. In the summer of 2010, she bought her first car. It was an old car, manufactured in 2000, which they affectionately named Maggie. Maggie has been brought from Germany by somebody who was living of this activity. He registered it with provisory plate numbers, used it for a couple of months and then sold it. Eastern Europeans bought cars brought from Germany like crazy. There was a general opinion that such cars were better taken care of. Now, the registration of a car was quite an epic venture. First, you had to go with it to the Auto Registry. Here you had to make an appointment by the phone. They had free appointment hours only three or four weeks away. On the established date and hour, you presented yourself with the car. If the car had the plate numbers expired, you had to take it there with a platform. You waited a little bit, half an hour, an hour (even though you had an appointment). Then you drove your car in a garage and you waited another 15-20 minutes. After this, they gave you a paper. With this paper, you went into the next building and you paid the tax. Then, you waited for another 20-30 minutes until they gave you the identity card of the car. After this, you had to go to an office which specialized in the elaboration of the car registration file. At this office, the nice lady told you what documents you need to bring her back for the file. First, you needed the calculation of the pollution tax. For this, you had to go the regional financial administration with a copy of the car's identity card and a filled in application form. You registered these papers and they told you that after 3 working days, you could go back to them to get the calculation of the tax. Then, you needed to pay the registration certificate tax, only at a certain bank and it cost around 10 euro. Then, you had to go to the city hall and apply for a financial certificate, which had to state that you had no outstanding debts toward the city hall. For this you paid a fee of about 3 euro and you had to wait 3 working days. After you got the calculation from the financial administration, you had to go and pay it at the treasury. Now this was a very high amount of money. Maggie cost Valerie 1.800 euro. She had to pay for it 1.200 euro pollution tax. Well, after the pollution tax was paid and she got her financial certificate from the town hall, Valerie went back to the office that elaborated the car registration file. The lady there filled in an application towards the head of police from Julestown, which was the county seat, asking for the registration of the car. She also made for Valerie the compulsory insurance, which cost about 100 euro per year. With the identity card of the car, the calculation of the pollution tax, the payment of the pollution tax, the financial certificate from the town hall, the payment for the registration certificate, the insurance and the application, Valerie had to go to the police department of Julestown to register her car. Now here there were queues of tens of people. One person stayed around 10-15 minutes at the counter. Therefore, you queued there for hours to register your file. When you got to the counter, a policeman checked your file and told you should return in about 3 hours to get your plate numbers and the provisory proof of circulation. After 3 hours of waiting, you stayed in another queue. They gave you the plate numbers and the proof and told you will get the registration certificate by post in about three weeks. In order to be able to circulate outside the town, you had to buy also the vignette which cost about 25 euro per year. Of course, all these institutions were open in the morning only, when Valerie was at work. Even when she received the registration certificate by post, it was by registered mail and she had to go to the post personally to get it and the post office worked only between 9 and 17. To get there, she had to miss from work a couple of hours. Every time she missed from work, there were the raised eyebrows and the sighs.

Valerie got her plate numbers on a Thursday. That same Saturday, at 4 a.m. she got in her car with her daughter and they went to Mineville. It was a long trip of 280 km and she was not used to drive. When they left Streamtown, Valerie sat writhed, bent forward and drove slowly and carefully. It was dark outside, but at least there was no heavy traffic. Victoria felt asleep very fast on the seat next to her mom, as she woke up at 3 a.m. to be able to leave from home so soon. Valerie did not want to tell her anything, but she was terrified. She never drove more than 20 km at once and now she had to drive 280 km. Her mind was racing «*Oh my God. What if I get into an accident? What if the car breaks down? What if I have a flat tire? What am I gonna do? Alright, alright, just calm down, calm down. Let's see. I have to drive 280 kilometers. From Streamtown to Julestown there are 20 kilometers. I drove many times 20 kilometers. Actually, now I will drive again 20 kilometers, only 14 times. Yeah, that's it! I'll drive the way from Streamtown to Julestown 20 times! Oh, God, help me! Take care of us!*" Victoria slept almost until they got to Mineville. She looked at her mom and said:

"*Hey mom. Where are we?*"

"*We have 40 km more and we arrive to Mineville.*"

"*When I fell asleep, you were so tense and writhe. Now, you're leaned back and very relaxed. I am very proud of you!*"

"*I love you, baby!*"

"*I love you too mom!*"

Maggie became a family member. Valerie started now to drive really much. She went to Mineville every two or three months. She went to work with her own car. After a few months they agreed to pay her the gasoline for this. She gained now more independence to move around then she ever dreamt she could have. It was the first time she had a car. Camil and Eva never had one, so until Maggie she never knew how great it is to have car. Of course, this independence came at a price. She paid a lot of money all together to buy it and register it.

The first time Alan heard that Valerie bought a car, he had nothing positive to say.

"*Why did you buy this type? The spare parts are very expensive. You should have bought another car, the spare parts are less expensive.*"

"*Did I ask for your opinion? Did I come to you to ask what car to buy? Did I come to you to ask for one penny to buy my car? No! So what the hell do you care what car I bought?*"

"*No, I'm just saying. And you know, it is useless to buy a car and then keep it in the parking lot.*"

"*What makes you think I will keep it in the parking lot?*"

"*You know you are afraid to drive and all.*"

"*I am not afraid to drive. I did not want to drive next to you because you always criticized every move I made while I was driving our car, which was paid more by me and used exclusively by you. Regarding the fact that I am not capable of driving. You know, how you and your family always said I was not capable of driving. Hell, you said I will not be capable to even get my driving license. Well, for your information, I am capable of driving. I even like driving since I had my driving classes. And you know why? Because my driving instructor had faith in me and he had patience with me. So please don't worry about the car staying in the parking lot. OK?"*

Then of course the car services. Now, in the beginning Valerie thought that professionals were working in the car services. What could have she thought? They could tell her anything, what did she know about cars? Was there any way she could check what they were doing with her car after she left it in their service? In time, Valerie realized this was very serious issue in her country. Nobody was checking the activity of the car services. These were mostly small workshops opened by one mechanic who knew how to change a battery or a light at a car. Now this mechanic hired some boys to help him. Usually, in these places came to work boys who could not find any other job. And the trusting people brought their cars in, hoping they will be repaired by this bunch of amateurs. What on earth makes us think that a guy who is so stupid that he cannot articulate correctly one sentence in his native tongue is able to fix a car, a complicated assembly of tens of thousands of components working together?

Right after she bought Maggie, Valerie spoke with some colleagues and they all gave her ideas what to check at her car. She noted everything on a piece of paper and went to the car service. She asked the owner of the car service to change the oil and the oil filter, to change the fuel filter, the air filter and the pollen filter. She asked him to change the distribution belt. She asked him to check the wheels and balance them. She also asked him to tell her if he sees anything unusual, she wanted to have a safe car. She drove it very much and she felt her life depended on the safety of the car.

Valerie and Victoria were doing financially OK, but the stress at Valerie's work did not decrease at all. Valerie was still looking for a different job. She spoke with the influent lady who helped her get this job. She begged her for help. She updated her CV over and over again. She created profiles on all the job sites. Still, she could not find anything better than the job she already had.

Victoria had a good friend whose family had a beautiful golden retriever. Every time Valerie went there, this golden retriever came in front of her and stopped. Valerie always pet her for minutes and minutes and the dog just adored it. Once Victoria came home from school and told her mom:

"Mom, the golden is pregnant."

"Oh, she is? God, I love that dog."

"Yeah, I know. I think she loves you too."

"You know what?"

"What mom?"

"Tell them we want a puppy."

"What mom? Really? Are you serious?"

"Yes, I am serious. I want a puppy of our own. Will you help me with it?"

"Of course, mom. Oh, mammy, I am so happy!"

Valerie felt she had to have a golden retriever puppy. She never had a pet in her life, but this breed simply won her over.

The pups were born on the 29th of May 2011. There were five pups, one of them was still born. Three of them were OK, and the fifth was not breathing. A completely white beautiful little she dog, just not breathing. The owner remembered what she saw in 101 dalmatians, so she held the little pup in one hand and started to rub her belly with the other. And soon, the little pup started to breathe. Valerie heard this story and said:

"That's my girl. She will be our dog. All the other are cream, she is completely white. And the fact that she was not breathing… Oh my God. She reminds me of Victoria. Victoria was not eating after she was born. I think both of them came into this world and thought « What on earth did I do? Am I crazy? Is it a good idea to be born in this world?»"

Valerie and Victoria decided to call her Lady. They took Lady home with them when she was 7 weeks old. Valerie has always been fond of animals. Actually, this was the only good quality her mother in law ever recognized in her. While she was living at her in-laws, many times they left her completely alone with the whole household. First thing Valerie did in the morning when she woke up was to go to the animals. And there were quite a few in that household: cows, pigs, chickens, ducks, rabbits, cats and dogs. As soon as she felt hungry, she thought «*How about the animals? If I'm hungry, I get something from the fridge, but the poor animals? What do they do if they are hungry?»* So she went and cleaned their places, put them fresh water and then feed them all. It took her more than an hour. Then she did her normal chorus around the household: cooking, washing the laundry, cleaning the house, sewing, if Alan's sister was home, helping her with the homework. Then, in the afternoon when she felt hungry, again her first thought was to go and feed the animals. Nobody ever thanked her for anything in that house, on the contrary she never did anything right, she never said anything right, she did not even walk right through their courtyard. So when her mother in law once said "Whenever we leave the animals in Valerie's care, we know they are fed and well taken care of." she took it as the greatest compliment ever addressed to her. With Lady however, Valerie took it to the next level. Both her and Victoria were nuts for Lady. She was a very quiet, calm and loving dog, with a wonderful energy. Everybody wondered:

"*Wow, she is so good and quiet! And how she listens to you!*"

Valerie always answered them:

"*Of course she is. God only gives good, beautiful, smart and loving girls. They compensate the fact that no man has ever loved me in my life. And you know what? I prefer it this way!*"

When Valerie was over stressed or overworked, she lied down in bed and took Lady in her arms. Lady did not even dare to breathe. She just laid there next to Valerie and did not dare to move a muscle until Valerie got up. Valerie never saw such a good-breeding in any human ever. If she coughed or felt really bad, Lady used to come in front of her and looked at her with those beautiful brown eyes all preoccupied and putting her muzzle on her knee. On the other hand, Valerie and Victoria tried to be good masters for Lady. Even though they did not live in a house, but in an apartment, they took out Lady for walks three times a day. Every day, Valerie cooked for Lady fresh food. Some rice cooked together with liver or kidney and vegetables. Lady received all her vaccines and medications in due time and she was a happy dog. Always playful and loving. Every day she discovered some new talent of her beloved dog. She never imagined she could grow so fond of an animal. She never had a pet before. But having Lady, a whole new world opened up before her eyes. She understood we humans are not smart enough to understand how smart dogs are, how much they can do to help us.

Valerie has been wanting for years to buy herself a piece of land. She wanted to have a little garden of her own, with trees and flowers. She has done a lot of gardening in her life, but it was always in somebody else's garden. While she was working in her in-laws' garden she always thought « *I work, I work, but do I gain out of it? Of course, it is ours and blah blah, but what do I get out of it? I think this is way the communism was. Working on the field in the cooperatives. Working and working and seeing how somebody else is rich and living well... I work and work and Alan is in Steville with his girlfriend, his sister receives good clothes and money and house and I remain with nothing. I know I should work only out of consciousness, but I'm not that advanced.* » Now, seven years after her divorce she bought herself a car and she finally could afford to buy a piece of land. It had 680 square meters and it cost 6000 euro. It was at about 300 meters from the paved road, in a village right near Streamtown. Practically it was at around 7 kilometers from the block with her apartment. She managed to buy this land without getting any credit from the bank, in fact she was able to pay back also for the mortgage credit she took to buy her little apartment. So Valerie was credit free, owning and apartment, a piece of land and a car. She could not save the way she did when Victoria was little, but she still made huge efforts to spend as little as possible. Growing up and going to school, Victoria had good, but very rich friends, children of doctors and notaries and public prosecutors. Valerie fought and worked hard to keep up with those pretentions. But for herself she still did not buy anything. She always went on holiday to Mineville, where she did not have to spend more money. She still dressed modestly and never spent money on alcohol or cigarettes or stylists or massages and what not.

For the land, Valerie met with the sellers at the notary. She gave them the money, after that they signed the contract. Few days after this, Valerie spoke with a topographer. He had to come with the instruments and put the stakes in the corners of the land. For this operation, all the neighbors had to be present, so that they see with their own eyes that their land is not being invaded. Now this was always a very delicate situation in her country. People went crazy in all issues related to the land. Everybody came punctually except for the topographer of course. Until he came, the interrogation unfolded. Who Valerie was, was she married, and where does she work, and to which university does Victoria want to go, and what topographer did Valerie call. Oooh, that one? He's too young. He does not know his job right. Valerie should have called somebody else, and each and every neighbor had his or her own idea. Finally the topographer came and did his job. It seems he did it right, as nobody commented anything to the final results. After a few hours, Valerie's land was marked with four stakes. She had only one neighbor with fence next to her, the other three sides of the land were free and needed fence. Valerie was going to have a lot of work to do with this land.

Victoria was a very good pupil. She always learned by herself, Valerie did not have to push her. She was determined to go to the medical university of Steville. It was the hardest admission competition of all and it was hard to be a medical doctor in her country. The system was totally abandoned by the state – as all other systems in fact. The doctors had small salaries and it was a generalized corruption. The locals were dying with the thousands because of this corrupted and rotten system. Even so, Victoria wanted to become a medical doctor.

"*Victoria, it is hard to be a doctor nowadays in our country. Look what is happening in the hospitals. You think being a doctor is like in 'Grey's anatomy'? Well, it's not. It's a huge responsibility.*"

"*I know, mom. But I made up my mind. I want to become a doctor.*"

"*You know what? If I make a mistake, we make a credit note and it is all solved. If a doctor makes a mistake, a human dies. This is what I am talking about. It is a huge responsibility my love. Why don't you want to become a pharmacist for example?*"

"*A pharmacist? And sell drugs behind a counter? I might as well finish high school and become a store clerk! Why graduate a university to sell drugs behind a counter?*"

"*Alright, my love, alright. I am behind you all the way and I will support you in every way that I can until I die and beyond. I just want to open your eyes before you decide something.*"

"*I have already decided mom. I'm going to Steville to the medical university. I love you mom.*"

"*I love you too, baby.*"

This was Victoria's second greatest good quality. She knew exactly what she wanted. Therefore, she always got what she wanted. Valerie always used to tell her:

"My love, God or the Universe, however you want to look at it, are looking at you and asking «What does this girl want? We want to give her what she wants. So, what does she want?» If you know what you want, they will give it to you. If you don't know what you want, how could they give it to you? Just think about it. If they see somebody who does not know what he wants they say «Hmmm, what does this guy want? He wants to be with his wife... But he also wants to be with his mistress... He wants money... But he also wants to lose most of his time chasing pleasures... What shall we give him?» Do you understand my love?"

"Are you talking about my father?"

"No, I'm just talking extemporaneously."

And they both started to laugh. Of course, Valerie was speaking about Alan. But in the end Victoria grew up knowing exactly what she wants and not being ashamed or afraid of asking it upfront.

Victoria's first greatest quality was her social intelligence. She was outgoing and friendly and knew how she has to behave with everybody and anybody. Of course, as a teenager, she did not appreciate it, but Valerie cultivated it as much as possible.

"Mom, why am I so fat?"

"You're not fat my love. You are just OK. How do you want to be? You are my daughter and I have never been only skin and bone. Why don't you like the way you are?"

"Because I have to lose some weight. Why do you cook so much? Why did you teach me to eat anything?"

"Because eating everything provides your body with everything it needs. I never fed you with junk food or sweets or soda and chips. I always gave you healthy food. This is the thanks I get?"

"No, you don't understand. It's not that I am not thankful for your great cooking. But you said I was a picky eater when I was small. You should have left the way I was. We are eating too much, mom. And why don't I sing as well as you do?"

"Not everybody sings well my love. Your father does not sing well. So what? You have other qualities. What's the problem?"

"The problem is I don't like the way I sing and I don't like the way I look. And what is with my skin? You promised me when I grow up my skin will be clear. And look! Look!"

"*Victoria, my dear, you are just fine. You are a beautiful, smart, hardworking, healthy girl. Your greatest quality is the social intelligence. Be thankful for what you have. Your social intelligence will help you in all walks of life. It will help you as a doctor. You will see. People will love you. You will heal them only with a smile and a good word. Trust me.*"

As she went to church since she was a little girl, Victoria got used to do it and liked it a lot. Valerie wasn't like most of the parents who keep telling their children to go to church, while they never go. No, Valerie went also to church and prayed on her knees, thanking God for all the blessings in her life. She thanked God also for Alan. Valerie realized after years of suffering that God had sent her Alan to force her to evolve. If Alan would have been a good man, Valerie, as lazy as she was, would have stagnated. She would have just become another house wife and that would have been pretty much it. By sending her Alan, God made her realize what a powerful woman she was and gave her the courage to face life on her own.

Victoria was the only grandchild Camil and Eva had. She was not the only grandchild Alan's parents had, but she was the best according to their standards. Unlike her cousins, she was well-behaved, learned well in school, she was friendly and she went to church. Once, Alan's parents came to the church where Valerie and Victoria went every Sunday. Usually they went to the church on their street, but now God knows for what reason they came to this one. Victoria sang the Apostle. This was a fragment of the Holy gospel that was sung by a singer, right before the Priest read the Holy Gospel of the day. For the orthodox, it is a great honor to sing the Apostle in the church. Victoria also sang in the church choir. When the Holy Liturgy was over, the priest noticed Victoria grandparents in the church. He has known them for tens of years and he was not capable to understand why they treated Victoria and her mother as they did. After the greetings, he asked them:

"*Well, what do you say? Are you satisfied how your daughter in law brought up your niece?*"

Of course, they acted innocently, as they did not understand what he wanted to say. But Valerie's heart almost snapped out of pride and joy. She understood what he said and thought «*Well, what do you say? Even though you treated us bad, even though you always criticized us and treated us as the Cinderellas in the family, even though you pumped all your resources in your other child and you always neglected Alan and his family, look how my daughter turned out to be! She turned out to be the golden child you ever dreamt to have as a niece! And this is the granddaughter you threw out on the street! You can know a tree by looking at its fruitage. You know if a mother is good, by looking at her child. If her child is healthy, happy, well adjusted, good citizen, than she is a good mother. You cannot tell a good mother by looking at her hair-do or the length and colour of her finger-nails. You know if a wife is good by looking at her husband. If he is happy, clean and well fed. I was never good for you. Never."*

Valerie was very open with Victoria since she was born. She tried to explain her about men and sex and all as soon as possible, just because she wanted Victoria to get good quality information, instead of junk from the street, the TV and the internet.

„My love, the most important thing is the open and honest communication between us. Please tell me everything. Anything crosses your mind. If you think I'm stupid, please say it to my face. If you think I stink, please say that to my face, don't keep it in your mind. Whatever happens, tell me about it. The sooner I know about it, the sooner we can find a solution. Any problem should arise, no matter how complicated, if you manage it, it can be solved. But you have to manage it. If you stick your head in the sand like the ostrich, it will just get worse and worse." Valerie was thinking when she was a teenager. When her period was late once and she thought she was pregnant, she thought the world will end. She thought her parents will throw her out of the house. Why should Victoria go through this hell?

„OK, mom."

„If you want to be with a boy, better tell me about it. I'll let you here in the house. Here it is clean, nobody will know. Why go in some sordid motels just to be together with him? It doesn't make sense."

„I don't want to be with any boy mom."

„I know, I know, but one boy could come up. I just want to tell you that I'm here for you no matter what should occur. No matter what. Do you understand my love?"

„Yes, mom."

„I have just one pretention regarding this."

„What is it mom?"

„If you get pregnant by accident, and it happens, it's not the end of the

world, please get pregnant with an intelligent man. Stupid people are all around us. They multiply exponentially. So please, do not have a child with a stupid man. You owe me that much. You owe it to your family, to your people and to your species. Alright my love?"

„*Alright mom.* "answered Victoria smiling. „*You're not quite normal, you know that?"*

„*I know, I know.*"answered Valerie also smiling.

Victoria's eighteenth birthday was coming up. This was the age when children became adults when they turned eighteen. With this occasion, it was customary to make a big party, usually in a restaurant and to invite all the classmates and the friends. It was all very expensive, but everybody did so. Valerie did not want anybody to say that she cannot afford the same thing for her daughter, so she decided to make it as big anybody of Victoria's class did.

Valerie hired a restaurant for the evening of her daughter's eighteenth birthday. She invited around 30 persons. She had to buy Victoria a dress and everything went with it: the shoes, the purse. She had to pay for the photographer and the DJ. Victoria had to go to a stylist for her hair and her makeup. As a present for her daughter, she thought to buy her a laptop and a smart phone. When she added all up, it came to the amount of 13000 crowns, which was around 2800 euro. It was quite an amount. Valerie also wanted to buy her daughter a car at her eighteenth birthday, but she couldn't yet. She sent an SMS to Alan with the amount she had to pay and asking him to contribute too. Wasn't Victoria his daughter too? Valerie wrote him the total amount and wrote he should pay for half of it. Alan was very surprised by this SMS and called her up.

"*Hey, I've got your message.*"

"*So? What are going to do about it?"*

"*I agree that I should pay half of it. I just have one tiny question.*"

"*Shoot.*"

"*What did you buy her as present? You wrote the costs for every item and you wrote her present cost 4000 crowns. What was this present?"*

"*It was a laptop that cost 2500 crowns and a smart phone that cost 1500 crowns. Alright? I think she deserves it. All her friends have such things and she is as good as any of them.*"

"*I see, I see. Well, can I pay in monthly installments? My part is 6500 crowns, can I pay you 1000 crowns a month? I don't have this kind of money all at once."*

"I don't have that kind of money either all at once, but I have no choice. I have to come up with it and that's all that it is to it."

Alan paid 1000 crowns once and that was it. Valerie paid on her own everything. It did not bother her she paid for everything by herself, she was used to it, what bothered her was Alan again promised something and did not do what he promised.

Chapter 15

The more Valerie aged, the more money she had. She did not look older, she looked better and better. However, she never forgot how hard it was for her in the beginning. She never forgot the washing of the laundry with her hands, therefore she was grateful she had an automatic washing machine. She never forgot the going out in the night, therefore she was grateful she had a warm, clean bathroom in her little apartment. She never forgot how much she had to carry in her arms and how hard it was to walk so much, especially when she was pregnant, therefore she was grateful for the car she had. Valerie thanked God for everything she had, all the time.

After she got Lady, having to walk her every day, Valerie lost a few kilograms. She was a little overweight. The truth was she liked to eat. There was no food in the world she did not like. She ate when she was stressed, she ate when she was tired. She ate when she felt lonely. Food remained her only consolation and pleasure in life.

Victoria was the one who pushed her constantly to improve her look, to lose some weight, to go and get a decent hair dye and hair cut. Valerie knew Victoria was right, but she felt nobody was interested in her, so why bother?

After the divorce, Valerie never got involved with another man. Even though her sister in law was looking at her tummy, as if she divorced because she got pregnant with the wrong man, it was the other way around. It was Alan who had a child outside wedlock, it was him who could hardly wait for the marriage to be over so that he can move in with another woman. Valerie remained alone. All those years. In the first five or six years after the divorce she did not even feel the need to have a partner. A woman struggling literally to survive, fighting every day to put food on the table and clothes on her child has no time and energy and no need to have relations with men, no matter what people thinks. Besides that, she was convinced whatever man she will chose, it will not turn out well. With her luck with men, she probably would have brought in the house some jerk who only would have abused her and worse, he would have abused her daughter. Valerie did not want to take that risk. It seemed to her men were too selfish. They think loving a woman means giving her and doing with her what you like. When, in fact, love means exactly the opposite of that. To love somebody means to give up what you want and do what your beloved one really needs. To love a woman does not mean to call her up and chat with her for hours on the phone, it means to go there where she is and help her cut the grass or clean the house, so that she finishes quicker and then you can both relax. To love a child does not mean to buy him or her sweets. It means to go out in fresh air and ride a bike or play with him or help him or her study. To love a dog does not mean to bother it within your yard, it means to take it out for a long walk. To love your parents does not mean to cry at their funeral and put beautiful flowers on their graves after they are gone, it means to help and respect them with all your strength while they are still alive.

Professionally, it wasn't any easier. Valerie was going every day to work thinking that same day she will get fired. In time, though, somehow, she got used to this feeling. Financially things were improving every month. Of course, they were not improving by themselves. She watched her expenses very carefully. She kept her job and she also translated in her spare times. There were months when she got around 300 euro only for her translations. Of course, this meant she went to sleep at twelve or one o'clock at night and woke up at four o'clock in the morning and went ten to twelve hours to work too, but this was the price. Now she also had the land, she had a lot of work to do there too, nobody was helping her except for Victoria. Still, in the rare moments when she caught her breathe, she felt lonely. She was always alone for Christmas and for New Year's Eve. While she was married to Alan, Victoria was too small and he was always spending the holidays with Isabella. After she divorced, Victoria grew up and spent the holidays with her friends. Valerie was encouraging her to do so. She wanted Victoria to have good friends, as she knew better than anybody how hard it is to get through life on your own. Valerie was OK with being alone for the holidays, she did not mind to be alone in general, but sometimes she missed being with a partner by her side.

What she wanted was a man to hold her like Peter Gabriel holds Kate Bush in "Don't give up" video clip. Valerie needed a man who helps her start up the car when it does not want to start up. A man that took the dog once a day out for the walk. A man who helps her dig the hole in the ground so that she can plant the tree. A man that helps her cut the grass. A man that helps her paint the log cabin every once in a while. She did not need a man who keeps her on the phone for hours when he is on duty and he is bored. She did not need a married man who cheats on his wife with her (of course he loved Victoria more than anything else, but, you know, he's married, now what could he do?). Valerie did not need a man who has time to meet her once every three months and the rest of the relationship takes place on the phone. For this type of relationships she already had her marriage, which took place on the phone and she saw physically her husband once a month and she ended it. She did not need a man who tells her that his wife spends more on the cigarettes than she earns, or a man that tells her every word his wife tells him, or how she does not do anything. Really, she didn't. She had so much work to do. What she needed was a man to be with her permanently as a serious, reliable partner.

This kind of man however she could not find. There were plenty of men interested in a short adventure, but nothing more. They were not interested to work with her, they were not interested to hear what she had to say, they were not interested in spending their lives with a woman that did not own, or at least had chance to inherit a decent house. After all, this is why Alan left her too. He chose Isabella because she had an apartment in Steville. While Valerie did not have anything, at least not when he left her. So, why waste his life on her? Just because they had a child? That was no reason to stay with his wife! He had a child with Isabella too, so he was better off with her!

Valerie's best cure was always work and more work. She sank so deep in her work, that she was able to forget about loneliness completely for days, weeks, even months. Her first concern was her job of course. Than the translations. Now she had also her piece of land to manage. She considered a property means responsibility. If you are not capable or not willing to manage a property, better sell it and keep the money in the bank, this way at least they will make some interest. She started with the fence and the gate. First, she called Alan. His motto was: "*If you need anything, just ask me. I will help you.*" Well, Valerie told him she needed help to make the fence. Alan answered "*If we have to, we'll do that too.*" After which he told her a long lecture about how a fence must be built, what materials are necessary, which are the steps to do it and so on. All this info Valerie could find on Google, what she needed was physical help, which she did not get. Then, she spoke with a couple of men who were prowling around her and also told her to ask them if she needs help. They told her that it is a lot of work to make a fence and they did not have time. Then, Valerie contacted a specialized company from the village where the land was and asked them if they can make her a fence. They told her to come to their office to discuss. Valerie went to their office. She explained what she needed, then they went to see the land. Valerie told them she could not attend the work, but they could go anytime they wanted to make the fence, the only thing was that the neighbors had to be notified, so that they could come and assist the operation. God forbid Valerie built a fence on their land.

Valerie spoke for the first time with this company in the beginning of October. She called them every week. Every week they had a different excuse. They did not have time. The machine broke down. They have a very important job. They did not have time. And so on and so forth. Finally, they made Valerie the fence a couple of days before Christmas. These ones that made the fence did not make the gate too, so Valerie spoke with another guy and coordinated him so that he installed the gate when they were working at the fence. The guy with the gate complained endlessly that it was cold in his garage when he manufactured the gate and it was cold when he went to erect it with the fence, and how much he worked in the cold and how his hands and feet were freezing. Unfortunately Valerie was not impressed. As a principle, Valerie did not feel sorry for men. Especially for those who hurt women. She did not feel sorry for those who live in a bigger house than hers. It's true that it was pretty hard to find a family that lives in a house with less than 10 sqm / head, but this was the situation. She did feel sorry for her colleagues who come back from a two-week vacation tired, with the after-vacation depression and complaining they don't have money, after she has been working all along.

Finally, when the fence with the gate were done, Valerie paid the workers thanking God it was finally over. The next step was the fountain. There was no source of water there and Valerie thought this the most important thing of all. So she called again the company who made the fence and asked them to dig a fountain. It took again several weeks and tens of phone calls, but in the end it was solved.

Valerie started to plant trees and a grapevine. She also made a little garden for vegetables and for flowers. It was very hard work. As there was no garden there before, the land was covered with grass and it was full of stones. Valerie started to dig it with a pickax, then with the spade. Only Victoria helped her. She had to cut the grass. She considered that she had to maintain her piece of land well taken care of, even if she could not afford luxury. She spent there every Saturday. In the morning at five she was out there, as she preferred to work at cooler temperatures. Many times she went also in the evenings too after work, in summer. She watered her garden and the trees with the bucket, from the fountain all summer long. Every time she went to her garden, she took Lady too. For Lady, this was the highlight of the day. She spent most of the time in the apartment. Valerie took her out for a walk in the morning, before work. After that, Lady stayed alone in the apartment until Victoria came home from school. They took another walk. In the evening another walk and that was pretty much it. Therefore, when Valerie took her to the garden, she was the happiest dog in the world. Valerie threw her little balls or pieces of wood and she ran to catch them and brought them back to Valerie. Right after Valerie cut the grass, she liked to lay down on her back on the grass and tried to bite her own tail, once at left and once at right. She barked and growled with great pleasure.

At work, things deteriorated even more. The company had serious financial difficulties, therefore, it sold the majority of its shares to a foreign guy. This guy appointed his man, Mr.Liqman, to be the general manager of the company. Consequently, Mr.Siegfedge and his brother stepped aside. Now this was the moment when hell broke loose. Mr.Liqman came convinced that all locals were stealing from the company and they had to be monitored very closely.

He was very careful to call Valerie up every twenty minutes and ask her some detail. Like how wide is a certain scotch tape they were acquiring. Or how many types of scotch tape are there in the world and what is the manufacturing technology for their production. She did not know all these details, so he had every reason to wonder:

"How come you don't know this? You are a chemist! What did you learn in school?"

They held meetings every day. One day they decided to acquire a certain type of a hot melt adhesive for example. Then, in the evening, when everybody was already home, Mr.Liqman re-discussed it with the production manager, who was also foreigner, and they decided to buy another type of hot melt adhesive, without informing anyone. The next morning, Valerie came to work and ordered the hot melt according to what she knew from the previous day. Right after that, she received the email from Mr.Liqman saying that she was out of the system. That she not informed and not involved as she should have been as manager in the company and that he was seriously thinking of replacing her and so on.

The manufacturing process was not going well. Lots and lots of scraps resulted because of the poorly managed production. Of course, these generated huge losses of materials, which led to material shortages. The foreigners never admitted there were huge quantities of material thrown away. On the other hand somebody had to be blamed for the losses. So they started the witch hunt against the suppliers. They stated that materials were missing because the suppliers sent less materials than they invoiced, instead of admitting the real root cause of the material losses. In the middle of this was Valerie, who had to fight all the time with the suppliers on the one hand to push them to reduce the prices and to force them to accept payments 3, 4, 5 even 6 months after the invoice date, on the other hand to check every incoming delivery – and there were tens and tens every day- and in the mean time to try to maintain a good relationship with them, because she always needed the materials very urgently. Every single day Mr.Liqman told Valerie:

"*You are incompetent. I will have to replace you.*" or "*Until you are still department responsible, you have to do this and that.*" or "*You are too slow, you don't react fast enough.*"

Another thing Valerie had to calculate was the cost of the materials that went into the finished goods. This seems easy to do, but not anybody understands how it has to be calculated. Valerie knew how to calculate it. So she did it over and over, several times per week. Then, she had to explain how she calculated it to Mr.Liqman. Then to the lady that had been hired to supervise the financial activities of the company and who had no knowledge whatsoever, except for the speaking of the foreign language. Her name was Aura. Then, the calculation was sent to the mother company abroad and when they asked for explanations, neither Mr.Liqman, nor Aura could explain it. So they called up Valerie. Whenever they felt like it. It did not matter it was after working hours, in the evening or on her day off. With these occasion, Valerie got again verbally abused and offended by Mr.Liqman on the phone, whose final conclusion was that she, Valerie, did not understand anything about anything and that she had to explain thoroughly the next day how she made the calculation. So the next day Valerie went to work and sent a 3-4 pages email, explaining in the smallest details, with formulas like in primary school how she made the calculations. An hour or two after she sent the email she went to her boss and asked him:

"*I have sent you the email with the calculation of the cost. Did you read it? Is it OK?*"

"*Ohh, I don't know, I did not have time to read it.*" was the answer of her boss.

Finally, Mr.Liqman's boss came to visit them and Valerie explained him the calculation and he said it was OK. Only then it was accepted that Valerie's calculations were good.

On one winter afternoon the managers were in a meeting. Mr.Liqman looked out on the window and he saw it was starting to snow. So he looked at Valerie and said:

"*It's snowing outside. It's your responsibility, you know that.*"

"*I know, I know*" answered Valerie.

This actually made her laugh, even though her boss did not joke when he told her this. She was so afraid not to be fired from her job, that she accepted anything he told her. She had to accept everything until she found another job. She needed money to raise her daughter, what could she have done?

Whenever they were talking about a supplier, Mr.Liqman looked at her and asked:

"*Are they your friends?*"

"*No, they are not.*" answered always firmly Valerie. She had no supplier friends. She never received one penny from any of the suppliers, but her boss continued accusing her of this. When in fact he was the one who had supplier friends, from his beloved native country. And he was the one forcing her to purchase from his friends. But this was OK. Because he was the general manager and he could do whatever he pleased.

Otherwise, he was just a drunk, divorced of his wife and wasting his life and his money with bimbos from Polville, where he lived in a rented apartment. He got drunk every night and some nights he drove drunk back to the factory with one of his girlfriends to show off that he is the general manager of a factory, just to impress her. The workers saw him, as the factory was working three shifts a day. A stupid boss however. An intelligent boss knows how to keep by his side the good, hard working employees. The stupid boss chases the good employees away.

The production manager was not better than him. In the morning he was sober, but as soon as the indirect personnel went home, he got drunk in the factory and acted rudely and shouted to the workers. Poor workers had to put up with this. The factory was far away from Streamtown and far away from Polville. There were villages all around and at least this factory sent a bus to bring them to work. They were simple people, they could not afford to commute to work in Polville or Streamtown. So they looked at this production manager and wondered how low he can sink. The working conditions were bad. In the summer it was very hot and there was a lot of dust inside the factory. Many of them worked on the production line, standing in foot for straight 10 hours. One of the women was pregnant and the team leader put a chair near her to be able to sit down every now and then. The production manager saw the chair so he lifted it up and throw it far away from the line. The chair broke and the pregnant lady got scared and started to cry. She had to be taken to the emergency room.

Valerie was continuously under the pressure of reducing the costs. For this, she had to search for new suppliers for materials. No resources were given her for this, she just had the internet and the phone and, of course, in the mean time, she had to do her daily job too. Which was ordering materials, insist for payments to the suppliers, checking incoming materials deliveries, ordering transports for all incoming materials, ordering spare parts, keeping the warehouse clean and in good order and so on. Valerie understood she had to fight to reduce the costs, she understood that she had to constantly find new suppliers and negotiate lower prices all the time, what she did not understand was what could she have done more so that her work will be appreciated. Amongst many mind games, Mr.Liqman had one with finding new Chinese suppliers. He found on the internet tens and tens of suppliers with contact persons. He forwarded the contact to Valerie. If Valerie did not send in the next ten minutes a price quotation request, with all the details of volumes and characteristics of the raw materials they needed, her boss sent her immediately an email:

"Did you contact this?"

"What about this?"

"You are too slow Valerie. You always react with delay. I will have to replace you with a younger person. We cannot wait until you wake up."

When this supplier search game came over her boss, Valerie was afraid to stand up of her chair or go to the bathroom either or drink a cup of coffee. As soon as he sent the contact, she immediately sent the quotation request, copying her boss so that he saw she contacted them. One day, while he sent these emails with the tens, he called her up to the first floor to speak with him. Valerie left her computer and went to his office. He was laughing. He was actually laughing with tears in his eyes. He was laughing together with Aura how stressed Valerie was, how afraid she was not to be fired, how fast she tried to contact the suppliers, just to please her boss. Valerie looked at him. He was laughing with tears of her. She just looked at him, with the same look she gave her father, when she was a small girl at home and he was threatening to kick her with his foot in her face. Males thinking they have power over females that economically depend on them. Dear males, you may think you have power over us until we economically depend on you, but as soon as we shall find another variant, we shall leave you. We are just temporarily using you. It's just like when you pay us to have sex with you. You do that because you don't have the brains to make us give you what you want for free. Think about it.

In addition to the hard times she had at work, there was the commute to her home and back. There still was no highway between Streamtown and Polville. Every 25 kilometer trip home from work took several hours. The queues of cars wanting to enter in Streamtown were stretching over 10-15 kilometers. This went on for years and years. At a certain moment, the local authorities decided to fix the railway crossing right at the entrance of Streamtown. They worked for months and months, this added to the queued of cars. The work did not last long, after a couple of weeks it had to be fixed again. All this out of the taxpayers money. The state did not care. They knew they could do whatever they wanted, the people could not do anything about it. There was nobody to protect them. All that mattered was for the few fortunate ones, the ones with the influence and the money, to get more money by granting the works to companies that bribed them. They remained with the money and the people were staying in queues for hours.

After months of search she found new suppliers for some materials. Of course they did not visit the Chinese suppliers, but when she found a new local supplier, her boss wanted to go to visit them and Valerie had to accompany him. Now this was particularly difficult for her, as she disliked him so much that it was very hard for her to sit in the car right next to him. But she did it anyway and listened him bragging about how great and rich and talented he was. On the way, somewhere between localities, they had an incident. Mr.Liqman, in his infinite wisdom, ran out of gas. The car was running at a high speed and suddenly he had no brakes. He panicked and started:

"*Valerie, Valerie, I have no brakes.*"

"*So don't stop.*" she answered smiling.

"*You don't understand, I have no brakes, I cannot stop. What can I do?*" he was really afraid and this caused Valerie an immense pleasure.

"*So reduce the speed by reducing the step on the manual gear.* "Valerie was having a great time seeing him how weak and stupid he was. She was not afraid. She was convinced God would not let anything bad to happen to her. And she understood that God has created this situation especially for her. God has put her boss show upfront his weakness and stupidity. Because the character of a person is revealed in the crisis situation. That is when each and every one of us show what we are capable of. Not back in the office when we are the great mega-galactic general managers. No, in these crisis situations that take us out of our comfort zone is when we show who we really are. The car stopped finally. Of course, Valerie had to solve the situation again, who else? The *man* with whom she was travelling? No way! She had to ask every truck passing by to give them some gas. Neither one of them wanted to give them gas. So they hitchhiked to the nearest locality, bought some gas in a small recipient, hitchhiked back to the car and got going again.

After the visit at the supplier, on the way back to the factory, Valerie's boss asked her:

"So, are you hungry?"

"No, thank you, I am not."

"How come? We did not eat all day and now it is afternoon."

"I don't know how, but I'm just not hungry."

"Would you like us to stop at a restaurant to eat?"

"No, thank you. I would like to get back to the office as soon as possible. I still have a lot of work to do."

"I know, I know, but we can stop to eat or at least drink a coffee."

"Thank you, but I really am not hungry and I don't want to stop."

For Valerie, eating has always been a social act. The older she became, it was harder and harder for her to eat with people that tortured her over and over again. She couldn't have swallowed a piece of bread in his presence. But how could he even invite her to eat? After the way he was treating her at the office, now he thought she actually will accept his invitation to eat in a restaurant at the same table with him?

Valerie could not possibly be friendly with Mr.Liqman. This was just as sickening for her like when being a child she saw her father feeling sorry and crying, after he beat up her mother until she dropped on the floor. The best she could was to do her job the best way possible, hoping she will not get fired and searching unabatedly for another job.

One a July morning, after walking Lady and preparing for another day of work, Valerie heard the phone ringing. «*Who could be so early? Probably Mr.Liqman found some problem in the factory and he wants to fire me over the phone.* » It wasn't her boss, it was Eva. «*Hmm, something is wrong, she never calls so early.*»

"Hello mom. What's up?"

"I'm afraid I have some horrible news." said Eva almost crying.

"What happened?"

"Eduard died."

"What? How? What do you mean died?"

"He died last night, in the evening. The paramedics said it was a heart attack, but the autopsy still has to be performed."

"Oh my God. Oh my God. And you? How are you? I hope you'll not going to die on me too!"

"No, no, don't worry. We're fine. Considering what happened... We'll tell you all about it at home. Can you come home?"

"I don't know if they will let me miss from work..." this is what Valerie actually said. She told her grieving mother by the phone that she is not sure she will be able to come home and burry her brother because she was afraid to ask for a couple of days off from work. Hearing herself she realized what an absurdity she said. *«How can I be so cruel? How could I say something like that to my own mother when she lost her child? Of course I'll go home. I don't care if he fires me, I will go home.»*

"Sorry mom. I didn't mean to say that. We shall come home today. I just go for a couple of hours to work to leave everything in good order and then we come home. In the afternoon we should be home. Can you manage until then?"

"Yes, dear, it's perfect. We arranged as much as we could, but there are still some things to do. You know how it is. But if you come, I know you will take care of everything. We need you."

"I know mom. I know. Is it OK if I come in the afternoon?"

"Yes, it's fine. And please drive carefully. It does not change anything if you come half an hour later, better safe than sorry."

"Alright mom. I'll call you when we leave from Streamtown. Get some rest if you can. Love you"

"Alright darling, we're waiting for you. Love you too."

Valerie went to work. She informed her colleagues about her brother's death and about the fact that she had to go home urgently. She could not cry, she was numb. With great effort, she tried to focus and to arrange everything before she went away. Later her boss arrived to work. She went to him and told him she had to go home the same day. She was prepared for the worst. She was convinced he will not accept this, but she was determined to leave whatever he said. Much to her surprise, her boss said:

"Of course you can leave. Do you need somebody to drive you home, to Mineville?"

"No, no, I'm fine. I will drive."

"Will you be able to drive in this state?"

"I have my guarding angel with me, my daughter. Thank you, but I will be fine."

This was probably the first human reaction from her boss's side after more than a year of working together. Strange what a deep effect had death on people.

Valerie's colleagues raised money and gave it to her to help her. It was customary to raise money for colleagues with deaths in the family, the expenses in these situations were astronomical. It was also stipulated by the law that the company had to give a financial aid to the employees with deaths in the family, but this particular company did not give a penny to Valerie with this occasion.

Valerie left everything in good order at work. She went home early, took Victoria and they both left for Mineville. It was a four hours drive, the traffic was horrible and Valerie felt she was losing it. The only thing that kept her attentive to the road was that Victoria was by her side and she did not want anything bad happen to her girl.

After they arrived home, Eva told them the whole story. On Wednesday afternoon Eduard called them on the phone. Each and every one of them. It happened rarely that Eduard called up both her parents, her sister and her niece. They could not understand well what he was saying, but they all thought the phone signal was weak. He spoke last time with Victoria, asked her when she was going to come to Mineville, how she finished school and so on and ended:

"*Alright, darling, I am going to go lay down a little. It's still early, but I don't feel so good. We'll speak tomorrow. Good night, my dear.*"

"*Good night, Eduard.*" answered Victoria.

Eduard laid down in bed and died of a heart attack. Even though she spoke just a few minutes ago with him, Eva felt something was not right. She called back Eduard but he did not answer.

She told Camil:

"*Pop, something is wrong. Eduard does not answer the phone.*"

"*Maybe he fell asleep. You know he does not hear the phone when he sleeps.*"

"*I know, I know, but something is not right. I am going to go over to him.*"

"*Alright, I'll go with you. We'll get a cab.*"

Eva took the keys to Eduard's apartment, they got dressed, called a cab and went to Eduard. They arrived in front of her door and knocked. No answer. Even though she had keys, Eva pushed simply the door. Strangely, it was not locked. They went in and found Eduard lying on the bed. Eva tried to wake him up, but she was not able to. They realized their son was dead. They called 911. The paramedics came immediately and declared him dead. The problem was he was too young to die, only 48 years old and the police had to be notified. The police came, took some notes and pictures. Then Eduard was taken to the morgue for the autopsy as the cause of death had to be found. Eva and Camil had to go to the police. The policemen asked them if they wanted to make the official statement that night or they wanted to come back next morning. Eva accepted to make the declaration right away. After they were over with that, at around 3 o'clock in the morning, they arrived home. Eva and Camil were over seventy years old when their son died. They both had cardiac problems and all this ordeal and the bureaucracy almost pushed them over the edge. They decided not to call Valerie so early, what could she have done in the middle of the night? They were going to call her in the morning.

After speaking with Valerie, Eva dressed up and went back to the police. She waited there for the result of the autopsy. From there, they sent her to the public prosecutor office, then back to the morgue, again to the police. Finally, she took the paper they gave her to the Civil register, so that they could issue the death certificate. It was a very hot summer, Eva could hardly stand on her two feet, shocked by the death of her daughter and ill, but she had no choice. She did all this by herself, Camil felt even worse and he did not even get out of the house. In the afternoon, after Valerie and Victoria arrived home, Eva felt a little relieved, at least she did not have to arrange everything by herself.

The next morning, they had to go to the morgue to take Eduard out and take him to the cemetery. They spoke with some guys who had a mortuary car. With some clothes for Eduard and with their hearts broken and frozen, they went to the morgue. Eduard was not ready yet to be released. They had to wait there more than an hour. Valerie had to sign the release paper. Then Eduard, was put in the mortuary car and they left. Neither of them was crying. Eva did not want to shock Valerie and Victoria more than they were. Valerie did not want to shock Victoria with her pain. Victoria was very afraid that Eva or Valerie will break down. Each of them was looking after the other two, so they behaved very quietly, unlike a typical conational would have behaved. Eastern Europeans are loud people. They like to show their emotions to the world. Some workers were renovating the morgue right in that period and saw when Eduard was taken out on the entrance hall and put down on the floor in her casket, right at the feet of the two women. They actually commented that they were not crying:

"*Look at them. They are destroyed! Look how they are weeping!*" said one of them ironically.

Valerie just looked at him. In normal conditions, she would have reacted, but now it was not the case. She thought «*How can they be so cruel? Even if they think it, how can they say it out so loud that we can hear them? And what do they care if we cry or not? Do they know what is in our heart? Why don't they mind their own business? May God repay them for this!*"

Several month before Eduard died, Valerie approached her parents with the issue of the places in the cemetery.

"*Don't get me wrong, but I really have to ask you something.*"

"*What is it?*" answered Camil. "*You know you can ask us anything.*"

"*I don't know what is the situation with the burial places in the cemetery. Does our family have something arranged for this? I know near grandma we have no place, right?*"

"*Right, it's true. Well, we have no places. Truth is the old cemetery where grandma is buried is completely full. There are no more places there. I have to ask around.*"

"*Can you do that, dad? Please. Please don't get me wrong, but I like to be prepared, at least to know what I have to do if something bad happened.*"

"*I'll ask around. You are right. We have to arrange this in time.*"

Camil did ask around. He found that a new cemetery was founded near the city, he went there and bought to places. He thought he will be the first buried there. But it was Eduard who was buried first there. In the tragedy that happened, at least they had this issue solved.

Camil called the cemetery to announce the death of his daughter, but this was not enough, Until the burial, the deceased had to be kept in one of the mortuary chambers, and those were managed by a private company, unlike the cemetery itself, which was run by the local authorities. After the mortuary car arrived with Eduard, the guys unloaded the casket with her and put her into the entrance hall. The owner of the mortuary chamber became very angry and started shouting:

"*What are you doing? Take this away from here. How dare you put something here without my permission? Nobody spoke with me about this. This is a private company you know."*

Valerie came running from her car:

"I'm coming, I'm coming. I was not able to speak with you, I did not have your number."

"Alright guys, take the deceased back in the car and you Madame come to my office."

Valerie went to his office, she paid for everything. She did not get any receipt and she did not have the presence of mind to ask for one. Only after that he gave the permission for Eduard to be brought into one of the rooms and he informed Valerie the burial will be on Saturday at 12 o clock at noon.

After this was solved, Valerie and Victoria went to the civil Register to get the death certificate. Another queue. After that they went to speak with a priest. Territorially, Eduard was belonging to one of the Catholic churches from Mineville. In principle, the respective priest had to bury Eduard. They did not find the priest at noon, they have been told to return in the evening. They just could pay for the contribution to the church and for the burial fee. This contribution was an amount of money every person had to pay per year at the church. If you did not pay it during your life time, when you were dead, your family had to pay it for you retroactively, otherwise the priest did not bury you. In the evening, Valerie and Victoria returned to church to speak with the priest. They waited for about an hour until he finished the Vespers. Finally, the priest accepted to speak with them.

"Now who was this man, your brother? I never saw him come to church."

"Well, he did not come to church it's true."

"Why didn't he come?"

"I don't know." answered Valerie. What could she have said?

"How can you not know? If you ask me something about a sister or a brother of mine, I can answer you. How come you don't know this about your brother?"

"I'm sorry, but I just don't know."

"OK, so tell me something about him. I see you brought the death certificate. I need to know something about him. Was he married?"

"No, he wasn't."

"Did he have any children?"

"No, he didn't."

"Do you have any other brothers or sister?"

"No, we don't."

"Do your parents still live?"

"Yes, they do. They are both over seventy and ill. This is why I came to speak with you, you can imagine in what state my parents are."

"Yes, I know."

"So please, can you be so nice and perform the burial ceremony on Saturday, at 12 at noon? I am sorry, I don't want to seem pushy, but the guys from the cemetery informed me about the hour, it was not decided by me. Could you come, please?"

"Of course, I'll come. Where is it?"

"At the new cemetery. You know, near the city."

"Yes, I know the place."

"Thank you so very much. We'll see you then."

"Yes, good night."

This was the life of a person, a short number of questions and yes/no answers. How simply it all ends. Valerie remembered how much Eduard was against the priests. Now here she was, begging a priest to come and bury him. «*What if he refused? Oh, how could he refuse? Yes, he could refuse. If a person never goes to church in his or her entire life and he or she always declares that priests and religion are worthless, how can you even have the pretention form a priest to come and bury them when they are dead? What if he refused to come? Eva would have been destroyed. I had to convince him to come, Eva would have been totally devastated if there was no Christian burial ceremony.*»

There was one more thing Valerie and Victoria had to solve that night. They had to buy some things as they had to serve something to the few persons who were coming to the burial. They did not want to invite them to the restaurant, as it happened many times. Some burials turned into real parties sometimes. After all the loud crying, people went to the restaurant and they drank and ate and finally you did not know what it was: a sad event or a party? Valerie and Victoria went to a supermarket and bought some drinks, soda, a few salty snack and cakes. They knew also they had to give half liter brandy to the guys who dug the grave. They bought everything, also paper napkins, plastic glasses. Valerie was making the highest efforts to focus, she did not want to forget anything. They carried everything in the car with no help from anyone.

Valerie and Victoria went home completely broken and feeling defeated. They could not even eat. Valerie could not sleep very much that night, but she did not dream of Eduard. Eva dreamt of Eduard, just as she was still alive. Victoria had nightmares in the short minutes she fell asleep. She kept on dreaming that Eduard was right next to them, but dead, and that they still had a lot of issues to solve before the burial. Then she woke up and she listened to her mom breathing, she was terrified something bad will happen to her mom with all the pain and the stress she was going through.

"*Do you imagine what could have happened if mom wouldn't have gone over to him?*" Valerie asked her daughter, the only reasonable person around with whom she could talk.

"*What mom?*"

"*You know how he disappeared for weeks. We all knew what was going on. We all knew he was drinking. We could not save him. I could not save him. I gave up when I was about 20 years old. This habit of him, this horrible illness, the drinking, was destroying me psychologically. So I gave up on him. It was making me sick, to think of him all the time, to think of what he was going through. With no job, no heating in her house. You know he lived tens of years with no income, no heating in his house? The door to his balcony was not even closing properly. Only his girlfriend gave him money, of course he used it to buy more booze. But, we, his family, gave up on her. If he disappeared for weeks, we did not even insisted with the phone calls anymore. We just assumed he was drinking and that was it. Can you imagine if mom wouldn't have gone over to him? How we would have found him after a few weeks? In July, in that apartment of his, up on the fourth floor? Can you imagine?*"

"*But it did not happen like that mom. Grandma felt something was wrong, they went over to him and found him right after he was dead. It is over. Don't stress yourself out over this mom. I need you. Please. I love you.*"

"*Yes, you are right. You are right my love.*"

Once again, Valerie rose up and continued walking, no matter how hard it was, just for the sake of her daughter. Just because her daughter needed her.

Next morning everybody was up early. As if they were happy the night was finally over. Eva said:

"Listen, Valerie. You know your brother was cut for the autopsy. I don't want the cut to be seen. Would you help me put this black scarf around his neck?"

"No way, I don't want to touch him. Leave me alone mom." This is what came out on Valerie's mouth. Obviously her filters were not functioning. The situation was saved by Victoria, who was acting the most mature and responsible way of all:

"I'll help you grandma. Don't worry. I'll go with you and we put together the scarf around his neck."

"Hey, I'm sorry. Please forgive me I reacted like this. I don't know why I have been so mean. Forgive me mom, I'll go with you, of course." said Valerie.

"It's OK darling. We're all in pain. We'll go all the three of us." Eva and Valerie and Victoria hugged each other.

Camil did not participate much to any of what was going on. He was visibly shaken and he mostly laid on the bed in his room. Everybody was shaken and shocked actually, but the three women had no choice, they had to take care of everything.

At 11,30 they were dressed and ready to leave the house. Valerie drove them to the cemetery's chapel. She unloaded with Victoria all that they bought for the people attending the funeral. It was a hot summer day, so hot you could hardly breathe. After unloading everything, Valerie asked the guys there to put the drinks in the fridge. Then, she braced herself and told her mom:

"OK, mom, let's go put the scarf on his neck. Come with me, we'll go together. Victoria, you don't have to come. I'll go with grandma."

"No, mom, I want to go with you. I want to see him. I'm not afraid or anything."

"Are you sure?" asked Valerie.

"Yes, mom, I'm fine."

Victoria was a brave girl. She wasn't afraid of nearly anything. Actually, the only thing that frightened both her and her mom was being separated of each other. But if they were together, they could conquer the world.

Now the chapel was a big and modern one and it was divided in ten rooms. Each room had around 25 sqm and it was with chairs, a table, a refrigerator so that a few people could stay there comfortable for a couple of hours. In each of these rooms, in one corner there was a small closed compartment where the actual coffin was. The little compartment with Eduard was very cold. The three women went in together. Eva stroked Eduard's forehead and his hands. Valerie only could stroke his hands. All the three of them put the black scarf around his neck and they put a little picture of Jesus Christ in his hand.

Slowly, people started to come. Valerie felt she will not be strong enough to look after her mom. So she asked kindly one of her mom's friends to take care of Eva until the funeral is over. The respective friend hesitated and Eva said:

"I'll be fine. Don't worry about me."

There was not the perfect moment now to get angry with anyone, but Valerie wondered what kind of friends are these? What kind of friends are those who only make a big case when they meet and they kiss you and they hug you like it's the end of the world, but when you need a little help, they back off?

The priest arrived right in time. Valerie was relieved to see him. The funeral started at 12 o'clock. There was a small ceremony place, organized so that different priests could perform the funeral service there. Eva was satisfied it turned out to be a beautiful Catholic ceremony. The priest sang beautifully and everybody behaved very politely.

Valerie acted quite courageously until they arrived with the coffin to the grave. That was when she lost it. She started to cry and shake uncontrollably. She felt she could not listen anymore to her ration. She was shaking so hard, she almost fell down. Fortunately, Victoria caught her and she was able to lean on her daughter. Victoria was terrified to see her mother like this. Valerie felt this, but she could just not control herself anymore. All of her life she tried to protect her daughter from violent manifestation of emotions. If there was a funeral in the family, Valerie did not take Victoria. First of all, she thought the local culture was too loud in expressing the grief at funerals. Nobody could benefit of it. The deceased person certainly did not benefit of it. The deceased needs peace and quiet, needs to be left to go in peace to the other Universe she or he is headed to. The children from the family did not benefit from it either. This violent expression of pain and sorrow just shocked them. The other persons attending the funeral did not benefit it. They felt embarrassed to see so close such a personal tragedy. So, why make such a great deal of it? So that people see how much you suffer? People don't care how much you suffer and even if they did, they could not grasp the depth of your sorrow. Only you and the Good Lord above know what's in your heart. Fortunately, nothing bad happened to Eva. She could control herself right to the end.

After Eduard was buried, Valerie needed quite some minutes to calm down. The priest retired quietly. Valerie ran after him and told him":

"*Father, thank you very much for coming. I am so grateful.*"

"*You're welcome.*"

"*We would be honored if you could come and have a piece of cake and a glass of wine.*"

"*Thank you, but I really cannot come. I have a meeting at the church with some members of our community.*"

"*Are you sure? A glass of water at least?*"

"*No, no, thank you, I cannot come.*"

"*Alright, thank you once again for coming.*"

Around twenty people came to the funeral. Mostly family and very close friends. It was a simple, elegant funeral, Eduard surely liked it from above.

Valerie tried to overcome rationally the pain she felt for losing her brother. The thing she could not understand is that her brother was gone forever. He did not live anymore. She thought « *How can this be? A person who was your flesh and blood, with whom you slept in the same bed, with whom you took baths together, with whom you ate from the same plate, who kissed you and hugged you and carried you in her arms to get away from your abusive father, now he's gone forever? He was here and alive and now he's not alive anymore? I cannot understand this. Nobody taught me how this is. I would understand if he went to Germany for a few months, or to America for several years, but I would know he is there, somewhere. Even if maybe I will never see him anymore, but he is still there. But for him to be gone, disappeared from this world and never coming back cannot be understood by me. This is our problem, we cannot really understand death. Nobody teaches us what death is, where does the person go and how should the ones remaining here cope with that.*»

Eva kept on dreaming with Eduard, as if he was still alive. Victoria kept on dreaming with Eduard, but with Eduard dead. The most powerful dream of Victoria was the one when he dreamt it was her birthday. Everybody brought her lots of presents. She got out of the apartment and found on the hall of the block a letter. It was Valerie's handwriting, but it was actually a long letter from Eduard addressed to her. Victoria took the letter, went back into the apartment and started reading it. The more she read, the more it made her cry. She asked her mom:

"Mom, this is your handwriting. Did you write this? Because it is a letter from Eduard, addressed to me!"

"My love, Edward cannot write anymore. He dictated me this letter, so that you receive his message from above."

Victoria read the entire letter several times and she thought this was the greatest gift she received for her birthday. She did not even care for the other gifts, this was the most wonderful thing she could receive.

Not even a year passed after Eduard's death and his married lover died too. Eva told Valerie:

"Well, now she died too. What do you think? Did they find each other up there?"

"I certainly hope not." answered Valerie.

"Why do you say that? They loved each other."

"No, they did not love each other. He loved her, she did not love him. She just used him. He wanted to be with her, she did not want to be with him. If she wanted to be with him, she should have moved in with him while they were still alive, on this earth. Clearly, she chose another man to stay with. So may she find that other man up there, she does not deserve to reunite with Eduard up there. After I die, I want to reunite only with Victoria, you and daddy up there. You wanted to be with me while I was here, I want to be with you up there. I don't want to reunite up there with somebody that did not want to be with me down here..."

Eva did not say anything. She understood very well her daughter's point, even though she did not agree with it.

Following the death of her brother, Eva, Camil and Valerie inherited her little apartment. Eva and Camil waved their rights, so Valerie became the only owner of it. Almost twenty years before, Valerie gave Eduard the money to buy it from the state. Now, it returned to her. Valerie always knew a new property means a new responsibility. She started sorting all the things remained. What was still good to use, she donated. Few very personal things she kept. Then, she renovated the place. She repaired what was broken, painted the house. Valerie did not want to invest in the small apartment situated of one the fourth floor in a poor neighborhood of Mineville. But she wanted to clean it and make it presentable before she sold it.

CHAPTER 16

Valerie continued to search for a new job. She improved very much her look due to Victoria's insistence. She lost weight with Dukan diet for several months. She arranged and dyed her hair a little bit and started to buy herself every now and then some new clothes, not the second hand clothes she wore all her life. It was just like she said to the Universe: "*Well, I'm ready. Bring it on.*" Valerie sent her CV to a serious German company that she admired a lot. The only problem was that it was located 50 kilometers away from Streamtown. To her huge surprise, a couple of hours after she sent her CV they called her and asked her to come to an interview.

Valerie had two interviews at this company and they hired her. When she was announced by them that she got the job, Mr.Liqman was away on holiday. She called him up and told him:

"*Hello, I'm terribly sorry to disturb you on your holiday, but I really need to speak with you.*"

"*No problem, Valerie. What happened?*"

"*I just wanted to inform you that today I will register my resignation. I found a new job, I will leave this company soon.*"

"*Why? What happened?*" asked her boss.

«*What happened? You tell me every day that you will replace me and you ask me what happened?*» thought Valerie. But she just said:

"*You have never been pleased with my work here, that is why I am leaving.*"

"*Alright, we'll talk about it when I get back, OK?*"

"*Yes, of course. Sorry again for disturbing you.*"

"*Alright, bye.*"

After Valerie spoke with her boss, she went straight to human resources with her resignation.

"Please register this and give me the registration number."

"Are you sure? I think we should just keep it, without registering it. Wait until he comes back, speak with him. Then you'll decided." said the human resources manager.

"I have already decided. I want to register it right now. Please give me registration number."

Her resignation got registered the same day. Valerie wanted to leave as soon as possible, so the sooner she registered her resignation, the sooner she could leave. According to the law a simple employee could leave two weeks after the date of the resignation and a manager could leave one month after the date of resignation. Valerie was a manager in the company, but this position was never registered official, no additional act was made to the work contract. She complained formally several times for this, but they never registered officially her position of manager. Now, the shoe was on the other foot. It was in Valerie's advantage that she was not legally registered as manager, therefore she could leave after only two weeks.

Her boss returned from holiday. He told Valerie they have to talk.

"So, you decided to leave us."

"Yes, I have."

"You lost some weight and now you found a nice job."

«*What an asshole*» Valerie thought.

"Well, it wasn't quite that easy, but if you want to put it this way..."

"I was just kidding" her boss continued.

«*Very funny*» she thought, but she did not even smile.

"So, you have found a nice job?"

"Yes, I have."

«*What is this? For this intelligent conversation I had to wait with the registration of my resignation? Thank God for not waiting for this. Oh, the things I could tell him... How bad he treated me, all his abuse and all his offences... But I have to keep calm. The calmer I am, the less I say, the sooner this charade will end. Patience, patience...*»

"Alright then, good luck. And if you ever need anything, we are here." her boss concluded.

"Thank you." Valerie ended too, turned around and left his office grateful to God this was over.

Her resignation was forwarded to her boss and he signed it. She had two more weeks and she was out of there.

She went to her office and announced everybody she was leaving. One of her subordinates immediately jumped up off her chair, went to her and stuck out her hand:

"*I bet you will not leave.*"

Valerie was surprised of this reaction, but she shook her colleagues hand and answered:

"*You're on.*"

Valerie did not say one word more, she just smiled. She knew what this was about. It was a common practice for people to frighten over and over that they were going to leave. Valerie never did this, even though she was searching for another job for years already. Her colleague thought she was just frightening to leave to get a raise. In fact, Valerie was very serious. She wouldn't have remained there no matter what raise they would have given her.

Valerie started to inform her acquaintances that she was moving to another job. She thought it would be fair to inform them, especially those persons who she begged several times to help her find a new job or at least inform her if they hear of a job opening. A few days after she dropped the stone on the clear lake, the wave started to show. One of her acquaintances called her back:

"*Hello, Valerie.*"

"*Hello, Ana.*"

"*Listen, I have spoken with my boss about you. I told him you want to move to another company. He asked me why are you going to work so far away from Streamtown, why don't you come back to work for us?*"

"*Well, you know how desperate I have searched for another job for months and months. I don't care how far it is from Streamtown, I need to work in a company where I am respected. You know how they treated me here, how they humiliated me. And I accepted everything because I had no choice, I needed the money to raise my daughter. But I don't have to take it anymore.*"

"*Well, yes, I know. I just want to tell you that my boss is willing to discuss with you about the possibility of returning to us. I cannot promise you anything, but I think you should come and speak with him. You've got nothing to lose, right?*"

"Right. Right."

"I have told him you have the salary of a manager now and a rented apartment from the company. I hope he will offer you at least the same from us."

"OK, thank you."

"Think about it. If you make up your mind, please call his secretary and set up a meeting with him. Alright?"

"Yes, yes, thank you. I'll think about it."

Valerie did think about it very seriously. It seemed strange to her that all those years while she was desperately looking for a new job, nobody was interested in her. Now, when this serious German company offered her a job, suddenly this other company, where Ana worked and where also she worked in the past, became interested in her. What happened? Her value increased all of the sudden? On the other hand, the offer was quite tempting for Valerie. The company where Ana worked was in Streamtown, 500 meters away from Valerie's block, while the German company that offered her a job was 50 kilometers away from her block. Even so, Valerie needed one night to make up her mind: «*I will call Ana and tell her I'm sorry, but I don't want to speak with her boss. These guys from the German company stuck out a hand to help me when everybody was turning away from me. They treated me very nicely at both interviews. It would not be fair to turn them down. Of course, it will be hard to work so far away from home. It will take me out of my comfort zone. But it's OK. I will grow, I will develop, I will learn. I'll manage somehow. I will go and work with them.*»

Valerie called Ana back and told her she made up her mind, she decided not to speak with Ana's boss.

Valerie started working in this modern German company when she was 43 years old. The company was very clean and well organized. It seemed you entered a totally different world when you entered their gate. First thing that struck Valerie was the clean appearance of the shiny new buildings, the grass cut all at the same size, the clean, marked alleys in the company, how clean the production hall, the offices and the bathrooms were. By then, Valerie had been working for ten years in multinational companies already, but the level of this company was the highest of all. Not only from the cleanliness point of view, but especially from the point of view of the respect for the employees. The working hours were very correctly accounted for and the working schedule was flexible. Nobody was humiliated in front of others. And most important of all: every employee had the right to express freely her or his opinion. Even if it was wrong. She or he was allowed to express it, as long as it was expressed in a civilized manner.

On top of all, Valerie knew a little bit of German and adored to hear the Germans speak. In her mind, hearing the German language raised very dear memories. It reminded her of good quality sweets like *Nutella, Haribo, Nussknacker, Schogetten, Toffifee* and so on, that Eastern European liked to bring from Germany. It reminded her of the *Rexona* and *8x4* soaps and deodorants that were smuggled in the country in the communist period, when there was no soap and deodorant in the communist stores. Having a good German soap back then was sheer heaven. It reminded her of the German TV channels Pro Sieben and RTL she was watching with the parabolic antenna right after the Revolution, that great sensation to see a foreign movie or some good quality music or even a nice advertising on TV. From her personal experience, of all the foreigners she worked with in her life, the Germans were the most friendly and respectful of all.

All this was the good and easy part in this turning moment of her life. The hard part was adjusting to the very young team that was already in the company when she was hired. The average age of the employees was under 30 year, while Valerie was already over forty. This, in addition to the highly sophisticated IT systems she had to learn there was a hard challenge for Valerie. Of course she tackled it very bravely for the sake of her daughter. She wanted to make her daughter proud of her. She wanted to prove that she was not too old yet to adjust to such a young and modern company.

A few months after she was hired, Valerie was sent to Germany for five months for training at the lead plant. She stayed in the southern part of Germany, in Bavaria, in a beautiful area during the winter of 2012-2013. Her German colleagues were friendly, well, much friendlier than her conationals back home. Valerie liked her stay in Germany. The region where she stayed was gorgeous. The country was clean. During her stay in Germany, she saw not even one stray dog. In her country, wherever you turn you stray dogs, dirty and only skin and bone. Before she had Lady, Valerie was not so passionate for dogs. But after Lady became a part of her family, Valerie fell in love with her dog and started to notice the suffering, the neglect and the abuse to which dogs and other animals were subjected in her country. Why in Germany the issue of dogs can be managed in such a civilized way and in her country not? Because in her country, the ones responsible to manage the dogs issue were stealing the money instead of using it to solve the problem. The roads in Germany were in perfect condition. In her country, you risked your life when you drove on most of the rods. In her country, it happened very close to her town, that on a recently built highway a car pile-up happened because it was not built right. It happened that a few months after it was built, the highway cracked and it had to be closed because it jeopardized the safety of the drivers. As she always lived in Eastern Europe, Valerie thought that the state of facts in Eastern Europe was the normal one. But after living and driving in Germany for a few months she saw this was not the normal state of facts. Why in Germany the roads could be good and in her country not? Because in her country, the representatives of the state who hired the highway construction companies did not hire the best companies to do the job, but the ones who were giving them as a bribe a percentage of the value of the contract. Why in Germany all the drivers were polite in traffic and respected the circulation regulations and in her country not? Because in Germany the law was respected by everybody. In Germany, the policemen were enforcing the law to everybody the same way. In her country, the law was enforced only upon the victims. In her country, the predators were above the law. In her country, the corruption was a constitutive part of the people's body. Like a huge, malign tumor. Her conationals lived for so long with this tumor, that they felt if the tumor was removed, they would remain with an empty body, unable to live.

The greatest challenge during the five months Valerie spent in Germany was to leave Victoria at home all by herself. Victoria was 18 years old and was attending her last year of high school. She had to learn for the high school graduation examination and for the admission examination to the medical university of Steville. She had to take care of the household and of Lady. She had to attend some private lessons of Chemistry and Biology to help her with the admission. Victoria has never been separated for one week from her mother. Now, she had to remain alone for months. Valerie was able to come to visit only once a month.

Victoria was a very courageous girl, just like her mom. She used to say she was much better in overcoming the challenges given her from outside that the ones she set for herself. She wanted her mom to be proud of her. Many times she said:

"All that matters to me, mom, is not to disappoint you. If you love and you are proud of me, the rest does not matter so much."

"Don't think like this, my love. You have to learn for yourself, not for me. If you learn, you will have an easier and better life. If you will learn and have a profession, something that you can do, nobody can take that away from you. You will not have to stay home and expect somebody to give you money for what you need. You will have your own money. Your goal must be your independence, ultimately your freedom. Don't ever worry about disappointing me. I am proud of you no matter what. No matter what you do, you cannot disappoint me. I will always love you, until I die and even after that."

Even so, Victoria still felt compelled to live up to her mother's expectations. This made her learn and behave impeccably. While her mom was in Germany, nobody helped her with anything, not her father, not her grandparents, not her aunts or uncles, not her cousins, not her friends, nobody. Nobody, except her mother from the distance, ever wondered *"Isn't that girl afraid to sleep alone? Does she have warm clothes to wear? Does she have food to eat?"* Everybody however was watching her. They all expected her to screw up. However, everybody saw she never had any boy sleeping with her while her mom was away. The house and Maggie were clean and well kept. Lady was walked and fed regularly, just like when Valerie was home. Victoria never missed one hour from school. She attended also the sport she attended during her entire high school period. She went to church every Sunday. Whenever her mom came home, she cooked for her. Victoria went through all this period brilliantly.

After her stay in Germany, Valerie understood that the fundamental difference between Germany and her country was that the German state loved its citizens, the German state was smart enough to make such laws that kept the good citizens inside the country. On the other hand, in her country the state hated its citizens. The state and law only protected the corrupted ones, the thieves and cheaters, it protected the abusers, instead of protecting the victims. The German state wanted its citizens to stay in the country, have children and raise them well for the best interest of the state. The state where Valerie lived was pretty much like Valerie's in-laws:

"If you don't like it here, you are free to leave."

Valerie expressed this after her return, at some discussions with her colleagues back home.

"I think Germany loves its citizens, while our state hates us. I think this is the most important difference between the two states."

One of her colleagues replied:

"Maybe it's the other way around."

"What do you mean?"

"I mean maybe the Germans love their state while we hate our state. Did you think about that?"

"I beg to differ. It's not like that. On one hand, the relationship between the State and the citizens is pretty much like the relationship between parents and children. Inside a family, the loving environment inside the family is not determined by the children, it does not depend on the children, it depends on the parents. The parents are the ones who set the mood. On the other hand, you cannot even say I don't love my State. I pay my taxes regularly. I go and stay in queue to pay my taxes to some clerks that look at me contemptuously from behind their counters. Why are they so contemptuous? Because I want to give them money? The least the State could do is to smile at me when I give it money and thank me. Right? What does the state give me back for my money? Bumpy streets, with queues of cars that stretch over tens of kilometers, corrupt leaders, hospitals full of infections, schools with no central heating and no bathrooms. I have risen a child that will be a good citizen, hard working and serious. What did the State give me to help me with that? 10 euro a month. This was the great help from the State."

As she managed very well the five months she was alone, Valerie wanted to reward her daughter as best as she could. She bought her anything that she desired and that they could afford. She even bought her daughter a car while she was in Germany. Victoria always wanted a car of her own. Of course, Valerie could not afford a new car for her daughter, but she could afford a twelve years old foreign car.

Since the dream of everybody in Valerie's country was to buy a second hand car from Germany, because the Germans take care of them, and since Valerie was in Germany, she bought her daughter a twelve years car with 2.600 euro. Valerie found the car on the internet. The dealer was around 100 kilometers away from where she stayed and he was of course Turk. Seemed like the majority of second hand dealers in Germany were Turks.

First, she went to see the car. The guy had all the documents and the history of the car, unlike the guy back home who sold her Maggie. Then, after a few days she decided to go and buy the car. She gave the money to the dealer and they signed a contract. After that, they went to a little town nearby where they registered temporarily. This took exactly fifteen minutes. Back home, it would have taken four working days. After the temporary numbers were on the car, Valerie and the Turk guy went back to his dealership and she took her daughter's car. In the following weekend, Valerie decided to take the car home to her daughter by driving it herself from Germany to her country. There were more than 1200 kilometers to drive, in winter, during nighttime.

Valerie was very afraid of this trip. What if the car broke down? What was going to do? What if she fell asleep? All she could do was trust God will take care of her and prepare herself the best she could for the trip. She checked the car he best she could: it started up OK. The tires, including the spare tire, were OK. The oil, water and washing fluid in order. She printed out a map with the road. She also wrote the names of the most localities by which she was going to pass by, printed them out with big letters and put the list on the chair next to her, so that she could look just in one second if she was on the right way. Also, she had a GPS with her. She bought six energizers and some biscuits, also water and she put everything on the chair next to the driver. She did not want to stop anywhere, except to buy vignettes and to fuel. Valerie left from Germany at noon, on a Thursday. It was still light when she arrived to the border with Austria. She got off the car, bought the vignette and left immediately. Somewhere, in Austria she stopped and fueled. When she was passing by Vienna, it was snowing very hard, she could hardly see 10 meters in front. The windshield wipers were working, but made a terrible noise. «*At least they don't let me fall asleep*». The radio was functioning. She did not know how to change the channels, but at least it was music on. At the border with Hungary, she stopped again to buy the vignette. She did not stop at all. She was driving respecting all the rules and speed limitations. Nobody stopped her, even though there were several police cars passing by her.

Finally, at around four o'clock in the morning she arrived at the border of her country. Here, everybody stopped and was checked. The checking area was covered, but not closed. There was a thick layer of dirty snow on the ground. «*Why don't they clean the snow? Don't their feet feel cold from staying on the snow? Hmm, I guess I got used to Germany. In Germany, the snow was cleaned, even on the small streets from the smallest villages.*» At that hour of the day, the customs was almost empty. The customs officers came to her and said:

"*Good morning. Please present your passport or identity card.*"

"*Yes, Sir, right away. Do you need also the documents of the car?*"

"*No, I need only need your documents.*"

Valerie showed him her identity card. The guy looked at it and said:

"*OK, Mam, you can pass. Welcome home.*"

"*Thank you.*"

Valerie stopped at a gas station right next to the border. She fueled, went to the bathroom and drank a coffee. She missed her country every time she went away. After relaxing for a few minutes, she left. The entire Europe was lit up. Even though it was night, there were lights on the highways and you could see where you were going. As soon as she entered her country, however, it was a totally different story. It was dark. The roads were terrible. The drivers were aggressive. At least, the radio found the national radio station and they were just starting the morning show. First thing they broadcasted was "*Our Father in heaven*". When Valerie heard the prayer, her eyes burst into tears, her heart was overwhelmed with gratitude for the Good Lord above for bringing her home safely on probably the hardest trip of her life.

Finally the sun rose and Valerie could see where she was driving. It started also snowing. There were huge queues of cars every few kilometers. It was a 280 kilometers drive from the border to Streamtown. Valerie crossed the border at 4 a.m. It was 9,30 a.m. when she got home. When she entered Streamtown, Valerie called Victoria. Even though it was a school day, Victoria did not go to school for the first three hours. She missed her mom too much. So when her mom called, she took Lady and they went outside in front of the block and waited for her mom. The reunion was the happiest. Victoria was grateful her mom brought her a car. Valerie was happy she found her daughter well and Lady expressed the general joy best of all.

Valerie brought a lot of presents for Victoria, clothes and sweets and of course some German cheese. Offenkäse was Victoria's favorite. She liked to heat it in the oven and eat it with a fresh baguette. After chatting for a few minutes, Victoria went to school. Valerie took a shower and went to sleep. She took Lady with her in bed and hold her tight in her arms. Lady did not move, she did not even breathe. She felt Valerie was exhausted, she knew she had to rest, so she kept as quite as possible not to disturb her. No human could possible take care of her like her dog did that day.

Valerie came home on a Friday morning. On Sunday afternoon she had to go back to Germany. Victoria had to take care of the car's registration. Valerie wanted the car to be Victoria's, so she wanted the car registered on her daughter's name. What she did not know was how much the insurance will cost. It cost 250 euro for a year, while if she would have registered the car on her name, it would have cost only 45 euro for one year. The pollution tax cost 800 euro. Valerie did not complain though. She wanted to ensure her daughter the means to be as independent as possible.

Victoria managed to register the car just as efficiently as her mother would have done. This enabled her to use her car before her mom returned definitively from Germany, but also gave her a sense of self-esteem that helped further on in her life. The very same year, she was going to have one of the hardest examinations of her, the admission examination to the medical school of Steville.

Valerie returned from Germany at the end of April. She started right away to work in her garden. She felt bad she could not take care of it while she was away, Victoria did not have time. She planted some tomatoes, cucumbers, some carrots and parsley and that year it was pretty much it. Victoria and Valerie focused the most on the upcoming exams.

First of all, Victoria had to take the high school graduation examination. If she got a good grade there, she could attend the admission examination. She was studying very hard, but besides that there were a lot of events going on in her life. As she was finishing high school, they were taking pictures of themselves, alone and together the whole class. They were organizing the prom. They were celebrating birthdays almost every week. It was a very busy and expensive period. Victoria was very involved in all the activities at school. She always volunteered and was the one who did the most of the work. This also took up a lot of her time, but she never complained. Actually, there were some of her colleagues and their parents who always complained about something, but they never took over things to organize them better. Valerie asked Victoria if she needed help:

"Hey, Vicky, are you able to do everything? I can speak with the other parents and tell them you don't want to do this anymore. I mean, you have so much to learn, you also organize all this stuff and in the end they are also unsatisfied..."

"It's fine mom. I'm used to it. I always have to ask some of them several times to give me money, even though we always agree before how much each one of us has to pay. I can do it and I like it too."

"Yes, I know, But doesn't it affect your learning?"

"No, no, mom. I promise. I have done this virtually since I started school. I'm used to it."

Eva and Camil did not feel very well. Their health deteriorated a lot after Eduard died. At a certain point, Eva's right arm went almost completely numb and after going to her general practitioner she did not learn what was wrong with her. She felt very bad several times and ended up in the emergency room in the hospital. Finally, one Saturday she ended up again in the emergency and they admitted her in the hospital. Finally, the doctors understood she had a stroke without knowing it and a big blood clot was still in the left side of her head which caused the problem with her right arm.

This happened two days before Victoria first high school graduation examination. Valerie used to call her parents up every day. That particular Saturday Eva had the phone closed and Camil was not answering. Finally Camil called her back and told her:

"Valerie, there is a problem with your mom. Please don't get alarmed."

"What is it, father? Whatever it is, please tell me."

"Well, she did not feel very well again this morning. She said she wanted some air, so we went out for a walk. Suddenly, on the street, she got very sick. We sat on a bench. I told her we should go to the hospital. But you know her. She does not want to go. She is fine. What do the doctors know. And so on. But I insisted. You know, the hospital is very close to our block, I said we make a small walk, in 10 minutes we are there. So she agreed."

"What did the doctors say?"

"They suspect she had a stroke."

"What? When did this happen?"

"We don't know when. You know how upset she was with Eduard and all. Well, we both were upset. And around spring, you were still in Germany, she started not to feel her arm. Our general practitioner kept on saying it's rheumatism. She used that balm against rheumatism. But of course it did not help. Anyway, now they kept her in the hospital. She has to do a RMN. The problem is that for making a RMN, you have to wait your turn for weeks and weeks. The doctor said however that if she is admitted in emergency, she could do the RMN in a couple of days."

"So, she will make the RMN test in a couple of days and we'll finally know what is wrong with her. That's good."

"Yes, this is why I told you, there is no need for you to worry."

"Alright, dad, what about you? How are you coping with everything?"

"We'll be fine, don't worry. You just stay calm. You know, I always told you. If something can be fixed, no need to get stressed, it'll get fixed. If it cannot be fixed, again there is no need to get stressed, because no matter what you do, you cannot fix it. OK? You just prepare with Victoria for the graduation. First exam is on Monday, right?"

"Right, dad, on Monday. Alright then. This is what we'll do. Tomorrow morning we come home. We'll try to leave at 3 in the morning. This way, it will not be heavy traffic and it will be still cool outside. At around 7 or 8 o'clock in the morning we should be home. Alright?"

"There is no need for you to come. You have to be back on Monday."

"Yes, yes, we are coming. I have decided."

"What about Victoria? She will be tired. All day Sunday on the road and on Monday exam…"

"She'll sleep in the car, she'll be fine."

"Alright, if you want to come, come. Then we'll go together tomorrow morning to the hospital to your mom, OK?"

"Yes, of course. What I want you to do, dad, is ask mom what she needs. Make a list. Then tomorrow we'll take her what she needs. Alright?"

"Yes, I'll call her later and ask her."

"Alright, dad, sleep tight, see you in the morning."

"Alright. Drive carefully. Bye."

"Bye."

The next day, Valerie and Victoria left home at 3 o'clock in the morning.

At 7 o'clock in the morning they were in Mineville. They knocked at the door. Camil opened the door and he was visibly happy to see them home.

He had the list from Eva. She did not want food. She was not eating so much and they received some food in the hospital. She just wanted some coffee, milk and drinking water. She could not drink the tap water there. She already had slippers and a pajamas, but she needed a clean one. Valerie also took some biscuits and fruit for her. They packed everything and went to visit her. Fortunately, on Sunday the visiting hours were longer, so they could all three go up without having to bribe the doorman.

Eva seemed to be fine. She was happy to see the girls. She gave them back some dirty clothes to take home and wash. After two hours of chatting, Camil, Valerie and Victoria left from the hospital. Back at her parents' house, Valerie cooked something for her dad, arranged a little bit things in the kitchen and after they had lunch together, they headed back to Streamtown. Victoria slept on the car both ways. They arrived home in the evening.

The next day Valerie went to work and Victoria went to her first exam, it was of language. The same week followed the Math exam, the Biology exam, also the evaluations for English and digital competencies. Victoria did great at all exams. She was the thirteenth in the entire county. Valerie was very proud of her and felt no matter how much she worked and did for her beloved daughter it was not enough. Valerie still felt guilty because Victoria never had a father. She felt she should have done more to keep Alan with them. She felt she should have bought a bigger house, instead of living in that small apartment. But this is all that she could do, without any help and only by hard work. Victoria knew all this and she was grateful for everything. She was a very well adjusted teenager, actually it was Valerie who was more affected that her daughter grew up without a father, than Victoria was. These were Valerie's demons, not Victoria's and Valerie had to fight with them. Victoria fought with a different kind of demons. Victoria struggled all her life to make her mother proud of her.

After a month, the examination for admission in the medical university of Steville followed. Almost all the children that went to university had a second option, in case they were not admitted at their first option of university. Victoria's first option was the medical university. Her second option was the law university. She registered to both admission examinations. The examination at the medical university was consisting of a grid of 50 questions from Biology and Chemistry. The examination at the law school was consisting 70 questions of logical reasoning. The examination for law university was on Monday 22nd of July in the afternoon and the examination for medical university was on Wednesday in the morning 24th of July. Victoria and Valerie had to stay in Steville for several days, so Valerie booked a room at a guest house check-in day on Monday and check-out day on Thursday. For Valerie, it was very helpful she could book the room online, this way she could solve the problem with a few clicks, instead of calling on the phone over and over again. Usually, all the children from the region had relatives and friends in Steville and when they had to stay in Steville, they just stayed with their relatives, not in those expensive guest houses. But Valerie did not have this luck. She did not even ask around, for her it was just easier to stay in a guest room. Of course, after the event was way passed, there were always a few that said:

"*Why didn't ask us? You could have stayed with us?*"

Valerie always thought «*Why didn't you offer in advance? You knew we are coming to Steville…*» but she just answered:

"*Ohh, thank you so much, but we did not want to cause any trouble.*"

They left from Streamtown on Monday morning and arrived in Steville before noon. They found the guest house, parked the car and checked in. Even though she had her doubts, the online booking worked and the guest house knew about their reservation. The guest house was clean and in a quiet area, in the east side of Steville. They unpacked quickly, put all the things in place and went to the mall, as it was very close to where the examination for law school took place. Even though Valerie has never been to Starbucks before in her life, now she thought she should pamper her daughter and offer her something special. All of her life she was very careful with her expenditures as the money was always short and she needed to ensure everything for her daughter's upbringing. And even if now her living level improved a lot, she still was very careful with what she spent. There were moments however when she felt she had to pamper her daughter, just like this one. So she told her daughter:

"*Order whatever you like.*"

"*Really, mom? Are you serious?*" asked Victoria, knowing her mother's spending habits.

"Yes, seriously. May I suggest you buy yourself a good coffee too, you will need a little caffeine for the exam."

"Alright, if you say so."

Victoria looked around and decided what she wanted. She asked her mom:

"What do you want mom?"

"Ohh, don't worry about me, I don't want anything." Valerie never wanted anything in these fancy places, she tried not to spend so much."

"Come on, get something. Get at least a coffee."

"Ohh, no, no, I had too much coffee as it is already. Don't worry about me."

But Victoria insisted:

"If you don't get anything, I don't want anything." Victoria knew only this worked with her mom.

"Alright, alright, I'll get a simple coffee, short, no sugar, no milk. OK?"

"OK. Let's go on the terrace mom."

They went on the terrace and chatted until they had their drinks. The time passed by quickly and they had to go to the university.

Inside the university there was a big hall, clean and fortunately with air conditioning. The only problem was there were no chairs to sit, so everybody was sitting on the steps. You had to wait for hours there. First, the candidates arrived with their parents about an hour before the exam started. Then, the parents waited in the hall until the candidates finished and came out. But it was not so bad, at least they did not have to wait outside in the hot July sun.

Victoria felt very good. As she was not used to caffeine, the coffee she drank at Starbucks gave her a real boost of energy. She had nothing to study for this exam, as there were questions of logical reasoning, so all she had to do was concentrate on the question and try to give a correct answer as quickly as possible. There were 70 questions and the exam itself was 60 minutes. There was not much time to think about the answer.

The exam started punctually. The candidates were distributed in different examination halls, in alphabetical order. In order to get in the examination hall, the candidates had to wait in front of the examination hall on which their name was written until somebody came out and called their name. So a large group of people gathered in front of every examination hall, candidates and the persons who accompanied them and, as it usually was when several locals had to wait in one place for something, a little rush was created. At some point, the guy at the door called Victoria's name, she presented her ID and the examination badge and she went. Finally, all the candidates went it and the parents settled down, each one finding something to do, as they had to wait for more than an hour until the kids were out. Most of the accompanying persons spent their time with their smart phones. It was very trendy and people spent a lot of money on these phones. Besides the fact that they were expensive, they also needed internet, so the 5 euro subscription with the phone company was not enough anymore. They had to have a subscription of at least 20 euro to have internet too on the phone and they all considered this was absolutely necessary for them to do. Valerie did not have a smart phone and she did not want one. She usually took Victoria's phones after she got bored of them. Finally, after many insistences from Victoria, she agreed to have a new phone, but a simple classical one, with qwerty keyboard which was inexpensive and therefore very hard to find in the shops. Valerie did not spend much time playing on her phone either. She rather read a book or made to-do lists in her notebook, which was always with her. In this notebook, she had everything written down. What she had to buy. What she had to do in the garden. What she had to do at home. What she had to take to Mineville and what she had to bring back from Mineville. Everything.

After almost two hours, Victoria came out of the examination halls. She was amongst the first ones to come out and she managed to answer all the questions.

"Wow, mom, it was hard."

"I imagine it was hard my love."

"There were 70 questions. In 60 minutes. Of course, some questions were easy and I could answer in a few seconds. But others not. And it's not that they were hard, but the phrasing was so tangled, on purpose, you know, to mislead you. Anyway, if I could not answer right away, I passed on to the next question. Just like you taught me."

"Well, yes, this is how you have to do in an exam. You don't have to waste time. If you don't know a question and you lose time to think about it, maybe in the end you solve it, maybe you don't. But you remain with no time for the next questions. It's better to pass over the questions you don't know, to do all

that you know and then, if you still have time, to come back and think about the hard ones."

"Yes, yes, I did like this and I gave an answer to all the questions. For three or four questions I simply did not know what to answer so I just circled one answer by chance. Statistically, it's a 25% chance to get the right answer, right?"

"Yes, much higher chance to get a point than not to write anything, right?"

"Yes, this is what I was thinking."

"You are a very smart girl and I am very proud of you." Valerie continued.

"Yeah, well, I hope I did good."

"I'm sure you did good my love. Now let's go home. Do you want to go some place to eat?"

"No, mom, you know I don't want to eat in the evening. We have some fruit in our guest house room, I'll eat a fruit and I'll be fine."

Victoria was very careful with her diet. And Valerie got used to this too. They rarely went to restaurants when they were away from home. Usually, they ate some fruit, a yoghurt or a piece of cheese and that was it.

Next day they slept late. At least Victoria did. She slept very well. She was not disturbed by noises and lights. When she was a little girl, Valerie always let her sleep in the normal conditions of the house. She did not keep silence, she did not put on the shades. She wanted her child to get used to sleep with the normal sounds and activities of the house. Moreover, there was always a radio singing and presenting the news somewhere around. Victoria got used to this she was little and now she had no problem to sleep no matter the conditions. On the long term, this was a good thing for Victoria. Unlike the others who grew up in the paternal grandparents' house, Victoria was used to live in any conditions. The other grandchildren were not. They were overprotected and over pampered, fed with unhealthy food and raised with unhealthy principles. Victoria remembered after the son of her sister-in-law was born, there had to be perfect silence in the house. They had to watch how they were walking outside in the courtyard, not to disturb the little prince. When Victoria was little, they were laughing and watching TV right next to her when she was sleeping and there was no problem. When her sister-in-law was pregnant, she could not walk more than ten steps, because:

"She has labor pains if she walks too much." Valerie's mother-in-law used to say.

And Valerie used to answer:

"She can only have labor pains only when she is in labor." And she was thinking «*How about me? I could walk in Steville kilometers and kilometers and it was fine, plus your son told me he wanted to divorce, but of course, who am I to compare myself with your daughter?*»

It has been painful for Valerie and Victoria to be treated as Cinderella in that house, but in the long run, it did them good. It made them tough and resilient and adaptable. It all turned out fine in the end. The unfolding of life showed who in fact achieved what in their lives.

Valerie also slept well when she was young, but after Victoria was born, her sleep deteriorated a lot and never got back to normal. All that waking up every night for a few times. In the beginning, she went back to sleep. But after a while, after she woke up three or four times the same night, she could not get back to sleep anymore.

The guest house was clean and nice and with air conditioning, the only problem with it was that it was very noisy. The employees of the guest house were speaking and laughing loudly on the staircase. Valerie woke up early, at six o'clock in the morning because of that. «*What are they thinking? Why does a person come to a guest house? On a holiday? Right, this means he or she needs peace and quiet to rest. On a business trip? Right, this means he or she needs peace and quiet to rest. Who on earth does not need peace and quiet when in a guest room?*" Valerie never complaint upfront for this. She knew from her experience she wouldn't have solved anything by this. She complained right on the website, this way she was sure she will hit them right where it hurts more.

If she woke up anyway, Valerie took a shower, she brushed her teeth and dressed up. She drank an instant coffee. She brought some instant coffee with her, with a little hot water from the tap, her morning coffee was ready. After this half an hour was over and the bathroom was free, she woke up Victoria. After they both were ready, they went for a walk in town. It was a long trip until down town, but they walked it. They adored walking together, no matter how much. They had a chance to speak about everything, plus they were burning a lot of calories, right?

"First of all, we go to the examination hall. I want to see where it is."

"I know where it is, mom."

"Have you ever been there?"

"No, I haven't."

"So how do you know for sure where it is?"

"Because I saw on the front door of the university where I was distributed."

"Yes, but you know, with the medical school there isn't just one big building, the university. There are a lot of small buildings, with all kind of room and examination hall. It will take time until we find it. And I don't want to run around all morning searching for the right hall. I want to see today the examination hall, I want to see on its door your name, with my own eyes. Get it?"

"Alright mom, we'll go there." answered Victoria. She did not like her mom when she was like this, no other moms were like this, but on the other hand, she knew from her experience that her mom was always right. If her mom said something could go wrong, it was better to listen to her, because most likely it was going to go wrong.

Valerie knew her daughter did not like her like this, but she also knew that she was right. So she tried to sweeten the deal:

"After that we go to the mall, do some shopping, OK? Or whatever you want, but first I want to see the door of the hall where you will take the exam tomorrow."

They went straight there. Now, the respective address actually consisted of a lot of buildings. They were a lot of medical establishments with alleys and stairs, as it was situated right on a hill of Steville. Victoria said she knew the building where it was supposed to be. They searched for it for about 20 minutes. Finally, they found it. There was no indication about the room the exam was going to be in. It was a two storey's building, so they went on each and every storey and asked about the examination hall. Nobody knew about it. Finally, they realized the examination was going to be held in a different building, in the Forensic Medicine Institute building. After getting there, they finally found the examination hall, it was on a side hall way, right in the end of the hall. Valerie saw Victoria's name on the door, so she finally settled:

"Alright, so here it is. Now we know where to come in the morning."

"Yes. It was quite hard to find it too. It took us one and half an hour. Sorry mom I didn't want to listen to you in the morning. You were right."

"Hey, no problem, no problem. Important thing is in the morning we'll not waste any time."

In the afternoon, they were back in the room of the guest house. After all that walking, they fell asleep, when Victoria's phone rang. It was a friend of hers:

"Hey Victoria. What are you doing?"

"I'm with mom, we just got to the guest house."

"Do you know the results from law university?"

"No, not yet, They said we'll get the results today. Hmmm, I have to check their web site."

"I have checked it already. You're admitted!"

"What? Come on? Are you for real?"

"Yes, yes, check it out on the site if you don't believe me. You are the 33rd on the list with admitted candidates. There were 800 candidates, only 80 places with state budget and you are on 33rd position! Congratulations!"

"Thanks, thanks. Well, I'll check the site. Thank you for telling me."

"You're welcome. Well, see you tomorrow at the other exam."

"Yes, when are you coming to Steville?"

"We'll come tonight to Steville."

"OK, then see you in the morning at the medical university. I checked the examination hall where we have to do. It is where the gynecology Clinique is. You where that is, right?"

"Yes, we get in through the front central gate, right?"

"Right, right. Look, you know what? Just call me when you enter the gate, I'll guide you. It is a bit tricky to find it."

"Alright. Then see you in the morning. Bye."

"Bye."

Victoria checked out immediately the law university site. It was true. She got in.

"Oh, God, you're so smart my love! Imagine that, of all those candidates, you are the 33rd!"

"Yes, that's right" said Victoria. "Well, I'm in!"

"Yes, no matter what you do at the other exam, in autumn you're a student my love."

"Yes, but I want the medical school, mom. You know that. This is just my second option."

"I know, I know, you'll get in there too, don't worry."

"I don't know mom, it's a difficult examination. What if I don't know the questions? Do you know how hard it is?"

"I know, but I also know how smart you are. At the simulation you did great, didn't you? So, why worry? You studied a lot, seriously, you took the private lessons, just be attentive and you'll do fine. The most important thing is your attitude, your morale. All the candidates that go to medical school are hard working and serious. If they weren't, they would have gone to the management faculty. But they wanted to study seriously and work hard, so they went to medical school. They all learned a lot, they all had private lessons, they all sacrificed a lot of evenings out with friends and vacations just to stay in house and study some more. What makes the difference is your morale. If you want to beat them, you have to be calm and composed. You have to be very attentive and smart. Do you understand my love?"

"Yes mom. Thank you."

"For what? I didn't do anything. This is your work, your studying, your future ultimately."

"Thank you for nagging me with the learning. Thank you for telling me every day how important it is to learn. Thank you mom for everything."

Valerie felt her eyes filled with tears when Victoria spoke like this with her. It's true, she told Victoria these lectures several times every day. She told them so many times, she made her own self sick with them. But it paid off finally. Victoria took learning very seriously. She wanted to succeed in life by her own hard work, not by receiving something from somebody. She was strong and ambitious.

"Just doing my job. I love you and I am very proud of you." Valerie answered.

Next morning they got up early. They left home again by foot. They stayed on a bench downtown Steville, which was five minutes away by foot from the examination hall. Victoria was very nervous.

"How come everybody is so damn relaxed, mom? And where are they all going?"

"They are going to work, my love. It's eight o'clock in the morning."

"Yes, but all these cars? Don't they know how important this exam is for me?"

"No, my love, they don't. Listen, my love, don't you want to have a bite to eat? Maybe some pastry? There are some nice shops here downtown."

"No mom, I don't want to. Leave me alone."

"Alright, alright." Valerie knew Victoria was stressed, so she was very calm and composed. No matter what her daughter said, she did not get angry. To the same things, she would have reacted, but not now. Nothing had to disturb her daughter's composure.

Half an hour before the examination, they went in front of the building where the exam hall was. Soon, Victoria's friends called her, Victoria explained them how to get there. Much to their surprise, Alan called Victoria. He asked where she was, he wanted to come there.

Right a few minutes before Victoria went in, her father showed up. He kissed her and wished her good luck.

After one and a half hour Victoria came out.

"Mom, it was hard. I did not know everything."

"Don't worry, not everybody knows everything. You'll be admitted."

"I don't know. Come on, help me calculate my grade."

"Alright. Let's see."

Valerie was recalling the question and discussed the correct answers with her friends. She evaluated how many points she will get, she told it to her mom, Valerie added up the points.

"Well, I hope I'll be admitted. I don't know. We'll see."

"You'll be fine. Don't worry. OK, so what shall we do the rest of the day?"

"We'll go to the mall?"

"Yes let's go to the mall."

Everybody agreed. There were couple of Victoria's friends who also wanted to attend the medical school and they have just got out form the exam, with their parents. They all agreed to go the mall.

"When are they going to give the results?" asked Valerie.

"They said that tomorrow, but they always give the results the same day. Late in the evening, it's true, but the same day. So probably tonight we'll know mom." answered Victoria.

"OK, so we'll just have to check their site, right?"

"Yes, first time they put it on the site. Then, they also print it and show it at the university."

"*Well, one of our friends is home and he promised us he will check out the site continuously. So when the results will come out, we'll know.*"

"*Alright then, let's go to the mall.*"

First of all, they ate. Valerie and Victoria something light of course. Then Victoria drank a smoothie, Valerie drank a coffee. After that, they visited every single shop of the mall. Valerie's feet were hurting from all that walking. Whenever she saw a chair somewhere, in a shop or on an alley between the shops, she had to sit down. She did not understand how all the others from the group could go on walking. Her feet were absolutely killing her. The girls were calling their friend back in Streamtown. He kept telling them:

"*I'm on the site. Oh my God, it's overloaded. They did not show the results yet. I check it again and again. I'll call you right away.*"

The, later on, in the evening:

"*I cannot find the site anymore. It disappeared. Do you get it? It disappeared from the internet!*"

It was nine o'clock in the evening. The shops of the mall were preparing to close. They were washing the floors. The mall employees were washing the floors of the alleys.

"*Well, it's time to go home.*"

"*Do we have results yet?*"

"*No, our friend is totally stressed out. He cannot find the site anymore.*"

All the group laughed.

"*Well, let's go home.*" the mother of Victoria's friend said. "*Where are you staying?*"

"*We stay at a guest house.*"

"*Why didn't you say something? You could have come stay where we stay. It's a friend's apartment. She is away and she let us sleep there for a couple of nights.*"

"*Oh, thank you, but we did not want to impose. It's fine.*"

"*Anybody finds out something, tells the others, alright?*"

"*Yes, we'll do so.*"

The girls had to walk a few meters together, wait at a few stops. Before they separated to go each on their way, Victoria's phone started to ring. She looked at Valerie:

"*It's dad. I wonder why he calls me.*"

"So answer him and you'll find out." Valerie said.

"Hello" Victoria answered the call.

A low and impenetrable voice on the other end, her father's:

"You're admitted."

"What? How do you know?"

"I'm on the site, I see you are admitted."

"Wow, how could you access the site? Our friend said it totally disappeared."

Valerie thought while her daughter was speaking with her father « *How strange. I also found out I'm admitted from my father.*»

"So, how about my friends? Find them too, please, please dad."

"Alright, tell me the names."

One of Victoria's friends was admitted and the other not. But Victoria and Valerie were on the top of the world. On the way back to the guest house, Valerie called Eva and Camil and a few of her friends to tell them the big news: HER LITTLE GIRL WAS ADMITTED TO THE MEDICAL SCHOOL OF STEVILLE!

CHAPTER 17

Valerie was in the parking lot of her block, trying to start up her daughter's car. It didn't want to start up. She tried over and over again, but with no success. «*How come no neighbor sees me now? They know exactly when I leave and when I come, they would like me to take them places with my car, but when my car won't start up, they're nowhere to find.*»

Valerie bought this car for her daughter, Victoria. Victoria was now a student in Steville and has been using the car for two years already, but now she did not want to drive it anymore. They had too many problems with it and now they were totally stressed out waiting for what will be wrong with it again.

Right after Valerie brought it home, she took it to the service she always went. She asked the mechanic whatever she knew needed to be checked, and as she always did, asked him to tell her if he saw some any issues with it. It cost some money, but Valerie did not mind. She always wanted to make preventive maintenance with her cars, she thought a good preventive maintenance would save her from more expensive repairs later on and from a lot of stress. Unfortunately, this preventive maintenance never saved her from anything with this car.

By now Valerie knew what was the key of survival in her country. The key of survival in life is to have the right expectations. For example, if you go to a car service, don't expect them to fix your car at a fair price. Expect that your car will function worse after you take it back and this will cost a lot, and after another week or two, you will go again to the car service and you will have to pay them to fix what they ruined the last time. If, for example, you want to have a little party and you invite to your house 20 friends at 8 o'clock, expect half of them at 7 o'clock, and the other half of them at 9 o'clock. If you get married, don't expect to get a loving supporting husband who will be by your side no matter what, expect him to run off with the first bimbo he meets. On the other hand, if you have an affair with a married man, don't expect him to act like your ex-husband, expect him to be the most loyal man on earth, that would never leave his wife, no matter what. If anybody ever tells you "*Please tell me if I can help you in any way.*" don't expect that person to actually help you, expect that person to find it hard to lift a finger for you.

After Victoria became a student, she insisted to go on a holiday to the seaside with her mom. Valerie rarely went anywhere on holiday, if she had a week off she went to Mineville to help her parents. This time though Victoria was able to convince her. They booked a hotel and decided to go by car. Victoria insisted they go with her car, so they did. They left Streamtown on a Friday evening. Few months earlier, during winter, a piece of highway was open to the public between Streamtown and Polville. A few days afterwards, a terrible car pile-up happened due to the poor quality of the highway. Then, in spring, a segment of the highway was closed down because the road began to break. It appeared that the land on which the highway was built has not been reinforced, so it was moving. For this reason, Valerie and Victoria could not go on the highway until Polville, which was 60 kilometers away from Streamtown. They were able to go only 20 kilometers, then they had to go back on the old road. Valerie drove all night. All the country was totally in the dark. In one county there had been some floods, so they closed down the normal route and re-directed the drivers. The girls did not know the road very well, now also being redirected made them feel uncomfortable. Luckily, Victoria had a smart phone and they used it as a GPS. When the sun was rising, they arrived to the capital. They went on the ring road. It was in horrible condition and already full of cars, even though it was still early in the morning. Finally, they got off the Highway, which connected the capital to Seaville, the biggest city at the seaside. This was also crowded, but at least they could drive a little faster. This is where the troubles with the car began. Suddenly, while they were driving with over 80 kilometers per hours, the car got out of the fifth gear. It went into the neutral point, turned to 4000 rotations. Valerie reacted as fast as she could, she stepped on the clutch, put the gearshift lever back into the fifth gear and continued to drive. A few seconds later it happened again. And again. She tried to keep it under

80 kilometers an hour, it seemed if the car was under 80 kilometers an hour it did not get out of the fifth gear. But with the aggressive drivers, always in a hurry, always overcoming and blitzing you from behind with their lights if you don't get out of their way, Valerie had to drive faster. As the lever kept coming out of the fifth gear, Victoria was holding it in the fifth gear with her hand, while Valerie was driving. This is how they went from the capital until a small resort by the sea, and of course this is how they returned to Streamtown one week later.

Valerie wanted to solve this problem as soon as she returned, so she called the car service already from the seaside. They always said you need to make an appointment by phone before you come with the car. She called on Thursday to say on the next Monday she will come with the car and describing the problem they had on the road. The mechanic said he did not know if one Monday he will have time to look at the car, how could he know from Thursday how many cars will he have on Monday to repair? So he told Valerie she should call again on Saturday between 10 and 13 a.m. and remind him. On Saturday, Valerie was already in Streamtown and she went to work in her garden. She remembered to call the mechanic only at 13,15 a.m. She called him three times, but he did not answer anymore. As she called later than the agreed time slot, and him being such a serious and precise person, he did not answer anymore 15 minutes later. On Monday morning, Valerie called him again. First she had to go for him to see what it is about. Then, she had to cal again to make an appointment for the actual reparation of the car. After all these calls and appointments, she still had to wait several days until the mechanic said he repaired the car. The bill was quite steep, it cost around 250 euro. He said the gear shift support and motor support were broken, that's why the gear shift lever bounced out of the fifth gear by itself at higher speeds. He said he had to change also the bushing of the back arm, the front arm right end, the front left pivot and that he had to fill up with oil the gear shift case. Valerie paid the entire amount, cash in full when he gave her back the car, without any comment. What could she have said? Could she check somehow if what he said was true? Was there any way to check if he actually did what he said? No, there was no way. Nobody was checking the quality of reparations done in the car services. There was no public authority to check this. Nobody ever wondered how come these guys, with no proper training whatsoever, could have all huge houses, when they were complaining all the time they were hardly surviving from one month to the other? The state never checked their incomes and the taxes they were paying.

«*Come on, come on, start up already! Start up, damn it!*» Valerie was still trying to start up the car. It was foggy outside and the darling did not like foggy weather. Whenever she knew she had to go with the car somewhere, Valerie's heart was beating faster when she opened its door and tried to start it up. « Will it start up*? Is it good weather for my car or it's too much moisture? Will it want to start up? I wonder what could be the problem with it?*»

After the reparation for the shift gear, while driving home her car, Valerie noticed the car had very serious trepidations. So serious, her hands were trembling on the steering wheel. «*What could it be? I just took it from the car service, it's wobbling like hell! What should I do? I cannot take it back to them! It's clear they have no idea what they are doing... Is there anybody in this county who knows something about cars? In the official dealership! Yes, they should know something about the car, right? I will take it there. It is in Julestown, no problem, it's on my way.*» So she did. She took it there.

Now this place was really scary. It was a nice, shiny new building. Empty, no queue of cars. Inside they were also selling new cars and they had a car service too. The mechanic from the service was very clean and looked intellectual. It looked totally scary. He was speaking very kindly with Valerie. She told him the problem, so he proposed a test drive. Which was good, because only this way he could see how the car was wobbling. He said the wheels were not balanced right and that he saw no other issue with it. Valerie asked him to put on the winter wheels as it was autumn anyway, and to balance them. She also asked him to check the antifreeze fluid. After this was done, the car was not wobbling anymore so Victoria took it and went to Steville with it. Now the thing in Steville was that the people of Steville hated every person that came there from a different county. So, when they saw a car with Julestown plates, they had to scratch the car or break a mirror or at least steel a windshield wiper or the plates with the number. With Victoria's car, they did everything. This time, they broke the mirror from the driver's side. They broke the mirror and also the support of the mirror, just so, to do a complete job. Valerie had to take the car again to the car service. She was terrified to take it back to the service where she was with the gear shift, she knew she will get the car back worse than she left it there. So she took it to the official dealership. It was steep again. A new mirror with a new support cost 200 euro.

After 20 minutes of trying, Valerie was able to start up the car. She was going to work with it. «*After all it cost me, at least I should use it a few more times to go to work!*"

This car did cost her. After the mirror incident, which wasn't the car's fault actually, but the "friendly" people of Steville's fault, in February, one morning Victoria could not start up the car. Of course, there was nobody available to help, the guys walking around the block were just laughing how the two girls were trying to start up the car. Valerie was pushing and Victoria was in the driver's seat. Finally, they called a friend of Victoria with his car, they wired the battery to the other car's battery and tried several times to start it up. It took around half an hour until they were able to start it up. As it was so difficult to start it up, they drove it directly to the dealership and waited to see what the problem was. This time, it was the camshaft sensor. The auto diagnosis and the reparation cost about 250 euro. This time, when Valerie wanted to start up the car in the parking lot of the dealership, it did not start up. «*Now this was a great reparation! It does not even start up when you take it out of the dealership!*» The guys from the dealership had to start it up with wires connected to a battery they had inside, so Valerie took the car and went to another service where they put on a new battery. One month later the periodical technical inspection had to be done. Now in Valerie's country, people usually paid a bribe so that authorized technical engineer let them get away with whatever problem they had with the car, so that they did not have to make any expensive reparations. This was not the case with Valerie. She wanted a real, serious check of the car. She considered her life and, more important, her daughter's life was depending on the safety of the car. This is why she wanted to do preventive maintenance of the car. She never played with the periodical checks or reparations of the car. The engineer who made the inspection told her there were several issues with the car, but the most serious was that the front right fuse was broken and it had to be exchanged. She made this reparation immediately, this time she went to yet another car service, for which she got great recommendations. She remembered last summer she had to change the right end of the front arm. This end was connected to the front right fuse. Didn't those idiots see that the fuse was broken, this is why the end of the arm was broken?

In June the same year, the ABS got broke. Valerie had it replaced in her latest car service. This mechanic also told her that the brake fluid had to be replaced because it was very used and only at a low level. After this, for a few days, the brakes seemed not to react so fast as usual, but eventually the problem disappeared.

Valerie was slowly losing her patience with this car. She was thinking only about it, searching on the internet what could be wrong with it. She decided to take one last final chance with this car. In August, she took it to the car service for a general revision of everything she could think of. She asked the mechanic to replace the distribution belt. He said also the water pump had to be replaced, he checked the antifreeze fluid, he replaced the oil, the filters (oil, fuel, air and pollen), he replaced some bushings in the back, he replaced the oil from the gear shift case, he replaced the bushings from the stabilizing bar, the plug. Valerie told him about the issue they had with the shift gear and asked him to check it too. This mechanic said the problem was not what the previous car service said, he said what they replaced had anything to do with the car bouncing out of the fifth gear. He said the problem was that the back cap of the case of the shift gear was broken and that he replaced it. The bill this time was 400 euro. In September, Valerie and Victoria went to Steville for a medical check. On their way back, another light lid up in the dashboard of the car. Victoria searched up the sign in the book of the car. This time, the ESP was burnt. Actually, this was the last drop. They both got really angry, Victoria said she will not drive it anymore. Valerie could not say this. If she had a car, she was responsible for it. So she started the soap opera of the burnt ESP.

First she took it to her service. They guy said he has to put the car on the tester. No mechanic knew anymore what is a wrong with a car, unless they put it on a tester. It actually happened that someone went with a small Tico to the car service that would not start up anymore and the mechanic told the owner he cannot check what's wrong with the car, because it was too small to put on the tester. They did not check anything. They just put the car on the tester, this is all they knew how to do. So the mechanic put Valerie's car on the tester. The tester said that sensor x, which was an ESP, was burnt. He could not find this sensor x at the auto dismantling garages and a new one was 200 euro. Of course, he charged Valerie for the dismantling of the sensor and the diagnosis. Now it's not that Valerie wouldn't have paid another 200 euro to get the new sensor, but in two months, something else would have been wrong with it, so what was the point? She started to search herself another sensor, hoping she will find it at a better price. She asked around at work. Several colleagues promised to help her, of course, nobody did. One of her colleagues told her about a website where she could buy online second hand spare parts. Valerie entered the code of the sensor and she found one for sale, at the price of 50 euro. She ordered it and the part arrived the next day. Valerie was at work, Victoria was at home as she was in exam session and she was learning at home. So Valerie called the mechanic and told him she bought a second hand sensor and she asked him kindly to mount it on. He did not seem extremely delighted by the phone, but he accepted to do it. Victoria went with the car to the service. Half an hour later, Valerie received a call from the mechanic. He said the sensor order by Valerie online was no good. Valerie bought this spare part with no invoice and no guarantee. It was written on the site, that the parts were second hand and that they did not provide any guarantee for them. So what could she have done? She thought about it for a few hours and it finally hit her. She was going to write on the site that the guy sold her a bad spare part. As he had a lot of spare parts to sell, it meant this was a business for him and a bad review was not going to do him any good. It worked pretty quickly. In half an hour, she got a call from the guy who sold her the spare part. He told her the spare part was good and most likely the mechanic did not know how to mount it. Valerie called back the mechanic and told him what this guy said. The mechanic said he did everything he had to do and the part was no good. Valerie called back the guy who sold her the spare part and told him what the mechanic said. He said he will buy back the part, provided that she deleted the bad review from the site. Valerie agreed and sent him back the part. She got back her money and she deleted the bad review.

But something was not leaving her alone. Something told her it was not over. So she took the car to the authorized dealership. They put the car on their tester. This again cost another 75 euro, but the result was different. They also said and ESP was burnt, but with code y this time. Valerie told the whole story to Victoria:

"You know what? I don't want another car of this type again in my life. Not even if they give me a new one for free. And don't get me wrong: it's a great car, just great. The problem is it breaks down every two months, and here, in our county they have no idea about it. They don't know the car. I assume they have a technical book of the car, but it is probably written in foreign language and they don't know the language so well. Also, they don't give it to an authorized translation company, because you know, mechanics, they are so poor, they hardly get by from one month to the other. I mean, look at where they are living. I work from dusk to dawn, right? And I have a 20 square meters apartment. Now take a look to the house of a mechanic. It looks like a drug lord's house, massive, arrogant, with one storey."

"OK, mom, whatever."

"Of course, I could take it to the country of origin to be repaired, I suppose they know this damn car they built. But on the other hand, I don't think it's worth to take a car to its country of origin every two months for reparations, what do you say?"

"I say it was just bad luck. Get over it. You did not find a good car. It happens."

"Yes, you're right. I mean I thought that being a foreign car and all, it would be great. All men are raving how good the foreign cars are. I mean it is full of them, anywhere you turn, you can see this type of car. Right? Because foreign technology is great. And you know what?"

"*What mom?*" Victoria could hardly listen to her mom anymore, but if she learned something in her life was that when her mom was pissed off about something, the best thing was to let her release the steam and not say anything until it was over.

"Foreign technology is great. It's just marvelous. And the local mechanics are great too. They really are. The problem is that they don't go well together. You know? Just like me and your father. Taken separately, your father is a great guy. Look how great he is with his current child and family. On the other hand, I am great too. But we just cannot function together. You know?"

"I understand mom."

"In the beginning, I thought there was a problem only with my car. So, I invested and invested in it. You know all the times I took it to the service. But then, I got into the cars of others. Each and every one of them has the dashboard lit up as a Christmas tree. They all say it's working this way too. But it's not

OK, it's not OK to drive your car if some sensors don't work. On the other hand, how can they ask 200 euro for an ESP sensor? All the cars of this type I saw manufactured in 2000 have the ESP burnt out and nobody replaces it of course at this price… And it's not just this. Always a door is blocked. The oil is leaking. The water is leaking. For the life of me, I cannot understand why do they all like this damn car so much!"

"I'm sorry mom. I'm sorry it did not work out. I just want to tell you that I am very grateful you bought me this car. And while it was working, it helped me a lot to have it. I'm sorry you are upset, but it was great to have it and I thank you for it."

"I am sorry my love that I was not able to buy you a good car. I bought you this piece of junk that obsessed me for years now, that occupied every free cell of my brain and that gave me palpitations. And you know what? This car made me understand what annoyed me the most about your father. More than the fact he had a child with another woman nine months after you were born. What annoyed me the most was that he was playing with my mind. Just like this damn car. And this I cannot forgive and I will not accept."

"I understand."

"So, I am going drive this car to work and back until March when the insurance expires and I'll give it away."

"Are you going to sell it?"

"No, I will not sell it. I don't want to scam anybody. This car has serious problems. I took it so many times to the service and these idiots just don't know what is wrong with it. I don't want to create problems to others with it. What goes around comes around. I believe in this with all my heart."

"So, what are you going to do about it?"

"I'll use it until the insurance runs out and then I'll give it to the junk yard where it belongs. I know, I know, it cost thousands of euro and I will give it away for a couple of hundreds. But it is better like this. At least, from now on it will not cost me anymore. Just the simple fact that I will not have to maintain it anymore, will make me save money."

"Alright mom. Whatever."

Valerie continued to use the car. In the morning, when she went into the parking lot, her heart always beat faster. « *Will it start up?*» Sometimes she was thinking so much what was wrong with it that she started to have palpitations.

If she drove longer and then stopped, it started up again. But after a shorter drive, the car did not start up. Valerie knew the car service would not solve her problem, still she called her mechanic, just to see what he will tell her:

"*Hello, I'm Valerie. You know, I was several times with my car at you. Last time with the burnt ESP.*"

"*Yes, m'am, how can I help you?*"

"*I was wondering why my car does not start up. I mean the battery is new, it has been put on the car three months ago. What do you say?*"

"*I don't know. I don't know why it does not start up.*"

"*I mean maybe the alternator is not working?*"

"*If the alternator would not work, the tester would have shown it.*"

"*Ahh, the tester. Right. Or maybe the alternator does not charge the battery? Or maybe there is some contact problem somewhere?*"

"*I don't know.*"

"*Alright then, thank you for your time. Bye.*"

"*Bye.*"

Eventually, Victoria took the car one time to Steville and back. It caused no problem. After she returned, in the parking lot, Valerie saw the car was leaking some fluid. She took some fluid on her finger. It did not smell as gas, it was not oil either. It was a waterlike fluid, a little reddish. Valerie looked it up on Google immediately. She learned that the brake fluid looked like that. She remembered her mechanic told her that the brake fluid was very old and low in her car and he repaired some cap so that it does not leak anymore. That was when he ruined the whole thing. «*So what? What can I do?*» Valerie could not even get really angry in front of Victoria. But she was in rage inside. «*Now if I go back to him, he will keep the car for a day or two, tell me he repaired it and ask for some more money. When in fact he does more wrong than good. My God, these people are playing with our lives. And the problem is they are all the same. I was in four car services with this car and still there is nobody who knows what is wrong with it. What? What can we do to protect our lives against these criminals? Shouldn't the state protect us some way?*»

Valerie wrote a message to the Auto Registry. Asked them if they can check a repair that was done to her car. She got no reply. The Auto Registry was not interested in stuff like this.

Valerie never let Vitoria use the car again. She continued to use it until spring. Then the time has come to solve the problem. Valerie never liked the ostrich policy. She believed strongly that any problem can be solved if you deal with it, if you tackle it. Maybe some problems will be harder to solve, maybe some problems will be more expensive to solve, some problems will take up more of your time, still you have to find a solution for them. If you stick your head into the sand and pretend the problem does not exist, it will just get worse. She did not want to let her car rust in the parking lot, like so many others do. Two weeks before the insurance ran out, Valerie started to give some phone calls to get rid of it. There were some dealerships that bragged how they take over your old car. The car buy back companies. Again, Valerie forgot she had to have the right expectations. She should have known that the advertisement they were making on their website that they buy back your old car, check the condition of the car, then help you sell it or just give you the amount of money the car is worth or you can buy a new car from them and they deduct the value of your old car is just bullshit meant to attract stupid customers like herself. She called them. Then sent photos of the car, gave them details about all the problems the car had. Of course, in the end they told her they were not interested to buy her car. What bothered Valerie the most was that they made her lose her time. They were making publicity for themselves, that was not true. So what? Who could Valerie turn to in this case?

Finally, she started to give some phone calls to the guys who were taking over old cars and dismantled them. She spoke with three of them. They did not sound very glad to take over her car on the phone. « *What is this? Some cheap way to make me give away my car for nothing? It cost me thousands and thousands of euro. Buying it, registering it, then repairing it every other month. I know it's a worthless piece of junk, Shouldn't they at least make an offer?*»

Finally she found a guy who was willing to buy the car from her and give her the destruction certificate. She needed that to erase the car from circulation. The guy gave Valerie 250 euro. After her marriage, this car was probably the second most damaging business of her entire life. «*When I think about it, Alan is a kind of like this car. Useless, costly, unreliable piece of junk.*» Valerie could hardly control herself. She was so angry, she felt she was getting sick. Then, her subconscious started to dictate her as always

« *Do what you have to do to survive. You must survive. You must be strong. You must be healthy. Your daughter needs you.*» Valerie breathed in deep. In and out. In and out. «*I have to forgive Alan. No matter how unacceptable it seems. No matter how sick I feel to my stomach when I think to all that he did to me. How he stole my best years. How he abandoned my child for some whore. No matter how my entire being is opposing this thought, I have to forgive him. After all, I have forgiven my dad, right? My dad who beat up my mother right in front of me. Right? So I have to forgive Alan too. My hatred against him does not do anything wrong to him, it just does me wrong. He doesn't care that I hate him, but I get sick hating him. I am the one losing my mind trying to understand him, while he doesn't give a shit. He just finds it funny nobody understands him. I have to forgive him. My God, it is hard. Maybe I should make this in smaller steps. First step, stop hating him. Just ignore him. Then, slowly, I have to try to forgive him. Really, truly just forgive him. The little boy inside of him. With his lying, cold, rejecting mother and abusive, violent father. I have to forgive him.*»

Valerie needed a good reliable car. She had to drive every day 100 kilometers to work and back. She had to go every month to her parents to Mineville. She had to go to Steville to her daughter. She decided to buy a brand new locally produced car. Valerie thought maybe if it is a local car, the car services of her county will know something about it. At least it had four years guarantee. And being a new car, at least for a few years she will not have to go so often to the car services, because her nerves were not able to handle the car services anymore.

This decision of hers started to shape up at the single pleasant surprise she had in her life as a driver.

It was hard to be driver in Valerie's country. The drivers were aggressive. If they thought you were not driving fast enough or you were just in their way, they drove real close to your back and signaled you with the lights and then passed you over. The worst of all drivers were the ones driving BMWs, especially older BMWs, and those that drove Volkswagens, also those that drove company registered cars and the ones with the 1,5 tons vans. They were totally insane in traffic. Seeing them, Valerie always thought «*The way you are driving, you will kill yourself. Then, at your funeral, women will pull their hair out weeping that you died so young. And if you only kill yourselves is one thing. My worry is that idiot as you are, you kill other people in traffic too, innocent people who drive like normal persons.»*

Now, it was one thing to be aggressively followed by another small car while you were driving a small car, but when you were driving a small car and you were followed closely and aggressively by a big truck, you just feared for your life. If you reduced the speed, for any reason, the big truck coming with speed from behind you could very well kill you right there. This happened several times with Valerie. She did not even know whom she had to complain. She wrote again to the Auto Registry. Nothing. Then to the Road Authority. Nothing. Finally, she filed a complaint to the Police. Actually, they answered. They answered in cases like this, she has to call the emergency phone number 911. Unfortunately, when something like this happened to her, she just drove for her life, she could not even think of picking of the cell phone and dial 911. Couldn't they just check on the guy who drove the respective car if she gave them the plate number? The drivers were not polite either. Before she went to Germany, Valerie thought this was the normal way. Not be polite, to cut off others in traffic. To be as rude and aggressive as possible. But in Germany, when she saw how polite the drivers were, when she saw how everybody was respecting the rules, not only those who did not have relatives and friends within the Police force, she started to think why in her country drivers could not be like that? Why in Germany, if you got into an intersection and you did not know way to turn, you could take out your map, put it on the steering wheel and look for a few seconds, even if the traffic light turned green and there were several cars waiting behind you, they were not signaling you with their lights, nobody honked their horn, they just waited patiently until you started to move your car? Why in her country if you would have done this, they would probably get out of their cars and drag you down off yours and beat you up? Valerie knew this was because of the corruption of the Police, which ultimately was one of the representatives of the state. The state was corrupt, the police was corrupt. They enforced the law and the rules only to those who had no connections, no influence. The powerful people, the ones with money and influence did not have to follow the rules.

Driving in Valerie's country was like finding your way through the jungle. In this jungle, Valerie had only one single pleasant surprise. She was driving back home from work with her car. At a certain point, she had to drive up on a hill, on some pretty strong curves. From the opposite direction, a big truck was driving down, loaded in the back with gravel. Right when he passed by Valerie's car, one of his tires exploded. The explosion was so powerful, that Valerie, while still driving, lowered her head as much as she could. She could not believe nothing had happened to her. She drove up a few meters more, than she pulled over to check what happened with the car. The truck did not stop, he continued driving like nothing happened. Few meters before Valerie, a white local car was driving up the hill too. To Valerie's great surprise, the driver pulled over too. A guy came out of it and asked her:

"Are you OK, mam?"

"Yes, I am fine, thank you."

"What about the car? Did something happen with it?"

"I cannot see anything wrong with it. The tires look fine, nothing lit up in the dashboard. Everything looks in order."

"Are you sure, mam? If you need anything, please tell me."

"No, no, I am fine. Just a little frightened. That's all. Thank you very much for stopping!"

"No problem. Take care. Bye."

"Bye."

Valerie got back into her car and started driving again. She thought « *Are you kidding me? A man actually stopped and asked me if I am fine? Now this is a surprise. Normally, a male driver would have been pissed off that I pulled over at such a short notice, he would have cursed me and passed me over. What was wrong with this man? Hmmm...*»

Valerie remained with a good impression about the local car.

Then, there was a discussion she had once with Alan. Trying so hard to forgive him, she started to speak him whenever he called her. She never called him, but Alan sometimes called her. Like he was sensing she was not so much against him anymore. With one occasion, she said:

"I don't even know what car to buy myself."

"What do you mean?"

"I mean Victoria's car, the one I had to get rid of. It was a piece of junk. Maggie is old, I cannot use it very much more. I need a good car. I don't even know what to buy."

"Why don't you buy a local car?"

"A local car? Hmmm.... I'll think about it."

Normally, if Alan told her she should do something, she did right the opposite. She remembered back when they were still married, once she cut her hair short and died it red. Alan told her:

"See? This is how I like your hair. It really becomes you."

"Ohh, you like my hair? Hmmm..." and she thought « *This means I'll never wear it like this anymore in my life.*»

Now she changed. She was trying really hard to forgive him. She was making huge efforts to talk with him and not get angry for every sentence that came out his mouth. She checked out the idea with the local car too, which turned out to be good after all.

When she ordered her new car, she had to pay 5% of the price and they told her the car will arrive in three months. After about two months, she decided to tell Camil and Eva that she was buying a new car. Valerie knew that when the car came from the factory, she will have to pay the 50% of its price, as she has promised.

"Dad, mom, I want to tell you something. Please stay here both of you."

"Yes, what is it Val?" Camil came and sat by her and Eva.

"I want to buy a new car. A local car."

"Aaa, the local car. I saw they are advertising it like crazy." said Eva.

"Yes, that is the one." said Valerie.

"What are you going to do with the other two?" asked Camil.

"Well, I gave away Victoria's car. I am still keeping Maggie, at least for a while. Then, we shall see."

"OK, then, we want to tell you something too." said Camil.

"What is it, dad?"

"Your mother and I, well, we have saved some money. You know we are not spending so much. The medicines cost a lot, plus what we spend for food and utilities. But that is pretty much it."

"Yes, but you are giving us money too, Victoria and me. Every time we come home."

"That is nothing. Don't even mention it."

"Are you sure? Do you have enough money?"

"We are fine, don't worry about us. Anyway, we were able to save a bigger amount of money and we want to give it to you. You do what you want with it. Spend it or keep it. It is yours."

And Camil gave Valerie the money.

"*It is from your mother and me.*"

Valerie jumped literally at her father's neck. She was not very used to receive such gifts, she rarely received anything from anybody without having to work hard for it.

"*Dad, this is too much! Are you sure? Do you have money? For what you need?*"

"*Yes, yes, don't worry. Take the money, it's yours. Once again, I want to thank you for the time you helped us with money. Remember? When we installed the central heating in this apartment and we had no money? You gave us the money. I will never forget that. Nobody ever helped me like that. Or when you bought your mother the automatic washing machine? Even though I still don't understand why your mother did not ask me for the washing machine. I would have bought it for her.*"

"*She did not ask me either for it, but I felt so sorry for her when I saw how she was struggling with the laundry. Remember mom? You bended over in the tub to rinse them, you support yourself on one elbow on the edge of the tub, with your other hand you rinsed the clothes in that cold water? Your knuckles were swollen from all that cold water?*"

"*Yes, I remember*" Eva said. "*I will be forever grateful for that washing machine. Your father does not understand that even if a person does not complain, if you have eyes to see and ears to listen, you can find opportunities to make his or her life easier.*"

"*Of course I helped you. You needed the heating and the hot water and the machine and everything, didn't you? And after all, isn't that what families are all about? To help each other out?*"

"*Yes, you are perfectly right*" concluded Camil.

The next day, on Sunday, Valerie and Victoria returned to Streamtown. On Tuesday, she got the call from the dealership:

"*Hello, we are calling from dealership, I am Adela.*"

"*Hello.*"

"*I am just calling to tell you that your car is ready.*"

"*Heeey, this is a good surprise.*"

"*It is?*"

"*Yes, initially you told me I will receive my car in three months. And it is ready after two months?*"

"*Well, we did our best. So, are you prepared?*"

«*She means if I have the money ready, the 50% advance payment.*» thought Valerie.

"*Yes, I am ready.*" Valerie answered. "*Can you send me the amount to pay?*"

"*Of course, we will send it to you today. When will you make the payment?*"

"*I need a couple of days. That is all.*"

"*Alright then. Hear you soon.*"

"*Yes, bye!*"

Before her father gave her money, Valerie had almost the entire amount prepared. Now, with that money too, she had all the amount ready. So she paid the 50% advance payment. In a couple of days after that, the documents of the car were all prepared and they called her to the dealership to get her new car.

Valerie always wondered how a new car smells. Well, her car smelled like plastic. She took it with 5 kilometers on board. Victoria could not come with her mom to pick up the new car and Valerie did not even ask anybody else to come and help, everybody was very busy every time she needed help. So she went with her Maggie, left it in a parking lot in Julesville which was very close to a bus stop. From there, she took a taxi, went to the dealership and took her new car and drove it home. The next day, she left her new car at home, went with a bus to Julesville, to the parking lot where she left Maggie, took Maggie and went with it to work. Then, from work she came home with Maggie. This way, she brought both her cars home. Like so many times in her life, she had these logistic games to solve, which took very much after the little logistic problem Camil was always asking her to solve when she was little girl: "*You have one boat and you have to cross a river. You have one wolf, one goat and one cabbage and you have to cross them the river too, with your boat. Now, you cannot get the goat and the cabbage in the same time with your boat, because the goat will eat the cabbage. You cannot get the wolf and the goat in the same time in your boat, because the wolf will eat the goat. How do you do it?*"

The first drive with the new car. The radio was singing a new song. The tank was empty, first thing Valerie had to do was to go and fill with gas. Then, slowly she drove out of the gas station. Valerie was trembling. She was afraid. «*My God, what if I crash the car? It is brand new... God help me! Ohh, I'll be fine. I have been driving for 6 years now, I'll be fine. Plus I have insurance and Casco and everything. I'll drive slowly and carefully. Hey, this car runs smoothly... By the way, what is my speed? With Maggie I can tell without watching the dashboard, when I go over 70 km/hour she makes such a big deal out of it. But with one, I can't tell... Hey, look at this, I am driving with 90 kilometers per hour and I can't even feel or hear anything. And it passed so smoothly over the bumpers. Great car, God it feels good to drive such a great new car*» Valerie was driving with a big smile on her face, totally relaxed. Driving her old cars was always a great stress, always expecting some breakdown. But now, she could drive relaxed and confident.

Nothing wrong happened to her or her car on the first drive home. On Sunday Valerie asked the priest to make a small ceremony for blessing the car. She saw many risen eyebrows for this, but she always did this with her cars and nothing bad ever happened to her. Of course, there were breakdowns, as with every car, but she never was involved in any car accident ever. Valerie knew God was looking after her and no risen eyebrows could convince her else.

There were also envies risen by the purchase of her new car. "*How could she afford this new car? Where does she have all that money from?*" people were talking behind her back. Even though nobody asked her this upfront, she saw the envy in their eyes. She always thought «*Just ask me how do I have all this money. Just ask me... I'll ask you to come every day to work with me, to see how it is. I'll ask you every evening to continue to work with me on my computer until you barely see with your tired eyes anymore and your head aches. I will ask you to wake up on Saturday at 5 o'clock and come with me to my garden to work some more. I'll ask you to come and spend every day off work you have to work some more at home, and not spend money having a good time in resorts and restaurants. Come on, just ask me into my face...*»

Then the men of her block. Several men have started to greet her only after she purchased her new car.

"*You know, I don't even care when men don't greet me.*" Valerie was chatting with Victoria. "*I mean he looks at me, he knows me, but he doesn't greet. Sometimes, I greet somebody one of them by reflex, because I know them. Usually, they greet me back. Well, except for those from Polville. Now the only men who are so rude that I greet them and they don't greet me back are from Polville. It is not an accident that Polville has been the capital of good manners. You know?"* Valerie started to laugh and Victoria too. "*Then, when I think about it, he is a man, he should greet me first, so I don't greet them first anymore. There are a lot of men who know me and since they don't greet first, we don't even look at each other when we meet. Funny thing is some of them started to greet me only after they saw* me *with my new car. Isn't that funny?"*

"*Yeah, it is funny, mom.*" Victoria laughed together with her mom.

"*Because, you know, men are telling us since the beginning of time that we women only stay with them if we have an interest to do so. That we look at them only if they have money. But they are no different from us, are they? Here is the proof. All those men who started to notice me only after I got my new car. I mean, there are so few men left who actually build a home for their family. Like my grandfather, you know? He was a miner, yet he was able to build a house for his family. My father never built anything, he just drank. The communist state gave him the home. Look at your father. Whom he chose to live with? Isabella of course, over me. Out of uninterested love? I don't think so. Just because she will inherit from her mother an apartment in Steville. Look at the boys your age... How they all have several girlfriends, but whom will they choose to get married with? The girl with the house, of course!*"

"*You are probably right mom.*"

"*I am right, I am! This is how they are! And what annoys me the most is how they try to take us out as the bad ones, when in fact they are much worse than we are.*"

Valerie was getting close to the age of 50. She could afford to buy a brand new car. Financially, she was doing very fine. She thanked God every day for all that she had and never forgot how short money was while she was a young woman. And even though now she could buy pretty much anything she desired, she always continued to keep a very strict control over her expenses.

Her life, on the other hand, was not getting easier at all. Her job was very demanding. A lot of work and stress and over time. At night, after she arrived home, many times she had also translations to do. Her day started at a quarter to five in the morning and ended at eleven o'clock at night. The weekends were even harder. Everybody was looking forward to the weekends. For Valerie, the weekends were traumatizing. On Friday afternoon she went shopping and cleaned the house. On Saturday morning, at dawn, she was out in her garden. In the afternoon, she cooked for her daughter. Every weekends she cooked for her daughter for the coming week. On Sunday morning, she continued with the cooking, because the package with food for her daughter left on Sunday afternoon. If she had a little time, she went to church too. Then, Sunday afternoon was for ironing the laundry.

Once a month she went to her parents, to Mineville. She cleaned up her parents' house as well as she could. It was a big house and many times she felt she just could not finish the work. But then, she thought «*If it is so hard for me to clean this window too, imagine how hard it is for mom. And how can I leave them with a dirty house? Don't they have the right to live in a clean, comfortable house after all they worked? On the other hand, I want to treat them just like I want to be treated when I'll be old. So, I'll sit down for a few seconds, and then I will continue cleaning.*»

Victoria was grown up, now she went on holidays with her friends. Valerie gave her money and frankly, she was happy her daughter had great vacations to which she did not have to participate. Valerie virtually never went on holidays. For her, holidays were just an additional expense and fatigue. The packing before the trip, all the preparations to leave everything in order at home, leaving the dog at friends who of course loved Lady, but Valerie felt nobody took care of her dog like she did, then the long trip, many times the driving for ten, twelve hours, then the driving back, unpacking at home, picking up everything again. Plus the money spent for the holidays. All this, was not a means of relaxation for Valerie. Many times she thought «*Maybe I am not able to relax anymore. I became a workaholic. If I take it easy, for one afternoon even, I feel guilty afterwards. What would relax me anyway? Knowing my daughter is fine and has everything she needs, knowing my parents are fine, in a clean house and well taken care of, knowing my dog is fed and she did her walk of the day, knowing at my little garden everything is in order, the little cabin is clean, the grass is cut, the weeds are pulled out. If all this would be in place, maybe I could relax. How could I go on vacation? If I have a few days off, I have to go to my parents and help them. Who knows how many months do they still have to live? I've seen so many cases of people with parents who had terminal illnesses, with only weeks to live, but they still went on holidays. Then, after their parents died, they made a great circus at the funeral with their crocodile tears how much they regret they lost their parents and what wouldn't they do just to have their parents for one more day... I will not do that mistake. I will spend time with my parents as much as possible while they are still here. I will give my mother flowers as much as possible while she is still alive, not after she is dead. I don't want to put flowers on her grave so that the neighbors see how much I miss her, I want to give her flowers now while she still enjoys them.»*

The winter holidays were the worst for Valerie.

"*When you were a few months old and we were in Stevillewith your father, I spent Christmas crying in the window, waiting for him to come home.*"

"*Why do you have to remember everything?*" asked Victoria.

"*You know what? This is what your father always asks me. I don't want to remember everything, that is just the way I am. Still, I am home alone for the holidays. You go with your friends and it's normal for you to go with your friends, but I am still alone. Well, with my Lady. So always on Christmas Eve and New Year's Eve, to show her how much I love her I take her to a long, long walk into town. There are no cars on the street, it is very nice. And I look to all the houses with all those Christmas lights. And I just want to take a big bat and hit all those lights.*"

"*Why mom?*"

"*I hate all those people with the big houses. I think I'm living in a twenty square meters apartment. We hardly have place to turn around. And others have big houses. I think what did I do wrong? My child does not have the right to live in a big house like those other children? Your cousins live in houses, all your cousins. You live in this dump. I think to myself: what did I do wrong? Didn't I work hard enough? Do I spend too much for rubbish?*"

"*You do everything just fine mom. Those who have houses inherited them most probably. Or they stole a lot of money and that's why they are rich. Don't worry, we are just fine. I have everything I need. Don't worry about a thing.*"

"*There is another thing I don't understand. I never saw Isabella come and work for his parents. Well, they died, I know, but she never came to work for them while they were alive.*"

"*Why should she come to work for them?*"

"*Why did I have to work for his parents? Because I was with your father. I want to see her milk the cows. I want to see her going with the herd of cows on the field. I want to see her digging in the field. I want to see her gather the dried grass on the field. I want to see her washing their laundry with her hands. I want to see her carrying the tiles and the cement when they renovate the house.*"

"She's not going to come to do all this."

"Why not? She is with your father. She has a child with your father. Why did I have to do all this and she does not have to do it?

"Because you were his wife. She is his girlfriend. She has no obligation."

"And I did have this obligation? How come I only have obligations in this life and others only have rights?"

"I don't know but it's absurd to expect her to come and work here."

"Why are you on her side?"

"I'm not on her side, I'm just telling you the reality."

"What reality? That I am a stupid idiot of whom your father just took advantage and she is the one who got the best of him?"

"You don't know what she got of him."

"I know she did not have to live with their clan for eight years. With all the joys involved."

"Mom, I don't want to fight with you over this. But sometimes you're absurd."

"No, I'm not absurd. Life is absurd. Just like Kafka described it. There is another thing I understood over the years."

"Please tell."

"I realized the way your parents treat you, that is how you will be treated your entire life. I cannot explain it, but it is true. I have been used, abused and mistreated by my parents. That's the way I was treated during my entire life. Your grandma always put me do the things she did not like to do. The dirty jobs. In my life, the same thing happened to me. With your father. At work. I have been put to do the dirty job. I have never been appreciated. I have never been pampered. I have never been considered worthy for the finer things of life."

"I'm sorry mom."

"It's OK, I'm just saying. This is one of the reasons I always wanted to treat you the best I could. Buy you the best clothes and things. Give you the best education. Take you to the best doctors and all. I want this for you for all your life. You know that in Mineville area, where we were born, people treat their children with the utmost respect? They call them young masters. The children are the most important persons in the family. And the results can be seen, you know? They turn out serious, hard working, clean, dependable people when they grow up"

"I love you mom."

"I love you too my dearest."

Valerie's life has become work and more work. She was a mother, a daughter and an employee. As she got older though, she started to feel the need to find herself again. She just needed to be herself, not that she wanted to drift away from her daughter or her parents, but she needed to think about herself too. Since Victoria was born, she never thought of herself. That was more than twenty years ago. Though she was not young anymore, she did not feel old yet. And although she was alone, she appreciated the fact that she was strong and independent. The holidays spent alone did not bother her anymore. Victoria was always away with her friends. Valerie thought this was best for her daughter, on the other hand she had her dog and with Lady, so she never felt lonely.

Valerie started writing. First as an experiment, just to see how it felt. She wrote some short texts about the times spent with Alan. After writing them, Valerie felt relieved. To much her surprise, it helped her forgive him much more easily. «*This is what I'll do*» thought Valerie. «*I'll write a book. I'll write there all my struggle and my pain and the hardships. Art has always been the best catharsis after all, right? And maybe, somebody will read it, some other single mom out there fighting all by herself. Maybe reading my book, she will feel better, she will understand she is not alone. Wouldn't that be extraordinary? If I could write a book that could help one woman out there, only one woman, it would already be a great personal success for me. Because I felt alone and I felt lonely and I felt nobody reaches out a hand to help me. And finally now I feel proud of what I achieved. And I don't mean the financial status I'm in right now, I mean I raised a child that turned out to be a hardworking responsible person. And this achievement nobody can take away from me."*

Writing had a strong effect on Valerie. The greatest transformation she felt was the change of type of men that attracted her. Valerie did not want to be alone. She never wanted to end up alone, just things turned out to be that way for her.

"*You know, my love*" Valerie confessed to the love of her life, her daughter. *"I finally understand what the problem is."*

"*What, mom?*"

"*The problem is with me. If a man is normal, he's just not attracted to me. Only if he is some kind of a sick bastard he is attracted to me."*

"That's not true mom."

"Yes, it's true. If I analyze all the men I met in my life, I never attracted a normal man. Never. So, I just give up. I am cursed in love. I don't even want to meet somebody anymore. I finally understood I was meant to be without man."

"It's not true mom, Don't say that. You should try and find somebody. I am grown up now. I'll go away. And I promise I will not be jealous."

"It's fine, my love. Thank God I don't even need it anymore. But since I've been writing, you know, the funniest thing happened."

"What mom?"

"I think I am finally cured of your father. I dare to say I finally got him out of my system. And you know how I know that? You know how I always have been crazy about Keanu Reeves?"

"Yes, I like him too. He's so cute and sad..."

"Now, see, that is a mistake. You should never make the same mistake I made. I was attracted to our father – and Keanu Reeves – because they are so mysterious. How they play that role with the sadness. Nobody understands what's the matter with them. I was fascinated to understand what is beneath that mask. I always thought under that sad mask there is a deep ocean of feelings and interior struggle. But I was wrong. There's nothing beneath. They are just cold and empty. This is why nothing you can see nothing at them, because <u>there is nothing</u> to see. Whenever you find a guy you cannot read within the first half an hour after you meet him, just dump him. He will just play with your mind, you'll just waste time and affection with them and never get anything back. Also stay away from the boy-men. Like your father and Keanu Reeves. Like they are still little boys and missing their moms. When I saw that face of your father's. It was long before you were born. I suppose I had a wild maternal instinct and I found somebody looking for his mom. Can you imagine? Well, that boy-man, still missing his mother's love, ruined my life. He destroyed me."

"Don't worry mom. I am not attracted to this kind of men. I am attracted to guys older than me. Beautiful, intelligent and rich." said Victoria laughing.

"It figures..." mumbled Valerie. *"With the father issues you have..."*

"Yes, right..." Victoria laughed again.

"Anyway, what I wanted to tell you is that I don't like Keanu Reeves anymore. Now I like Gerard Butler. He is a totally different kind of man and I adore him. And the best is that this shows the change that took place in my

mind. This proves me I am on the right path, I am changing. I am happy I am not attracted to that kind of men anymore, those like your father!"

"*Ohh, mom, but I like Keanu Reeves.*"

"*You just like him because I liked him. But I don't like him anymore.*"

"*I don't care, I still like him.*" concluded Victoria.

CHAPTER 18

Alan was playing on his computer. This is what he liked to do most. Of course, now he was fifty years old. He thought «*So what if I like to play on my computer? Whom am I bothering with it? I am working, aren't I? I have a salary and I am able support myself. Well... Valerie would ask me now when shall I grow up. I would ask her why should I grow up? I like it like this. I like to play on my computer. It's all simulated, no responsibility, no stress. I like it when she gets angry with me. I miss her cooking. And the love making. Hmmm... If I like being with her, how did I end up here? Living with an evil woman, who wants to control every move I make. Ohhh, how I liked my independence. How Valerie left my independence intact, even though we were married and we had a child. How I liked my mother in law when I was married with Valerie. Eva cooked me my favorite meals. She always respected me. Left me sleep as much as I wanted. Isabella's mother does not respect me, she bashes me verbally in front of my family and the ones I know. Something's gone wrong... I did not want to end up here. I just wanted to play on my computer. Well, it seems I'm not as smart as I thought I was. Actually, I am quite stupid. Hmmm... Hey, however it is, in the end I have inspired a great woman write a book about me. I mean, how many men can brag they accomplished something like this?*"

Alan has been living with his son Samuel, his girlfriend Isabella and her mother for 15 years now, in an apartment in Steville. He never got married with Isabella. He always did what she asked him to, everything. Isabella was quite a control freak. Except for this. No matter how much she insisted, even if she brought it up every day, Alan did not want to get married to her.

"*I had a bad experience with marriage. It did not end good. Why should I repeat it?*"

"Because you are have been living with me all these years. Why not?"

"Didn't you always say you did not believe in marriage? I mean, back then, when I was married with Valerie and had an affair with you, didn't you always say that marriage is just a piece of paper that doesn't mean anything?"

"I meant that not that piece of paper keeps two people together."

"You're right. That piece of paper did not keep me together with my wife and my child..."

"What? Now you regret your wife? Go back to her!"

"I do regret that I'm not with her anymore. And I'm sorry that she left me. But I cannot go back to her." answered Alan. And he thought «*I don't deserve her, you stupid bitch. I deserve to suffer, I deserve to be with you.*» and he continued:

"If I go back with her, I will not be able to see my son anymore. You know she cannot stand him."

"So what? Your son grew up without you. So did your daughter. Both of your children are very well without you. If you're gone, they don't even miss you."

"You're right dear. You're always right."

"Don't say that, you idiot."

"So, what do you want me to say?"

"Nothing, nothing. Shut the hell up." Isabella got angry and did not want to continue the discussion. She was not happy and Alan was not happy. But, as long as he was away from Valerie, it was fine. Isabella did not even want anything else from life.

Alan had some feeble attempts to win back Valerie in his forties. Feeble because he did not have the energy to do something meaningful. And OK, not win her back as a wife or anything. He knew what she thought about him, how she spoke of him all those years. He could not face all those people who knew what he did wrong. When he was young, he did not care very much what people said about him. But now, he needed respect. Just like Valerie said once:

"You know, when I was young, everybody did whatever they wanted with

me. I ate shit with a big spoon. But now, as I am getting older, I cannot eat all that shit anymore. I need respect."

He did not want that aggravation. But at least to get her sleep with him one more time. All exes do that, right? He thought if he fooled her once, he could fool her again if he applied himself. But it did not work out.

One year he went to visit her and Victoria in Streamtown on the anniversary of their wedding. He thought this would have a great effect on her. You know, how women take a slight hint and turn it and twist it, and give it a bigger and bigger meaning until they reach the conclusion that you are crazy about them? That is what he tried to do too. He knew Valerie was very sensitive to subtle hints so he tried to send her a subtle hint. But it had no effect on her whatsoever.

«Why didn't she react to my hint? Why is she so smart and strong? I mean, she always was smart and strong, but getting older she became even smarter and stronger. I did not get any better with age, why did she? I thought if she listened to my advice with the car, maybe she opened a little door for me to get in. Well, at least I finally was able to give her a good advice. It is something, right?»

Alan was working as a field agent for a company specialized in IT services for other companies. He liked his job. First of all, because he was working with computers, which he loved most to do. Secondly, because he did not have a fixed schedule. He had to leave whenever they called him and wherever it was necessary. He always was away from home. Which was great. His son ignored him, Isabella was nagging him, Isabella's mother attacked him every time she had the chance. Why would he want to be home?

One night he was preparing to return to Steville. He has just finished a job 30 kilometers away from Steville. His phone started to ring. It was Valerie.

"Hey Alan, it's me."

"Hey Valerie. What's up?"

"I am terribly sorry to bother you. I have a problem and I wanted to ask for your help."

"Tell me, how can I help you?"

"I am driving to Steville with my car. And I got a flat tire. I have a spare tire, but no key. Could you help me please? I know I am out of line here, but I did not know who else to call."

"Where are you? I am heading home right now, in half an hour I am in Steville."

"I pulled over here in a village, ten kilometers away from Steville. I found a little parking spot. Should I wait here for you?"

"Yes, I am coming as soon as I can. Don't worry, we'll work this out somehow. OK?"

"Yes, thank you. Thank you very much."

Alan could not believe what just happened. Valerie asking for his help? Lately she did not even want to talk with him. What could have happened with her? Did this mean she was slowly forgiving him? Whatever happened, he was happy she asked for his help. He drove as fast as he could and together, they changed the tire. And more important, they had a chance to talk. Well, mostly he had a chance to talk. He missed so much talking with her. Valerie knew how to listen to him. Even though most of the times she had a different opinion, at least she did not share her opinion unless she was asked to.

Victoria spoke with her father, almost every week. They did not meet very often, even though both of them were in Steville. Alan was not bothered by this. They both were used living without each other. Alan thought « *I did tell her I love her once. I cannot tell her every day like her mother that I love her, but I told her once. Right after she got admitted to the university. I'm sure Valerie said I just loved after she got admitted to the university. But it's not true. I always loved my daughter. It's just that I did not express it very well. What about her, what about my daughter? She never told me she loved me. When I told her I love her she replied with "Thank you." She could have said "I love you, too, dad." Right?*»

Alan was 43 years old when his mother died. She died of a terrible disease. She has known about her condition for one year. One year of struggle and pain. Horrible pain. Two surgeries. Nothing could help her. Alan did everything in his power to help his mother. He took her to the best doctors in Steville. He paid for all the medical procedures. His sister said she had no money at the time, but she promised she would pay him as soon as she could. In the end she never had the money to pay him back their share of their mother's treatment and surgeries. The same story as with the inheritance left by their parents. The sister of Alan all got her share of inheritance, but Alan didn't. All he got was her promise to pay him her share in money. Nothing else.

«It's strange. I got absolutely nothing from my parents. Did this happen because my children got absolutely nothing from me? Was Valerie right when she said what goes around comes around? Is this how God punishes me for abandoning my wife crying, with our child in her arms?»

Alan loved his mother. Her death affected him terribly and the worst part was that he was not even capable of expressing his grief.

At 35 years of age, Alan was being sued by his wife Valerie. She wanted to divorce him. When she told him, he said:

"*Whatever you say.*" and a few tears fell off his eyes. Deep down he never thought she will have the strength to go through with it. The signs have been there. If he wanted, he could understand a long time ago that this was going to happen.

First sign was she was not jealous anymore. He could flirt with other women, she just turned her head in another direction. Of course, there were many women who were not jealous, but not Valerie. Valerie has always been a jealous person. She got angry even if he looked a little more to another woman. But not anymore.

Then she did not want to sleep with him anymore. Valerie, whose sexual appetite was wearing him out while they were together, now she was avoiding by any means to go to bed with him. Of course, he only came to visit her and their child once a month, but he still wanted to sleep with his wife. But she organized everything so that she went to bed much earlier than he did, with Victoria in her arms. And she pretended she was sleeping when he came to bed.

Finally she started looking for a rented apartment and moved out from his parents' house.

Alan knew what all this meant. It's not that he wanted to divorce too. It was just that he did not have the energy to fight for their marriage anymore. He could not provide a home for his family. He never stayed with them. He had a son with another woman. He simply felt he did not deserve to be with Valerie and Victoria. So why fight for it?

Alan was living alone in Steville. His wife and their daughter were living in Streamtown, with his parents, his mistress and their son lived in Steville. It was a little bit too much for him, so he chose the easiest variant: ignore both women, with their children too. Good old ostrich policy. What scared him the most was the hatred he rose in Valerie. He thought if she met with the other child, maybe she will sweeten. He asked Valerie:

"*So, do you want to come to meet my son?*"

"*What? Are you kidding me?*"

"*No, I'm not kidding you. Want to come?*"

"*No way. I'd rather be dead than to go meet your son.*"

"*Alright, then let me take Victoria meet him. He is her brother by the way.*"

"*Victoria will visit her brother over my dead body.*"

"*Why? Why are you so mean? Why do you hate my son so much? What fault does he have in this story?*"

"*First of all, let us establish what fault does my daughter have in this whole story. After all, she was born first, right? What fault does she have that you screwed up her life before she was even born? After we establish this, then we can pass to your second child and see what fault does he have. Alright?*"

Half an hour passed by, Alan broke the silence.

"*What are we eating today?*"

Valerie did not answer him.

Alan insisted:

"*You're not speaking with me?*"

"*We fought, remember?*"

"*We did not fight. You fought with me. I did not fight with you.*"

"*Speaking of fighting. I wanted to tell you something.*"

"*Shoot.*"

"*On the 14th of February I got a message from you. Happy Valentine's day and I love you. I wanted to tell you to be very careful when you text people. It's one thing to say something. But if you write a text message, be very careful whom you send it to. Instead of sending it to your mistress, you sent it to me."*

Alan remained stunned. «*She cannot believe I still love her.*»

He just said:

"I made no mistake. It was addressed to you."

"Yes, right. At least be a man and admit you made a mistake."

"Whatever you say dear."

Alan was visiting his wife and parents in Streamtown once a month. His wife and their daughter have been living in his parents' house for six years now and the relationship between them was deteriorating day by day.

As soon as Alan parked his car in the courtyard, his brother-in-law got in it and drove away to attend his business.

"Why do you let him take your car?" Valerie started.

"He is my brother-in-law. Of course I let him take the car."

"He has his own car. Why does he take yours?"

"Why not? I don't understand why does it bother you."

"Does he give you money for the gas? I'm sure he doesn't. Or your car goes without gas? Is that it?"

"We have to help each other. Don't they tell you in church this?"

"Yes, they do, and I agree, but why doesn't your brother-in-law and parents help me then? They also go to church. If I have to go to work and the bus is not circulating, I go by foot. You know that? They said they will drive me there if I pay the gas. How come he can take your car without paying for the gas?"

"What do you care? I buy the gas, so what's your problem?"

"Yeah, you buy the gas. From the money your mother takes from me and gives to you. Remember, right? When you don't have money for gas, you ask your mother, she goes to the wardrobe and takes from my money and gives it to you. Of that money are we talking about?"

"I don't understand how can you be so bad."

"Well, I had to adapt to the people that surround me. You know, survival stuff. When in Rome, act like Romans."

"Whatever."

"And another thing. Do you have any idea how much you mother spends on your sister? For you, she never has money. When I met you, you one pair of pants, one thin jacket, even though it was winter, two blouses, a sweater and two pieces of underwear. Look at how your sister is dressed. See? Doesn't that bother you?"

"You're just imagining things. What you say it's not true."

"Really? And you think I will change my opinion only because you tell me I'm wrong? For your information, only the facts can change my opinion."

"When I brought you here, I thought you will get along with my parents. Obviously, I was wrong."

"So why did you bring me here?"

"You wanted to get away from your father, remember? Didn't you always complain you wanted to get away from your father?"

"Ohhhh, that's so sweet. So you heard me complain and out of your good, loving heart, you took me here, to live with your loving parents, while you live in Steville with that whore. How nice of you. May God reward you for this."

Alan's second child was born when he was 26 years old. This second child was born by his girlfriend, Isabella. He has been married for 5 years already, he had a nine months old daughter with his wife and now his girlfriend was giving birth to his son. He felt terrible in confront with his wife. Alan thought «*Why do I have to feel like this? Did I commit a crime or something? I mean didn't she always tell me if I am a man I will take full responsibility with my actions? Well, this is my son, he should have my family name. Oh my God. She's gonna kill me. How am I going to tell her? I have to tell her. She always told me if we do something, we should tell each other. She always said she did not want to find out from others, she wants to find out from me. So I'll have to tell her. Somehow, I'll have to tell her. But not right now. For now, nobody should know.*»

"So, when are you going to introduce me to your family?" asked Isabella a few weeks after their son was born.

"You mean my wife and my daughter?" answered Alan.

"I mean your mother, your father and your sister."

"I cannot introduce you to them. I am married. They don't know I have a girlfriend and a child with her."

"OK, but you do have a girlfriend and a son. So what's the big deal?"

"No big deal, it's just you said you only wanted a child. Remember? I told you I am married and I love my wife and you said you did not want to break my family, you said you just wanted a child. Why do you want to meet my family all of the sudden?"

«Don't worry, we'll get there. A few more years and we'll get there. Your wife will find out about us and she'll dump you. You don't want to get back home, to work on the farm with your parents and you'll end up with me. We'll get there…» thought Isabella.

Alan was waiting for his wife in the railway station of Steville. She had been at her parents, in Mineville the last couple of months and now she was returning to Steville, to her husband. Luckily the train arrived punctually. Valerie saw from the train window Alan waiting for her. She remembered, the nice warm feeling she used to feel whenever they were reuniting this way. She was returning by train and he was waiting for her in railways station of Steville.

"Hey, Alan."

"Hey, Valerie."

Few minutes of silence.

"So, how was your trip?"

"It was OK. We had heating in the compartment, so it was not so bad. How's everything here?"

"Fine, fine. Same o' same o'" answered Alan.

"How are things at work?" asked Valerie.

"Fine, nothing new."

They went to the tram station. That was the closest to the railway station, right in front of it. The tram took them right to Alan's aunt, were they were living for the last months.

"I'm not quite sure yet, but I think I am pregnant. We are going to have a baby."

Alan's mind computed the news in fractions of seconds: *«Wow, finally.*

Well, sorry Valerie, but this is my chance. I'll tell you I don't want the child, you'll get mad and tell my parents. Finally, I have the chance to hurt them, just as they hurt me. They want a grandchild? A grandchild is what they are <u>*not*</u> *going to have!»*

"*Now you got pregnant? Now, when I have just decided to divorce you?*" answered Alan.

Alan was finishing university when he was 24 years old. He had already been married for three years. Everybody told him he got married to young. He thought this too, but his mother insisted so much for him to get married. How could he turn down his mother?

Now he was a student in Steville, with a wife. Financially they were not doing so well, but he hoped this situation will be solved as soon as they finished university and got jobs. Alan wanted to remain in Steville after he finished his study. This was not easy to achieve. First of all, it was very hard to find a job in Steville. They were not so welcoming with people coming from other counties. Secondly, the real estate market in Steville was probably the most expensive in the country. Even in the capital of the country, you could find an apartment at a lower price than in Steville.

Alan's parents had two children. They wanted their children settled down as soon as possible. Alan got married the first, he was the oldest. They had a piece of land. They thought to sell it and give the money to Alan, so that he and Valerie could buy an apartment in Steville.

Once, when Alan and Valerie came to visit them in Streamtown, Alan's father started the discussion:

"*Listen, we want to talk something with you.*"

Alan and Valerie came closer and said:

"*We're listening.*"

"*Your mother and I have been talking. We know you would like to remain in Steville.*"

"*Alan wants to remain in Steville, I'm not so fond of it, but OK.*" said Valerie.

"*Well, we have a piece of land. We want to sell it and give you the money. But not for you to waste.*"

"*We never wasted any money.*" Valerie couldn't help herself.

"*No, I mean we want to give you this money and you have to buy an apartment in Steville. What do you say?*"

"*OK, fine.*" said Valerie. It's not that Valerie did not trust the old man, but she just did not trust him.

"*There is one condition though.*" continued Alan's father.

"*Do tell.*"

"*You will have to sign us a paper waiving all your other rights to anything else from our side.*"

"*OK, give us the money and we'll sign this paper of yours.*"

"*So this means I should start looking for an apartment?*" asked Alan.

"*Yes, start looking and inform us when you find it. We'll come to Steville and finalize everything.*"

"*What amount are we speaking about? Just to know what to look for.*" Continued Alan.

"*We could give you around 6.000 dollars. You should try to find something around that price.*"

So Alan started looking for an apartment in Steville. He looked and he looked. For months. Finally, he found an apartment that fit the price condition and that also was in an acceptable neighborhood. He called his parents, happy:

"*Mom, I found an apartment. Finally. I found it. Do you have the money prepared?*"

"*I'll talk with your father and we'll call the buyer for the land. As soon as we have the money, we'll let you know.*"

"*You mean you don't have the money yet?*"

"*We don't have the money. We have to sell a piece of land.*"

"*But you said it's all prepared, I just need to find the place.*"

"*Don't worry, we'll solve this right away.*"

Alan's happiness was very short. He started to realize something was not right. After one week, he called his mother again.

"*Well, mom. Do you have the money? Can you come with the money to Steville? These guys who are selling the apartment are not willing to wait much longer.*"

"*Alan, we need to talk. You should come home to Streamtown. We need to talk.*"

Alan and Valerie went to Streamtown. Alan's parents explained them the guy who wanted to buy their land changed his mind and he did not want to buy it anymore. So they did not have the money to give them.

To the rest of the world, Alan's parents said they wanted to give them the money, but Alan refused. When Valerie heard this story from one of Alan's mother's brothers, she exploded:

"And you believed this?"

"This is what she said. It is true?"

"Are you stupid? Now tell me one person who would turn down money to buy an apartment in Steville. Tell me one person! How could you believe such a story?"

"She is my sister! Why would she lie to me?"

"I don't know why your sister would lie to you, but if you asked me if it is true, it means you she's been lying to you also in other occasions. So let me tell how it happened. They promised us they would give us money to buy an apartment under the condition that we shall waive all our other rights here. Alan has been looking for an apartment for months. And finally when he found a place that fit the budget, they said they did not have the money, because the guy who wanted to buy their land changed his mind. OK? This is what happened."

Alan never exploded. He just kept everything to himself. He thought «*Mom, dad, you hurt me. You hurt me bad. I'll hurt you back. Let's see. What is it that you want the most in the world? To see your children married, at their homes, right? Right. Well, you're not going to see this son of yours married at his home. You never did anything to help my family settle down. All you did was insist that we get married, but then, nothing. Nothing! OK, so this son of yours will not remain married. I'm sorry for Valerie, I'll have to sacrifice her. But she's strong. She'll get over it. And she'll be better off without a loser like me, who is not even capable of providing her with a home. So, I'll find myself a girlfriend and I will screw up everything, just like you screwed up everything for me. Mom and Dad."*

Alan was 21 years old when he got married. He felt he was too young to get married, but his mother insisted. «*Why does she insist so much? As if*

she wants to get rid of me. She does not want me to be her son anymore? Well, in the end, it is not so bad. I have a beautiful wife who takes care of me, cooks for me and I love her.»

Alan's wedding was arranged by his parents. There were 200 persons invited, Alan's wife did not know virtually anybody. They were sitting at the front table and everybody was staring at them, analyzing them, gossiping.

"*God, I can hardly wait for it to be over.*" said Valerie.

"*Hang on there. We have a few more hours to resist. I'm sorry, but this is tradition around here.*" answered Alan.

"*It is too hot. I am drenched with sweat, my dress is stuck to me. I hate this stupid traditional music which is so loud I can hardly hear my thoughts. And all these idiots whom I don't even know are staring at us like we are some scarecrows.*"

"*I'm sorry you feel so uncomfortable. This is the way it is at weddings here in Streamtown.*"

"*Well, it sucks. And by the way, your mother promised me nobody will shout how much money each guest gave as gift. Still, the coordinator shouted out all the amounts we received. It was despicable, I felt humiliated.*" Valerie finished off the idea in her mind *«I gave up my name. I gave up my religion. Most of all, I gave up my freedom. I hope it was all worth.»*

It was on a Friday afternoon. Alan and Valerie were students in Steville and they came to Streamtown to visit Alan's family. Valerie did not want to come.

"*Why do I have to go visit your family?*" asked Valerie the tenth time.

"*You don't have to go. It's just that I told them about you and they said they would like to meet you. That's all.*" explained Alan patiently once again.

"*Yes, but if I go to your parents' house, it seems so official. Why does it have to be so official? I don't want anything official from you. We are together, we love each other, why do your parents have to be involved?*" continued Valerie.

"*It's nothing official. We just go for a couple of days to see them. You can eat cherries. You know how you like cherries. We have a big cherry tree right in our courtyard. And it is ripe right now, in May. What do you say?*"

"OK, alright, let's go. But only for this weekend. That is it."

"Only for this weekend." Said Alan and he thought « *For now. Then for another weekend. Then for the holidays. And then for the rest of your life. Just wait and see.*»

After a few weeks of convincing, Valerie agreed to come to Streamtown. They went by train from Steville to a nearby locality, then took another train to Streamtown. They got off the train in a small halt, few hundred of meters away from the house.

They were walking slowly, hand in hand. As soon as they entered on the street were Alan lived, Valerie stopped suddenly.

"I have such a bad feeling."

"What's wrong? Do you feel sick? Maybe from that filthy train?"

"No, I'm not sick, but I had such an awful foreboding. Oh my God. I just feel like turn around and go back to Steville."

"What? Are you serious? What's the matter?"

"I don't know, I don't like this street. My entire being is against this place, this street and this house."

"Look, it's fine. If you don't want us to go in, we turn around and go back to Steville. I cannot force you."

"Yes, but your parents are waiting for us. What shall we tell them? That we came until here and then turned around and went back to Steville? Never mind, let's go in."

Alan's parents were living in a house. Alan's grandparents had given them money before they got married to buy a house on their street. They bought the house, but it was old and small. Alan's parents has renewed and expanded it. They built 2 other rooms and a bathroom. The expansion of the house came in handy, as during their marriage they had two children. Alan was their first born. He left very early the family house, as he wanted to study Chemistry. Valerie always teased him on this subject:

"I still cannot understand why did you want to study Chemistry."

"Because I like it."

"No you don't. You are not even so good at Chemistry. You are great in Math and Informatics. I'll give you that. But not in Chemistry. Why on earth did you want to study Chemistry? Hmmm, I think you did this only for the chicks."

"What chicks?"

"90% of the pupils in Chemistry high school and 80% of the students in Chemistry Faculty are girls. I think that is why you wanted to study Chemistry."

"It's ridiculous" always answered Alan, smiling.

As in Streamtown, there was no Chemistry high school, he went to another little town, 30 kilometers away to attend highschool. Alan did not commute every day, during school time he lived there, in the pupils' dormitory. He left from home when he was 14 years old and never came back.

Now, at 20 years of age, he was a student and he was coming home visiting his parents, with his girlfriend Valerie. They entered the courtyard. Alan's parents and his sister were all in the garden, behind the house. Alan's parents were having regular, full time jobs, but also a very large garden, a lot of animals and also some parcels in the field. Considering that they also have risen two children, it was a lot of work in the house. Alan and Valerie arrived home in the evening and just as they coming close to the entrance door of the house, also Alan's parents were coming in the house from their garden. Alan's mother looked at Valerie, smiled and went into the house. But Alan's father was clearly expressing his surprise. He remained staring at Valerie for a few seconds, as if he did not understand what was going on. Valerie greeted both of them and then went into the house. She went to the bathroom, washed her hands and asked Alan's mother if she could help her with anything, as she was starting to prepare dinner for the whole family. Alan's sister also came into the kitchen, sat on the sofa and they were all staring at Valerie. Valerie thought «*Hmmm, he said they were expecting us! These guys did not even know about me! Alan lied to me. I did not want to come here... They are all looking at me as if I am a ghost. Especially his father... Haven't he seen women before in his life?*» Alan's mother was turning around the kitchen to prepare everything as it was evening and everybody was very hungry. At a certain point, she dropped a ceramic plate of her hand. Everybody became very attentive, as there was a superstition that if the mother-in-law breaks a dish when the daughter-in-law comes the first time in the house, they will not get along. So everybody started to comment and laugh:

"You dropped a dish, you dropped a dish!"

But Alan's mother replied:

"But it did not break. So it doesn't count! Shut up all of you!"

Only Alan and his father remained outside, in the courtyard.

"Who is she?" Alan's father asked him.

"She is my girlfriend. Do you like her?"

"That's irrelevant if I like her or not. She is not for you."

"Why not?"

"She is too beautiful for you. Look at her. She is a very attractive young woman. How can you think she is suitable for you? Such a beautiful woman like her means trouble. Where is she from?"

"She is from Mineville. And she is Catholic."

"What? No way! No way! You should find yourself a girl, from our county or from Steville. We are Orthodox! You should find yourself and Orthodox girlfriend! She is a city girl too. I can tell. We have to work here in the field, we have to milk the cow! Does she know how to milk the cow?"

"No, she doesn't but I am not marrying her to milk the cow. I want to marry her because I love her."

"What marriage? Are you out of your mind? You are twenty years old! You are too young to get married!"

Alan's father was very much against the whole story. As he was staring to raise his voice – he brought up his children, especially Alan, because he was the oldest, with the raised voice – he went back into the garden, so that nobody from the house can hear him. Alan wanted to convince him, so he ran after his father in the garden.

"Father, stay, don't go away. I'm telling you I want to marry her. If you don't agree I will not marry her, but be aware I will not get married with any other woman. So think about it. You want to see me get old unmarried just like my uncle?"

Alan's uncle, his father's brother too wanted to get married when he was young with a woman, but his mother did not agree with that the marriage to that particular woman. So, he did not get married with her, but the problem was he never got married afterwards. Alan used this example successfully now with his own father.

Finally, his father said:

"Alright, alright, we'll see."

"Will you think about it?"

"Yes, I will. Now let's go in. I'm hungry. Your mother is preparing dinner."

"Most likely Valerie is helping her. Valerie is a great cook. She cooks me all the time, all the dishes I like."

"What else does she do for you?"

"I am not going to discuss that now with you..." Alan closed the conversation smiling.

Alan was ten years old when his sister was born.

Although his family was living in the outskirts of Streamtown, their family had a very rural kind of life. In the meantime, both the parents had full time jobs, so there was not much time and energy left to fool around.

Alan was the first born and he was a quiet, serious boy. His parents were using him for all kind of works, most of them too hard for his age. He also had to take care of his younger sister until the parents came home, and this was the most difficult job, as all his sister wanted was to play.

Alan wanted to study. This was all he wanted. He knew that if he studied, he will be able to get away from the hard life he had at home. It was too much work there, no time to breathe, to think even. His father had a very bad temper. He got angry very easily and immediately started shouting. As he did not want to beat his wife or the younger children, he always ended up beating up Alan, for whatever happened around the house.

Alan's mother was overloaded, drained of energy. She always held in her arms the sister of Alan, even though Alan was craving for her love too. The little boy needed his mother badly, but she did not have the time and the energy for him. Moreover, she also loaded Alan with the young one and he loved her so much, he could not refuse her. So he did everything his mother asked him, hoping secretly that one day she will have time for him too.

Whenever Alan had a free moment or it was a religious holiday and the family was not working, he retired in a silent room and studied. Sometimes, girls were coming to the gate and asked for him. As he was always sad, always unhappy, girls have always been attracted to him. Alan has always triggered the maternal instinct of the females around him, as if he did this to compensate the fact that he was not ever able to trigger his mother's maternal instinct towards him. So when girls came looking for him, he just sent his mother to the gate.

"*Go tell her I'm not home.*"

"*Why? Why don't you go to her? What could happen if you speak for a few moments with her?*"

"*I don't want to, OK?*"

"*But they are coming all the time and ask you out and you never go. Some of them bring chocolate and candies just to please you!*"

"*So take the chocolate and the candies and tell them I'm not home. How hard can it be?*"

"*Sometimes I'm worried about you...*"

"*What? You are worried I'm not working enough?*" he asked his mom ironically.

"*I'm worried you'll end up alone. Like your uncle.*" Alan's mother was really concerned about her first born son. «*He's strange. I'm afraid he'll never be able to have a family if he runs away like this from girls. I'm afraid we'll get stuck with him all his life. I can't have that. I hardly have energy for the other one, that came after him. I have to be very careful. If I see some girl, any girl, that comes even a little bit close to him, I have to insist that they immediately get married. The sooner the better. I have to be very attentive.* » she thought.

Alan was born in the sixties. His father was from Streamtown. As he could not find a job there, he went working to another town, 30 kilometers away. He commuted every day train. The train made the 30 kilometers trip inone hour and a half hour, so he spent a lot of the time commuting. Also, the train was in a horrible state. The windows and the doors were not closing well. In winter and in summer, it was hell on earth.

While working there, Alan's father met his wife to be. She was a young woman, 10 years younger than him. She was born in Steville county and came there also for the job.

They got married not long after they met, but the young woman had a very hard time adjusting to her new family. The only good thing was the young couple did not have to live in the same house with their in-laws, at least they had a house of their own, even though it was still a lot to work to get this house in shape and it was only a few meters away from their in-laws' house.

Nine months after the marriage, she gave birth to her first son. They called him Alan. The birth was a very difficult one. Alan's mother hoped that at least she gave birth to a beautiful son if she had such a hard time giving birth to him.

Alan was not a beautiful child though. First of all, his father was not beautiful. Secondly, the umbilical cord was twisted around his neck and he hardly had oxygen in the last hours before his birth. The doctor noticed this problem, but he did not perform a C section. Even though after the nineties C sections became very fashionable as women did not want to feel any pain whatsoever giving birth, back in the sixties everybody was still trying to give birth naturally to their children. People thought that it was healthier for the mother and for the child. So the doctor took Alan out using a forceps. This deformed his little soft head. His face was blue and black because of the lack of oxygen.

After he was born, Alan was given to his mother. When she saw him, she started to weep:

"*Oh my God, how can he be so ugly? Look at him! I cannot hold him, I just can't!*"

"*But he is your son. You must breast feed him!*"

"*I cannot breast feed him. Take him to another woman, I cannot look at this child.*"

And she did not look at him. For several days, she was not able to even hold him in her arms. That was when Alan started to miss his mother's love terribly.

Lightning Source UK Ltd.
Milton Keynes UK
UKOW05n1620220617
303899UK00002B/37/P

9 781504 372091